The Church That God Intends

*Reconsidering the
Reformation Heritage of the
Church of God Movement
(Anderson)*

Compiled and Edited by

Barry L. Callen

Emeth Press

The Church That God Intends
Copyright © 2009 Barry L. Callen
Printed in the United States of America on acid-free paper

All rights reserved. No part of this book may be reproduced, or stored in a retrieval system or transmitted in any form or by any means, electronic, mechanical, photocopying, recording, scanning or otherwise, except as permitted by the 1976 United States Copyright Act, or with the prior written permission of Emeth Press. Requests for permission should be addressed to: Emeth Press, P. O. Box 23961, Lexington, KY 40523-3961.

Library of Congress Cataloging-in-Publication

Callen, Barry L
  The church that God intends : reconsidering the reformation heritage of the Church of God Movement (Anderson) / compiled and edited by Barry L. Callen.
    p.   cm.
  Includes bibliographical references and index.
  ISBN: 9780979793578 (alk. paper)
  1. Church of God (Anderson, Ind.) --History.
    BX7025 .C48 2009
    289.9–dc22
                                              2008048984

Contents

Introduction: A Modern-Day Reformation Movement 5

I. A Risking God; a Daring People

1. The Open and Risking God
   Barry L. Callen 11
2. Joining Together Holiness and All Truth
   Barry L. Callen 29
3. Reconciling Clashing Ecumenical Visions
   Barry L. Callen 49
4. Building a Young Reformation Movement
   Merle D. Strege 71

II. Human Walls; Kingdom Doors

5. Race Relations in the American Holiness Movement
   James Earl Massey 85
6. African-American Worship: Pentecostal
   and Holiness Movements
   Cheryl J. Sanders..97
7. William J. Seymour: Follower of the "Evening Light"
   B. Scott Lewis 113
8. Women in Ministry: A Biblical Vision
   Sharon Clark Pearson 131
9. An Analysis of Autobiographies by Holiness Women
   Susie C. Stanley 163

III. Divided World; United Church

10. A Wesleyan Perspective on Christian Unity
    David L. Cubie 181
11. An Ecumenical Vocation for the Wesleyan/
    Holiness Tradition
    Elizabeth H. Mellen 211
12. Practicing the Unity Being Preached
    Merle D. Strege... 237
13. Holiness Church Participation in the Larger Church
    Gilbert W. Stafford 259

IV. God's Intentions; the Church's Challenge

14. The Biblical Ministry of Reconciliation
    James Earl Massey 275
15. Becoming a Community of the Spirit
    James W. Lewis 293
16. "Place" and Higher Education in the Holiness Tradition
    Merle D. Strege 317
17. Relevance of the 19th-Century Holiness Paradigm
    Douglas M. Strong 331

Index of Persons 345

About the Contributors 353

Introduction

God, as revealed in the Bible, intentionally brought creation into being. It was an unnecessary but lavish act of divine love. Ever since the fall of this creation into sin, God is reported to have demonstrated another intention, the calling into being of a people, a church, a "chosen race, a royal priesthood, a holy nation, God's own people" (1 Pet. 2:9). The purpose of this calling has been—and still is—for this church of God to be an instrument of reconciliation and healing for the nations. It is to be a reflection of the very character of God, the actual community of the Spirit, the current body of Jesus that proclaims "the mighty acts of him who called you out of darkness into his marvelous light" (1 Pet. 2:9).

The Church of God movement (Anderson) came into being in 1880 through the inspired ministries of many people, particularly Daniel S. Warner (1842-1895). A keynote of this reform movement has been a deep concern about the status of God's church in this troubled world. To this movement's pioneers, the church had deteriorated over the centuries into a welter of divisive denominations reflecting much more human arrogance and compromise than the holy, united character of the church that God intends.

There have been many movements on behalf of church reform over the centuries. This particular one, arising in the late nineteenth century in the midst of a larger American holiness movement, honored those Christian reformers who had gone before. The new movement soon reflected on its own role in the flow of church history and saw itself, in some sense, as the "last reformation." The "last" was based in part on belief that the return of Jesus Christ was relatively near and that God was moving to prepare his troubled bride, the church, for this culmination of history. The preparation centered in a restoration of the intended holiness and unity of God's people. This restoration was to be built on the earlier work of others, including Martin Luther and John Wesley, and thus was on the end of a parade of God's people who were being freshly faithful to the upward call of God.

But there was more. The "last" also meant that God's intention, the heart of the final reform, was not to be focused merely on the correction of a particular doctrine or the realignment of a particular church body. Daniel Warner's 1878 covenant with God was nothing less than to "to join *holiness* and *all truth* together and thus build up the apostolic church of the living God."

Holiness, all truth, and the apostolic church were keynotes of the reforming dream of the early Church of God movement. All of the human, the partial, and the non-biblical were to be shed from the church's life. Sanctified believers, "the saints," were to "come out" of it all and stand together, purified, empowered, gifted, governed, and sent by God's Spirit. God wants nothing less for those called to be his people! The church brought into being by God is not to be the church *of people*, any people for any of their limited agendas, but the church *of God* and God's intention in this world.

The initial implementation of this grand vision occurred within the womb of the Holiness Movement in the United States in the final decades of the nineteenth century. Daniel Warner became an impassioned holiness leader, but soon he broke with the formalized holiness movement over the issue of "denominationalism." The larger holiness movement was seeking a revival of the holiness emphasis, thus reinvigorating the established churches in the Wesleyan tradition. Warner, however, considered the very establishment of these churches as part of the prevailing unholiness, and thus sought to "come out" of them instead of reinvigorating them from the inside. True holiness, he believed, could not exist "upon sectarian soil."

Warner broke with the formalized holiness movement in May, 1881, insisting: "We wish to cooperate with all Christians, as such, in saving souls—but forever withdraw from all organisms that uphold and endorse sects and denominations in the body of Christ" (Barry Callen, *It's God's Church!*, 1995, 93). The Church of God movement has now been on the scene for one hundred and thirty years. The return of Christ has not yet occured. The constituency of today's reform movement lives in a very different time in the life of the world and broader church. Its radical idealism, its come-out call, and its reliance on the Holy Spirit to administer church life apart from human denominations have become stressed by sociological realities that, over time, seem to temper theological visions.

By the 1990s, a few of Warner's later followers had rejoined what then represented the older formalization of the holiness movement, the Christian Holiness Association and its Wesleyan Theological Society. If fact, one of them, Barry L. Callen, was elected as the editor of the *Wesleyan Theological Journal* and has served in this capacity ever since. Under his editorship, a series of Church of God writers, and a few others addressing the reforming vision of the Church of God movement, have appeared in this journal's pages.

These significant *WTJ* materials form the heart of this present volume. The original publication of each article is carefully noted. They attempt in various ways to revisit, refine, and renew the heart of the reforming heritage of the Church of God movement. The focus is on a risking God who calls into being a daring people who accept the Spirit's several invitations. These include being filled with the Spirit, breaking with racial and gender discriminations in church life, championing the perspectives, power, and gifting of the Spirit that together enable a holiness of and unity among believers which can result in a presentation to the world of the church that God intends.

I acknowledge the Editorial Committee of the Wesleyan Theological Society and am grateful for its encouragement of this publication. The writers, most but not all affiliated with the Church of God movement, have provided valuable reflections on a rich teaching heritage in the holiness tradition. They are reflections that deserve fresh prominence for new readers. After all, they are reaching for the fullness of what God intends for today's church!

Barry L. Callen
Anderson, Indiana
February, 2009

DEDICATION

This volume is dedicated to the memory of the late Gilbert W. Stafford (1938-2008). A revererd and loved leader of the Church of God movement (Anderson). Dr. Stafford was an outstanding educator, minister, author, ecumenical participant, and personal friend. For more than three decades he served the church through Anderson University School of Theology as Professor of Christian Theology, Associate Dean, and Dean of the Chapel. He longed for the fuller realization of the church that God intends in this troubled world, and he contributed effectively toward that possibility. May the churdh of today and tomorrow share his gracious spirit and learn from his inspired thoughts and actions. See chapter 13 for a sample.

In loving memory,
Barry L. Callen

Dr. Gilbert W. Stafford
1938-2008

Part I
A Risking God; a Daring People

Chapter 1

The Open and Risking God

by
Barry L. Callen

A proper understanding of the nature of God determines how all else in the Christian faith is viewed. The Wesleyan/Holiness tradition has tended toward an "open" view of God, one recognizing that God has granted meaningful freedom to humans and that emphasizes the "relational" nature of truth and the church. The following study looks at the current tension in the "evangelical" Christian community over the issue of the openness of God. Written by Church of God theologian Barry L. Callen, it affirms the biblical view of God by tracing the significant theological journey of Clark H. Pinnock. Openness lies at the base of the Church of God movement's understanding of the church that God both intends and makes possible. It enables a significant role for spiritual "experience," the present role of the Holy Spirit in church life, and a non-creedal approach to viewing Christian truth. Originally appeared in the Wesleyan Theological Journal *(36:1, Spring, 2001).*

By the eighteenth century much Calvinistic theology had solidified into dogmatic assertions about the being of a sovereign God and God's relations to the fallen creation. Formalized at the Synod of Dort (1618-1619), this "TULIP" solidification had become firmly scholasticized Calvinistic dogma. Hardly a fragrant flower lacking rigid and defensive thorns, this particular TULIP consisted of the five affirmed articles of Dort issued in response to the Arminian Remonstrance of 1610. These articles were: (1) **T**otal depravity; (2) **U**nconditional election; (3) **L**imited atonement; (4) **I**rresistible grace; and (5) **P**erseverance of the saints. These five petals of the theological TULIP are tightly interconnected as the logical chain that would become standard theological thinking for much of evangelicalism in the twentieth century.

John Wesley carried on a long debate with Calvinists, especially the Calvinist George Whitefield. Certainly endorsing the fundamental concepts of a sovereign God and a fallen creation, Wesley's view of the relational and redeeming nature of the sovereign God disallowed any unqualified unfolding for him of at least points 2-5 of Dort's TULIP. In the North American evangelical community of the last half of the twentieth century, this debate continued. Wesley's view managed to gain only a minority position. This now may be changing, at least to some significant degree. A Wesley-sensitive school of thought, often called "Free-Will Theism," has been pioneered by Canadian theologian Clark H. Pinnock.

Since the 1970s, the theological work of Clark Pinnock has taken up the daunting and often controversial task of renewing evangelical theology.[1] In large part this renewal has proceeded by Pinnock's effort to freshly champion key theistic and soteriological insights similar to those of John Wesley. As it was in the eighteenth century, Pinnock's contemporary path often has been hazardous since dogmatic (scholastic) Calvinists remain fixed on the TULIP of Dort.[2] Even so, considerable progress is now being made to "liberate" God from certain non-biblical and rationalistic strictures. Emerging again is the sovereign but also "open" and "risking" God in whom Wesley rejoiced and about whom the troubled world of this new millennium needs to know.[3]

The present task of Pinnock and others is to replace TULIP with what is perceived by them to be the more biblically authentic and pastorally satisfying ROSE (God is **R**elational, **O**pen, **S**uffering, and **E**verywhere-active). The new floral rubric reflects the heart of Wesley's work, has been at the center of Pinnock's work since the 1970s, and is a source of hope for contemporary Christian theism. What follows is a brief tracing of the theological journey that has brought Pinnock to this revised (recovered) theism and the central elements of the new theological ROSE as it has emerged in his pioneering work. The journey began with (1) the results of the "reciprocity principle," led to (2) a revising of "classical" theism, rediscovered (3) the God who is "open" and risks the historical process, and now has generated (4) a passion that emerges from the new metaphor for God.

The Results of Reciprocity

Although at first absorbing the whole theological ethos of the widely privileged position of Calvinism among evangelicals, Pinnock later would deal forthrightly with several related issues and free himself from much of the TULIP theological model. The significant changes in Pinnock's thinking, especially during the 1970s, were enabled primarily by gaining and then actively pursuing "the insight of reciprocity."[4] Although not at first consciously aware of or intentionally motivated by particular Christian traditions that are reciprocity oriented, Pinnock soon realized that his emerging biblical insights had deep roots in various Christian traditions. They pointed to a "ROSE" theism that had a coloration and fragrance significantly different from the old TULIP.

New perspectives came to Pinnock similar to those typical of theologians like John Wesley and the ancient Orthodox tradition of the East. This tradition does not assume that the human fall into sin has deprived persons of all divine grace or responsibility for responding to God's offer of restored relationship with Christ. Salvation necessarily involves cooperation in divine-human interrelations.[5] While Western (TULIP) theologians typically have shied from such reciprocity, fearing an undermining of the sovereignty of God in favor of a works-righteousness heresy, Eastern theologians have insisted that, while never *meriting* God's acceptance because of human action, it nonetheless is the case that God's freely-bestowed grace empowers humans for *responsible cooperation*. Wesley affirmed the universal gift of "prevenient grace," probably deriving this view largely from early Greek theology (especially Macarius).[6] Pinnock now joined this long and more dynamic trail of church tradition, freshly championing a divine-human mutuality that would stimulate a wave of theological innovation (recovery) in evangelical circles. If Wesley had united "pardon" and "participation" motifs, resulting in what some judge his greatest contribution to ecumenical dialogue,[7] Pinnock now was beginning a similar journey that he hoped would make a significant contribution to the renewal of contemporary evangelicalism.

The first link in the Calvinistic chain to break for Pinnock (the first TULIP petal to fall) was the doctrine of perseverance of the saints. At the time of this breaking, Pinnock was teaching at Trinity Evangelical Divinity School (1969-1974) and giving attention to the book of Hebrews. Why, he wondered, are Christians warned not to fall away from Christ (e.g., 10:26) and exhorted to persevere (e.g., 3:12) if they enjoy the absolute security taught by five-point Calvinism? In fact, he concluded, human responses to God *are taken seriously by God.* Is there not a dialectic of divine and human interaction, a relationship of reciprocity? The garment of strict Calvinism thus began unraveling for Pinnock with this realization of the truth of reciprocity. A believer's security in God is linked to the faith relationship with God that must be intentionally maintained. There is, in other words, a "profound mutuality" between God and believers.[8] God allows the divine will to be frustrated by human intransigence. A believer's continuance in the saving grace of God depends, at least in part, on the human partner in the divine-human relationship. Pinnock now began to understand that, once the factors of reciprocity and conditionality are introduced, the landscape of Christian theology is altered significantly. On this terrain he could begin to "regard people not as a product of a timeless decree but as God's covenant partners and real players in the flow and the tapestry of history."[9] Human responses actually do matter to God.

Two forces now were at work in Pinnock. First, himself an experienced apologist in the Calvinistic tradition, he tended to think logically, seeing a systematic sequence of results naturally emerging from his new premise of reciprocity. Second, and he insists more basic in his own case, was biblical teaching. When reconsidered in light of the God-human mutuality, the Bible—surprisingly to many "evangelical" believers—presents itself as highly congenial to the fresh insights being inspired by the reciprocity principle. Five doctrinal moves thus occurred for Pinnock during the 1970s, all results of affirming and applying the reciprocity assumption.[10] They may be summarized briefly as follows.

   1. **No "Terrible Decree."** John Calvin had used the phrase "terrible decree" in relation to his belief that God as a sovereign act had destined some people to eternal lostness (*Institutes* 3:23). He reasoned: God wills all things. Since some people will be lost according to the Bible, logic compels the conclusion that God wills such lostness. But with the premise of reciprocity, Pinnock now could see and accept the biblical teaching that God's desire and will are that *all people* be saved (1 Tim. 2:4; Titus 2:11; Rom. 5:18). Lostness happens only by human choice, not by divine decree.

   2. **Corporate View of Election.** What, then about divine election? It is a corporate category, Pinnock concluded. God has chosen *a people* and individuals enter into God's election as they choose by faith to join the elect body in Christ (Eph. 1:3-14). Election thus encompasses all people, at least potentially, and is a cause for rejoicing rather than for having to defend God from the charge of acting in a morally intolerable way by choosing some people and damning others. Pinnock was helped to see this corporate focus of God's election by the writing of Robert Shank.[11]

   3. **Predestination and Theodicy.** If the biblical narrative reflects a dynamic and interactive pattern of God's dealing with people, then pre-

destination focuses on God setting goals rather than enforcing preprogrammed decrees. The primary goal for those elect in Christ is that they be conformed to the image of God's Son (Rom. 8:29). The future is a realm of possibilities for believers who are to be co-workers with God. This view helps greatly to avoid any suggestion that God is the author of evil.[12] Here is the personal witness of Pinnock: "In the past I would slip into my reading of the Bible dark assumptions about the nature of God's decrees and intentions. What a relief to be done with them!"[13]

4. **Free Will of the Sinner**. Calvinists had defined human sinfulness as total, leaving no room for human freedom to function in relation to potential salvation. But, if there is a divine-human reciprocity, would there not be some room for the functioning of human free will? Pinnock was appreciatively aware of John Wesley's doctrine of universal prevenient grace (God graciously compensating for a fallen humanity unable to respond otherwise)[14] and he recognized that the Bible treats people as though they were responsible and able to respond to God. The gospel of Christ and the evangelistic efforts of the church certainly address people as though they are free and responsible. Therefore, Pinnock concludes that such is actually the case.

5. **Atoning Work of Christ**. What then about the very source of human salvation, the atoning work of Jesus Christ? Put simply, Jesus really did die for the sins of the *whole* world, contrary to the more restrictive Calvinian (TULIP) logic. Given the premise of reciprocity, where does human response fit in? If Christ died for all people and no human response is possible or necessary, one would be at universalism (all will finally be saved) or at the old Calvinism (those few who are saved must be saved by God's electing choice). But such are not the only options if stress is placed on the needed human appropriation of the saving act of Christ. Those who are finally saved are those who, in their relative freedom, choose in faith to reach out and accept the divine grace offered—and, of course, persist in their acceptance. Pinnock had become convinced that there is a real reciprocity in the salvation process.

Into the Eastern and Wesleyan Streams

By the 1990s Clark Pinnock had developed fresh appreciation for key aspects of the Eastern, Wesleyan, charismatic, and even process traditions of Christian life and thought. His theological journey may be pictured as a new turning toward select perspectives of the Eastern tradition of Christian thought. This focus has become Pinnock's integrating perspective, largely replacing the previous Latin focus of the West. By contrast with his earlier rationalistic theological patterns, he now exhibits the characteristics of the relational, therapeutic, transformational, and cooperative approaches to Christian faith.

Like John Wesley before him,[15] Pinnock has come to give increased priority to aspects of the Eastern tradition of Christianity, while at key points retaining the *language* and *evangelical audience* of the West, language like the "inerrancy" of the Bible and audience like the Evangelical Theological Society. Pinnock recognizes a helpful addressing of this altered approach in "the so-called quadrilateral of Wesleyan theology"[16] which retains biblical centrality while recognizing key roles for the experience of true transformation of the believer and the continuing wisdom of the church's tradition (including that of the ancient East). In his 1997 keynote address to the Wesleyan Theological Society, Pinnock observed that there is shallowness in the rhetoric of "scripture only" and announced that over the years he had come to realize "how Wesleyan my moves in method and theism were." His conclusion? "I think we need to move to a larger concept of method (as represented by the Wesleyan quadrilateral) and to a more dynamic model of the nature of God (as intimated also in Wesley's thinking)."[17]

In recent years there have evolved significant similarities between the theological work of John Wesley in the eighteenth century and Clark Pinnock in the twentieth. Both have strong ties to England and significant impact in the "new world." Both in their times grieved over the lostness of the masses and the desperate need for renewal in the church by the power of the Spirit of God. Both wrote extensively without being "systematic" theologians in a technical and rationalistic sense. Both affirmed most foundations laid by the Protestant Reformers, but each also struggled against hardened scholasticisms within the Protestant ranks. Mildred Bangs Wynkoop says that Wesley unlocked "the scholastic doors to allow the vibrant 'Word of God' to illuminate and vitalize the cold, correct Reformation theologies."[18] Philip Meadows explains that Wesley was...struggling to find a more acceptable balance between the freedom of nature and the sovereignty of grace that can satisfy a truly biblical life of faith....[For Wesley] the idea of divine justice involves a limitation of God's sovereignty in respect of and response to the genuine creaturely freedom of choice between good and evil.[19]

Wesley, much like the contemporary Pinnock, concluded that God is a "loving personal agent whose gracious power is exercised not at the expense of human agency but in order to set persons free to love."[20] The issue of human freedom is key. Traditional Protestant teaching has understood "original sin" to mean total corruption of the image of God in humans, so that apart from grace humanity has no freedom to respond to God (leading to the logic of determinism since God alone can and does choose who will be graced with response-ability). Again, joining Wesley, Pinnock has come to believe that the loving God of the Bible "preveniently" graces *all people*, hoping that *all* will respond and be saved. Pinnock also is open to the Eastern Orthodox position on sin and grace which includes real freedom for humans, so that salvation requires the joint functioning of divine grace and human free will—God's intent, provision, and risk. Randy Maddox has concluded that the closest resemblance between Orthodoxy (early Eastern) and Wesley likely lies in "their respective doctrines of deification and sanctification."[21] Similarly, Clark Pinnock has been on a journey of renewal that has come to the centrality of relational theological categories that focus on actual transformation into Christlikeness and the importance of walking closely with the Spirit.[22]

Pinnock's book *Flame of Love* (1996) sets the reader on a journey with the Spirit, a journey of true transformation. Both Wesley and Pinnock experienced a theological journey that led away from scholastic Reformed determinism with its rationalism that commonly pictures God in ways other than the way Jesus portrayed the Father—loving, gracious, sacrificial, wounded by human transgressions, prepared to risk on behalf of all who are lost. As Colin Williams observes, Wesley "broke the chain of logical necessity by which the Calvinist doctrine of predestination seems to flow from the doctrine of original sin, by his doctrine of prevenient grace."[23] For Pinnock, the tight Calvinistic logic had also unraveled and has led to a revising of "classical" (TULIP) theism.

Revising Classical Theism

An adequate Christian doctrine of God, according to the more recent work of Clark Pinnock, would be "a distillation of what we believe God has told us about himself....Although the Bible does not present a systematic doctrine of God that can be easily reproduced, it provides building blocks for such a doctrine."[24] In order to formulate what he was coming to accept as an adequate theistic view, Pinnock gathered these building blocks that both criticized elements of "classic" Christian theism (resident in the "TULIP" logic) and warned that the metaphysics of the currently popular "process" theology alternative does not represent adequately the broader biblical vision of the divine that is now enriching his own thought and Christian life (since it tends to violate divine sovereignty in favor of a too-extreme view of reciprocity). God surely is more than the earth-bound gods of modern thought. God is transcendent in a way that can really satisfy today's urgent questions about meaning and significance with answers that have roots in a reality beyond the restricted and momentary horizons of this world. God clearly transcends and reigns, but in a way that does not negate the creation's divinely-given freedom to be and choose. Indeed, in very "ROSE-like" fashion, Pinnock now insists:

> To say that God is the sovereign Creator means that God is the ground of the world's existence and the source of all its possibilities. But he is not necessarily the puppet master who pulls all the strings. It is possible for God to make a world with some relative autonomy of its own, a world where there exist certain structures which are intelligible in their own right and finite agents with the capacity for free choice. Thus, God gives a degree of reality and power to the creation and does not retain a monopoly of power for himself. His sovereignty is not the all-determining kind, but an omnicompetent kind. God is certainly able to deal with any circumstances which might arise, and nothing can possibly defeat or destroy God. But he does not control everything that occurs. God honors the degree of relative autonomy which he grants the world.[25]

How, then, is God best understood? The answer lies at the foundation of all Christian theology and, for Pinnock, is explained well in his essay titled "From Augustine To Arminius: A Pilgrimage in Theology."[26] Biblically speaking, God at least is the Lord, sovereign and free, the mystery who transcends all time and worlds and all that they contain. But "classic" Christian theism came to add to such affirmations that *God's glory* is the ultimate purpose that all creation serves, that God controls all that happens, and that God's sovereign will is irresistible. According to the Westminster Confession (1646): "God from all eternity did, by the most wise and holy counsel of his own will, freely and unchangeably ordain whatsoever comes to pass" (3:1). After World War II evangelicalism in North America was dominated by this "classic" (TULIP) view that God is understood best as the One who is all-controlling and ordains all things, the One who is timeless, changeless, passionless, unmoved, and unmovable. This was the very teaching environment of Clark Pinnock's earliest years as a Christian and a view he now refers to as "a power-centered theology requiring deterministic freedom and no-risk providence" [no risk to God].[27]

What then is the biblical understanding of God and how God relates to the concerns of ordinary human life today? By the 1980s Pinnock was identifying as a significant theological problem key aspects of the classical theism found in Augustine, Aquinas, and Reformed scholasticism generally. The problem was said to be that God is understood as a closed, immobile, unchanging structure rather than the more biblical view of God as a dynamic personal agent who by choice is deeply and vulnerably involved in human joys and sorrows. To many ancient minds a god who is immutable and impassable suggested a divine being who is stoic, stable, even untouchable. But Pinnock now was convinced that the divine determination of all things, meaning that the future is already settled and divinely known, "has a definite tendency to diminish the dynamic dimension of God's nature and to threaten the reality of creaturely freedom."[28] Such diminishing and threatening were serious theological and practical matters. The classic tendency is to "prefer to speak more of God's power than of weakness, more of God's eternity than of temporality, and more of God's immutability than of living changeableness in relation to us."[29] Pinnock had come to believe that the Calvinist argument for God's exhaustive foreknowledge is tantamount to predestination since it implies the fixity of all things. Further, the rigid categories of scholastic Calvinism are inadequate to contain the radically relational God revealed in the Bible. After all, the Word *became* flesh—a dramatic statement of God's changing unchangeability!

Pinnock proceeded to initiate fresh thought about the "social Trinity." He judged that reluctance to recognize a truly social model of the Trinity has been a major theological problem over the centuries. For instance, while making the doctrine of the Trinity central to his theology, Karl Barth elevated unity over diversity, insisting on speaking of three modes of divine functioning rather than a triunity of the divine being. For Pinnock, "such agnosticism regarding the immanent Trinity has led some of his [Barth's] disciples into unitarianism" and has deprived Christians of "the revolutionary insight concerning God's nature represented by the social analogy of the Trinity." Naturally one wants to make it easier for Jews and Muslims to appreciate Christianity in the context of monotheism; thus, in order to avoid any suggestion of tri-theism, "we say that the Trinity is a society of persons united by a common divinity." Of course, there is only one God, eternal, uncreated, and incomprehensible. But

Pinnock further insists that biblical revelation offers this key insight: God's nature is "internally complex and consists of a fellowship of three. It is the essence of God's nature to be relational."[30]

In a dynamic biblical context that reveals a relational God who chooses loving reciprocity with creation, it had become possible for Pinnock to engage in the reconceptualization of God similar to the reforming work of John Wesley two centuries earlier. Wesley argues in his "Thoughts upon Divine Sovereignty" that integral to the divinity of God as God is the necessary association of divine justice and mercy with divine transcendence, power, and sovereignty. By insisting on such a necessary association, Theodore Jennings, Jr., suggests that Wesley "sought to overcome a bifurcation in the conceptualization of the divine being which seemed to be the consequence, on the one hand, of a deistic conception of God and, on the other, of a Calvinist reflection on the divine sovereignty....[Thus] the question of the poor, of the violated and humiliated of the earth, is decisive for the doctrine of God."[31] After all, the distinctive place where the God of the biblical witness intersected the life process of creation was at the point of pain. Israel experienced great pain in its Egyptian slavery and through the pain came a distinctive discernment of the God who identifies with, shares, and redeems (the exodus) in the midst of the pain (Ex. 6:6-7). Here was God interactively involved, relationally engaged with the human historical process in ways hardly fitting TULIP rigidities.

Clark Pinnock has thus been critical of any "classic" theism that fails to recognize biblical relationalism. However, he has not wanted to overdo his criticism of classical theism. After all, in his judgment the "classic" evangelical view is far better than radically liberal or extreme process views of God, although he readily admits to having learned a few important lessons from process thinker Charles Hartshorne. One lesson was that God, although unchanging in character and intent, surely is able and intends to change *operationally* in response to a changing creation that possesses genuine freedom of decision. Pinnock confesses that, without being a process thinker himself, "God has used process thinkers to compel me to change certain ideas which I had and bring them up to scriptural standards."[32] He admits that modern culture generally has also influenced him in this matter, encouraging in him a new emphasis on human freedom and a viewing of God as Self-limited in relation to this present world. At least at these points, he is sure that modernity has drawn Christian theological reflection in the direction of restored biblical teaching.

Pinnock's approach to the doctrine of God shows his continuing evangelical identity, regardless of his affinity with select insights of process theism. He will not relinquish the ontological transcendence of God. God *is* even when the world *is not,* he insists. Contemporary Christians should resist the "interiorization of faith where Christianity becomes an ideal of life rather than a truth claim about an objective God beyond the natural world."[33] He places much responsibility on Immanuel Kant for the negative trending today that seeks to shift the grounding of theological concepts to the realm of human experience. By contrast, commitment to biblical revelation rather than to modern experience and ideology inclines Pinnock toward using biblical categories and even language. The controlling criterion of judgment is:

> ...the foundational symbols of the Bible cannot be replaced, though they may be supplemented and interpreted. The symbols cannot be replaced because they are not based upon cultural experience but on a divine intrusion into history....We do not feel entitled to resymbolize Christian theology to suit ourselves, based in the ostensive authority of human experience.[34]

As he journeys from the TULIP to the ROSE model of Christian theism, Pinnock's general intent is to retain as much as possible of the biblical portrait of God as taught faithfully in the ecumenical tradition of the church, except at the points where the conserving tradition is found to be preserving elements not truly biblical. If his critics are right about Pinnock's "openness" views of God being largely reflections of modern philosophical and politically-correct assumptions, he would find such criticism devastating. To him, the primary criterion of truth for the Christian is fidelity to the Scriptures. But, in fact, he judges that the critics are wrong in this regard and that an "openness model" of God is more biblically adequate than several aspects of the conventional Christian theism of evangelicalism that are reflected in the TULIP theological model.

The God Who Risks the Process

The proper view of Christian theism is now thought by Clark Pinnock to be a carefully balanced model that is both sensitive to select insights of contemporary "process" thought and also retains the core biblical elements of theism. This equilibrium model must both insure true divine transcendence and celebrate a social triuneness that comprises God's very nature and characterizes God's dealings with a wayward creation.

Calling this balanced model "classical free will theism," he explains:

> It means that we affirm God as creator of the world as classical theism does and process thought does not, and also affirm the openness of God as process theology does and classical theism does not sufficiently. This leaves us with a model of the divine which sees God as transcendent over the world and yet existing in an open and mutually affecting relationship with the world. It is a doctrine of God which maintains mutuality and reciprocity within the framework of divine transcendence.[35]

Pinnock wishes to be clear that, in projecting this new model of Christian theism, it is really very "old." The Bible and not modernity is being given the primary and final voice. As the whole Bible narrative reflects, human history is to be seen as much more than "the temporal unfolding of an eternal blueprint of the divine decisions." In fact, by divine choice, human history is "the theatre where new situations are encountered and fresh decisions are made, the scene of divine and human creativity."[36] God tested Abraham to see what he would do. Only after the test did God conclude: "Now I know that you fear God" (Gen. 12:22). Commenting on the wickedness of Israel, God says in frustration: ". . . nor did it enter my mind that they should do this abomination" (Jer. 32:35). The flow of fallen human history yields results which God does not dictate and to which God reacts.

The mistake of TULIP theism is its denial of the gracious choice of the sovereign God to grant real freedom to humans and to enter the human arena vulnerably and redemptively so as to affect and be affected by the flawed historical process that persists prior to the final triumph of God over all evil. God feels the pain of broken relationships (Jer. 31:20). This surely is at the heart of the meaning of the Incarnation and is symbolized dramatically by the cross of Christ. On that old tree of divine sacrifice is revealed this: love instead of coercive power is the primary perfection of God. God works "not in order to subject our wills but to transform our hearts."[37] There emerges from the Bible a distinctive view of God, a dynamic theism that sees God as simultaneously sovereign over creation and suffering with creation. God is involved, interactive, responsive, and compassionate. God should not be understood either as immune to the evil and suffering of our fallen world or trapped in an ongoing codependence with this world. Pinnock has come to join John Wesley in understanding God's power

> . . . fundamentally in terms of empowerment, rather than control or overpowerment. This is not to weaken God's power, but to determine its

character! As Wesley was fond of saying, God works "strongly and sweetly." That is, God's grace works powerfully, but not irresistibly in matters of human life and salvation; thereby empowering our response-ability, without overriding our responsibility.[38]

The doctrine of God as "Trinity" is crucial for reflecting adequately the very nature of God and, consequently, God's chosen relation to the creation. Pinnock now teaches a relational ontology, a social trinitarian metaphysics that views God as both ontologically other (not part of or dependent on creation) and at the same time relating actively and responsively to the creation with unmerited love. God has chosen to create "an echo in space and time of the communion that God experiences in eternity, a reflection on the creaturely level of the loving movement within God." Since God by nature is "socially triune," the creation is designed to be "an ecosystem capable of echoing back the triune life of God." God exists as a communion of love and freedom, is "an open and dynamic structure" which, while wholly Self-sufficient, "delights in a world in which he can interact with creatures for whom his love can overflow."[39] God's involvement with the world is characterized by the unchanging nature, essence, and intent of God, but also by God's responsive and therefore changing experience, knowledge, and action. Never is God subject to change involuntarily, but God allows the world to touch and affect him—the very world over which God is truly transcendent and in which much happens in opposition to divine intent.

The issue of divine sovereignty, when understood as "nothing happens except what is knowingly and willingly decreed by him" (John Calvin, Institutes, 1.16.3), can be very troubling for modern people who wonder about the supposed divine purpose in the death camps of the Holocaust or the killing fields of Cambodia. So Clark Pinnock now concludes that "history itself seems to call the sovereignty of God into question and to require us to rethink it." Further, the Bible "seems to portray more genuine interaction and relationality in God's dealings with creatures than theological determinism allows." Therefore, "it would seem that we need a better model of divine sovereignty than that of total control." If God is a loving Parent, sensitive and responsive, evidently God has chosen "to actualize a world with significantly free agents and to exercise sovereignty in an open manner."[40]

Such divine openness calls for a new view of divine power. God chooses to delegate power to the creature, willing that human history flow from the decisions of free persons who, because of their freedom, are capable of both evil and lovingly responding to a loving God. God by a deliberate choice becomes vulnerable to human choice and normally does not choose to override human decisions—at least not immediately. Jesus says that God's rule is near but not yet in full effect since the powers of darkness still resist. Paul says that the Spirit waits and groans with us on the way to final redemption (Rom. 8:23). God clearly is sovereign, meaning that all ability exists within the divine being, but not meaning that there is any divine tyranny involved. God can and will manage, whatever the resistance to the divine will, and one day will triumph. Even so, risk, frustration, and pain lie along God's chosen way.

With love as God's reigning attribute, the sovereign God, truly transcendent, has chosen to make room for others and to seek real and mutually responsible relationships with them. Accordingly, the wonderful truth is that "God is so powerful as to be able to stoop down and humble himself, and God is so stable and secure as to be able to risk suffering and change."[41] This sovereign God has created a world populated by free agents who are drawn by the Creator's love, but who also are capable of rejecting God's love. God is willing to work within this risky historical process, choosing to accept a future that is open and a world that is dynamic rather than one that is static and predetermined.[42]

Passion from the New Metaphor

The "loving heart of the Father" brings into focus the now controlling metaphor for Pinnock's understanding of God. Many of the alterations in his theological perspectives over the last twenty-five years have emerged from this one central paradigm change. The shift has been a move from the root metaphor of God as "absolute monarch" (TULIP model) to the "loving Parent" (ROSE model) who is at once transcendent, triune, "open," and gracefully engaged with a fallen creation. The result is that he now is "filled with passion for explicating the tender mercies of God more convincingly in our day and for lifting up the divine relationality more effectively."[43]

Change in "classic" Christian theism of the strict "TULIP" variety will not come easily among evangelicals generally. Pinnock has proceeded nonetheless to journey along a path that he sees as biblically illumined and vital for the credibility and effectiveness of Christian life in the postmodern and pluralistic world of the twenty-first century. Out of a heart of love and in the chosen context of freedom granted to fallen and yet beloved humans, the transcendent and loving God reaches, risks, suffers, relates, and redeems. There emerges the beautiful "ROSE" of the **R**elational, **O**pen, **S**uffering, and **E**verywhere-active One. Committed to belief in the triune God whose Spirit is everywhere active, Pinnock has become convinced that God is striving for life and wholeness among all peoples. This "inclusivist" view is a natural response to belief in the boundless love that God is by nature. This view brings vision, challenge, and significant implications for the Christian theological enterprise and evangelistic mission.

Notes

[1] See Barry L. Callen, *Clark H. Pinnock: Journey Toward Renewal* (Nappanee, Ind.: Evangel Publishing House, 2000).

[2] One modest exception is the Calvinist Norman Geisler who nuances aspects of the "TULIP" model into a "moderate" instead of an "extreme" Calvinism. He judges an extreme Calvinist to be one who is more Calvinistic than John Calvin himself (*Chosen But Free*, Bethany House Publishers, 1999, 55).

[3] See especially Clark H. Pinnock and others, eds., *The Openness of God* (Downers Grove, Ill.: InterVarsity Press, 1994), John Sanders, *The God Who Risks* (Downers Grove, Ill.: InterVarsity Press, 1998), and Gregory A. Boyd, *God of the Possible* (Grand Rapids: Baker Books, 2000).

[4] Clark H. Pinnock, "From Augustine To Arminius: A Pilgrimage in Theology," in Pinnock, gen. ed., *The Grace of God and the Will of Man* (Zondervan: Academia Books, 1989, Bethany House Publishers edition, 1995), 19.

[5] See, for instance, Daniel Clendenin, *Eastern Orthodox Christianity* (Baker Books, 1994) and Bishop Kallistos Ware, *The Orthodox Way* (St. Vladimir's Seminary Press, rev. ed. 1995).

[6] Randy L. Maddox, "John Wesley and Eastern Orthodoxy," *Asbury Theological Journal*, 45:2 (1990), 35. Maddox develops Wesley's whole theological vision around the concept of "responsible grace" (*Responsible Grace: John Wesley's Practical Theology*, Kingswood Books, Abingdon Press, 1994).

[7] See, for example, Albert Outler, "The Place of Wesley in the Christian Tradition," in *The Place of Wesley in the Christian Tradition*, ed. K. A. Rowe (Metuchen, NJ: Scarecrow, 1976), 30.

[8] Pinnock was influenced by I. Howard Marshall's examination of the security issue in his book *Kept by the Power of God: A Study in Perseverance and Falling Away* (London, 1969; Minneapolis, 1975).

[9] Pinnock, "From Augustine To Arminius...," 18. Pinnock's colleague and friend John Sanders was traveling a similar road. The shift in theistic view first came to Sanders through his own Bible reading, especially in relation to petitionary prayer. Why pray in a petitionary way if God already has determined everything? To the contrary, Sanders observed, there is a divine-human mutuality (see Sanders, *The God Who Risks*, InterVarsity, 1998). While Pinnock was supplementing his Bible reading with Wesleyan, pentecostal, and process theological sources and finding there much support for an open, free-will theism, Sanders was finding similar support by reading some Dutch Reformed sources,

especially the work of Vincent Brümmer.

[10] A former student and now critic of Pinnock, R. K. McGregor Wright, turns "results of reciprocity" into the negative of "accommodating the assumption of human autonomy" (*No Place for Sovereignty*, InterVarsity Press, 1996, 12).

[11] Robert Shank, *Elect in the Son* (Springfield, Mo.: Westcott, 1970).

[12] See Gregory A. Boyd, *God At War: The Bible and Spiritual Conflict* (Downers Grove, Ill.: InterVarsity Press, 1997). Boyd assumes the reality of an active reciprocity between God and a fallen world that has the freedom to choose against the will of God. Boyd argues that theologians still draw too heavily on Augustine's approach to the problem of evil, an approach that attributes pain and suffering in this world to the mysterious "good" purposes of God. Pinnock is highly appreciative of Boyd's extensive work, the most recent of which is the book *God of the Possible* (Baker Books, 2000).

[13] Pinnock, "From Augustine To Arminius. . . ," 21.

[14] See Randy L. Maddox, *Responsible Grace: John Wesley's Practical Theology* (Nashville: Kingswood Books, Abingdon Press, 1994).

[15] Randy L. Maddox has concluded that "Wesley is best read as a theologian who was fundamentally committed to the therapeutic view of Christian life, who struggled to express this view in the terms of the dominant stream of his western Christian setting, and who sought to integrate some of the central convictions of this setting into his more basic therapeutic viewpoint" ("Reading Wesley As Theologian," *Wesleyan Theological Journal*, Spring 1995, 16).

[16] Ibid., 71.

[17] Clark H. Pinnock, "Evangelical Theologians Facing the Future: Ancient and Future Paradigms," *Wesleyan Theological Journal* 33:2 (Fall 1998), 12-13. Pinnock had been invited to keynote the 1997 annual meeting of the Wesleyan Theological Society by Douglas Strong of Wesley Theological Seminary in Washington, D. C. Strong was the WTS program chair that year and invited Pinnock in part because Pinnock's "scholarly trajectory places him in close proximity to our [Wesleyan] tradition" and in part because he is recognized as "one of the leading North American theologians today and is viewed as a spokesperson for the broad umbrella of American evangelicalism" (email letter from Douglas Strong to Barry Callen). His invitation was supported enthusiastically by the WTS Executive Committee and led to the Society's support of the publication by Barry L. Callen titled *Clark H. Pinnock: Journey Toward Renewal* (Evangel Publishing House, 2000). The keynote address is found in the Fall 1998 issue of the *Wesleyan Theological Journal* under the title "Evangelical Theologians Facing the Future."

[18] Mildred Bangs Wynkoop, "John Wesley: Mentor Or Guru?," *Wesleyan Theological Journal* (Spring 1975), 7. See Appendix D of Barry Callen, *Clark H. Pinnock: Journey Toward Renewal* (Evangel Publishing House, 2000) where Pinnock reflects on the trauma experienced as he has sought to renew in more relational categories the view of God's nature and way with humans. He observes: "Had I been a Wesleyan, I might have had an easier time of it."

[19] Philip R. Meadows, "Providence, Chance, and the Problem of Suffering," *Wesleyan Theological Journal* (Fall 1999), 72, 62-63.
[20] Henry H. Knight III, *A Future For Truth: Evangelical Theology in a Postmodern World* (Nashville: Abingdon Press, 1997), 172.
[21] Randy Maddox, "John Wesley and Eastern Orthodoxy," *Asbury Theological Journal* 45:2 (1990), 39.
[22] Note H. Ray Dunning, *Redefining the Divine Image: Christian Ethics in Wesleyan Perspective* (Downers Grove, Ill.: InterVarsity Press, 1998). He writes chapters on the "Image of God" as relation to God, others, the Earth, and self.
[23] Colin Williams, *John Wesley's Theology Today* (N. Y.: Abingdon Press, 1960), 44. Wesley remained on the edge of Calvinism in the sense that he also attributed all good to the free grace of God and denied the presence of all natural free will and human power antecedent to divine grace.
[24] Clark H. Pinnock, in Pinnock and Delwin Brown, *Theological Crossfire: An Evangelical/Liberal Dialogue* (Grand Rapids: Zondervan, 1990), 61, 63.
[25] Clark H. Pinnock, "God Limits His Knowledge," in David and Randall Basinger, eds., *Predestination & Free Will: Four Views of Divine Sovereignty and Human Freedom* (Downers Grove, Ill.: InterVarsity Press, 1986), 145-146.
[26] This pivotal Pinnock essay appears in Clark Pinnock, gen. ed., *The Grace of God and the Will of Man* (Minneapolis: Bethany House Publishers, 1995, original edition 1989), 15-30.
[27] Clark H. Pinnock, "Evangelical Theologians Facing the Future: An Ancient and a Future Paradigm," *Wesleyan Theological Journal* 33:2(Fall 1998), 22. In 1998 there appeared *The God Who Risks: A Theology of Providence* by John Sanders (InterVarsity Press). Pinnock refers to this book as a competent and detailed argument that God indeed is relational in nature. In the manner of working with the creation, God is relational and loving to the extent of taking real "risks". Says Sanders: "The almighty God creates significant others with freedom and grants them space to be alongside him and to collaborate with him" (137).
[28] Clark H. Pinnock, "Between Classical and Process Theism," ed. Ronald Nash, *Process Theology* (Grand Rapids: Baker Books, 1987), 315.
[29] Clark H. Pinnock, "Systematic Theology," in Pinnock and others, *The Openness of God: A Biblical Challenge to the Traditional Understanding of God* (Downers Grove, Ill.: InterVarsity Press, 1994), 105.
[30] Clark H. Pinnock, *Flame of Love: A Theology of the Holy Spirit* (Downers Grove, Ill.: InterVarsity Press, 1996), 33-35.
[31] Theodore W. Jennings, Jr., "Transcendence, Justice, and Mercy: Toward a (Wesleyan) Reconceptualization of God," in Randy L. Maddox, ed., *Rethinking Wesley's Theology for Contemporary Methodism* (Nashville: Kingswood Books, Abingdon Press, 1998), 65.
[32] Clark H. Pinnock, "Between Classical and Process Theism," 317. Another evangelical, Gregory Boyd, embraces elements of the fundamental vision of the process world view and constructs an interpretation of the Trinity with

careful modifications of this process vision (see Boyd, *Trinity and Process*, New York: Peter Lang, 1992).

33Clark H. Pinnock, in *Theological Crossfire*, 67-68.

34Ibid., 72.

35Clark H. Pinnock, "Between Classical and Process Theism," 321.

36Ibid., 323.

37Clark H. Pinnock, "Systematic Theology," 114.

38Randy L. Maddox, *Responsible Grace: John Wesley's Practical Theology* (Nashville: Kingswood Books, Abingdon Press, 1994), 93.

39Clark H. Pinnock, "Systematic Theology" (1994), 108, 110.

40Clark H. Pinnock, "God's Sovereignty in Today's World," *Theology Today* 53:1 (April 1996), 16-18. Richard Muller recognizes that contemporary evangelical theology needs to express the profound involvement of God with creation (just as Pinnock does). Contrary to Pinnock, however, Muller remains convinced that the structure of classical theism is still the best option. He insists that "incarnation and the divine immutability are not contraries" ("Incarnation, Immutability, and the Case for Classical Theism," *The Westminster Theological Journal*, Spring 1983, 25).

41Pinnock, "Systematic Theology," 105.

42This line of thought is appreciated by Philip Meadows ("Providence, Chance, and the Problem of Suffering," *Wesleyan Theological Journal*, Spring 1999). Speaking of the paradox of providence and chance, Meadows explores the resources in John Wesley's theology for constructing a contemporary theodicy. He concludes that God loves the world by setting it free. Seen in the cross and resurrection of Jesus is the deeply personal and relational nature of God's vulnerable love.

43Clark H. Pinnock, "Response to Daniel Strange and Amos Yong," *The Evangelical Quarterly* 71:4 (October 1999), 351. With this passion comes Pinnock's acceptance of the controversy that accompanies it.

Chapter 2

Joining Holiness and All Truth

by
Barry L. Callen

The Church of God Movement (Anderson) does not acknowledge any "founder" other than Jesus Christ and, at Pentecost, the Spirit of Christ. The movement emerged rather spontaneously in a variety of settings (especially, at first, in Ohio, Indiana, and Michigan), with the prophetic ministries of a series of men and women who felt that God was doing a special thing in these last days. The primary pioneer of the movement could be identified as Daniel S. Warner (1842-1895). Only by understanding him and his vision and ministry can one understand the dynamics of the movement's earliest generation. This material originally appeared in the Wesleyan Theological Journal *(30:1, Spring, 1995).*

In its earliest decades the Holiness Movement in America sought to be a reforming force within existing church structures. Eventually many movement adherents, often reluctantly, became separatists, judging themselves forced out of the churches because of their commitment to holiness.[1]

The Holiness Movement was "reformationist" early; elements of it later became more "restorationist" based on "primitivist" ideals often associated with the holiness emphasis. Daniel Warner (1842-1895) and the Church of God movement (Anderson, Ind.) he helped inspire came especially early in this "separatist" process, although his motivation was anything but the further dividing the church by setting up another human organization, even one justified by a concern for holiness. As early as 1880, Warner became an aggressive, idealistic "separatist," not only from the established churches, but also from the formal structures of the Holiness Movement that seemed insistent on supporting them.

Warner's come outism was inspired by a vision of the church outside all denominations, enabled by the dynamic of holiness. He cared deeply about the unity of believers, saw holiness as the way to it, and judged the continuing existence of multiple and often competitive denominational structures to be an evil among God's people that God intended to end.[2] Years later many other holiness people would feel "pushed out" of their denominational homes by the nominalism of unresponsive church establishments. They would organize their own alternatives. Warner, by contrast, "came out" in response to his own vision of what he had come to understand as God's higher will for the sanctification of the church itself.

Sounding the Trumpet

Participants in the early Wesleyan/Holiness Movement apparently were avid readers. Holiness papers were common, sometimes competitive, and often ceased publication altogether or merged with others. For example, the official paper of the Church of the Nazarene, *Herald of Holiness*, was established as this denomination's official organ in 1912, but its history stretches back into Warner's time. Four papers lay behind this one, and "each of these had at least two direct ancestors."[3] A similar pattern is seen in the earliest editorial work of Daniel Warner.

The first issue of the *Gospel Trumpet* appeared January 1, 1881. It originated from Rome City, Indiana, and was a merging of *The Pilgrim*, published in Indianapolis by G. Haines, and the *Herald of Gospel Freedom*. Warner was founding editor, with publishing supervision provided by the Northern Indiana Eldership of the Churches of God (Winebrennerian) through whom Warner was ministering. Warner's subsequent ministry would be felt by the world largely through the medium of this new holiness paper. Although he did not know it at the time, he was "standing on the threshold of an exciting adventure for both himself and the whole Christian church" (Smith 1965, 9).

The new paper carried this statement of purpose: "The glory of God in the salvation of men from all sin, and the union of all saints upon the Bible." Expressed here were the major burdens of Warner. He had been "disillusioned with the shortcomings of the denominational system of his time-the fierce and unbrotherly rivalries, the rigidity of creedal systems, the lack of any real and deep commitment to serious Christian living on the part of so many nominal church members. With Bible in heart and hand, and by faith, Warner saw something better than this..." (Phillips 1979, 21).

Only two issues of the new *Gospel Trumpet* were published in Rome City. Haines owned a job printing business in Indianapolis, the state's rapidly growing capital city, so he suggested moving the *Trumpet* there. Seeming a progressive opportunity, in February, 1881, this modest holiness periodical found a home at 70 North Illinois Street, Indianapolis, very close to the railroad station and the new statehouse then under construction. This was an exhilarating setting, certainly different for Daniel and his wife Sarah whose backgrounds were in small Ohio farming communities. Maybe now, it was hoped, the publishing of holiness would move more to the center stage of public life.

By the summer of 1881 the Haines Warner partnership had dissolved. Warner paid Haines $100 for his share of this obviously modest operation. The negotiation led to the reluctant agreement of Haines not to launch a rival holiness paper in Indianapolis. He soon did, however, even sending samples of his new paper to *Gospel Trumpet* subscribers. All was not "perfect" in holiness circles!

Warner soon wrote of this awkward circumstance. He deplored such a development as necessarily hurtful to the holiness cause. Haines is said to have brought to the previous partnership "a chilling iceberg, an austere, worldly, complaining, and mere money policy." Warner notes that the primary time commitment of Haines had been to his other role as Indianapolis agent for the *Cincinnati Times Star*.[4] Already beginning was what has been called "the miracle of survival,"[5] a miracle that would have to last for decades, clear to the present time. Publishing the holiness message, especially in opposition to the denominational establishments, was hardly a lucrative or persecution free business. It required very dedicated and sacrificial servants. Daniel Warner was prepared to be one of these.

Warner managed on his own the best he could. He moved the printing office to his home at 625 West Vermont Street near downtown Indianapolis and built a makeshift office beside the house by using lumber from an old horse stable that he tore down himself. There he began printing the paper, setting all type and doing all the folding and addressing by hand-and by himself at first. There were only a few hundred subscribers to serve in this tedious way. When winter came, the drafty little office was not at all practical and there was no money to plaster the walls so that the cold could be kept out. There seemed only one option. He moved the noisy and ill smelling printing press into the kitchen of his home, reporting that "Dear Wife tendered her kitchen to the Lord for the use of publishing salvation. Praise the Lord!" An independent report from Sarah is not available, but one wonders how thankful she really was to have her kitchen so invaded.

Sarah Warner had just given birth to their second child, son Sidney. There they were, with little money, a new baby, a press in the kitchen, and few people who seemed to care. About the only bright spot was a subscriber in Michigan, a Joseph Fisher who was so enthusiastic about the *Gospel Trumpet* that he sent generous support and voluntarily sold subscriptions. Soon Warner was listing Fisher on the masthead as the co publisher.

Growing Come-Outism Conviction

As the issues of the *Trumpet* kept coming, in spite of all obstacles, a conviction of Warner's kept growing. In part it was rooted in the theological emphases of John Winebrenner (1797 1860) that had shaped him from his earliest life as a Christian. Winebrenner loomed large in Warner's mind as "a spiritual father," to the extent that "his very mental furniture bore the Winebrennerian stamp."[6] This stamp centers in a five point theological transformation that Winebrenner experienced across the 1820s[7] and led by 1830 to the rupture of his relationship with the German Reformed Church in Harrisburg, Pennsylvania. These five points are:

1. The Bible is the Word of God, the only authoritative rule of faith and practice. This "only" left no place for church tradition, including human inventions like creeds, catechisms, rituals, etc.;

2. Spiritual regeneration, being born again, always is necessary for a person to become a real Christian and church member. Thus the Christian faith is rooted in the Bible and in such spiritual experience;

3. Humankind possesses free moral agency and the ability, with the Spirit's assistance, to repent, believe, and be saved. Thus denied were the Reformed doctrines of predestination, providence, and perseverance;

4. Baptism and the Lord's Supper became seen as symbolic "ordinances" rather than grace conveying "sacraments." Baptism necessarily is to be preceded by belief and regeneration and is best administered by immersion (eliminating the appropriateness of infant baptism). Feetwashing also joined the list of the church's ordinances;

5. Regarding the church, the only requirement for membership in a local congregation is having been born again and the true

Biblical name for a local congregation or for the Body of Christ as a whole is "Church of God."[8]

Warner's own spiritual conversion was in a revival meeting being held near Montpelier, Ohio, in 1865. The evangelist was a minister of the General Eldership of the Churches of God (Winebrennarian). Warner then received his ministerial license from the West Ohio Eldership in 1867, having decided that this body represented best the true faith and practices of the New Testament church.[9]

After years of ministry, Warner's relationship with the West Ohio Eldership would also rupture, deepening his suspicion that human structures and creeds are a human intrusion into the life of God's church. This suspicion would deepen further as he became involved in the holiness movement and saw in this the experiential means whereby Christians could counter the evil of sectarian chaos. In addition, in 1868, near the very beginning of his ministry, Warner had purchased a copy of the book *Discourses on the Nature of Faith* by William Starr (1857). Starr was a Congregational minister in Illinois who felt his ministry stifled by a restrictive church establishment. Sometime before 1880, Warner wrote this annotation in his personal copy, alongside Starr's call for believers to rise up against sectarianism and bring to reality a "holy and unified church":

> If this holy man, perceiving only the eavil [sic] of division, is thus moved to cry out, what must be the guilt of one who sees both the eavil [sic] and remedy and yet will close his mouth and see the world go to ruin? (231).

The conviction that God was calling for a freedom of the church from denominational division, on the basis of Christian holiness, had matured in Warner's thinking.[10] It was time to act.

The New Commission

By 1880 Daniel Warner himself was ready to cry out and act out against sectarianism. An increasing number of leaders of the holiness movement were feeling significant tension between their passion for church renewal and the viability of continuance in their home denomi-nations. Soon there would be new holiness oriented denominations, one way of finally dealing with the holiness movement's "search for order" (Dieter 236 275). Another way was that of the more "radical" holiness reformers who soon became known as "come outers." Prominent and one of the first among them was Daniel Warner.[11]

Warner now was growing impatient with compromises to his vision. He was gripped increasingly by the "new commission" that he felt God had given him. According to the March 7, 1878, entry in his personal journal:

> The Lord showed me that holiness could never prosper upon sectarian soil encumbered by human creeds and party names, and he gave me a new commission to join holiness and all truth together and build up the apostolic church of the living God.

This new commission carried major implications that, at least in Warner's judgment, could not be ignored any longer. Like a growing number of others, he "sought to apply the logic of Christian perfectionism, with all its ultraistic inclinations of the perfectionist mentality, to the church question" (Dieter 246). The first compromise that Warner called into serious question was his own participation in the Holiness Association. By doing so, he was "the first to propose such radical applications of the revival's promise of unity among all true Christian believers" (Dieter 246).

Both Warner's affinity with and his questioning of the reform from the inside approach of the mainstream holiness movement can be seen in one setting in 1880. A convention of the Western Union Holiness Association convened from December 15-19 in the Brooklyn Methodist Episcopal Church in Jacksonville, Illinois.[12] The planning committee said that this gathering, comprised of about two hundred holiness leaders from a range of denominations and states, would only be in the interests of holiness. Thus, it was to be "strictly and purely undenominational." People were to come not representing any particular denomination, but only to celebrate and strengthen "the holiness cause."

One delegate was to represent each holiness periodical, with all delegates to be in agreement with the doctrine of holiness "that sets forth entire sanctification as an instantaneous work of God, wrought in the heart through faith, subsequent to conversion." Likely Daniel Warner was present both as a representative of the *Herald of Gospel Freedom* and because he had been asked to make a formal address, an honor in this select ecumenical crowd. He also was appointed to the program committee charged with the responsibility of planning the next convention.

The topic of Warner's address to the convention was "The Kind of Power Needed to Carry the Holiness Work." The main point he made was that "it is the power of God Himself that is needed for this work." He warned that "the devil is set against this work....We need God's power to the fullest degree promised to meet this adversary." "God is looking around to find someone he can trust," announced Warner. God "generally finds them among the holy ones."

Some of the statements by other speakers heard by Warner at this convention stirred the evolving struggle within him. For instance, Thomas Doty from Cleveland, Ohio, editor of the *Christian Harvester*, said that "if you belong to a church, it is your duty to promote holiness right in it: in the Presbyterian church, as a Presbyterian; in the Baptist church, as a Baptist, etc." Doty admitted that he disliked the whole denominational idea, but said God "permits it, and so must we." Warner did not address this issue in his formal remarks, but M. L. Haney (Methodist Episcopal leader) did. He attacked come outers "who insist on the silly dogma of no churchism, and favor the disorganization of all Christian forces."

But J. W. Caughlan, editor of *The Good Way*, realized that there was a real problem to be addressed somehow. Holiness believers needed encouragement and support between holiness camp meetings, especially when and where denominational leaders were unsympathetic to the holiness cause. When the organized church comes into conflict with Christ, suggested Caughlan, maybe that "church" should be "consecrated" on the altar of sacrifice. By endorsing the idea of holiness associations and bands, this Western Convention "was a first step toward creating a potentially separatist group within the church" (Jones 55).

It may be that, as Warner heard such men speak in these ways, "the conviction was being cemented in his heart and mind that there was no room for him and for the burning message he felt in a situation where denominationalism was being exalted and continued membership in a denomination was being made a requirement of continued fellowship and acceptance."[13] The message beginning to burn inside Warner tended to question the easy, status quo assumption that God passively permits rampant division of Christ's body, the church.

Maybe being a "come outer" was the way to go. Warner saw the charge of no churchism as very wrong, unfair, and demeaning of the unifying potential of the promised sanctifying power of the Spirit. He believed deeply in the church and refused to accept the claim that genuine reliance on the Holy Spirit to establish and guide the church inevitably is the way of anarchy. Is God the author of confusion? The church is, after all, God's church! God is capable of constituting, gifting, and governing believers who are fully yielded to the Holy Spirit. Is that not exactly what the New Testament says? Since holiness cannot prosper on sectarian soil, Warner judged, his new commission to "join holiness and all truth together" impelled him to take definitive action.

I'm Coming Out!

The strength of Warner's convictions grew and began to be acted out. In April, 1881, he was elected an Adjutant General in the Salvation Army in Indianapolis. He promised that the *Gospel Trumpet* would carry reports of some "battles and conquests of the Lord's Salvation Army." But the February 8, 1882, issue reported an apparent end of this relationship. Being joined to anything but the Lord now was said to be a trick of Satan.

This vigorous come out view rooted in a pivotal event in April, 1881. While conducting a revival meeting in Hardinsburg, Indiana, Warner reported that he "saw the church." No longer would he be patient with church bodies that organized their lives on the basis of sect recognition and requirements. For years Warner had been troubled about the inconsistency of his repudiating "sects" in principle and yet continuing to belong to organizations that insisted on basing their memberships on formal sect recognition. Now he no longer would condone the disjunction between his holiness generated unity vision and the standard acceptance of sect division. What he now "saw" was God's intended alternative, a Spirit inspired, Spirit enabled, Spirit governed, and Spirit unified gathering of all God's people. Holiness also is to extend to the church, not only to the inward experience of individual believers. Visible unity is a key aspect of the church's intended holiness.

Instead of passive acceptance of the usual compromises, Warner determined to be faithful to a fresh vision, a new way of conceiving how things might be for the church of the Spirit. The Israelites of the Exodus and the Babylonian Exile finally were able to see dramatic new possibilities in the worst of circumstances. Their seeing opened their imaginations, inspired their faith, and generated new hope. God always has been in the business of regathering the faithful. God intends a church that is visible in this world, not one that is *invisible* (the typical Protestant theory that the true church is inevitably buried out of sight, somewhere within the spoiled "churches" of our sinful world).

Warner now chose to walk the ancient prophetic path that announced God's higher intention. As Merle Strege puts it, Warner rejected "the American religious *status quo*, the business as usual way of denominational religion" (96). Since the church really is God's, surely there is a better way of showing it to the world than settling for a network of quarreling and divisive denominations.

This prophetic position brought an immediate crisis in Warner's relationship with the National Holiness Association.[14] "The Spirit showed me," he wrote, "the inconsistency of repudiating sects and yet belonging to an association that is based on sect recognition."[15] No longer would he be patient with the placing of *human* conditions on membership in God's church. He went to a meeting of the Indiana Holiness Association in Terre Haute, Indiana, and tried to get changed the "sect endorsing clause" of the association so that its membership would be open "to all true Christians everywhere" (whether denominational adherents or not). The effort failed. Many holiness people persisted in believing that abandoning the "churches," with all their obvious faults, was not the best way to renew the people of God. So Warner reported in the *Gospel Trumpet* (June 1, 1881): "We wish to co operate with all Christians, as such, in saving souls-but forever withdraw from all organisms that uphold and endorse sects and denominations in the body of Christ."

The stance of the Holiness Movement at first did not generate for itself the dilemma faced by Warner. Its purpose was to be a transdenominational renewal force. Its primary concern was not the evil of denominationalism as such, although some leaders were uncomfortable with all the formalized division; it was the evil of nominal Christianity. The intent was that participants in the holiness associations would remain loyal members in their respective denominations so that they could be renewed by the holiness emphasis and return to their denominational homes to broaden the renewal impact.

By the 1880s, however, frustrated by attempts to renew existing churches, many holiness converts had begun considering the possibility of one or more distinctively holiness denominations. Warner was a pioneer of this "come out" trend, although he opposed the very idea of denominations, *even new ones organized under a holiness banner*. The extent of Warner's renewal vision was greater than this, thus the inevitable clash.[16]

Reported church historian Henry Wickersham in 1900: "Before this he [Warner] was in good standing with many editors and sectarian holiness workers, but because of his decided stand for the truth, he was denounced in their papers, set at naught by the ministry, and rejected by his former friends" (300). According to sociologist Val Clear (36):

> It was in the small cells of the holiness minded individuals scattered about the country in the 1870s and 1880s that the future adherents of

Warner's movement were to be found. Most of the holiness people stayed within their denominations, forming a type of church within the church. But many others were disaffected, felt that Old Ship Zion was sure to sink. For many of these latter persons, D. S. Warner became a spokesman, and the *Gospel Trumpet* was his voice.

The significance of Warner is clear. In this earliest phase of the life of the Church of God movement, "it was Warner who was prophet, teacher, evangelizer, poet, advisor, theologian-the voice of the reformation. Since the *Gospel Trumpet* was the only formal organizational entity, it was Warner's dominant personality and the Trumpet that kept the movement from disintegrating into a thousand isolated and disconnected parts" (Reardon 24). So far as the larger holiness movement is concerned, Warner is the one who brought to the movement clear elements of the Anabaptist tradition. These elements came in part from his reliance on the central teachings of John Winebrenner and partly from his close association with the Evangelical United Mennonites in northern Indiana.[17]

Having ruptured his formal tie to the holiness movement, Warner wasted no time in questioning his future with the Northern Indiana Eldership of the Churches of God by which he was licensed as a minister. In October, 1881, he attended a meeting of the Eldership in Beaver Dam, Indiana. There he tried and again failed to have accepted the radical implications of his holiness unity vision. He proposed that this body "conform more perfectly to the Bible standard with reference to government" by ending the practice of granting ministerial licenses and eliminating formal church membership procedures so that all who bore the fruit of true regeneration would belong automatically by the action of God. When this body said a firm "no," five people walked out of the meeting with Warner, declaring that they were "coming out" of all sectism. Thus was constituted in Beaver Dam the first congregation of the Church of God movement.

This walk out was repeated later in the same month in Carson City, Michigan. Joseph and Allie Fisher, staunch *Trumpet* supporters, had asked Warner to come to Michigan to speak to a special holiness meeting being held prior to the annual camp meeting of the Northern Michigan Eldership, also a breakaway from the General Eldership of the Churches of God (Winebrennerian) over issues like Freemasonry. The local congregation objected to the holiness meeting, so the Fishers and twenty others, finding this the last straw, left the Eldership.

So a second group had separated from sectarianism. The "Carson City Resolutions" that they agreed to include this: "That we adhere to no body or organization but the church of God, bought by the blood of Christ, organized by the Holy Spirit, and governed by the Bible....That we recognize and fellowship, as members with us in the one body of Christ, all truly regenerated and sincere saints who worship God in all the light they possess, and that we urge all the dear children of God to forsake the snares and yokes of human parties and stand alone in the 'one fold' of Christ upon the Bible, and in the unity of the Spirit" (see Callen, 1979, I, 295 96).

Here were elements of the rationale for a new movement, one intending to be truly trans denominational in the sanctifying and unifying power of the Spirit. Joined were the passion for Christian holiness, the dream of Christian unity, and the belief that the first enables the second, but only when free of the artificial restrictions of human attempts to organize and "run" the church. Human hands must be taken off of God's church!

Warner's thrust was echoed by John Morrison[18] as he addressed the International Convention of the Church of God movement convened in Anderson, Indiana, in 1963. He told the crowd of thousands that "Christian fellowship ought to be wide enough and warm enough to take in a Christian wherever you may find him." Then Morrison concluded:

> So go home loving all Christians; but for heaven's sake don't join any of them! That's right! As I understand it, D. S. Warner's major contention was that a person can be a good Christian and cooperate with other Christians in proper fashion without joining any of the religious organizations known as churches. You do not join the Church-you are born into it! (see Callen, 1979, II, 651).

With the Beaver Dam and Carson City walk out events, a new "movement" now was gaining momentum and definition. The *Gospel Trumpet* was the movement's primary medium of conveyance, with Warner its tireless visionary and mouthpiece. The initial purpose of this holiness paper changed because of the dramatic events of 1881. Before then the *Gospel Trumpet* had been one of many holiness papers; but after Beaver Dam and Carson City it became Warner's major vehicle for furthering a "cause" extending beyond the goals typical of the larger holiness movement.

This cause drew considerable sympathy from many Christians longing for more vision and power, more holiness and unity than they had found to date. Judges Melvin Dieter: "Warner's promise of a group, gathered together under the guidance and instruction of the sanctifying Spirit, free of denominational and sectarian trammels, as he pictured them, combined with a reformatory, eschatological thrust, carried a certain populist magnetism" (256). Indeed it did, as the last years of the nineteenth century made very clear.

Most holiness people who separated from their denominations during the last quarter of the nineteenth century thought of themselves as "pushed outers," not "come outers." They judged themselves chased off by the increasing "carnality" in the churches, a sin situation intolerant of a holiness renewal.[19] Warner was both pushed out (West Ohio Eldership) and later intentionally came out of the Holiness Association and the Northern Indiana and Northern Michigan Elderships. In all instances, holiness was the key issue. At first, holiness was an unwelcome emphasis. Then holiness generated a unifying vision that called believers out of the compromised and unresponsive denominations. This vision also was intensely opposed by many who judged it idealistic, impractical, even arrogant; but it was embraced enthusiastically by thousands who saw it as the will and direct action of God.

New Movement of the Church of God

Daniel Warner would devote the remaining fourteen years of his life to restoring the unity of God's people through the sanctifying work of the Holy Spirit. He was a "come outer." He and soon many others "saw the church," a vision of the seamless, undivided body of Christ. Warner began sprinkling the pages of the *Gospel Trumpet* with testimonies of fresh sightings of the church beyond division.[20] One of his many poems soon became a central vehicle for singing and celebrating the vision of the Church of God movement concerning the relationship between holiness and the God intended unity of the church. Reads verse one and the chorus:

> How sweet this bond of perfectness,
> The wondrous love of Jesus!
> A pure fore taste of heaven's bliss,
> O fellowship so precious!
> Beloved, how this perfect love,
> Unites us all in Jesus!
> One heart, and soul, and mind: we prove
> the union heaven gave us.[21]

The "perfect love" of sanctification, it was argued, enables Christians to live above sin, including the sin of rending the body of Christ. Human lines of denomination, race, sex, and social status are to be discounted, even ignored in the face of the transforming grace of God in Christ. The emphasis should be on *seeing*, not arrogantly claiming to be the whole, pure, undivided church. The vision calls for refusing either to erect or recognize human controls on Christian fellowship. God sets the members in the church. It's God's church! The church exists for mission, and disunity is hurtful to the church's attempt to bear a credible witness in the world.

Warner finally had found a church home. It was not one of the Winebrennerian elderships or the Holiness Movement as such. It was *the whole body of Christ*. He sensed God moving to complete the sixteenth century Protestant reformation and the eighteenth century Wesleyan revival in a "last reformation."[22] There was a new sense of liberty and joy, inspiring Warner to compose many new songs that express the fresh vision. Testifies one song by Warner and his faithful colleague Barney Warren: "My soul is satisfied; my soul is satisfied; I am complete in Jesus' love, and my soul is satisfied."[23] Another announced, "There's music in my soul."

So strongly did Warner feel about the new movement that he later renumbered the volumes of the *Gospel Trumpet*, repudiating its first three volumes when it had appeared under earlier names and in connection with the Northern Indiana Eldership of the Churches of God. He explained:

> Since the *Herald* was started back in the fogs of Babylon, and died before it saw the evening light clearly, we have desired to drop off its three years and cast it back into the burning city where it belonged, and have our volume indicate the actual number of years that the *Trumpet* has been sounding. For when a person gets clean out of Babylon, that should be the beginning of months and years to him.[24]

Historian John Smith summarizes Warner's "enlightenment" experience this way:

> He had found the freedom in Christ for which he had so long sought. A new ingredient entered his life. It was as if he had been released from a great load and for the first time was able to stand erect. He felt as though he had stepped from the condemnatory shadow of his own and all other sectarian walls and now stood in the full light of truth-the "evening" light of which the prophet Zechariah had spoken. There was indeed cause for rejoicing. God had begun a new work in the church.[25]

These breaks from traditionally organized Christian denominations focused on (1) rejecting all sects, (2) refusing to form another, (3) in part by not defining or limiting the new cause by any set creed. The emerging movement was similar to many previous movements by its (1) seeing the church as a voluntary gathering of all and only the truly regenerate (like the Anabaptists, Campbellites, etc.) and (2) highlighting the Bible and the Spirit as together the sufficient guides to all truth (Quakers, etc.). The *distinguishing feature* of this new "cause" was primarily that Warner and others "put all of these emphases in a single package and then wedded them to the Wesleyan doctrine of holiness" (Smith 1980, 48).[26]

The early tone of this new cause was celebrative in nature and aggressive in style. In the new year's greeting for January, 1882, the *Gospel Trumpet*, that is, editor Daniel Warner, was very plain:

> To Babylon and all her concomitants, we promise nothing but fire, sword and hammer, and confounding blasts from the armory of God's Word. We have scarcely begun the bombardment of the wicked harlot city. By the grace of God, we expect to deal with sin and sinners as we never yet have done....We know no man after the flesh, and we seek to please no man.

Propositions Still Worthy of Note

Several editors of other holiness papers, themselves now targets, reacted with criticism of Warner's new stand that claimed to be outside the presumed evils of sectism. Warner sought to answer them at length.[27] The new freedom had its own dilemmas—and certainly its detractors (soon even to include Mrs. Warner!). It still does. It also has its vision, its hope, its determination to release the church back into God's control.

In more recent years, and in a more irenic tone, various leaders of the Church of God movement have reflected on the new commission of Daniel Warner and have sought to state ways in which "joining holiness and all truth together" continues to have relevance for the contemporary church's quest for Christian unity. Of particular note are the writings of Charles E. Brown (1939), Barry L. Callen (1969, 1979, 1995), James Earl Massey (1979), John W. V. Smith (1954, 1980), Gilbert Stafford (1973), and Merle Strege (1993).

A former historian of the Church of God movement, John W. V. Smith, recalled (1) that holiness groups have tended to remain aloof from general ecumenical activity and (2) that the work of Daniel Warner is a clear exception to the pattern of holiness leaders giving only marginal attention to the matter of Christian unity. He then offered six "concluding propositions" about the relationship between holiness and unity that reflect the "new commission" of Daniel Warner and remain worthy of careful consideration. They are:

1. Believers in holiness must not be too ready to accept easy answers in rationalizing division in the Church. Even "liberal" Christians pray God's forgiveness for participating in the sin of division.

2. A passionate concern for personal sanctification should not subvert an equally great concern for the doctrine of the Church. It is well to keep in mind that the Apostle Paul used the word *sanctify* in regard to *both* persons and the Church.

3. In the light of Christ's prayer for the Church (John 17), the concepts of "spiritual unity" and "invisible oneness" are inadequate and inconsistent with the apparent implications of "perfect love."

4. Associationalism and conciliarism are abortive approaches to Christian unity in that they only mitigate the evils of division and do not remove it.

5. Nondenominationalism is an inadequate concept for the full realization of Christian unity in that it expresses primarily a negative rather than a positive character to the Church.

6. This time in Christian history seems to be an especially propitious one for all proponents of holiness to dedicate themselves to giving major attention to the relational implications of this doctrine to the end that, under the leadership of the Holy Spirit, we may be able to lead the way toward unification of the whole Church so that, indeed, the world may believe.[28]

Works Cited

Brown, Charles E. 1939. *The Church Beyond Division.* Anderson, Ind.: Gospel Trumpet Company.

Brown, Charles E. 1951. *When the Trumpet Sounded.* Anderson, Ind.: Gospel Trumpet Company.

Byers, Andrew. 1921. *Birth of a Reformation: Life and Labors of D. S. Warner.* Anderson, Ind.: Gospel Trumpet Company.

Callen, Barry. 1969. "Church of God Reformation Movement: A Study in Ecumenical Idealism." Masters thesis, Asbury Theological Seminary.

Callen, Barry. 1979. *The First Century.* 2 Vols. Anderson, Ind.: Warner Press.

Callen, Barry. 1992. *Guide of Soul and Mind: The Story of Anderson University*. Anderson, Ind.: Anderson University and Warner Press.

Callen, Barry. 1995. *It's God's Church!: Life and Legacy of Daniel Warner*. Anderson, Ind.: Warner Press.

Clear, Valorous. 1977. *Where the Saints Have Trod*. Chesterfield, Ind.: Midwest Publications. Revision of his Ph.D. dissertation, University of Chicago, 1953.

Dieter, Melvin. 1980. *The Holiness Revival of the Nineteenth Century*. Metuchen, N.J.: The Scarecrow Press.

Jones, Charles. 1974. *Perfectionist Persuasion: The Holiness Movement and American Methodism*. Metuchen, N.J.: The Scarecrow Press.

Kern, Richard. 1974. *John Winebrenner: Nineteenth Century Reformer*. Harrisburg, Pa.: Central Publishing House.

Massey, James Earl. 1979. *Concerning Christian Unity*. Anderson, Ind.: Warner Press.

Phillips, Harold. 1979. *The Miracle of Survival*. Anderson, Ind.: Warner Press.

_____. *Proceedings*. 1881. Western Union Holiness Association (meeting in Jacksonville, Illinois). Bloomington, Ill.: Western Holiness Association.

Reardon, Robert. 1979. *The Early Morning Light*. Anderson, Ind.: Warner Press.

Smith, Frederick. 1913. *What the Bible Teaches*. Anderson, Ind.: *Gospel Trumpet* Company.

Smith, Frederick. 1919. *The Last Reformation*. Anderson, Ind.: *Gospel Trumpet* Company.

Smith, John. 1954. "The Approach of the Church of God (Anderson, Ind.) and Comparable Groups to the Problem of Christian Unity." Unpublished doctoral dissertation, University of Southern California Graduate School of Religion.

Smith, John. 1965. "D. S. Warner: Pioneer Leader," in Vital Christianity (July 11, 18, 25).

Smith, John. 1975. "Holiness and Unity," Wesleyan Theological Journal (Spring).

Smith, John. 1980. The Quest for Holiness and Unity. Anderson, Ind.: Warner Press.

Stafford, Gilbert. 1973. "Experiential Salvation and Christian Unity in the Thought of Seven Theologians of the Church of God (Anderson, Ind.)." Unpublished doctoral dissertation, Boston Univ. School of Theology.

Stanley, John. 1990. "Unity Amid Diversity: Interpreting the Book of Revelation in the Church of God (Anderson)." *Wesleyan Theological Journal* (Fall).

Starr, William. 1857. *Discourses on the Nature of Faith and Kindred Subjects.* Chicago: D. B. Cook and Company.

Strege, Merle. 1993. *Tell Me Another Tale: Further Reflections on the Church of God.* Anderson, Ind.: Warner Press.

Warner, Daniel. 1880. *Bible Proofs of the Second Work of Grace.* Goshen, Ind.: E. U. Mennonite Publishing Society.

Warner, Daniel. 1885. *The Church of God, or What the Church Is and What It Is Not. Gospel Trumpet* Company.

Warner, Daniel, and Herbert Riggle. 1903. *The Cleansing of the Sanctuary: Or, The Church of God in Type and Antitype, and in Prophecy and Revelation.* Moundsville, W. Va.: *Gospel Trumpet* Company.

Wickersham, Henry. 1900. *A History of the Church.* Moundsville, W. Va.: *Gospel Trumpet* Company.

Notes

[1] For a tracing of this process, see Melvin Dieter in the *Wesleyan Theological Journal* (30:1, spring, 1995).

[2] For a full presentation of the evolution and application of the come outism vision of Warner, see Barry Callen, *It's God's Church!: The Life and Legacy of Daniel Warner* (Anderson, Ind.: Warner Press, 1995).

[3] Paul Bassett, in *Wesleyan Theological Journal* (Spring/Fall, 1993), 104.

[4] *Editorial, Gospel Trumpet,* June 1, 1881.

[5] See the history of the *Gospel Trumpet* Company (Warner Press) by this title (Phillips 1979).

[6] L. Leon Long, "To What Extent Was Warner a Winebrennerian?" in *The Church Advocate* (February, 1976), 6.

[7] This transformation of Winebrenner was encouraged by his involvement in revivalism and his interaction with leaders of groups like the United Brethren in Christ that reflected roots in German Pietism and other "radical" elements of the Protestant Reformation that had been transplanted to America.

[8] J. Harvey Gossard, "John Winebrenner: Founder, Reformer, and Business-man" in *Pennsylvania Religious Leaders* (Historical Study No. 16, The Pennsylvania Historical Association, 1986), 89 90.

[9] For a recounting of this whole story, see Barry Callen, *It's God's Church! Life and Legacy of Daniel Warner* (Anderson, Ind.: Warner Press, 1995).

[10] The major published expression of this conviction at the time was Warner's *Bible Proofs of the Second Work of Grace* (1880). There also soon would be his booklet *The Church of God* (1885) that reflects key themes of Thomas Campbell's classic restorationist *Declaration and Address* (1809) and bears close

resemblance to John Winebrenner's booklet *The Church of God* (1829, rev. ed. 1885, Harrisburg, Pa.: Board of Publication, General Eldership of the Churches of God).

[11]Others were John P. Brooks, leader of a movement in Missouri that became the Church of God (Holiness), and James Washburn, leader of the Southern California and Arizona Holiness Association from which the Holiness Church was organized. See especially John Brooks, *The Divine Church: A Treatise on the Origin, Constitution, Order, and Ordinances of the Church; Being a Vindication of the New Testament Ecclesia, and an Exposure of the Anti Scriptural Character of the Modern Church or Sect* (Columbia, Mo.: Herald Publishing House, 1891).

[12]See the published *Proceedings* (1881) now housed in the archives of Anderson University. Also see John Leland Peters, *Christian Perfection and American Methodism* (Nashville: Abingdon Press, 1956, 136), and Charles Edwin Jones, *Perfectionist Persuasion: The Holiness Movement and American Methodism* (The Scarecrow Press, 1974, 55).

[13]Harold Phillips, editorial in *Vital Christianity* (October 20, 1974), 8.

[14]Warner's specific involvement focused primarily in the Indiana Holiness Association, which at one point named him as a vice president (Dieter 255). He also had significant contact with the larger holiness movement in both Ohio and Illinois.

[15]*Gospel Trumpet*, June 1, 1881.

[16]In 1993 Barry Callen, a contemporary leader of the Church of God movement, became editor of the *Wesleyan Theological Journal*, current publication of the holiness body from which Warner withdrew more than a century earlier. A sect endorsing clause no longer is required by this holiness body. Warner's vision is admired in principle by today's Christian Holiness Association, but it still is not actively pursued as such. The primary agenda remains more the Christianizing of Christianity by in depth renewal through the holiness experience and the holy life.

[17]Says Melvin Dieter (254): Warner's "development of the church as the dwelling place of the Spirit, the baptism of believers only, the centrality of the Word of God in the midst of the congregation as the 'universal law,' the strong sense of mission as a reformer, the strongly apocalyptical tone, and even the retention of the rite of foot washing as an ordinance of the church—all may be closely identified with the Anabaptist tradition."

[18]From 1925 to 1958 Dr. John Morrison was president of Anderson College (University). For detail, see Barry Callen, *Guide of Soul and Mind: The Story of Anderson University* (Anderson, Ind.: Anderson University and Warner Press, 1992).

[19]See Paul Bassett, *Wesleyan Theological Journal* (Spring/Fall, 1993), 74. A good example is the formation of the Free Methodist Church in 1860 following the experience of Rev. B. T. Roberts being "pushed out" of the Methodist Episcopal Church. See L. R. Marston, *From Age To Age a Living Witness* (1960) and Clarence Zahniser, *Earnest Christian: Life and Works of Benjamin Titus Roberts* (1957).

[20]For examples, see Charles Brown (1939, 1951) and Barry Callen (1979, I, 123 240).

[21]Daniel Warner and Barney Warren, "The Bond of Perfectness," verse one and chorus, as in *Worship the Lord: Hymnal of the Church of God* (Anderson, Ind.: Warner Press, 1989), 330.

[22]Late in Daniel Warner's ministry he increasingly couched his view of the evolving new movement of the Church of God in terms rooted in a church historical interpretation of the Bible's apocalyptic literature (especially the books of Daniel and Revelation). See *The Cleansing of the Sanctuary* (Warner and Herbert Riggle, 1903), Frederick Smith's *What the Bible Teaches* (1913) and *The Last Reformation* (1919), and John Stanley, "Unity Amid Diversity: Interpreting the Book of Revelation in the Church of God (Anderson)," *Wesleyan Theological Journal* (Fall 1990).

[23]The full text is found in the current hymnal of the Church of God movement, *Worship the Lord* (Anderson, Ind.: Warner Press, 1989), 649.

[24]*Gospel Trumpet*, August 1, 1889.

[25]John Smith, in *Vital Christianity* (July 25, 1965), 8.

[26]Also see John Smith's unpublished doctoral dissertation, "The Approach of the Church of God (Anderson, Ind.) and Comparable Groups to the Problem of Christian Unity" (University of Southern California Graduate School of Religion, 1954).

[27]See the *Gospel Trumpet*, Jan. 16, 1882. Also see Byers, 1921, 299ff.

[28]John Smith, "Holiness and Unity," *Wesleyan Theological Journal* (Spring, 1975), 35-36.

Chapter 3

Reconciling Clashing Ecumenical Visions

by
Barry L. Callen

Early leaders of the Church of God movement (Anderson) were highly critical of the significant human compromises they saw burdening the Christian community of their time. Organizationally speaking, they were "come-outers," abandoning the denominationalized community of divided Christians and seeking harmony among all believers through the dynamic of God's sanctifying and unifying power. Struggle naturally developed between this "radical" holiness movement and a body like the Free Methodist Church that shared the holiness passion, but pursued it within a denominationalized structure. Dealing with such tension over time has helped the reform movement refine its concepts of how best to conceive and pursue the goal of Christian unity. Originally published in the Wesleyan Theological Journal *(37:1, Spring, 2002).*

The Free Methodist Church was formed in 1860 and essentially duplicated the polity of the church body from which its first members were departing. The Church of God (Anderson) movement evolved two decades later and rejected the legitimacy of humanly operated polities in general. These two new bodies, both vigorous holiness representatives with much in common, nonetheless differed widely in their views of the church and its intended life. This difference in how the Bible is to be read in regard to church governance persists yet today and is at the root of some of the diversity present in the Wesleyan Theological Society. The sharp nineteenth-century rhetoric of this difference is greatly muted today, bur remembering the awkward path from then to now is worth the effort.

J. Paul Taylor, former bishop of the Free Methodist Church, explored in his 1960 book *Goodly Heritage* the great tradition shared by all Protestants. He wrote out of an abiding conviction that "the present cannot be severed from the past without jeopardizing the future. The Church has a family tree, and it would be as fatal to cut the tree down for firewood as to sleep self-complacently in its shadow."[1] Accordingly, the study at hand intends neither the firewood nor the complacency attitude toward the church's past. Instead, recalled here is an awkward era of strong polemics between two holiness bodies, the positive shift in this relationship in more recent decades, and the lessons that appear important for the future. It is a study of clashing ecumenical visions, differing visions of how authority should be configured in church life, and avenues to reconciliation.

It certainly is the case that organizations, including church organizations honored by God, have their human sides and experience their own life cycles. The early twenty-first-century versions of the Free Methodist Church and the Church of God movement (Anderson) are significantly different in many ways from their organizational, cultural, ecumenical, and rhetorical lives at the beginning of the twentieth century. Even so, recalling how it was then offers perspective about how things got to be the way they now are and may yield some wisdom about how the Holiness Movement might better proceed in matters of church form, freedom, and unity. In the 1880-1900 period, there appeared to be a rather volatile continuum on the "church question." For most involved, the question was whether or not committed holiness advocates should remain in "the mother church" or form new holiness sects. Some like Daniel Steele and Henry Clay Morrison never withdrew. Others like Daniel Warner withdrew completely and disdained the whole sect-making scene, helping to set off a strenuous debate in the holiness movement. Many holiness leaders decried come-out-ism and favored remaining loyal to the established church and being holiness leaven from within.

One extreme of this "church question" continuum was Methodism's episcopal church government model, a disciplined connectionalism to which holiness advocates were called to be loyal in the midst of their reforming enthusiasm. The other extreme was represented by John P. Brooks and Daniel S. Warner (Church of God, Anderson). Theirs was a cry of "democratic" reaction that idealized a strong congregationalism in active opposition to the "Babylon" of divisive and intolerable denominations. They called holiness believers to abandon all sects and stand free in God's one church, unencumbered by heavy human hands. Martin Wells Knapp represented the attempt to find a middle position. A loyal Methodist, Knapp, W. B. Godbey, and other vigorous holiness advocates increasingly felt pressure to move away from their unqualified denominational loyalty. They decried the anti-sectarianism of a Warner as itself highly sectarian, something promoting religious anarchy, but recognized that true holiness is an interdenominational reality. Thus, they tried to effect holiness fellowship on a non-sectarian (not anti-sectarian) basis, being open equally to denominational loyalists and come-outers.[2] The result in part was an eventual moving back into denominationalism (formation of the Pilgrim Holiness Church), although *The Revivalist* holiness publication and God's Bible School have sought to continue representing Knapp's middle way.[3]

Four decades before the opening of the twentieth century, some holiness advocates including B. T. Roberts had been "put out" of Methodism and had moved immediately to form a new denomination, the Free Methodist Church. Such seemingly unqualified acceptance of denominationalism by dedicated holiness people (one extreme of the continuum) set the stage for a clash with the later anti-sectarians (the other extreme).

Reluctant Denominationalism: The Free Methodist Church

In the 1880 to 1910 period, any denomination like the Free Methodist Church that understood itself to be a holiness body in the historical stream of orthodox Christianity would clash with a reform (even "restorationist") movement like the Church of God (Anderson). This movement was insisting that no "denomination" could possibly be a contemporary representation of the church God intends—the pure and undivided New Testament Church. A survey of the tension-filled relationship between the Free Methodist Church and the Church of God movement during the decades 1880-1920 demonstrates the sharp contrast that inevitably arose when a holiness denomination with a positive view of its own existence and role under God was challenged by highly motivated Christian reformers who were "caught up" in the zeal of an ecumenical ideal based on a "second work of grace" (largely as taught by Free Methodists). The Church of God lacked patience with what it saw as the Free Methodist Church's church-compromising and mission-hindering sectarianism. Free Methodist leaders responded with their own impatience over what they saw as an excessively idealistic movement that was itself dividing the church by its ecumenical extremism.

The spirit of prosperity, the growing social respectability of being a Methodist, and the many second and third-generation Methodists who had come into the church on convictions passively accepted from their families, were causing great unrest in the religious world of America in the middle years of the nineteenth century. Holiness revivalism had evolved values, patterns, and relationships that were expected to characterize committed believers. Urbanizing America and the increasing "establishment" position of Methodism was experiencing a contrasting evolutionary pattern. This pattern was viewed increasingly by many holiness people as disturbingly negative. They saw a drift toward "worldliness" and an abandonment of Wesleyan foundations.

This erosion was perceived by some to be at a serious stage in the Genesee Conference of the Methodist Episcopal Church in western New York. Beginning in the early 1850s a division had developed between a group of ministers pastoring the larger city churches, especially in the Buffalo area, and the more conservative ministers of the small town and rural churches. The two parties within this conference were the "Buffalo Regency," distinguished by their "liberal" standards of conduct and belief, including a non-Wesleyan view of entire sanctification, and the "Nazarites" who contended that

> Methodist rules as to amusement and dress were disregarded; that there was no insistence upon conversion; that the doctrines of Methodism were obscured; that the secret-society men had control of the conference; and above all they felt that the doctrine of holiness as taught by John Wesley and the early Methodists was neglected and sometimes rejected.[4]

Benjamin T. Roberts (1823-1893), a Genesee Conference minister and "Nazarite" leader, had been influenced in his early years by revivalism, abolitionism (slavery), and holiness perfectionism.[5] In 1857 he published an article titled "New School Methodism" in *The Northern Independent*, a religious news journal devoted mainly to the reform of slavery. His comprehensive criticism of the prevailing condition of the conference was taken by the "Regency Party" as the opportunity for a showdown. Donald Bastian recounts the grim story:

> Roberts was charged at the annual conference and committed to trial. He was convicted and reproved by the bishop. What charge could be leveled for the publication of an article which no one

was even willing to refute? Nothing less than "immoral and unchristian conduct." Then, at the same annual meeting he was appointed to serve a church at Pekin, New York, to which he went without complaint (it was generally thought to be a "dead-end" congregation)....But the fracture was beyond healing. A second charge was brought against him when a layman, without Robert's permission, republished "New School Methodism."...Roberts was expelled from the Methodist Episcopal Church along with another clergyman....Besides, hundreds of sympathetic layman had been deprived of their membership for no reason except that they were in sympathy with an effort to keep the doctrines and practices of historic Methodism alive.[6]

Roberts and hundreds of like-minded laypersons, having no desire to separate themselves from their parent church, found themselves involuntary "spiritual nomads," destitute of any church home. But they were too deeply committed to the Methodist principles of fellowship and doctrine to remain disconnected indefinitely. Accordingly, with hesitation and only following a final appeal to the General Conference in 1860, a group of laypersons and fifteen ministers met in conference at Pekin, New York, on August 23, 1860. There, on the farm of I. M. Chesbrough, they took what they saw as the only course left. They organized a new denomination. The new group was named the "Free Methodist Church" because the adjective "free" reflected the crucial issues of the denomination's origin. Its founders agreed that it was to be marked by freedom from human slavery, secret societies, purchased seats in churches, and any human binding of the Spirit in worship. Roberts was elected as the first superintendent.

The Free Methodist Church was a body with a positive sense of group identity. This is seen in its 1862 *Discipline* where the denomination's stated mission was "to maintain the biblical standard of Christianity and to preach the gospel to the poor." A positive sense of identity also is seen in a more recent editorial in the Free Methodist that refers to this denomination as "this truly New Testament church."[7] In *A Future with a History*, David McKenna speaks of the founding of this denomination in 1860 as the "reluctant" birthing of a "free church." He adds: "Pulled by conviction and pushed by injustice," this new church body emerged and could be categorized as a "sect" because of its "revivalistic fervor, its emphasis upon personal holiness, and its freedom from the constraints of an institutionalized structure."[8] Howard Snyder reports this:

It would be inaccurate to conclude that this schism occurred solely, or probably even chiefly, over doctrinal issues. It appears that a schism was inevitable, regardless of the issues. The division between the urban-liberal and rural-conservative ministers was so deep that it could scarcely have been healed. On the one hand, the liberal group felt threatened because of the increasing effectiveness and popularity of Roberts and others; on the other hand, the closely-knit liberal group, bound together by widespread membership in the Masons, was increasingly violating what Roberts and his followers felt to be essential standards of Christian and church life.[9]

This new Methodist body was seeking to "spread holiness across the land" (a denominational slogan and priority) and attempting to do so with a sense of freedom from former ecclesiastical bondage—"freedom" and "holiness" were its key words. A clear conviction of the group was that the denomination was not the result of schism in the popular and negative sense. Interprets Donald Bastian, "ours is a church born of necessity!"[10] Serious believers had found a bond of fellowship in holiness rather than in ecclesiasticism and social compromise. And they grew. By the 1880s, the Free Methodist Church was widespread over the geographical area in which the Church of God movement was by then beginning to take significant root (Pennsylvania, Ohio, Indiana, and Michigan in particular).

The increasing contact of the young Free Methodist Church with an even younger and also fast-growing holiness reform movement, the Church of God, was characterized by considerable friction between them. The core of the clash involved somewhat differing group agendas and a contrasting assessment of the rightness and inevitability of denominations existing at all within the body of Christ. So far as early Free Methodists were concerned, they were in existence as a distinct body of believers because of New Testament conviction and the thrust of circumstances that they did not create. Wrote B. T. Roberts in 1883:

> If being filled with the Spirit splits the church, then it ought to be split. If a church is in danger of becoming a charnel house, full of dead men's bones, there should be a resurrection....When Christians cannot, in conscience, agree with those with whom they are associated, in matters of primary importance, they should separate from them....This should never be effected unless it becomes strictly necessary.[11]

Despite this willingness to effect separation among Christians under some circumstances, the Free Methodist Church featured what it judged a legitimate "ecumenical" dimension. B. T. Roberts insisted that "the division of the church into sects tends to promote its unity and efficiency." One can "belong to a sect without being a sectarian." Pointing a critical finger at groups like the young Church of God movement, he added that "the most unrelenting sectarians are among the advocates of no-sect principles."[12] Roberts had an irenic spirit and represented the Free Methodist Church in 1883 as it became a charter member of the new World Methodist Council. Soon after, this denomination also became a stalwart member of the National Holiness Association. To the Church of God movement, this was hardly the direction for nurturing true Christian unity.

The Church of God in Active Opposition

The young Church of God movement had an ecumenical vision that decried organizational alliances as an appropriate approach of to the dilemma of Christian disunity. It tended to see as self-serving nonsense the assertion that dividing the church into sects actually can promote Christian unity and efficiency. One of the initiating acts that launched this movement of the Church of God was Daniel S. Warner's leaving the National Holiness Association in 1881 because of its insistence on members holding valid denominational credentials.[13] He then reported the following in the *Gospel Trumpet* (June 1, 1881): "The Spirit showed me the inconsistency of repudiating sects and yet belonging to an association that is based on sect recognition....We wish to co-operate with all Christians, as such, in saving souls—but forever withdraw from all organisms that uphold and endorse sects and denominations in the body of Christ." The early years of the Church of God movement featured the stridency of a prophetic voice, not the gentleness of an irenic spirit. True and divinely-intended unity among Christians was understood to be a by-product of heart holiness, not an engineered arrangement among humanly originated and dominated church structures. The result of this view was a clash of ecumenical visions by two holiness bodies with much in common otherwise.

The Church of God movement, much like the Free Methodist Church, came into being only reluctantly. Its primary pioneer, Daniel S. Warner (1842-1895),[14] had lost his ministerial credentials, in large part because he also was loyal to the serious preaching of Christian holiness.

In his case, the body that rejected him was the Churches of God of North America (Winebrennerian).15 There, however, the similarity with B. T. Roberts tends to end. The holiness ministry of Warner included a call for the renewed holiness of individual believers and of the church itself, understood in part as a complete rejection of the denominationalism that burdened and divided it. To Warner, being holy as individual believers and together as Christ's body had dramatic implications for the chaotic Christianity he observed on all hands. His was a holiness-inspired ecumenical vision not prepared to tolerate quietly other holiness teachers who professed the holiness experience and yet remained blind to much of the corporate implications that should flow from it. Warner intended to form no new "church," being determined to avoid compounding the arena of division. He claimed to "see" the one church first formed at Pentecost and intended to live in it alone.

A "movement consciousness" soon evolved among the "evening light saints," even though standard denominational characteristics were resisted vigorously and were critiqued sharply when existing in other Christian settings.16 The early publications of the Church of God movement, for instance, were prone to attack the Free Methodist Church by name. Many *Gospel Trumpet* articles and editorials imply or boldly state that in numerous ways the "F. M. Sect" was sufficiently akin to the Evening Light, and yet so fundamentally different at the key point of the unity of God's church, that it was to be recognized as an especially dangerous and subtle trap of sectarianism. Holiness denominations so smacked of the ideal without being the ideal that they appeared to leaders of the early Church of God movement as especially undermining the ideal itself.

On one occasion B. T. Roberts offered a definition for "sect" which was soon made notorious thanks to D. S. Warner and some of his reforming colleagues. Roberts defined a "sect" as follows:

> The word "sect" is from the Latin "secare," to cut off, to separate. The word "section" is from the same root. Hence, a section is a portion cut off, or separated from a body of which it forms a part. A sect of Christians is a part of the entire Christian body, separated from the rest by some peculiar doctrines or tenets, which they hold exclusively or to which they give especial prominence.17

Warner readily admitted that this definition is accurate, but he could not understand "how any man of ordinary intelligence can thus define sects, as separate, cut-off portions from the body of Christ, by some exclusive party doctrines, and then turn around and say it is right thus to sever the general body of Christ into fragments....It well demonstrates the fact a heretic (i.e., sectarian) 'is subverted and sinneth.'"[18]

B. T. Roberts, hardly considering sectarian division as ideal in church life, nonetheless could see it in a light far more positive than "sin." An editorial in the *Free Methodist* clarified the attitude of the Free Methodist Church about denominationalism:

> Notwithstanding the fact that the existence of religious bodies under different names or denominations has been the subject of attack...nevertheless, such denominations have played a very important part in the permissive providence of God both in aggressive work and in conserving true doctrine. True, that which has been accomplished largely under the incentive of denominational zeal ought to have been accomplished from other motives—from the love of God and our fellows; but it is better that it were accomplished under denominational zeal than not at all.[19]

Roberts insisted on the following in another editorial in *The Earnest Christian* (1885):

> Any religious organization or association composed of Christians, that acts and worships permanently together and does not include all the Christians of that place or country is of necessity a sect. There is no possibility of avoiding it. It may call itself by the most general name that can be found [Church of God?]. That makes no difference....The one who makes opposition to sects the pretext for trying to get up another sect presumes most wonderfully upon the ignorance and the credulity of mankind....[20]

Regardless of such justification of sects and accusation of sect opposers, leaders of the young Church of God movement used the Free Methodist stance as fuel for their anti-sectarian fires. J. W. Byers quotes the definition of Roberts in his tract entitled Sects[21] and A. B. Palmer refers to it in the context of his lamenting that "it seems so strange that GREAT men, such as Johnson, and Alexander Campbell of the Christian and Disciple orders and many others teach either directly or indirectly that sectism is not of God, and then remain in them."[22]

Bishop Sims of the Free Methodist Church reintroduced the definition of Roberts when he wrote a tract titled *No-Sectism*. He thought that his own denomination was distinguished from other Christians only because a bold stand for truth (holiness) had forced it to be so. Could this be sin? Hardly. He argued that the no-sectism antagonizers from the Christian fringe (Warner in particular) ought to be answered. Warner reacted quickly and forcefully to this tract with a fifty-page booklet, also called *No-Sectism*, in which he responded point by point to Sims' attempt to clarify and justify Roberts' definition of a sect. Note, for example:

> All sect-apologists, as far as we have known, until F. M. zealots, have fought for their party idol under the cloak of the church. But since Mr. Roberts has written a book in defense of his young daughter of the harlot family [reference to the imagery in the Book of Revelation], in which he unguardedly called it a sect; and since men have become more enlightened by the present truth [vision of the Church of God movement], they find it impossible to longer deceive the people. Therefore they are forced to confess that what they, and their creed falsely call a church [such as the Free Methodist denomination], is nothing but a human fraud, a "cut off" from the body of Christ. And yet they have the audacity to wink at the sin of sectism....They are therefore the boldest heretics we know on earth.[23]

Sims had defined "no-sectism" as "the theory of those who believe that all sects are of the devil, and, consequently, that it is a sin for one to belong to them."[24] Warner clearly represented this definition, but he vigorously disassociated himself from all "isms," even "no-sectism."

Some groups, Warner explained, make the idea of separation from modern sects their central emphasis. But he did not. His own understanding was that Christ and not "come out of her" was the center and genius of his own teaching and that of the group he represented.[25] Nevertheless, Sims and the other Free Methodists seem to have seen the movement's anti-sectism more than its Christ and thus they could not comprehend the practicality of Warner's idealism regarding being free from all "isms"— no matter how desirable that might be. Sims argued that the protection of the rights of individual Christians demands that there be a visible organization, and hence sects. Further, in an editorial in *The Earnest Christian*, B. T. Roberts, while arguing that church organization is essential for the orderly protection of the rights and privileges of Christians, made reference to an editorial in the *Gospel Trumpet* that Roberts described as "the name of an organ of the sect no-sect."[26] This editorial apparently discussed two evangelists that were being exposed for earning their livings "under a hypocritical holiness garb." Roberts admits that he is unaware of the true facts in the case being discussed, but challenges the right of the editor to condemn fellow Christians in such a manner. Even if they were guilty,

> ...what right has the editor to try, condemn and execute those parties, without citing them to trial and giving them a chance to be heard in their own defense? Are they under his authority? Who placed them there?...Are the professed children of God to be governed by lynch law? Yet under the no-sect theory no other government is possible.[27]

Bishop Sims concluded his argument with the contention characteristic of most Free Methodists both then and now:

> It is utterly impossible for them—such as come out of sects—to prove that they are not a sect....Are there any Christians in the world besides yourself, and those with whom you are associated? Then you are a sect.[28]

D. S. Warner responded by insisting that it is simply deception to insist either that the organization of sects is essential to the visibility of God's church or that the church cannot be organized for its mission without the emergence of sects.[29]

From the Free Methodist side, little else can be documented which states opinions of and reactions to the Church of God movement as such. Sims and Roberts apparently said what they felt needed to be said. But the movement was certainly not through with its critique of Free Methodism! Continued criticism of the Free Methodist Church in particular and of sectism in general was grounded in this affirmation:

> This gathering of God's people out of sect Babylon back to Zion [the movement seeing itself as one example of a spontaneous and widespread moving of God upon His divided people everywhere], into one fold, was foretold by the prophets ....What are God's people who are yet scattered there commanded to do? What saith the Scripture? "From such withdraw thyself: from such turn away." No honest soul can remain there after hearing this solemn command.[30]

W. H. Cheatham's declared in the *Gospel Trumpet* that the devil often counterfeits the true church.

> And after the dark age and reign of this Roman beast, we can see traces of the true church appearing again. As she advances in the true light (word of God), the devil brings forth his churches, and his Bible, which is this discipline, creeds, etc. ...So about the year 1861 he brought forth one they called Free Methodist. The devil, no doubt, thought that this young daughter

of the beast family would palm off for the genuine church; but soon the detector was laid on her and she was found wanting.[31]

W. A. Haynes, in an article in the *Gospel Trumpet* entitled "A New God," tried to discredit Free Methodism by being "creative" in his quoting of an article by George Fitch in which Fitch had tried to set forth the origin and doctrines of his denomination. Quotes Hayes (and the internal parentheses are his additions):

> In the Genesee conference of the M. E. church, about the year 1858, several preachers and many members were excluded from the church (M. E. sect) for their adherence to the principles of Methodism (not God's word), especially to the doctrine and experience of "entire sanctification." Appeals were made to the general conference (instead of God) which were denied....Therefore, they (not Christ) felt compelled (because of their ignorance of God's word) to form a new (dis)organization....The Free Methodist church was organized by a convention of laymen and ministers which met at Pekin, Niagara County, New York, on the twenty-third day of August, 1860.

At this point Haynes interrupts his own quoting to explain:

> Christ said in A. D. 32 he would build his church....How is this, this heavenly church, compared to F. M.-ism which was not thought of until eighteen hundred and twenty seven years after Christ completed his organization?...Oh what contrast! And, my dear reader, will you take warning and flee from sect confusion to the church of the living God?

Hayne's quoting of Fitch is resumed:

> All hope of obtaining anything like justice was cut off. What could be done? To stay in the M. E. church was impossible. We had not left. We were unjustly and cruelly turned out. To what other church could we go and find a home?

Haynes then bursts in—

> Oh, ye poor victims of tyranny, you were without a home, you were away from Father's house, and not acquainted with our mother. Galatians 4:26. You knew no church where "you would be welcome." Then you were outside the church of the first-born, and did not know where to look for it. Why did you not repent of your ungodliness? Then Jesus would have let you in his church. But you did not think of him, did

not know he had a church....You ran from a lion and a bear caught you....[32]

By the 1890s it had become common for Church of God leaders to read church history as a pattern of apostasy led (according to a reading of the Book of Revelation) by the "Beast" (Roman Catholicism) and the "Second Beast" (Rome's many sectish Protestant daughters). Speaking of the Wesleyan reform of the eighteenth century, for instance, Herbert Riggle reported this in 1912:

> After a great body was thus called out, they became deceived because God was specially favoring them, and organized into a sect...an image to the old, or papal, beast. As soon as they did this, they lost their spirituality, and today they are a dead, formal body. The very doctrine with which Wesley started his reform is today rejected by a large number of the Methodist divines. A number of years ago B. T. Roberts and several other Methodist ministers began to preach holiness, and the result was an excommunication. These preachers then began to shout, "We are free! We are free!" But not willing to give up the name Methodists, they organized an image that they term "Free Methodists." These people are now as dead spiritually as their mother. Their work is accompanied by much noise but little power of God. So it has been throughout the entire Protestant age.[33]

Riggle and his Church of God colleagues understood themselves to be part of God's rising above "the entire Protestant age" in the "evening light" time of the church. They were privileged to be in the vanguard of the "final reformation" of the church.[34]

Despite the several similarities between the Free Methodist Church and the Church of God movement (and there are more similarities than the differences being emphasized here in their most extreme forms),[35] there obviously was considerable friction between them a century ago. The major source of this friction seems to have been that they were both engaged in spiritual warfare, although they were not always fighting the same foes. Free Methodism was challenging "world-worship" within the churches, and the Church of God movement, in addition to opposing worldliness, was directing substantial energies toward a reformation of the churches themselves—"sect-worship." These differing orientations made it exceedingly difficult for each to adequately appreciate the contribution of the other. Free Methodism, while recognizing the danger of severe self-orientation, saw the Church of God as offering no satisfactory alternative to some organized form of "sectism." The Church of God, on the other hand, seems to have pictured "F.M.-ism" as the hapless defender of the Maginot Line against worldliness while the hoards of sectism were striking and smashing from the undefended rear.

One can understand why Free Methodism was unable to appreciate another "holiness" group that was determined to associate "entire sanctification" with a vision of church unity that Free Methodists judged impractical and not worthy of propagation. At the same time, one finds it difficult to discredit a priori the insistence of the Church of God that Christians acquainted with the "deeper life" should pause to reconsider the divinely inspired implications that ought to follow on a corporate level the individual's being graciously renewed by the presence and power of the Spirit of God. In an atmosphere of clashing rhetoric where the spirit of reconciliation had not yet appeared, mutual appreciation was unlikely.

Whatever one's final judgment in this regard, at least one thing appears certain. The sometimes harsh and blunt polemical language sampled above is more understandable when placed in the context of the times in which it was employed. Further, if the testimonies of the early pioneers of the Church of God movement are accepted at face value (and evidence generally indicates that they should be thus taken), then the ethics involved in calling Christians out of denominationalism into God's only, divinely-organized church is above question. They did not issue a call for others to come and join a new sect, even a "no-sect" sect, whether or not these pioneers soon were drawn subtly into a sect pattern in order to consolidate their gains and propagate their message. The initial call was for God's people, scattered and stunted by many human barriers, to free themselves of all such bondages so that they might enter into a fellowship of the whole of God's people. These pioneers were vibrating with a vision and were on the march, not for themselves, but for God on behalf of God's people, "in order that the world may know." No less than a frank recognition of this ideal does justice to the vision of the reformation movement of the Church of God.

Changing Attitudes and Retrospective Wisdom

By 1900 Henry Wickersham, an early church historian in the ranks of the Church of God movement, signaled a softening of the previous pattern of harsh anti-sectarian rhetoric. He reported that "the Free Methodist sect, though small compared to the Methodist Episcopal Church, has considerable zeal and demonstration of power, and does considerable evangelistic work."³⁶ H. M. Riggle, after his famous days of public debating on behalf of his religious views, came to this fresh conclusion in 1924:

> Personally, I question the wisdom of Christian ministers making it a business publicly to discuss points of theological difference. In the past, when certain religious cults emphasized their distinctive doctrines, public debates were common. A Disciple minister once told me that as soon as his converts were immersed they came out of the water "ready for dispute." But this spirit of controversy is rapidly disappearing and God-fearing men everywhere are rising above their petty differences and seeking a common ground where all can work together in evangelizing the world.³⁷

In this more congenial spirit, Riggle almost affectionately tells an amusing incident recalled from those early years of tension between the Church of God movement and the Free Methodist Church.

> Two Free Methodist preachers with whom I am well acquainted were holding meetings in Greensburg, PA. In a special service a man was seeking holiness. Their method emphasizes dying out to sin. The seeker at the altar became desperate and cried at the top of his voice, "Kill him, kill him, Lord." A man on the street heard this and supposed that a murder was being committed. He ran and rang the police alarm, and soon the place of meeting was full of officers in blue coats ready to arrest the murderers, who proved to be harmless holiness preachers.³⁸

Charles E. Brown, a prominent editor, theologian, and historian in the Church of God movement, indicated in 1966 that "it is almost unbelievable the hostility we [Church of God Movement] had toward other church groups in the early days—even with the holiness people."³⁹ But time has properly lessened the emotional atmosphere so that the Spirit of Christ can more easily guide former "contestants" into becoming present and future "companions" in the quest for the whole truth of God as it is in Jesus Christ. This new atmosphere of increased objectivity has permitted one to understand better the tension-filled relationship of these two church groups in earlier generations. There was the unbounded and unrelenting, even awkward and impractical, vigor of a unity ideal in its youth clashing with a force occupied largely in other concerns and generally unimpressed with what it considered dramatic pronouncements and restorationist fancies. Now there is more humility arising from an increased historical consciousness. In a common statement made by leaders of the Church of God movement and the Christian Churches/Churches of Chirst in 1996 after nearly a decade of intense conversation about these similar yet differing church traditions, there is this: "We have learned that the roles played by the Enlightenment [for the Christian Churches] and American Holiness/Revivalism [for the Church of God] have shaped the theological perspectives of our respective heritages. This awareness now influences our attitude and helps us to transcend certain limitations coming from our histories."[40]

James Earl Massey wrote *Concerning Christian Unity* in 1979 and through it offered many Church of God people a fresh way of viewing this crucial subject. He repeated the classic concern of this movement that "membership in denominational families has made Christian believers far more conscious of separate traditions than of the true nature of the Church." However, he conceded this: "Although the Church is a spiritual fellowship in which Christ is the central and uniting figure, we all experience that fellowship in connection with some denominational or denominated group." Denominations are "mainly patterns of partnership in which believers have tended to cluster....No one group is the complete historical embodiment of the Church as Jesus planned it, even if its emphasis is more nearly apostolic or embraces a greater area of the original teachings that undergird the Church." Even so, since "denominational separatism limits fellowship and hinders having a visible unity," and since "every Christian has a legacy in every other Christian," "we experience that legacy only as we receive each other and relate, moving eagerly beyond group boundaries." Unity is "one of the Lord's imperatives for his people." In a study of Ephesians 4, Massey concludes that Christian unity is a given, "but our experience of it must be gained."

Such intentional gaining of functional unity has become part of the newer perspective of the Church of God movement. In 1984 the Church of God in North America convened a "Consultation on Mission and Ministry" to establish goals for the movement to the end of the twentieth century. One stated goal established was "to expand ministries through voluntary relationships with Christian groups outside the Church of God Reformation Movement and to seek to live out the vision of unity through broader interdependent relationships that serve mutual needs for training, fellowship, and witness." It was in this spirit of fresh openness that in 1984 Gilbert W. Stafford began representing the Commission on Christian Unity of the Church of God in meetings of the Faith and Order Movement. He explained in 1997 his view of the importance of such representation and called for wider involvement by

Holiness churches in ecumenical exchanges.[41] The following year David Cubie wrote about a Wesleyan perspective on Christian unity [see his whole article in this volume]. He observed: "A principle that has largely been lost by the present holiness denominations, except for the Church of God (Anderson), is that the unity of the church is an essential part of eschatological hope."[42]

In 1987 the officers of the General Assembly of the Church of God invited the late Bishop Clyde Van Valin of the Free Methodist Church to function as an observer in its annual sessions and then address the Assembly with his honest evaluative comments. He said to the Assembly that the Church of God movement's focus on Christian unity is "a message that we all need to hear expounded and demonstrated."[43] For the June 2000 General Assembly, a similar observer invitation was accepted by a former Free Methodist leader, Dr. Kevin Mannoia, who at the time was president of the National Association of Evangelicals. In the 1990s the Free Methodist Church convened two of its General Conferences on the campus of Anderson University (1995 and 1999), which is the largest of the institutions of higher education of the Church of God movement and is located adjacent to the general offices of the movement's North American cooperative ministries. The hosting relationship was congenial indeed. At the 1995 General Conference, Barry L. Callen of the Church of God served by invitation on the four-person Findings Committee that observed the Conference at close range and prepared an analysis of it for the Board of Bishops. The Committee of was comprised of three prominent Free Methodists, was chaired by David McKenna, and included Barry Callen as an "outside" observer-analyist. There have been several other joint relationships of various kinds, including cooperation in publishing the "Aldersgate" church curriculum and the fact that a recent General Director of Church of God Ministries (North America), Robert Pearson, received his undergraduate education on a Free Methodist campus (Seattle Pacific University).

One "ecumenical" activity of each of these holiness bodies in recent decades is worth noting because of the differing goals that reflect a continuing difference of ecumenical vision still held. From 1907 to 1919 there had been an unsuccessful set of conversations about church union between the Free Methodist Church and the Wesleyan Methodist Church. Then from 1943 to 1955 such conversations were revived in the hope of creating a new holiness denomination, the United Wesleyan Methodist Church. Even though a detailed draft of a proposed new Discipline was completed for the new denomination and the 1955

General Conference of the Free Methodist Church was highly affirmative, the Wesleyan General Conference defeated the union process by a 96-62 negative vote. This attempt at increased unity had proceeded along organizational lines—how to blend church structures and agree officially on the wording of beliefs and practices. The thought was that a congenial merger would have enhanced the unity among the involved Christians. After considerable effort, it was not to be.

By contrast, for a period of years beginning in the late 1980s, Church of God (Anderson) leaders engaged in serious "ecumenical" dialogue with leaders of the Christian Churches/Churches of Christ of the Campbellite or Disciples tradition. Neither of these bodies is "connectional" organizationally and neither thinks of enhancing Christian unity primarily along organizational lines. Neither has anything like a Discipline and neither would want one, let alone trying to negotiate a common one. One is not a "holiness" body and both were anxious to make clear that "merger" was never a consideration (a concept at odds with the nature of the strong Christian unity traditions of both groups). Their vigorous unity visions are fellowship and Christian-identity oriented in ways leading away from organizational approaches to Christian unity. A book growing out of these conversations is titled *Coming Together in Christ* and was co-authored by a representative of each dialogue partner.[44] Unity in Christ is a concept compatible with both groups, as opposed to unity in formalized doctrine or church organization. What came from this effort was not a failed legislative vote, but warm Christian friendships, better self-understandings, and a series of cooperative ministry and mission efforts that would not have happened otherwise.

Currently appearing on the web site of the Free Methodist Church are ten defining values of that denomination. Here are two of them:

> *Connectional*: We are a church which recognizes and values its nature as a connectional church united with others in the ministry of Jesus Christ, and not possessing an independent mind set.
>
> *Movement*: We are a church which aggressively seeks to make Him [Jesus Christ] known by putting mission above self-preservation and status quo and are not concerned primarily with our own existence, comfort or organizational operations.

The "movement" designation and most of its Free Methodist description reflects well the Church of God heritage.[45] The only exception is the "church" self-designation. The Church of God has emphasized the concept of "movement" to the point of avoiding any claimed "church" identity for itself—such identity being seen as the institutional demise of a true movement. The Church of God admittedly has struggled with an "independent mind set" that is not countered, as it is for Free Methodists, by the "connectional value." It aspires to increased and mutual accountability, but continues to resist any formal "connectionalism" that creates a network of "ecclesiastical control" that, it is thought, usually moves quickly to human domination of God's church. Both of these holiness bodies value the "free" word and agree on it as an appropriate adjective for most aspects of church life. Both of these holiness bodies are seeking a better balance between form and freedom. The Free Methodist Church carries an episcopal heritage and seeks increased flexibility in the midst of structured accountability; the Church of God carries a free-church heritage and seeks more structured accountability without violating the heritage of freedom in the Spirit of Christ.

These quests continue, now in a spirit of constructive cooperation rather than in the older spirit of rhetoric-laden critique. The Church of God now talks about putting the "move" back into the Movement while Doug Newton, coordinator of the 1999 General Conference of the Free Methodist Church (that convened on the Anderson University campus of the Church of God) began this way his February 27, 1998, letter to Free Methodist pastors:

> The question is being asked across the Free Methodist Church, "Can a movement be restarted?" No one doubts that the early days of the Free Methodist denomination qualified as a bona fide movement of God. All of the characteristics were present. Energy. Enthusiasm. Fruitfulness. Creativity. Expansion. Progress. Strong identity. Passionate focus. There's a unanimous desire across the North American church to be part of a movement again. But can it happen?

This is a crucial question. The answer is yet to be seen, but at least it is being asked seriously and simultaneously by both the Church of God Movement and the Free Methodist Church.

Two holiness bodies have been on differing ecumenical journeys. At first the contrast between them was sharply drawn. Now, with each body much changed, the considerable congruities between them are most prominent. Reconciliation has been in the wind for decades and surely will proceed.

Notes

[1] J. Paul Taylor, *Goodly Heritage* (Winona Lake, IN: Light and Life Press, 1960), 3.

[2] In fact, this middle way of Knapp is not very different from the early position of Daniel S. Warner. However, when Warner was refused full fellowship with the holiness association in Indiana merely because he no longer held formal denominational credentials, he became a radical come-outer.

[3] See the centennial history of God's Bible School by Wallace Thornton (*Back to the Bible*, 2000).

[4] C. L. Howland, *A Brief Story of Our Church* (Winona Lake, IN: The Free Methodist Publishing House, n.d.), 9.

[5] Howard A. Snyder, "Formative Influences on B. T. Roberts," *Wesleyan Theological Journal* (34:1, Spring 1999), 177-199.

[6] Donald N. Bastian, *The Mature Church Member* (Winona Lake, IN: Light and Life Press, 1963), 18-19. The Genesee Conference of the Methodist Episcopal Church, at its 1910 session in Rochester, New York, made full acknowledgement of the wrong done to B. T. Roberts fifty years before. The credentials unjustly taken from him were restored to his son.

[7] Editorial, *The Free Methodist* (November 22, 1966), 4.

[8] David L. McKenna, *A Future with a History: The Wesleyan Witness of the Free Methodist Church* (Indianapolis, IN: Light and Life Press, 1995), 12, 17-18. McKenna, when speaking of a "sect" in this way, refers to the definition of Ernst Troeltsch in his *The Social Teaching of the Churches*, 1981, 1:331-342.

[9] Howard A. Snyder, "Unity and the Holiness Churches," Bachelor of Divinity thesis presented to Asbury Theological Seminary, 1966, 29.

[10] Bastian, op. cit., 22.

[11] B. T. Roberts, "Church Organizations," editorial in *The Earnest Christian* (June 1883), 167-168.

[12] Ibid.

[13] See Barry L. Callen, *It's God's Church!: The Life and Legacy of Daniel S. Warner* (Anderson, IN: Warner Press, 1995), 90ff.

[14] No one is accorded the title "founder" since the early pioneers of this movement were intending to return to the early and one church, not to "found" anything.

[15] See Richard Kern, *John Winebrenner: 19th-Century Reformer* (Harrisburg, Pa.: Central Publishing House, 1974).

[16] See John W. V. Smith, *The Quest for Holiness and Unity* (Anderson, IN.: Warner Press, 1980), chapter 5.

[17] As quoted by Daniel Warner, *The Church of God or What Is the Church and What Is Not*, 25.

[18] Ibid., 25-26.

[19] Editorial, *The Free Methodist* (February 3, 1886), 8.

20Editorial, *The Earnest Christian*, XLIX:6 (June, 1885), 184-85. If the idealism of the early Church of God movement is to be taken seriously, the one thing it was not doing was intending to "get up another sect" for any reason!

21J. W. Byers, *Sects* (Gospel Trumpet Company, n.d.).

22A. B. Palmer, "Extracts," *Gospel Trumpet* (January 28, 1892), 1.

23Daniel S. Warner, *No-Sectism* (Moundsville, W. Va.: Gospel Trumpet Com-pany, n.d.), 11-12.

24Ibid., 5.

25Ibid., 5-6.

26Editorial, *The Earnest Christian*, XLII:5 (May, 1882), 160.

27Ibid.

28Warner, *No-Sectism*, 33.

29Warner, *No-Sectism*, 33.

30Daniel Warner and Herbert Riggle, *The Cleansing of the Sanctuary* (Moundsville, W. Va.: Gospel Trumpet Company, 1903), 395-396.

31W. H. Cheatham, "Beware of Counterfeits," *Gospel Trumpet* (May 16, 1895), 4.

32W. A. Haynes (Flag Springs, Mo.), "A New God," *Gospel Trumpet* (March 21, 1895), 1.

33Herbert M. Riggle, *The Christian Church: Its Rise and Progress* (Anderson, IN: Gospel Trumpet Company, 1912), 190. Reprinted 1997 by Reformation Publishers, Clarksville, TN.

34See F. G. Smith, *The Last Reformation* (Anderson, IN: Gospel Trumpet Company, 1919).

35Not only are these similarities seen in basic doctrinal and aesthetic-prudential standards, especially in the decades being considered above, but one even sees like terminology and concepts of evangelism when comparing such volumes as H. M. Riggle, *Pioneer Evangelism* (the 1924 recollections of an early Church of God movement evangelist) and J. W. Sigsworth, *The Battle Was the Lord's* (a history of the Free Methodist Church in Canada).

36Henry C. Wickersham, *A History of the Church* (Moundsville, W. Va.: 1900), 263.

37H. M. Riggle, *Pioneer Evangelism* (Anderson, IN: Gospel Trumpet Publishing Company, 1924), 116. Note that Riggle, one of the more forceful of the early evangelists of the Church of God movement, saw no compromise involved in open cooperation with other Christians who differed with him. This is one key aspect of the unity ideal.

38Ibid, 92.

39Charles E. Brown, in David Telfer, "Interdenominational Cooperation in the Church of God," Anderson School of Theology (unpublished, March 30, 1966).

40The full statement is found in Barry L. Callen and James North, *Coming Together in Christ: Pioneering a New Testament Way to Christian Unity* (Joplin, MO: College Press, 1997), Appendix I.

[41] Gilbert W. Stafford, "Faith and Order: Holiness Church Participation," *Wesleyan Theological Journal* 32:1 (Spring 1997), 143-156.

[42] David L. Cubie, "A Wesleyan Perspective on Christian Unity," *Wesleyan Theological Journal*, 33:2 (Fall 1998), 227.

[43] For a record of the comments of Bishop VanValin and other observers over the years, see the documentary history of the Church of God (Anderson) by Barry L. Callen, compiler and editor, *Following the Light* (Anderson, IN: Warner Press, 2000), 323-326.

[44] For a detailed account of this extended ecumenical conversation, see Barry L. Callen and James North, *Coming Together in Christ: Pioneering a New Testament Way to Christian Unity* (Joplin, MO: College Press, 1997).

[45] The new "Membership and Covenant" adopted by the 1995 General Conference of the Free Methodist Church was intended to equate as closely as possible the New Testament model of entrance into the church (Body of Christ) with requirements for membership in the denomination. This intention is very compatible with the ecumenical vision of the Church of God tradition.

Chapter 4

Building a Young Reformation Movement[1]

by
Merle D. Strege

In the opening years of the twenty-first century, the Church of God movement (Anderson) is comprised of a diverse constituency. So much is this the case that, combined with its minimal institutionalization, many fear for its holding together at all. This circumstance was much the same at the opening of the twentieth century when the movement was only a few years old. Merle D. Strege explains that the movement was held together "by some rather frayed threads." He explores some personalities and events that prepared the way for a wave of cautious institutionalizing of the movement, especially between 1917 and 1930. How can a "radical" reform movement, committed to resisting "man-rule" in church life, deal with heretics, backsliders, and biblical interpretation? What holds together a movement determined to "come out" of all the standard organizational controls of the denominational world? Originally published in the Wesleyan Theological Journal *(36:2, Fall, 2001) under the title "Quilting a Church: The Church of God in 1900."*

When Editor Enoch E. Byrum greeted readers of the *Gospel Trumpet* on the eve of the twentieth century, his note of confidence belied the condition of a movement held together at that moment by some rather frayed threads. After twenty years of existence as a radical holiness reform movement, the Church of God (not yet located in Anderson, Indiana) looked toward a new century while, intentionally or not, it sewed together practices of several different origins to create the Church of God movement. The men and women who often referred to themselves simply as "The Saints" were in the initial stages of stitching together the first patches on the quilt that was become the movement.

I examine here some aspects of the life of the Church of God movement around the year 1900. Personalities and events of those years prepared the way for the rapid institutionalization of the movement that occurred between 1917 and 1930. In fact, the rapid proliferation of boards and agencies during that later period finished a work that in some instances had begun not in 1917, but roughly two decades earlier. These are important matters in the history of the Church of God (Anderson) because of the movement's original and sharp repudiation of all forms of church organization.

The first steps toward the institutionalization of the Church of God movement were the approbation and development of practices that were essential to the theological instruction and formation of the movement. Many, if not most, of these practices were not created ex nihilo. Some were new, but many were packed in the theological and ecclesiological baggage that the first generation of movement adherents carried with them into the earliest fellowship of "The Saints." All the members of the movement's first generation were "come-outers." They abandoned their memberships in denominations and rejected what they termed "denominationalism," "Sect Babylon," or "sectism."[2] In some instances they simultaneously abandoned certain religious practices as worn-out vestiges of a failed human system of church life.

For example, Daniel S. Warner, primary pioneer of the movement, repudiated his ordination in the Northern Indiana Eldership of the Churches of God (Winebrennerian), finding it necessary to be ordained anew according to a simpler form he judged more in keeping with the simplicity and purity of the New Testament church. But the Saints did not forsake all the practices of sect Babylon. Thus, from the General Eldership of the Churches of God Warner retained the practice of footwashing. That this was an ordinance of the true New Testament church made perfectly good biblical sense to the influential Byrum clan, H. C. Wickersham, and others who had come out of Brethren denominations that traditionally followed this practice.

It is not easy to determine the yardstick by which some practices were excluded while others were sewn into the quilt that became the Church of God movement. Without question, every practice had to conform to the group's understanding of what the Bible endorsed or permitted. But this general standard does not alone account for the persistence of some practices and the demotion or demise of others. What is offered here are case studies that illustrate some practices that were included by the year 1900 and others that eventually were shifted to the margins of the quilt of the movement's existence.

Theology and Practice: A Definition

Before examining these case studies, we need to establish a common understanding of the concept of a "practice" and its relationship to the teaching of the church's theology. Since the publication of Alasdair MacIntyre's *After Virtue*[3] in the early 1980s, theologians and religious historians, as well as people concerned for the life of the contemporary church, have paid increasing attention to the idea of practices.[4] MacIntyre explains a practice by such examples as "throwing a football with skill is not a practice; but the game of football is, and so is chess. Bricklaying is not a practice, architecture is. Planting turnips is not a practice; farming is."[5] As MacIntyre defines them, practices are socially established cooperative activities that aim at some desirable end and which require the development of virtues in practitioners if those practices are to be sustained.

Perhaps no theologian more than James McClendon has extended MacIntyre's understanding of practices and applied it specifically to the church's enterprise of teaching theology. Like MacIntyre, McClendon defines best by example:

> The practice of Christian teaching can best be understood in these terms. Just as "medicine" denotes not merely bottles on a pharmacy shelf, but a practice, and "law" not merely statutes, but another kind of practice, our practice of doctrine is far more than the individual doctrines involved. In each case the named practice is definitive for and inclusive of its ingredient doctrines, laws, or medicines. There is no "thing taught" without teaching; no Christian doctrines apart from the practice of doctrine.[6]

McClendon distinguishes this "practical" understanding of theology from the two major definitions of doctrine.[7] The first is the idea that doctrine consists in revealed truth being imparted to the church. While such doctrines are often said to be biblical or Bible-based, they are formally contained in distinct propositions (dogmas, doctrines) that convey the substance of divine revelation to believers. The second concept of doctrine is the one embedded in liberal Protestantism. It views doctrines as what appears in a church not as revealed dogmas, but as accounts of the Christian religious affections being set forth in human speech. So doctrines express human states, not states of mind, but of awareness, since awareness is the human faculty that apprehends God. Not only does McClendon argue that a practice offers a third understanding of the nature of doctrine and doctrinal teaching. He also lists several groups, the Church of God among them, that he believes illustrate this understanding in the history of Christianity.

The application of a practical understanding of theology to the Church of God (Anderson) is, of course, open to question. Since I think that McClendon's inclusion of the Church of God in such groups gives every appearance of a good fit, I will move on to examine some cases involving theological teaching in the Church of God in this practical vein.

Church Discipline: Dealing with Heretics and Backsliders

The issue that took priority in E. E. Byrum's retrospective view of 1899 was the "Zinzendorf theory." Among some holiness movement preachers within the Church of God and without, an alternative theology of sanctification had developed out of the teaching of Nicholas Zinzendorf. The details of this theology are not important here, save to say that Zinzendorf's view that the full cleansing of the soul in entire sanctification was attributed rather than real earned his latter-day followers among the Saints the label "Anti-Cleansers." A significant number of preachers in the Church of God appear to have espoused this view. These Anti-Cleansers arrived at the general campmeeting in Moundsville, West Virginia, ready for a showdown. In his report of this meeting, Byrum claims to have used the Scriptures to publicly refute their argument. Those who persisted in this teaching either left the Saints of their own accord or were barred from fellowship. Readers of the *Gospel Trumpet* were warned to have no dealings with these people so long as they persisted in their error.

Historian John W. V. Smith says that the "Anti-Cleansing Heresy" and its aftermath dealt a very serious blow to the young Church of God movement.[8] It is very difficult to accurately portray the number of men and women in the Church of God ministry at the turn of the century. Some estimates, likely exaggerations, put the number of defections as high as fifty percent of the ministry. Smith says that the departing group was significant both in number and in stature. Although names and numbers of defectors in 1899 continue to elude us, we do know the names and number of ministers who attended the Moundsville campmeeting of 1902. Three years after the campmeeting where Byrum repudiated the Zinzendorf theory, only 91 ministers were at Moundsville.[9] In 1905 a total of 393 ministers registered in the ministerial list that validated ministerial status so people could qualify as clergy for reduced rail fare. Clearly the departure of the "Zinzendorfians" dealt a body blow to the young movement.

Six months after the Anti-Cleansing campmeeting, Byrum was understandably still worried about the effects of this schism.[10] The Zinzendorf theory had been propagated to some extent and some of the saints were becoming confused, even "losing their experience." Byrum seems to have kept track of at least some of the Anti-Cleansers. He noted that some had repented while others persisted in preaching this doctrine. Sill others hadleft the ministry and "gone to work with their hands," a step "which is much better," opined Byrum, "than to go forth propagating something that would be detrimental to souls."[11] Byrum remained adamant in refusing fellowship to the sizable minority who remained outside the tiny fold. He encouraged the saints to pray for the restoration of the heretics, but he also took comfort in the fact that the Zinzendorfism episode "is only a fulfillment of the word of God." Byrum invoked 2 Peter 2:1-2 as a forewarning of such episodes.

Four years after the Anti-Cleansing campmeeting of 1899 movement leaders followed essentially the same procedures in dis-fellowshipping W. G. Schell. It was Schell who had delivered Daniel Warner's funeral sermon in 1895 and who some had thought would succeed him as editor of the paper. In other words, we are talking about a very prominent minister. But prominent ministers D. O. Teasley and H. M. Riggle collaborated on an announcement that warned all readers of Schell's apostasy.[12] As in the Byrum article, the two men cited a New Testament text that warned of days when some would depart from the faith (1 Tim. 4:1-2) and specified the heterodox views that Schell had come to espuse.[13] This announcement formalized the beginning of a seven-year spiritual, occupational, and geographical odyssey that culminated in Shell's restoration to the movement after a public and published repentance.[14]

These two episodes suggest that by 1905 there were clearly understood and applied procedures for disciplining people who deviated from the doctrinal norm. Before this date official minister's lists, complete with the name of an endorsing minister, identified the men and women who were in good standing in the church. Such lists and such procedures are the marks of a "church" rather than a movement of saints governed only through the gifting of the Holy Spirit. By about 1900, then, the movement's leaders had worked out a clear understanding of a theology of the church's ministry, what constituted fellowship within that ministry, and what constituted breaches of that fellowship. The leadership had also acted in accordance with these understandings; in a word, they were practicing what they understood and thought.

Biblical Inspiration and Interpretation

Unlike other groups with origins in the nineteenth-century Holiness Movement, some Bible scholars in the Church of God began employing the historical critical method of biblical studies in the 1930s and certainly by 1940. Again, around the year 1900 attitudes and practices set the stage for later developments. In this case it was biblical inspiration and authority.

In 1894 H. C. Wickersham published the second edition of his book *Holiness Bible Subjects*[15] including an essay entitled "What the Bible Is Not, and What It Is." This essay suggests that Wickersham had at least a passing awareness of recent developments in biblical scholarship related to authorship, etc. He seems to have steered a middle course between those developments on the one hand and a plenary view of inspiration on the other. When it came to inspiration, Wickersham insisted that God did not inspire the words or even the ideas of the Bible, but rather the people who wrote it. He followed a logic that said, "If God had inspired the thoughts and the words of the Bible, the Bible would have been written in the same style of words and expression of thought."[16] As far as inspired authors were concerned, Wickersham explicitly limited inspiration's effects. As he put the matter, "Remember, and the idea cannot be too strongly enforced, that inspiration is not omniscience. The apostle Paul could write the epistle to the Romans, but he never knew how to make a steam engine or a locomotive.... Look not to the Bible for what God never put in it—look not there for mathematics or mechanics, for metaphysical distinctions or abstruse sciences; but look there simply for the way of spiritual life and salvation from all sin, and you will find enough...."[17]

Little more than a decade later, E. E. Byrum published a book specifically on the authorship and transmission of the Scripture entitled *How We Got Our Bible*.[18] Apparently he thought that his brother in the faith as well as his uncle by blood did not have all the light that there was to be had on this subject. Byrum took the more conservative view that the words of the text were inspired and that the same Spirit guarded the transmission and translation of the text so that "we can clasp hands, as it were, with the apostles, and when we serach our New Testament, feel assured that we are speaking the same words that they spoke."[19] Clearly Wickersham and Byrum differed on this important point of church doctrine.

The practice of biblical interpretation in the Church of God before 1900 seems to have favored Wickersham's more dynamic view of inspiration. The last two numbers of the 1893 volume and the first number of the 1894 volume of the *Gospel Trumpet* ran a series of three articles from the pen of editor Warner dealing with the interpretation of several specific passages of scripture and the issues deriving therefrom. Warner clearly perceived the movement's practices of biblical interpretation to be a larger matter, of which the readings of specific passages were particular instances. While he spoke to the particular instances, he also addressed the larger question.

Warner adduced several texts to assert the idea that the ministers of God "agree in faith and doctrine, being in the one 'faith of the gospel.'" They are of the same mind. The sameness does not reside in what they have compiled in a creed and subscribed to, but in that mind, faith, doctrine and practice that is "according to Jesus Christ." This harmony of sentiment and teaching "is attained and only can be attained by having our former education and our wisdom destroyed and purged out; and be led of the Spirit of God into all truth, according to the promise of Christ (Jn. 16:13)."[20] Such harmony was the ideal, but Warner also recognized that not all of God's messengers possessed the same gifts and abilities, nor had they all attained to the same measure of gospel truth. Nevertheless, there is harmony in all that is taught as long as each teacher is confined within that measure of truth received by the Holy Spirit. How did this vision of hermeneutical harmony actually play out?

The first of Warner's articles was entitled, "Do the Ministers of God See Eye to Eye?" Within weeks he received answers to that question which led him to write a second article, entitled "The Ministers of God Must See Eye to Eye." The issue was that some ministers differed with Warner over the interpretation of Jesus' saying that a camel could sooner pass through a needle's eye than a rich man enter the kingdom. After adopting a literal reading of that text, Warner exhorted his ministerial colleagues:

> And now beloved, if we are going to fulfill the prophecy of a holy ministry returned from Babylon confusion, to see eye to eye, and teach the same things, be sure that you take up and teach nothing that has the traditions of sectism to sustain it. Only teach what you know by the sure Word and Spirit of God, and there will be harmony.[21]

It is interesting that, despite clear differences of interpretation, Warner did not use the authority of the editor's chair to enforce doctrinal uniformity. Instead he appealed to the Word and Spirit of God and implicitly trusted in an ongoing conversation between minister and minister and between minister and editorial office. This suggests a practice of Bible reading and interpretation wherein participants engaged one another in the common belief that the Word and Spirit would guide honest and sincere efforts, leading them into "all truth."

The final article in Warner's series was titled "The Ministers of God See Eye to Eye," wherein he continued to take up dissenting readings of biblical passages.[22] As in his previous articles, he claimed neither authority over his colleagues nor that he possessed greater light on the Scripture. Rather, Warner continued to follow an emerging practice of interpretation that allowed for divergent views in a conversation that trusted the Spirit to lead the church into all the truth.

At the beginning of the twentieth century the Church of God was divided in its theology of the inspiration and interpretation of the Bible. Authoritative voices spoke in favor of more dynamic theories of inspiration while others advocated more conservative views. But the example of a conversational style of hermeneutics suggests the greater force of the former view and the basis for the later acceptance of more contemporary views of biblical exegesis and interpretation.[23]

Theological Practices Established and Lost: Divine Healing and Pacifism

My final illustration of theology as practice involves two different doctrines, one that was sewn into the movement's theological quilt with very strong thread and another that, while it may never have been cut out of the quilt, certainly has faded over the years. I am referring respectively to the doctrines of divine healing and pacifism.

As E. E. Byrum peered into the twentieth century, he worried that the ministers of the movement were not sufficiently emphasizing the doctrine of divine healing. In fact, he believed that both the preaching and practice of divine healing had declined. Byrum was determined to reverse this tendency. He exhorted his fellow ministers to a re-dedication to this specific doctrine and its practice, warning them that their failure to do so would invite Satan into the camp of the saints, inciting all manner of false teachings and generally hindering the work of the Lord. Byrum also saw to it that the movement could not avoid the doctrine. During his tenure as editor the back page of the *Gospel Trumpet* was dedicated to articles and testimonies concerned with divine healing. He also insured that the practice of divine healing was embedded in the movement's life, even to the extent of praying over small hankies anointed with a drop of oil and then mailing the same to isolated saints who had no nearby elders to call for the prayer of faith.

At the same time that Byrum made divine healing an article of faith and practice in the life of the Church of God, the doctrine of pacifism came to be neglected. When the Spanish-American War erupted in 1898, the *Gospel Trumpet* initially paid scant attention to it, although Noah Byrum said that war news filled the secular newspapers.[24] But when a reader asked the Trumpet whether it was the duty of a Christian convert to desert the United States Army, the paper answered that desertion violated the teaching of Romans 13. Besides, "God can keep him saved where he is until he has served his time."[25] A few months later the Trumpet responded to what it called a number of letters concerning the question of whether or not a Christian should go to war:

> We answer no. Emphatically no. There is no place in the New Testament wherein Christ gave instructions to his followers to take the life of a fellow man. In olden times it was "an eye for an eye and a tooth for a tooth." "Love your neighbor and hate your enemy." In this gospel dispensation it is quite different. Jesus says: "But I say unto you, do good to them that despitefully use you," etc. (Matt 5:44). "Avenge not yourselves." "If thine enemy hunger, feed him; if he thirst, give him drink"—not shoot him.[26]

The paper did not comment further on the Spanish-American War. Nor did the publications of the Gospel Trumpet Company teach the doctrine of Christian pacifism at any point during the following decades. When World War I began, the paper took a compromise position that supported men who volunteered for military service as solidly as it encouraged pacifists. By the war's end the paper was endorsing the sale of Liberty Bonds.[27] A comparison of the doctrines of Christian pacifism and divine healing in the Church of God strongly suggests that the long-term weakening of the former can be attributed to the absence of what ensured the strengthening of the latter: a determination to practice a doctrine in addition to the formal pronouncement of it.

What all of this suggests is that, especially for a group like the Church of God, we know its theological life only superficially and in a distorted way unless we understand its practice of theology as well as its doctrinal statements. If we understand the movement's theological life as a matter of practices as well as formalized statements, we will discover some practices developing well in advance of related theological teaching. We may also discover that formal, printed statements of our theological commitments do not necessarily insure their reception into the life and habits of the church.

Notes

[1] This article was initially an address by Dr. Strege, historian of the Church of God, delivered as the presidential address to the founding meeting of the Historical Society of the Church of God (Anderson), convened in Anderson, Indiana, in June, 2000.

[2] By "sectism" the Saints meant the human practice of inappropriately dividing or sectioning the church universal.

[3] All references here will be to the 2nd edition (Notre Dame: University of Notre Dame Press, 1984).

[4] See, for example, James W. McClendon, Jr., *Systematic Theology*, vol. 2, *Doctrine* (Nashville: Abingdon Press, 1994); David D. Hall, editor, *Lived Religion in America: Toward A History of Practice* (Princeton, NJ: Princeton University Press); and Dorothy C. Bass, editor, *Practicing Our Faith* (San Francisco: Jossey-Bass Publishers, 1997).

[5] MacIntyre, *After Virtue*, 187.

[6] McClendon, *Systematic Theology*, vol. II, 28-29.

[7] Ibid., 28.

[8] John W. V. Smith, *The Quest for Holiness and Unity* (Anderson, IN: Warner Press, 1980), 185ff.

[9] File titled "Ministers Lists," Archives of the Church of God, Anderson University.

[10] "Words of Greeting," *Gospel Trumpet*, vol. 19, No. 51 (December 28, 1899), 1.

[11] Ibid.

[12] "Departed From the Faith," *Gospel Trumpet* (June 18, 1903).

[13] Schell was said to have stated to "reliable brethren" that he no longer considered the "present reformation" to be of Godly origin, in essence asserting the same view of the cultural and historical origins of some of Warner's ideas as were stated at the outset of this paper. Timing is everything. Schell also denied that footwashing was a NT ordinance and espoused triune immersion as the true NT form. Teasley and Riggle also made vague charges that "from time to time there has been manifest in his life that which is not consistent with the character of a pure New Testament minister."

[14] For detail on this odyssey, see Barry L. Callen, editor, *Following the Light* (Anderson, IN: Warner Press, 2000), 123-126.

[15] Grand Junction, MI: Gospel Trumpet Publishing Company, 1984.

[16] Ibid., 19

[17] Ibid., 20.

[18] Moundsville, WV: Gospel Trumpet Company, 1905.

[19] Ibid., 87.

[20] Daniel S. Warner, "Do the Ministers of God See Eye to Eye?" *Gospel Trumpet* (December 14, 1893).

[21] *Gospel Trumpet*, December 21, 1893.

[22] *Gospel Trumpet*, December 28, 1893.

[23] For a fuller discussion of this topic, see my "The Peculiar Impress of the Mind: Biblical Inspiration and Interpretation in the Church of God (Anderson)," unpublished paper (September, 1995).

[24] Noah Byrum, 1898 Journal, Noah Byrum Papers, Archives of the Church of God, Anderson University.

[25] "Deserting the Army," *Gospel Trumpet* (Feb. 10, 1898), 4.

[26] "Should We Go To War?", *Gospel Trumpet* (April 15, 1898).

[27] For a fuller treatment of this topic, see my "The Demise [?] of a Peace Church: The Church of God (Anderson), Pacifism, and Civil Religion," *Mennonite Quarterly Review*, vol. LXV, No. 2 (April 1991).

Part II
Human Walls; Kingdom Doors

Chapter 5

Race Relations and The American Holiness Movement

by
James Earl Massey

Although the Wesleyan/Holiness tradition has an admirable record of addressing certain social evils, its history on the American scene has not been exemplary in race relations. Like Christians in general, holiness people have suffered the impact of prevailing social stereotypes and prejudices. A notable exception, at least in part, is the Church of God movement (Anderson) that has enjoyed a prolonged and unusually fruitful involvement with the African-American community of Christians. The Wesleyan Theological Society gave its 2006 Smith/Wynkoop Book Award to James Earl Massey's African Americans and the Church of God *(Anderson University Press, 2005), which tells this story in detail. As Massey explains below, it has been the strongly relational themes of the Church of God movement and its unusual commitment to freedom and unity that have combined to enable such social fruitfulness. While the racial divide has not disappeared, even in this reform movement, significant strides have been made. Originally published in the* Wesleyan Theological Journal *(31:1, Spring, 1996).*

Some years ago I was privileged to take part in a special conference of Evangelicals, assigned to report about the contributions of African Americans to Evangelicalism—that perennially interesting and mosaic-like spiritual movement. It was not difficult to trace and comment on those contributions because, quite early in the history of the black presence in this land, blacks received the gospel of Christ with openness.

They rigorously tested and proved its viability, and began passing on the evangelical witness with concern, creativity, and gusto.

As an African-American Christian, I felt an understandable pride as I handled my assignment.[1] The pride had to do with the three particular contributions I sought to highlight at the time. One was the widespread development of evangelical churches within the African American grouping; a second was the continuing influence on the Evangelical music scene of the black church tradition of celebrative and self-expressive worship music; and the third contribution was the courageously prophetic witness African- American believers have steadily made in calling white believers to become more socially responsible in their concern to evangelize. The 1970s had just ended, and that decade was a pregnant period of years during which Evangelical Christianity had grown faster in America than any other religious movement, with a grouping that then numbered more than forty million. Yes, I felt a distinct pride in reporting about how African-American believers had responded to the gospel, and had eagerly busied themselves in passing on the Evangelical heritage with ready faith, steady creativity, and acknowledged contagion.

Sensitizing Evangelicals

Among the more than forty million reported at that time as comprising Evangelical Christianity in America were many African-American believers. The membership of most of these was in black evangelical churches which gave them a spiritual home, a meaningful social setting, and a political base from which to engage the contrary forces and patterns of a racist society. Their history of organized separateness from white churches in groupings designated as "African Methodist" or "African Baptist," etc., was due, in the main, to the problematic course of Evangelical Protestantism under the influence of those contrary forces and patterns in a racially partitioned society.[2]

Efforts to sensitize the evangelical conscience about racism and social implications of the faith have been as prolonged, persistent, and necessary as those to stimulate the national conscience. It is a matter of fact, and a matter for shame, that major changes regarding race relations and social action began taking place earlier on the social scene in America than they did within the churches of Evangelical Protestantism. To be sure, some change in evangelical social views was stimulated by Carl F. H. Henry since 1956 through his editorial writings in *Christianity Today* magazine and in 1964 through his pacesetting book *Aspects of Christian*

Social Ethics. Also in 1968 Sherwood Wirt called attention in his *The Social Conscience of the Evangelical* to several issues needing a decisively Christian response from evangelicals.[3] But one must not overlook the fact that Carl Henry and Sherwood Wirt, among others, were writing and publishing their views to the church during the era of the Civil Rights Movement of the 1950s and 1960s. Those were the strategic and stressful decades when the American social scene was being impacted by the charismatic presence of vocal and socially active African American leaders who unrelentingly kept calling the nation to make its "liberty and justice for all" motto a lived reality for all its citizens.

As for efforts to sensitize Evangelical believers for greater social and racial openness, I am reminded of something that happened during the first World Congress on Evangelism, a convention that brought evangelical leaders from around the world to Berlin, Germany, for a ten-day gathering in November, 1966. During the convention, those of us who were delegates heard many position papers which treated aspects of the Congress theme, "One Race, One Gospel, One Task." But, as the Congress continued across those ten days, some of us who were African American noticed that no attention had been devoted in any of the position papers to the first part of the theme, "One Race." Nor had any paper on that aspect been distributed to us for a private reading, as had some topics related to other aspects of the general theme. The Congress delegates had been drawn together from across the world, literally, and the vast assemblage represented the largest ecumenical and evangelical gathering of the Church since Pentecost in A.D. 33. Even though it reflected a great diversity of nationalities, geographical locations, and color distinctions, no major statement about the oneness of the human race had been given in any plenary session!

A few of us African-American delegates discussed this omission among ourselves and finally gained audience with Carl F. H. Henry, the Congress Chairman, to voice to him our question about this evident gap in planning. Interestingly, we later learned that some delegates from India, Africa, and South America had also noticed the omission. Chairman Henry listened to us with openness, and soon acknowledged to us that the planning committee had taken the "One Race" aspect of the general theme as a given, and therefore had not assigned anyone to treat it! Aware now of the problem as we had voiced it, he apologized on behalf of the planning committee and asked if we would be willing to work at developing a summary statement about "One Race" which could be included in the final report scheduled to be distributed to the world press as an outcome of the Congress. Although it was rather late in the day for anything like a major paper on the matter, six of us agreed to help develop such a statement.

Jimmy McDonald, Howard O. Jones, Bob Harrison, Ralph Bell, Louis Johnson, and I worked into the late hours of that night. We managed to finish a clearly focused statement on race. Our statement underscored human equality as a biblical principle rooted in the oneness of the human family under God as Creator. We stressed the imperative of *agape* love in our dealings with all humans, and the need to reject racial and national barriers which forbid full fellowship and cooperative ministry in the Church. As it turned out, the section the six of us prepared about the world-wide problem of racism was undoubtedly the strongest statement evangelicals had ever made on the subject until that time.[4] It was a basic statement that declared our biblically informed understanding about racism as an unjust attitude, a social evil, and a barrier to cooperative ministry as believers. Within another decade, by 1977, Evangelical Christianity in America would comprise a mosaic-like grouping of more than forty million members,[5] but its influence as a leader in fostering racial understanding and social harmony in the land would, sad to say, still remain negligible.

Relations Within the American Holiness Movement

The story has not been very different with the churches which comprise what I refer to here as the American Holiness Movement. This movement is comprised of those church groups with a history of an emphasis on Christian holiness and with some historical relation to the transmission of this tradition through holiness associations and conventions. In fact, in tracing the patterned story of the Holiness Movement in America one will discover that the number of blacks involved in its life and witness has been even more disturbingly meager than the number of blacks in the Evangelical Movement.

A significant number of black evangelical leaders have had ministries which involved them steadily in both black and white settings throughout Evangelicalism. They comprise a very distinct group whose spiritual concerns and emphases are rooted in the theology and cultus of the Bible school and biblical seminary movement which trained them. Although they have often differed with white evangelicals over how to answer certain social questions, and found it necessary to identify and sometimes redefine the issues for which white definitions were judged inadequate, they nevertheless have been respected and continued to serve as bridge-builders between the races.[6] The number of such leaders within the American Holiness Movement is considerably smaller. Let me trace the reason or reasons why I believe this has been, and continues to be so.

In my judgment, the black presence in the American Holiness Movement has been comparatively slight because this movement's major concerns have not seemed as appealing or germane to black believers as has the basic salvation emphasis articulated by the Evangelical Movement. Although it is clear that the Scriptures call for a dedicated life that honors God and the divine will—a call that is indeed known and heralded in the black churches, African Americans have been "grabbed" by other currents of truth and meaning in the Scriptures. One in particular is that strong and steady current in Old Testament thought that accents the importance of social regard and race uplift. When African-American Christians think and witness about renewal and restoration, or about Christian unity, they also envision what these should mean for those who have been victimized by a racist system. In addition, they reason that any personal quest for spiritual depth or closeness to God must inevitably include some concern for bettering the social process in America.

Given America's racist environment, one of the predominant issues with which African-American believers and their churches have been concerned is social survival. Along with the biblical message about salvation through faith in Jesus, they have been encouraged by the clarifying anthropology taught in the Scriptures, that validating message about all humans being children of God. Given our set of social circumstances in the chequered course of American history, the concern of black believers has been for salvation and survival, with the social implications of the faith being viewed as far more germane than an emphasis on a strictly personal pietistic inwardness. This is not to say that a concern for the deeper life is neglected; it is rather to say that the social and the spiritual are viewed in a more related fashion by black believers than by most proponents of the Holiness tradition.[7]

The concern for freedom, social equality, and general race uplift has so absorbed the energies of black church leaders in particular and black churches in general that sometimes little energy has remained for much else. To sense the extent to which this has been the case, one need only explore the various histories of the black denominations, on the one hand, and the studies which report about black membership in predominately white denominations, on the other.[8]

By and large, African-American believers tend to honor and promote what Peter J. Paris has aptly described as "the black Christian tradition." As Paris has explained it:

> The tradition that has always been normative for the black churches and the black community is not the so-called Western Christian tradition per se, although this tradition is an important source for blacks. More accurately, the normative tradition for blacks is that tradition governed by the principle of nonracism which we call the black Christian tradition. The fundamental principle of the black Christian tradition is depicted most adequately in the biblical doctrine of the parenthood of God and the kinship of all peoples—which is a version of the traditional sexist expression "the fatherhood of God and the brotherhood of men."9

In contrast with the emphases highlighted in the Evangelical and Holiness traditions, *this* is the emphatic tradition that became institutionalized in the African-American churches.

To be sure, African-American interest in revivalistic religion and a depth relationship with God has not been lacking, as those who have experienced a black worship service can readily testify. Nevertheless, blacks have never accented personal piety at the expense of a needed accent on the social meaning of a religious experience. The development of higher Christian graces, or a "closer walk with God" as it is popularly termed, continues as a concern and advisement among black evangelicals; but the perfectionist emphasis that prevailed in holiness circles in the nineteenth century did not gain as wide an appeal among blacks as among whites. For one thing, Christian perfectionism seemed "too Methodist-like" to those who were Baptist by orientation. For another, it seemed too unattainable to those who did not hear a clear enough explanation about the doctrine.

African-American believers always have insisted that true religion is essentially experiential. It has not been as necessary to blacks that there be a refined doctrinal system to expound this belief. Blacks were in tune with American revivalism at an early point in its development, and benefited greatly from its impacting influences, but they did not get as involved as whites in that wing of the American Holiness Movement which blended Pietism and Wesleyan perfectionism.10

The Church of God Movement (Anderson)

The following are holiness-teaching denominations which have had primary and extended contact with African Americans in the course of their history and witnessing in America: The Christian and Missionary Alliance Church, The Church of the Nazarene, The Pilgrim Holiness Church, The Holiness Christian Church, The Salvation Army, and the Church of God (Anderson, IN.). These groups are also among the larger Holiness bodies registered in the nation. Although the separate history of each of these groups has not always reflected the best social arrangement with the blacks who became members in them, it is of interest to report that their black members did not break away from these groups to form independent organizations, as did those blacks who experienced segregation in the Methodist Church, for example.[11] Perhaps among the reasons for their not breaking away might be the fact that most of the named groups have had so few black members in comparison with their white majorities.

A word is in order regarding the history of some of these groups in relating to African Americans. The Church of the Nazarene put forth well-planned and organized efforts during the 1940s to promote holiness evangelism among African Americans, but those efforts yielded rather meager results. In fact, during the total history of this group's contact with African Americans from the late nineteenth century to the early 1980s, there were never more than twelve black ministers associated with it.[12] The Salvation Army has not fared much better in attempts to promote the holiness theme among African Americans. Booker T. Washington, the noted Tuskegee educator and national race leader, was so impressed by the rich history of The Salvation Army in social outreach and group openness that in 1896 he wrote: "I have always had the greatest respect for the work of the Salvation Army, especially because I had noted that it draws no color line in religion."[13] And yet, despite such an endorsement from a leading black educator and race statesman, The Salvation Army never experienced widespread success in gaining African American members or in holding them.

Among those holiness-teaching groups that have had a rather prolonged contact with African Americans, the one that has been the most fruitful is the Church of God (Anderson, IN). In 1968 there was in this body a black membership of 16,703 within a total United States membership listing of 144,243. By 1974 the number of African American members had increased to nearly 20,000 among a total reported membership of 160,198. In 1980 the Church of God (Anderson) listed 472 predominantly black congregations, with 27,628 black members among a total membership in the United States of 179,137. These figures show a pattern of steady relationship between African Americans and the larger body of Church of God members in the United States and an instructive growth pattern among African Americans associated with the Church of God.

It is most enlightening to compare the race membership percentage in this holiness-teaching group with those percentages reflected within the main-line majority-white denominations, especially during the late 1970s when American Baptists reported a 12% black membership, the Episcopal Church 5%, the United Church of Christ 4.3%, the Disciples of Christ 3.8%, the United Methodist Church 3.5%, the United Presbyterian Church 2.7%, the Lutheran Church in America 1.7%, and the Southern Baptists a meager 1.0%.

African Americans are by far the largest ethnic minority within the Church of God (Anderson). In 1989, of 199,786 members listed for the Church of God in the United States, 37,435 were African Americans. The reason for this significant percentage is historical, theological, and social. It is due in no small measure to the appealing and promising unity ideal that is at the heart of the Church of God message; it is an ideal that has from this movement's beginning in 1880 been allied in the church's message and practices with the call to scriptural holiness. As church historian John W. V. Smith has explained it: "Many church groups avoided making a strong interracial stance. The Church of God reformation's message of unity of all believers, however, made a very strong interracial position inherent in the message itself."[14]

The message voiced by the Church of God about the unity of believers appealed strongly to African Americans who were otherwise restricted and segregated in a racist society. The message of unity provided promise for a needed affirmation of self-worth, on the one hand, and for needed social togetherness, on the other. Unlike other church groups whose doctrinal positions accented non-relational themes, the central theme of the Church of God was, and remains, a relational one: believers belong together, united by love. Although social relations within the Church of God have witnessed the same problems and stresses all other church bodies have faced, the challenge of the biblical insistence on unity has always been present in the group's heritage and message as a prodding factor toward freeing its life from racist concerns in the national environment and toward reform of its life as people of God called to practice holiness. To be sure, evidences that some persons within its congregations have yielded to prevailing social patterns of race distancing and polarization can be documented in the history of the Church of

God just as in the history of other church groups in America. Nevertheless, the unity ideal central to its heritage and reason for being has never allowed such lapses from the ideal to stand unchallenged.[15]

The two worlds of race have not yet disappeared from the Church of God, but some significant strides have been made in recent years which show an increased openness and intent to fulfill this movement's unity ideal. Among the many available evidences of this, the following will sufficiently illustrate this openness and intentionality. Since the early 1970s, several African Americans have served in full-time posts as staff persons for the major boards and general agencies of the Church of God. In 1988, an African American was elected by the General Assembly of the Church to serve as the body's executive secretary, a post that is the highest elective office within the church. Reelected following his first term, this leader continues to serve with distinction and wide regard. In June, 1989, the General Assembly of the church ratified an African-American educator, a former pastor within the group, to be dean of the church's graduate School of Theology. For many years in the recent past, the chair of the Board of Trustees of Anderson University, this movement's largest school, was a gifted black pastor and campus alumnus.

Like other church communions with a history within the American Holiness Movement, the Church of God (Anderson) is not yet perfected. It stands, along with these and multitudinous other religious bodies in America, between the alternatives of advance and decay, fulfillment and failure, witness and waywardness, significance and selfishness. The twin concerns of holiness and unity beckon us to full openness and obedience to our reason for being. If our obedience is full, and if our experience of holiness is thoroughgoing, then renewal will be the result—and our continuing witness may yet prove convincing to many others. May it be so, to the good of all whose lives we touch, to the good of this socially fractured nation, to a divided Christendom that needs our witnessing presence, and to the greater glory of God.

Notes

[1] For a published report, see James Earl Massey, "The Black Contribution to Evangelicalism," in *Evangelicalism: Surviving Its Success*, edited by David A. Fraser (Princeton: Princeton University Press, 1987), 50-58.

[2] Among the myriad of studies about this, see Albert J. Raboteau, "The Black Experience in American Evangelicalism: The Meaning of Slavery," in Leonard I. Sweet, editor, *The Evangelical Tradition in America* (Macon: Mercer University

Press, 1984); Gayraud S. Wilmore, *Black Religion and Black Radicalism* (Garden City: Anchor Press, Doubleday, Inc., 1973).

[3]See Carl F. H. Henry, *Aspects of Christian Social Ethics* (Grand Rapids: Wm. B. Eerdmans Publishing Co., 1964); Sherwood Wirt, *The Social Conscience of the Evangelical* (New York: Harper & Row, Publishers, 1968).

[4]The full text of the Congress Statement was published in *One Race, One Gospel, One Task*, Volume I, Edited by Carl F. H. Henry and Stanley Mooneyham (Minneapolis: World Wide Publications, 1967), 5-7. Personal reports about the Congress were published in books written by two persons from among the six who prepared the statement about race. See Bob Harrison, with Jim Montgomery, *When God Was Black* (Grand Rapids: Zondervan Publishing House, 1971), 145-146; James Earl Massey, *Concerning Christian Unity* (Anderson: Warner Press, 1979), 121-126.

[5]See the feature story in *Time* Magazine, December 26, 1977, 52-58.

[6]On this, see William H. Bentley, "Black Believers in the Black Community," in *The Evangelicals*, edited by David F. Wells and John D. Woodbridge (Nashville: Abingdon Press, 1975); William H. Bentley, *National Black Evangelical Association: Reflections on the Evolution of a Concept of Ministry* (Chicago: 1979). See also Tom Skinner, *Black and Free* (Grand Rapids: Zondervan Publishing House, 1968); William E. Pannell, *My Friend, the Enemy* (Waco, TX: Word Books, Inc., 1968); William E. Pannell, *The Coming Race Wars? A Cry for Reconciliation* (Grand Rapids: Zondervan Publishing House, 1993); Howard O. Jones, *White Questions to a Black Christian* (Grand Rapids: Zondervan Publishing House, 1975); Samuel G. Hines, with Joe Allison, *Experience the Power* (Anderson: Warner Press, 1996).

[7]This criticism does not apply to those proponents of Holiness who showed such social concern as to seek societal reform during the mid-nineteenth century. On this, see Timothy L. Smith, *Revivalism and Social Reform in the Mid-Nineteenth Century America* (Nashville: Abingdon Press, 1957).

[8]For examples, see the rather broad treatment of the major black Baptist groups in Leroy Fitts, *A History of Black Baptists* (Nashville: Broadman Press, 1985), esp. ch. 2, 41-106, in which he details how the socio-political needs of blacks spawned the various conventions which reflect and promote the black Baptist tradition. See also James Melvin Washington, *Frustrated Fellowship: The Black Baptist Quest for Social Power* (Macon: Mercer University Press, 1986).

[9]Peter Paris, *The Social Teaching of the Black Churches* (Philadelphia: Fortress Press, 1985), 10.

[10]On this blending of Pietism, revivalism, and Wesleyan perfectionism, see Melvin E. Dieter, *The Holiness Revival of the Nineteenth Century* (Metuchen, NJ: Scarecrow Press, Inc., 1980), esp. 3-10, 18-63.

[11]The experience of segregation within the Methodist Church led to the formation by blacks of the African Methodist Episcopal Church and the African Methodist Episcopal Zion Church. On the origins of the A.M.E. Church, see Harry V. Richardson, *Dark Salvation:* The Story of Methodism as It Developed Among Blacks in America (Garden City, NY: Anchor Press/Doubleday, 1976),

esp. 76-116. On the origins of the A.M.E.Z. Church, see Richardson, 117-147, and William J. Walls, *The African Methodist Episcopal Zion Church* (Charlotte: A.M.E. Zion Publishing House, 1974).

[12]See W. T. Purkiser, *Called Unto Holiness,* Vol. 2, The Second Twenty-Five Years, 1933-58 (Kansas City, MO: Nazarene Publishing House, 1983), esp. 197-200. For two additional and earlier reports regarding efforts by The Church of the Nazarene to evangelize blacks, see Raymond W. Hurn, *Mission Possible:* A Study of the Mission of the Church of the Nazarene (Kansas City, MO: Nazarene Publishing House, 1973), esp. 84-85. See also Roger Eugene Bowman, *Color Us Christian:* The Story of the Church of the Nazarene Among America's Blacks (Kansas City, MO: Nazarene Publishing House, 1975).

[13]Quoted by Edward H. McKinley, in his book, *Marching to Glory:* The History of the Salvation Army in the United States of America, 1880-1980 (San Francisco: Harper & Row, 1980), see 53, note 41. For the story of Salvation Army efforts to win blacks, see 50-53, 150-151, 183-184, and 196-201.

[14]John W. V. Smith, *The Quest for Holiness and Unity:* A Centennial History of the Church of God (Anderson: Warner Press, 1980), 162.

[15]For more about the history of race relations in the Church of God, see John W. V. Smith, *op. cit.,* esp. 161-169, 385, 389, and 403-406; David A. Telfer, *Red & Yellow, Black & White & Brown:* Home Missions in the Church of God (Anderson: Warner Press, 1981), esp. 42-53. See also James Earl Massey, *African Americans and the Church of God: Aspects of A Social History* (forthcoming).

Chapter 6

African-American Worship: Pentecostal and Holiness Movements

by
Cheryl J. Sanders[1]

In a significant sense, the Church of God movement (Anderson) is a "pentecostal" movement. While not in the "tongues" tradition, it always has been oriented to the centrality of the presence, power, gifting, and control of the Spirit of God. In addition, this movement has enjoyed a prominent African-American constituency that has blended into the whole of the movement its distinctive perspectives and styles of congregational life. Given, then, the movement's constituency, Spirit orientation, spiritual-experience focus, and anti-creedalism, personal testimony, inspiring music, and powerful preaching have been judged crucial. Theology has been put into hymns and songs composed especially for the movement to sing. Robert A. Adams has chronicled this major music tradition in his doctoral dissertation (Southwestern Baptist Theological Seminary, 1980). Cheryl J. Sanders, Church of God pastor in Washington, D.C., explores aspects of this tradition, prominent in some congregations and campmeetings of the Church of God movement. Originally published in the Wesleyan Theological Journal *(32:2, fall, 1997).*

Worship in the African-American Holiness and Pentecostal churches involves song, speech, dance, and other ways of knowing God and verifying spiritual revelation. This tradition thrives on the integration of aesthetics (cultural authenticity), ethics (implementation of Christian norms), and epistemology (ways of knowing) in its characteristic verbal and bodily articulations of praise. Worship practices and experiences are continually interrogated with reference to specific aesthetic expectations and ethical standards. When a soloist or instrumentalist has pushed the congregation to the brink of ecstasy with an inspired performance, when the preacher has brought the sermon to a dramatic climax, when the gatekeepers of pulpit and pew usher the people through the experience of the shout, it is understood as the "witness of the Spirit," the much sought-after manifestation of the Holy Spirit. The underlying ethical and theological context of Holiness-Pentecostal worship is the corporate testimony of being "saved, sanctified, and filled with the Holy Ghost."

Saved, Sanctified, and Spirit-Baptized

As used in this discussion of worship, "saint" is a term suggestive of both liturgical and ethical identity. The key testimony or confessional formula that characterizes the saints is "saved, sanctified, and filled with the Holy Ghost." Each denomination among the Holiness and Pentecostal churches has specific doctrines and disciplines governing the interpretation of the meaning of salvation, sanctification, and Spirit baptism, but some generalizations will be ventured here in an attempt to characterize the liturgical and ethical self-understanding of the tradition as a whole.

To be *saved* means that one has repented and asked forgiveness of sins, and has confessed Jesus Christ as Savior and Lord. This imparts a basic "entry level" of liturgical identity that distinguishes the saint from the unbeliever. To be *sanctified* is to receive some second form of blessing that conveys on the believer a distinctive ethical identity of being set apart for God, literally to be made holy. Some of the non-Wesleyan groups would not see sanctification as a separate process, but as an experience inherent in salvation. To be *filled* or *baptized with the Holy Spirit* is a declaration of liturgical identity which signifies that the saint has experienced total initiation into the worshipping community by a personal confession or manifestation of Spirit possession. The evidence of this is the major area of doctrinal difference that accounts in part for the vast multiplicity of denominations and church bodies within the Holiness and Pentecostal movements. Generally speaking, the Wesleyan-Holiness churches emphasize the infilling of the Spirit as manifested in a holy life, while the Pentecostal churches seek the pouring out of the Spirit in the ecstatic utterances of tongues.

James Tinney, for many years a professor of journalism at Howard University, testifies that he "got the Holy Ghost" during his adolescence in 1956, and offers a vivid portrayal of the experience of tarrying for

Spirit baptism in the black Pentecostal context:

> So the seeker prays loud and long as hard and as fast as he can to get this power. He sweats and cries and screams and physically throws himself, demanding that God do what he wants. He commands the power of God as his own. It is a violent scene—one which is carefully hidden from the casual visitor. The seeker will work himself into a state of possession if it takes hours upon hours of struggling. Hair will become matted, clothes will become dirtied, the flesh will become sick and feint until "the power comes"....The result will be a total rejection of American mainstream values, coming back full circle to the African heritage of possession. And it will be symbolized by a break with rational thought and language and an utterance in unknown tongues, among other manifestations.[2]

Because Tinney's account is part of a political science dissertation, his understanding of Spirit baptism is couched in the language of power. The social ethical focus of his interpretation entails a ritual return to Africa, and a concomitant rejection of American mainstream values, presumably both religious and secular. It is important to acknowledge that this ritual is conducted in secret, or at least removed from the view of the casual observer, as Tinney suggests.

While water baptism is ordinarily required only once in the life of the believer, the baptism of the Spirit may be understood as a ritual of initiation that can be repeated, replenished, or re-enacted as often as the saint becomes possessed by the Holy Spirit in worship. The fact that the possessing Spirit is Holy mandates that the saints manifest holy living both inside and outside the sanctuary. Thus there is a vital connection between the ethical and liturgical identity of the saints, as expressed in the exhortation of the Psalmist: "Rejoice in the Lord, O ye righteous: for praise is comely for the upright" (Psalm 33:1).

African-American Holiness and Pentecostal Worship Practices

There are numerous articles, books, and dissertations that describe in detail the worship practices of the Holiness and Pentecostal churches. James Shopshire (1975), Arthur Paris (1982), and Joseph Murphy (1994) have written descriptive narratives of black Pentecostal worship based on participant observation.[3] Moreover, I have analyzed my own observations concerning worship based on data gathered from 1990-1994 during visits to 75 churches and 28 college campuses in 21 states (and the District of Columbia), representing 25 mainline Protestant, Catholic, Pentecostal, and Holiness denominations. Based on this information, I have developed a composite portrait of worship in the Holiness-Pentecostal tradition, with attention to eight basic elements, as follows: (1) call to worship; (2) songs and hymns; (3) prayer; (4) offerings; (5) Scripture reading; (6) preaching; (7) altar call; and (8) benediction.

The *call to worship* includes acts which initiate the worship experience. It may be a simple and informal verbal signal to "stop chatting and settle down," or a formal combination of choral introit and litany recited by minister and congregation. The call to worship may be a brief reading from the Bible, the church's hymnal, or from some printed worship aid that encourages people to become focused on worship. In some cases it is preceded by a devotional service, including songs, prayers, and testimonies. Also, it may be immediately followed with a processional of the clergy and choir. In the church Paris describes, the devotional service comprises half of all that happens in the entire worship experience, if not also half of the total worship time. In the church Murphy depicts, there are no formal devotions as such. In all cases some verbal signal is given to invite the congregation to worship.

The *singing* of some combination of songs, hymns, choruses, and Negro spirituals is a vital part of all these worship services. It is difficult to denote the role music plays in worship with any degree of precision because music tends to undergird everything else that is done. Unlike some of the other elements of worship, music is interspersed throughout the service, and not at just one or two points in the order of worship. In the composite outline, however, the singing of songs and hymns represents a major component of congregational involvement in the worship experience. The sacred repertoire is inclusive of hymns of the mainline evangelical Protestant church, gospel songs, praise choruses, and Negro spirituals. Shopshire seems given to understatement when he judges that worship in the Pentecostal church he observes is much the same as "any of the Protestant denominational worship gatherings, with the probable exception that the singing was better than average."[4] The African-American Holiness and Pentecostal churches certainly are known for their enthusiastic singing and response, as worship finds expression across a broad range of sacred musical forms. The sung repertoire of the tradition includes classical anthems, arias, and oratorios, hymns, gospel songs, spirituals, shouts, chants, and lined-out common-meter sacred folk songs.

The Hammond organ is the instrument of choice for the improvisational style of worship music in many of these churches. Murphy gives special attention to the importance of the organ in the worship, noting at many points in his narrative the manner in which the organ shapes the mood and expresses the energy of the songs, speech, and dance. The organ takes the lead in providing the rhythmic and tonal texture of the worship experience, and it is the principal instrument used to accompany the chanted sermon. Both Murphy and Shopshire describe the call and response between preacher and organist, which is actually a three-way conversation involving preacher, congregation, and musician. In the hands of a skilled and accomplished musician, the organ sings, speaks, and dances.

Prayer is an individual or collective appeal to God, which includes praise, thanksgiving, confessions, and various petitions. As is the case with music, it is difficult to fix one point in the outline of worship where prayer occurs, because it typically is done repeatedly throughout the service. Prayers are sometimes chanted in the Pentecostal churches in a manner not unlike the chanted sermon. They are seldom read or recited from a printed source, with the exception of the Lord's Prayer, which the worshippers may recite or chant from memory. The use of the Lord's Prayer represents a vital ecumenical connection with the prayer rituals of the universal church.

Offerings are taken by having the worshippers march to the front of the sanctuary to deposit their monetary gifts for the church in baskets, plates, or on a table. Also, the ushers may pass the offering receptacles up and down the rows of seated congregants in a precise, orderly fashion. Most of the African-American Holiness and Pentecostal churches emphasize tithing, and sometimes special prominence is given to the tithers by having them come forward individually to place their tithes in a special receptacle. The offerings can consume a considerable amount of time if the minister makes an appeal for a specific cause or if people are asked to bring their offerings according to the specific dollar amount, as is the case in the churches described by Murphy, Paris, and Shopshire. Usually some form of prayer and/or doxology is offered in connection with the offering, either before or after the monies are actually received.

Scripture reading is another indispensable element in African-American Holiness and Pentecostal worship. One or more texts may be read near the beginning of the service, or shortly before the sermon is preached. The Scriptures can be individually read from the pulpit, or read responsively by minister and congregation. The Bible is accorded the highest respect and regard in these churches, and in some cases there are special ritual procedures for transporting and handling the particular Bible from which the sermon is preached.

Preaching is a climactic event in this worship tradition because it is believed that the preacher actually speaks for God. Often the sermons are performed in the sense that the basic message and content are amplified through chants, moans, dancing, and other ecstatic behaviors. Each of the worship narratives analyzed here describes the interaction between preacher and congregation in multiple dimensions. Preaching is more than the simple verbal communication of the gospel of Jesus Christ based on some Scriptural text; it involves emotion, physical movement, various modulations of the preacher's voice, and is designed to bring the worshipping community into some form of climactic expression—shouting, tears, praise, repentance, and/or tongue-speaking. In some of the churches, specific provision is made for the preacher (typically male) to have an attendant (typically female) whose responsibility is to assist him with his liturgical cape, to administer juice or water as needed, to wipe the sweat from his brow, etc., adding to the dramatic impact of the preaching performance. Sociologist Harold Dean Trulear has described the ritual aspects of preaching as follows: "The use of robes, capes, etc., to enhance the preacher's appearance and the attendant nurse with her ever-present orange juice and fresh handkerchiefs are all part of the props or staging of the ritual drama where 'God speaks to His children.'?"[5] Regardless of the size of the sanctuary, these churches all have electronic sound systems, some very sophisticated and advanced, and the preachers use hand-held and/or lapel microphones to enhance the modulation of the preaching voice. The sermon is always intended to elicit congregational response.

Altar call is a formal ritual of response to the preached word, which usually functions as an invitation to discipleship. Many African-American Holiness and Pentecostal churches adhere to the practice of issuing dual altar calls—the first an appeal for sinners to repent and receive salvation and the second an invitation for believers to receive sanctification or the baptism of the Holy Spirit. Altar calls may also include the ritual laying of hands upon the sick or distressed, and anointing with oil, with the purpose of achieving healing or deliverance. Prayer is always a key element of this ritual, which may occur at some other point in the service, even prior to the sermon. In some churches the major objective of the altar call is to invite the worshippers to have hands laid on them so they can be "slain in the Spirit." The dissociative experience of temporary loss of consciousness represents a form of ritual empowerment. The altar call may serve a variety of purposes in worship. It is used to invite sinners to repentance, new converts to church membership, hurting persons to wholeness, and saved persons to sanctification and other forms of spiritual empowerment and blessing. For some worshippers, the altar ritual is as pertinent and significant to them personally as the sermon itself, if not more so. There are preachers who invest as much time and energy in directing the altar call as in preaching the sermon.

Benediction is a prayer or formula of blessing signaling that the worship experience has ended. It may include a final exhortation or commission of the worshippers to implement some particular truth or principle that has been preached. The minister who offers the benediction may raise one or both hands, and in some cases the worshippers also raise their hands while receiving the benediction.

There are some additional aspects of African-American Holiness and Pentecostal worship that distinguish these churches from the white North American Protestant mainstream. The list would include: (1) the holy dance; (2) the "Yes" chant; and (3) the use of white uniformed liturgical attendants. Many or most of these marks and symbols can be found in traditional black denominational churches, and definitely in "neo-Pentecostal" Baptist and Methodist congregations. These aspects of worship are rooted in African cultural identity, and may be reflective of specific worship patterns and cultural practices associated with slave religion in the rural South. As each of these practices is defined and illustrated here, an assessment will be offered of the specific ethical and aesthetic meaning ascribed to them within the community of the saints.

The **holy dance** is best exemplified as the ritual of the shout, the climactic expression of individual and collective Spirit possession that is especially characteristic of the black Pentecostal congregations. In her article "Dancing to Rebalance the Universe: African-American Secular Dance and Spirituality," Katrina Hazzard-Gordon comments that dance serves as a "kinetic vocabulary" through which the needs, perceptions, impressions, and responses of African-American people are articulated.[6] Her description of the juxtaposition of the "chaotic, the uncontrolled, and the unconscious" movements associated with the onset of full possession with the "ordered, contained, conscious, and controlled" conduit step is reflective of the static/ecstatic dialectic in Holiness-Pentecostal worship.[7]

In this perspective, the concept of liturgical dance can be expanded to include choreographed choir processions and a whole host of bodily gestures by choir and congregation, such as swaying, patting of feet, clapping of hands, raising one or both hands, and spontaneous standing on one's feet. In the Holiness churches, there are saints who do not do the "shout step" associated with the Pentecostals but rather leap straight up and down when they "get happy."

In his worship narrative, Shopshire gives some indication of the aesthetic and ethical norms the saints associate with the holy dance. His account is illustrative of the tension that sometimes exists between the static and ecstatic in fulfillment of the expectations of the worship leader:

> Not being satisfied with the response, [the bishop] said in a scolding tone, "I can't understand how anyone can remain quiet and seated in such a spirit-filled gathering as this. Get up, and dance!" Speaking especially to the constituent members of the gathering, he took time to remind them that to dance is indicative of a meaningful experience in worship, and they "need not try to be cute" by not talking back and dancing....As he talked he was moving back and forth across the length of the pulpit platform with a very agile gait, ever so often initiating a brief dance step and then stopping. By the time the point had been made about dancing being integral to meaningful worship experience he had reached a vocal peak, and performed a dancing frenzy for about 15 seconds.[8]

Clearly this bishop has mastered the technique of inciting the holy dance through measured demonstration. He seems to have a definite sense of the aesthetic requirements of the ritual dance. Moreover, he seeks to convince others of the ethical propriety, even necessity of ecstatic expression in worship.

Another of the salient marks of African-American worship in the Holiness-Pentecostal tradition is the ***chant of affirmation***, originated by Bishop C. H. Mason in the early days of the Church of God in Christ, and later written into an anthem by Dr. Arenia C. Mallory. Pearl Williams-Jones observes that the chant of "Yes, Lord" typically follows and brings closure to the shout:

> Shouts may conclude informally through the intuitive consent and feeling of tensions released by the collective body, or may give way to a chant in slow tempo such as, "Yes, Lord" which is an unmetered chant originated in the early days of the Church of God in Christ....Bishop Charles Harrison Mason was heard to enchant, "Yes, Lord, Yes, Lord, Yes to your word. Yes to your will. Yes to your way." The congregation chants in heterophany.[9]

The chant of affirmation has already been cited above in the excerpt from Shopshire's narrative where the bishop exhorts the worshippers to say "yes" and dance. Murphy also describes the chant of affirmation in his narrative of worship in the Church of God in Christ:

> Mother Hall chants the Church of God in Christ national anthem, "Yes, Lord." In a sure, husky voice she asks the congregation to affirm the wonders of creation, the saving deeds of Jesus, and the power of the Spirit. With each pause the congregation affirms "Yes, Lord." As the enthusiasm grows, more and more people shout "Yes" and "Yes, Lord" as they feel moved. One woman comes out into the aisle to spin about with back bent, feet pumping in place, and hands raised high, fingers spread. "Oh Yes, Lord!"[10]

The chant of affirmation is sung with attendant gestures of submission such as lifting up holy hands, shouting, cries of "Hallelujah," "Glory," "Thank you, Jesus," or simply "Yes." Ethically speaking, there is a dialectic inherent in these signs of surrender—to say yes to God is to become empowered to say no to the world, and especially to the powers of evil and deception that would hinder the believer from having peace with God. Thus, the worshippers are exhorted repeatedly to drop their inhibitions and release themselves to follow the lead of the Spirit in worship. This release requires the full assent of the individuals. In this light, the inhibiting factor is ultimately sin or self-centeredness or even class consciousness. To say or sing "Yes" to God is to affirm God's acceptance of the sacrifices of praise, and to signal divine approval of the saints' worship in all its culturally aesthetic concreteness and particularity.

A visually striking feature of African American worship is the performance of specialized liturgical roles by women, e.g., deaconesses, ushers, attendants, and nurses. These *uniformed attendants* almost invariably wear white, a color which signifies purity and consecration. Most ushers and nurses are women, and most preachers are men, but there is sufficient flexibility in fulfilling these roles to allow men to serve as ushers or nurses, and women as preachers, even in the churches that do not ordain women. Even so, the women more consistently wear white when performing the liturgical roles of deaconess, usher, nurse, and preacher. White is almost always worn by deaconesses, especially on those Sundays when they are responsible for preparing the Communion Table, and is typically worn by women preachers. Candidates for baptism by immersion usually wear white.

Women's Day, an annual observance first instituted in the churches of the National Baptist Convention by Nannie Helen Burroughs in 1907 "to raise women, not money," is observed today in almost all black churches.[11] It is the one Sunday in the year when all the women worshippers are expected to wear white. In no way is the wearing of white an indication of a preference for white culture or assent to the biased color symbolism of a racist society. In ethical perspective, it seems to be more indicative of a desire to surrender all marks of personal style and distinctiveness in order to become totally identified with the worshipping community and its God—white is the one color that makes it possible to achieve complete aesthetic uniformity.

Static and Ecstatic Forms of Spirit Possession

Spirit possession is an important feature of virtually all the diasporic religions of New World Africans. For example, devotees of Cuban *santeria*, Haitian *vodou*, and Brazilian *candomble* enact elaborate rituals of possession and acknowledge a corresponding pantheon of possessing spirits and deities of African derivation. What separates the African-American Holiness and Pentecostal tradition from the others, however, is the belief that the possessing spirit bears the exclusive identity of Holy Spirit.

The perennial objective of Holy Spirit possession is achieved in some combination of ecstatic and static forms. Ecstatic worship forms have as their salient feature a trance resulting from religious fervor. Ecstasy literally means "out of place." In static worship forms, on the other hand, worshippers are at rest or in equilibrium. Static literally means "causing to stand." However, as is the case when the term is used to describe a form of electricity, it should not be assumed that static worship is necessarily dead or lifeless. Static electricity is electrical force produced and accumulated as potential energy; current electricity moves and flows in the form of kinetic energy. Static energy is stored, kinetic energy moves. The two are interdependent, because kinetic energy is the discharge of static energy through some conductor or channel. Yet, as anyone who has observed a thunderstorm can attest, static energy can be discharged at random, without conductor or channels, with a force that is not only impressive in magnitude, but frightening and potentially lethal in impact. On the other hand, the flow of kinetic energy can be entirely predictable and controlled. The two distinct forms of electrical energy suggest an analogy which can bring enhanced insights to the study of Holiness and Pentecostal worship, a dialectic of static/ecstatic worship structures and forms of spirit possession.[12] Along the continuum of Holiness-Pentecostal groups, the Holiness churches tend to favor the static forms and ideals of Spirit possession, while the Pentecostals insist upon ecstatic expression in worship.

To define ecstatic worship as worship "out of place" necessitates formulating some understanding of its dialectical opposite, worship "in place." Static worship is the state of equilibrium out of which the ecstasy flows; it is the requisite platform for the trance ritual to occur. In no way should this scheme be understood as indicative of the relative inferiority or superiority of static and ecstatic forms of worship. However, the fact remains that practically every Christian worship tradition tends to favor one over the other, sometimes to the exclusion of the other. Yet, the two are neither equal nor mutually exclusive in this sense; ecstatic experience absolutely depends on static structures, but static structures may or may not produce ecstatic experience. In fact, static forms and structures can be intentionally used to deny or suppress spirit possession. The ecstatic state may be forthrightly suppressed, scorned, or forbidden. So there can be static worship without spirit possession in any state or form. But it is not possible to have worship of any kind without some static structure to initiate and organize the ritual interaction of the worshippers. In other words, to say that static structures sustain ecstatic forms of worship is merely to agree that one cannot dance without a floor, sing without a scale, or speak without a language.

Static structures are those elements in worship that represent a state of equilibrium or rest. They include: hymn singing, Scripture reading, corporate prayers (esp. the Lord's Prayer), offerings, sermon, altar call, announcements, benediction. These are designated here as static structures because they embody the potential energy of the worshipping congregation to explode into ecstatic expression—shouting or holy dance, tongue-speaking, spontaneous utterances, lifting holy hands. Most of these structures can serve as a platform for ecstatic movement. For example, people may shout during hymn singing and sermons, speak in tongues during or after prayer, and engage in call and response as the Scriptures are read. The call to worship and the benediction are also static structures that frame the worship ritual by marking the boundaries of sacred time. Generally speaking, the offerings and announcements do not support ecstatic activity or evoke ecstatic response.

Thus, worship has fixed and fluid forms, rehearsed and unrehearsed, scripted and improvised, prepared and spontaneous. To make matters more complex, it is clear that some forms and events in worship reflect both fixed and fluid elements at the same time. For example, the quintessential ecstatic expression in Pentecostal worship is the shout, or holy dance, which usually occurs as a spontaneous eruption into coordinated, choreographed movement. There are characteristic steps, motions, rhythms, and syncopations associated with shouting. It is not a wild and random expression of kinetic energy. Rather, there is a culturally and aesthetically determined static structure which sustains the expression of ecstasy in a definite, recognizable form, whose existence may not be apparent to the casual or uninformed observer. Similarly, speaking in tongues may appear to be a strictly spontaneous and unrehearsed verbal expression, but in reality the practice is evoked by "tarrying" or other repetitive patterns of activity designed to encourage tongue-speaking. Glossolalia is not the only ecstatic speech used in worship. The vocabulary of utterances spoken spontaneously in worship is not random or undefined. There is a definite lexicon for intelligible ecstatic utterances in the sanctuary, which may manifest cultural and regional variants, but is nevertheless known to the group. Usually, these are terms found in the Bible with reference to the praise and attributes of God: "Hallelujah," "Amen," "Glory," "Holy," and "Praise the Lord." In the ecstatic state, the worshipper may repeat one or more of these expressions many times, in a loud or subdued voice.

Alternative Styles of Worship

Among black Protestant churches in general, there are two basic orientations toward worship that set the tone for worship in particular congregations: quietistic and lively. The quietistic congregations give priority to static structures, while the lively congregations value ecstatic expressions in worship. Quietistic worship traditions may exclude or control ecstatic worship forms in several ways, for instance by insisting that everything in worship be scripted, read, and timed; by restricting rhythm and repetition, especially in singing; or by direct intervention or verbal rebuke by authorized figures such as ushers or preachers. Lively worship traditions may devalue static worship forms by making statements such as "We are not here for form or fashion, we are here to praise the Lord" or by vigorously exhorting persons to speak aloud, stand, raise hands, shout, etc., and subjecting them to verbal ridicule if they refuse, as in "You think you're too cute and too sophisticated to shout." The quietistic worship leader imposes silence and stillness upon the congregation; the leader of lively worship invokes noise and motion.

Interestingly, the task of setting the tone for worship, whether quietistic or lively, is not always totally determined by the minister, singer or preacher who is standing in the pulpit—leadership may be exercised indirectly, but to great effect, by the one who organizes, reproduces, and distributes the order of worship, or by some individual or group in the congregation to whom the worship leader looks for cues and approval. Or the congregation as a whole may be predisposed to one or the other style of worship, and collectively by their silence or their utterances indicate approval or disapproval of what is taking place. For example, if one individual is given to loud utterances in a quietistic congregation, the response may be staring, frowns, or hushing actions. On the other hand, in a lively congregation the individual who prefers to remain still and silent may feel uncomfortable and self-conscious, and may even attract unwelcome public criticism or ridicule. In his study of black worship, Trulear defends the integrity of quietistic worship in black middle-class churches as a legitimate ritual verification of a particular concept of humanity:

> If being human means to be dignified and intellectual, under control and logical, all patterns of behavior that this society has said Blacks are incapable of, then these congregations will model these ideas of human virtue in the context of worship. This is still a function of Black humanity. Those who would deny this as in some sense legitimate would have to eliminate people such as Du Bois and Daniel Payne from the Black religious world.[13]

In this perspective, it is helpful to bear in mind that competing ideals of black humanity may be at stake in debates between lively and quietistic worshippers concerning appropriate forms and expressions of black-worship.

Gatekeepers

Static and ecstatic worship have their distinctive sets of gatekeepers. Ushers, nurses, deaconesses, i.e., uniformed attendants with some designated title and role, are the gatekeepers of the static aspects of worship. Singers, preachers, and to some extent dancers are the gatekeepers of ecstatic worship, the people who "usher" the congregation into and out of the ecstatic state. Ushers attend to the physical movement of worshippers in and out of the sanctuary, and demarcate the temporal and spatial boundaries that encompass the sacred space. In other words, as ushers greet and seat each worshipper they are defining and managing the ritual space; their tenure of duty spans the entire worship time, from prelude to benediction. The preachers and singers direct the emotional and spiritual dynamics of the worship experience, and ushers participate in this process by attending to the special needs and security of persons experiencing the transition from static to ecstatic worship.

With respect to gender roles, in general the African-American Holiness and Pentecostal churches tend toward a peculiar egalitarianism in assigning gatekeeping roles based on gender. The gatekeepers of static structures can be men, just as the gatekeepers of ecstatic expression, the preachers and worship leaders, can be women. Both men and women serve as lead singers and dancers, according to gifts and ability. For obvious reasons, the persons chosen as ushers, nurses, and attendants tend not to be easily and readily inclined to ecstatic spirit possession. Similarly, the other gatekeepers, including preachers, singers, and instrumentalists, are normally expected to know and honor the rules governing the static forms and structures of worship, and to maintain spiritual equilibrium whenever the congregation is swept into the ecstatic state. The biblical principle invoked as an explanation for the need for gatekeepers to maintain equilibrium is taken from 1 Corinthians 14:32, Paul's letter addressed to an early charismatic Christian congregation: "the spirits of the prophets are subject to the prophets."

In the World, But Not of It

Given that the ultimate objective of worship in the African-American Holiness and Pentecostal church tradition is some form of Spirit possession, the aesthetic and ethical norms that govern movement toward this objective are derived from the Bible and black culture. The distinctive songs, speech, and dances of these churches symbolically "usher" the saints "out" of this world and into a more authentic one discerned within sacred time and space. There is a connection between the saints' rejection of the world and the world's rejection of the saints. The saints reject the world on the basis of biblically-derived ascetic commitments, i.e., the mandate to holiness; they are themselves "rejected" by the dominant host culture because of their race, sex, and class. When the saints sing "Holy" unto the Lord, lift up holy hands, do the holy dance, in effect they are expressing their allegiance to a world where God has determined who is accepted and who will receive power. Moreover, their worship shows that they believe God is accepting of the praise, performances, and aesthetic standards that are characteristic of Africans in diaspora. The Holy Spirit has freed at least some of them from the pressure to conform to the worship styles of the dominant culture.

The saints are "in" a world that is sinful, oppressive, and discriminatory; they demonstrate that they are not "of" this world by purging themselves of its secularizing influences through rituals that meet their own criteria for cultural authenticity and biblical interpretation. In worship, the saints replicate the "other" world, the place where the oppressed outsider can be at home. Ethically, their allegiance to this "other" world requires them to be loving, honest, and pure, even in relation to their enemies. Just as the sanctuary or temple is the place of ritual possession, their bodies are temples of the Holy Spirit. Ritual purity in the sanctuary requires purity of body, mind, and spirit outside the sanctuary. By their worship the saints manifest the holy character of the God they serve; by clean living they demonstrate to the world that they possess the Spirit that possesses them in worship.

Notes

[1] Portions of this present article are dependent on select material by Dr. Sanders that appeared originally in her book *Saints In Exile: The Holiness-Pentecostal Experience in African American Religion and Culture* (New York: Oxford University Press, 1996), especially chapter three. Used by permission of Oxford University Press.

[2] James S. Tinney, *A Theoretical and Historical Comparison of Black Political and Religious Movements* (Ph.D. dissertation, Howard University, 1978), 240-241.

[3] See James Maynard Shopshire, "A Socio-Historical Characterization of the Black Pentecostal Movement in America," Ph.D. dissertation, Northwestern University, 1975, 170-183; Arthur E. Paris, *Black Pentecostalism: Southern Religion in an Urban World* (Amherst: University of Massachusetts Press, 1982), 54-70; and Joseph M. Murphy, *Working the Spirit: Ceremonies of the African Diaspora* (Boston: Beacon Press, 1994), 158-169; and my book *Saints in Exile: The Holiness-Pentecostal Experience in African American Religion and Culture* (New York: Oxford University Press, 1996), esp. chapter 3.

[4] Shopshire, 172.

[5] Harold Dean Trulear, "The Lord Will Make a Way Somehow: Black Worship and the Afro-American Story," *Journal of the Interdenominational Theological Center*, Vol. XIII, No. 1, (Fall 1985):100.

[6] Katrina Hazzard-Gordon, "Dancing to Rebalance the Universe: African American Secular Dance and Spirituality," *Black Sacred Music* 7:1, (Spring 1993), 17.

[7] Hazzard-Gordon, 19.

[8] Shopshire, 180-181.

[9] Pearl Williams Jones, "The Musical Quality of Religious Folk Ritual," *Spirit*, Vol. 1, No. 1 (1977), 29.
[10] Murphy, 160.
[11] *Women and Religion in America*.

Chapter 7

William J. Seymour: Follower of the "Evening Light" (Zech. 14:7)

by
B. Scott Lewis

The mixed relationship that the Church of God movement (Anderson) had with Pentecostal movement of the twentieth century is seen clearly in a study of the experiences and ministry of William J. Seymour (1870-1922). A catalyst of the famous 1906 Azusa Street Revival that helped launch the modern Pentecostal movement, Seymour had come to champion some perspectives and experiences not commonly affirmed in the Church of God movement. However, he had been nurtured spiritually by this movement and had absorbed some of its key emphases, vital to his own future ministry. He had encountered and affirmed the quest for holiness and unity of the "Evening Light Saints" (the name by which he had known the early Church of God movement), and he had heeded its come-out call. His ecclesial-theological convictions were impacted directly by these "Saints," including their focus on the cleansing and unifying power of God's Spirit. Originally published in the Wesleyan Theological Journal *(39:2, Fall, 2004).*

The catalyst of the 1906 Azusa Street Revival, William J. Seymour, is well known within Pentecostal and Charismatic circles. Knowledge about Seymour's life prior to the Azusa Revival, however, is sketchy, except for Seymour's contact with Charles Parham in Houston in 1905 where he learned of Parham's doctrine of speaking in tongues as the evidence of the Baptism of the Holy Spirit. These events are well documented and much historical evidence is available. Prior to these events, however,

Seymour's contact with the Holiness movement is much less developed as a source of influence for his thought and practice.[1] Therefore, in the following essay, I explore Seymour's association with the "Evening Light Saints," now known as the Church of God movement (Anderson, Indiana). The key question addressed is: What influence did the "Saints" have on William Seymour's life and theology?[2]

William J. Seymour: Seeker of the Light

On May 2, 1870, William Joseph Seymour was born to former slaves, Simon Seymour and Phyllis Salabarr Seymour, in Centerville, Louisiana.[3] William Seymour's family during the late nineteenth century probably experienced some of Louisiana's severest treatment of slaves. For instance, it was typical for Louisiana slaves to work very long hours in extremely humid weather.[4] In the years following 1865 after the 13th Amendment was ratified, southern slaves enjoyed emancipation; however, the years 1865 through 1867 witnessed some of the worst violence experienced in the South, with a total of 243 Blacks murdered and over 300 assaults.[5] Seymour's life met the cruel realities of racism in the South and probably he experienced the toils of living and working on a plantation to keep the family's needs met. Seymour's ecclesiastical commitment during his youth in the South, according to Vinson Synan, was Baptist.[6] However, Seymour's "African religious heritage" would have influenced his Christianity. This was a heritage in which "spiritual practices were communally oriented; worship focused on rhythm, spontaneity, and evocative preaching; the indwelling of the Spirit was experienced through a Christ-centered conversion; and symbolic imagery, derived from the Bible, became the foundation of their spirituality."[7]

Seymour moved north to Indianapolis at age twenty-five and at a time when 90% of Blacks lived in the southern states.[8] While in Indianapolis he waited on tables in a hotel restaurant and lived at two downtown addresses during his stay (127 1/2 Indiana Avenue and 309 Bird Street).[9] While living in Indianapolis, Seymour became a member of the Simpson Chapel Methodist Episcopal Church. This church was racially inclusive and active in outreach to Blacks, even letting them attain leadership positions.[10] Interestingly, an African Methodist Episcopal Church was also in downtown Indianapolis, but Seymour chose to attend the interracial church for the reason that Nelson notes: "[It] was the first clear indication he gave of seeking interracial reconciliation."[11] While in Indianapolis, as Rufus Sanders has shown, oral tradition tells of Seymour attending the Simpson Chapel when he first became associated with the "Evening Light Saints."[12] Only after the M. E. Church became racially divided, according to Nelson and Sanders, did Seymour then become dissatisfied with the Methodist Church.[13] In 1900 "racial attitudes in Indiana were beginning to harden" and many churches began to racially divide along color lines.[14] Moreover, the *Indianapolis News and World* paper tells how "in recent years there has been a growing hostility toward the black man. He has continually had fewer friends and more enemies."[15]

Most scholars suggest that William Seymour left Indianapolis to escape the racial prejudice and went to Cincinnati in hopes of finding his "promise land."[16] His move to Cincinnati is not well documented. Douglas Nelson relies heavily on oral tradition for Seymour's stay in Cincinnati.[17] In fact, according to Rufus Sanders, Seymour "never mentioned Cincinnati in any known conversations, but neither does he talk about Indianapolis."[18] The exact year he moved to Cincinnati is not clear.[19] His name appears in the Cincinnati City Directories in 1901, 1902, and possibly in 1904.[20] Perhaps Seymour's racial experience in Indianapolis probably was less than desirable and he went to Cincinnati in search of increased racial inclusiveness. Whatever our speculation about the reasons why Seymour moved to Cincinnati, the circumstance needs to be reconstructed in light of his association with the "Evening Light Saints."

William Seymour: Follower of the Light

The first contact with the "Evening Light Saints" was in Indianapolis while Seymour was attending an M. E. Church. His association with the Saints led him to experience conversion. The "Evening light Saints," who latter became designated as the Church of God movement (Anderson, Indiana), emphasized experiential conversions and the holiness doctrine of entire sanctification. Moreover, the Saints were very tolerant of blacks, and advocated interracial worship. In fact, James S. Tinney notes, "when Seymour heard the testimonies of these Saints, he could not resist. He went to the altar and 'prayed through' to salvation. Then he went back a second time and prayed until he testified to being wholly sanctified, as he tells us."[21] Perhaps his conversion with the Saints was the result of interracial inclusiveness that attracted the young Seymour. If Seymour left the M.E. Church in Indianapolis for the reason of its increasingly "color line" split, as Nelson and Sanders seem to assume, it is reasonable to suggest that the "Saints" had a radical influence in his decision. Furthermore, because the Saints advocated a strict "come-outism," Seymour would have left his "sect" immediately. Therefore, it is unlikely, as Nelson and Sanders suggest, that Seymour attended the M. E. Church and "Evening Light" services simultaneously. The holiness-and-unity message of the Saints would have influenced the young Seymour to rethink his ecclesiastical commitment to the M. E. Church.

The Light of Racial Unity

James Earl Massey observes that Blacks were typically dissatisfied "over the sectarianism in which they as members of various religious bodies were involved...and were quick to see and claim the spiritual and social implications inherent in the Movement's central message of Christian fellowship."[22] In fact, Blacks "embraced the Movement's essential theological forms, sentiments, opinions, faith, and practices."[23] While vast amounts of racial prejudice abounded during the late nineteenth-century, the "Saints" abhorred such notions and upheld interracial worship as an indicator of the true church functioning in holiness and unity. During the early years of the "Saint's" movement, Merle D. Strege says:

> It was not uncommon for members of both ethnic groups to attend the same tent meetings and revivals, on occasion drawing the ire of local residents for transgressing such racial taboos as mixed seating. In some instances Whites served as ministers to biracial gatherings; in other cases Black ministers took the lead. The pattern of racial unity in the movement's early decades was driven by a literal reading of Galatians 3:28 as the normative status of the true New Testament church: "In Christ there is neither Jew nor Greek; there is neither bond nor free, there is neither male nor female: for ye are all one in Christ Jesus."[24]

Notably, Daniel S. Warner and his early followers, according to historian Charles E. Brown, "were more rigid and stern in their stand...for justice to the Negro" than most holiness churches.[25] In an article written in the *Gospel Trumpet* on December 20, 1906, W. J. Henry writes:

> There is no room for prejudice of any kind in the hearts of sanctified people. If you, as a white man find any of this in your heart toward the black man as an individual or toward his people, you need to go to the Lord for cleansing; to the black brother, I will say the same. All prejudice of every kind is outside the church of God.[26]

There is no question that Blacks were attracted to the early Saints movement; they had found their "light" in the darkness of racial prejudice.

Perhaps Seymour's conversion experience was the result of the racial inclusion witnessed within the Saint's meetings. Tinney suggests that, upon hearing the "testimonies of these Saints," Seymour experienced entire sanctification.[27] His experience was common in the early meetings of the Saints. In fact, some of these meetings were commonly reported in the *Gospel Trumpet* by stating that souls were saved, sanctified, and prejudice removed. Interestingly, in Illinois and especially Indiana, several such reports were recorded. One field report in the *Gospel Trumpet* (August 25, 1898) records that "Prejudice was removed, a few souls saved, and friends won to the truth….Our labors will be for a time in Indiana near Indianapolis, thence to the northern part of the state."[28] Another report in Bryant, Indiana, says: "A few souls were saved, a few believers sanctified, and many were convinced of the truth….Much prejudice was removed from the hearts of the people at that place."[29]

Many of the traveling ministers among the Saints frequented Indianapolis and area towns. Such was the case with J. N. Howard, A. J. Kilpatrick, E. Bragg, Bro. and Sis. Craft, and Bro. and Sis. Cheatham between the years 1898 and 1900. A. J. Kilpatrick was one white evangelist who spent six weeks in Augusta, Georgia, with Jane William's congregation, converting large numbers of Blacks.[30] Conceivably, Seymour could have had contact with one or more of these individuals, including Kilpatrick, while living in Indianapolis. If Seymour was searching for racial unity, a "promise land" as Nelson and Sanders suggest, then the quest for racial inclusion would have been found with the "Evening Light Saints."

The Light of Holiness

Perhaps Seymour embraced the "holiness" and "unity" quest of the Saints and heeded the call to "come out" from the M. E. Church in Indianapolis. The early Saints preached a radical holiness message, inherited from Daniel S. Warner who advocated "coming out" of "whatever human structures and traditions impeded the free flow of God's Spirit."[31] Warner's message suggested that people leave their holiness traditions and join the true church, whose organizer and true unifier was the Holy Spirit.[32] The Saints identified themselves as living in the "evening time" or the "last days" when God would cleanse and unify his church prior to Christ's soon return.33 Thus, the call was "to all the truly redeemed to abandon the sinful sects and to come out of spiritual darkness into the light."34 Evidently, Seymour followed the "light," abandoned his former ties with his holiness sect, the M. E. Church, and became an "Evening Light Saint."

Warner and others in the early Saint's movement thought "sin" was the cause of denominations or sects, "and the only cure for this plague was a through-going experience of sanctification that would melt believers into a spiritual and physical union."35 The very foundation of the Saint's vision for unity, therefore, was holiness. The Saints believed that the experience of sanctification, subsequent to justification, empowered believers to live a holy life, renewed the image and likeness of God, perfected love, and baptized them with the Holy Spirit.36 Historian John W. V. Smith notes:

> With Sanctification came "heart purity," "fullness of God," "fullness of joy," "assurance of faith," "full assurance of hope," "perfect love," "the more abundant life," and the "baptism of the Holy Ghost"....The importance of this experiential understanding of salvation in the minds of the pioneer leaders of the Church of God can hardly be overemphasized. It was related to all other aspects of their faith and practice, and especially to their view of relationships to each other, to the world, and to other Christians.37

The experience of sanctification was central to the message and vision of unity, for it was the cleansing of God's sanctuary that unified the Church, which set the stage for Christ's soon return. This motivated the early Saints toward "a God-ordained mission in the 'last days,' an urgency generating a self-conscious 'movement' now being driven by a prophetically fired biblical vision."38 William Seymour, as an "Evening Light Saint," would conceivably be motivated by the same vision of holiness and unity: a cleansing of the church prior to Christ's soon return. Perhaps Seymour went to Cincinnati in an urgent drive to preach "full salvation" to those in that city before Christ's return.39

Following the Light in Cincinnati

William Seymour's move to Cincinnati in 1900 or 1901 is contemporaneous with the Saint's vigorous evangelistic activity in that city. During this time a new church was planted in downtown Cincinnati, offering its inhabitants a "guiding light" in the "evening" of the last days. Most scholars place Seymour in Cincinnati with the Saints, but no direct evidence of this is available.[40] Nelson and Sanders suggest that Seymour was a "Saint" because he attended Martin Wells Knapp's Bible school.[41] They assume that Knapp was an "Evening Light Saint," which is incorrect.

Martin Wells Knapp was a "come-outer" from the Methodist church, but it is unlikely that he was associated with the early Saint's movement.[42] In fact, an article published in the *Gospel Trumpet* in 1901 accuses Knapp's school and his "Apostolic Holiness Union" of teaching false doctrine.[43] Moreover, in the same article, G. Tufts, Jr., who once associated with the Saints, was dis-fellowshipped for "joining" Knapp's holiness union.[44] In light of the *Gospel Trumpet* article, it is inconceivable to think that any Saint would attend the Bible school, much less William Seymour, unless he had split off from the movement.[45] In other words, if Seymour had associated with Knapp's holiness school, he would have "violated" the Saint's "come-out" doctrine and risked being dis-fellowshipped from the movement. If Seymour was still associated with the Saints, as many suggest, then most likely he did not attend Knapp's school. Moreover, Seymour's name does not appear in any of the attendance records at the Bible School nor does any "Saint" appear listed in the records.[46] Seymour's move to Cincinnati, then, if still associated with the Saints, as scholars suggest, would not be a move to associate with Martin Wells Knapp and his school, but possibly a move to help the new "Evening Light" ministry in Cincinnati.

During the year 1900 much "evening light" activity was present in Cincinnati where Seymour had moved. Montford L. Neal suggests that the earliest Church of God congregations in Cincinnati started in 1904 and 1907.[47] However, evidence from the *Gospel Trumpet* suggests otherwise. In fact, the earliest Saint's congregation was established prior to the time of Seymour's stay. For instance, in the year 1900 Robert Campbell writes from Cincinnati to the *Trumpet* stating:

> It has been some time since I have written to the *Trumpet*. I am praising God for salvation full and free, and for his power to heal the body as well as the soul. We have a few precious souls here who are out for God and the truth. We have opened a little mission at 4482 Sixth Street. Any of the saints passing this way will find a welcome. If the Lord so leads, we would be glad to have them stop with us.[48]

In June of 1900 John A. Vance, a traveling evangelist, writes from Cincinnati to the *Trumpet* stating:

I arrived here yesterday from Louisville, on my way to Moundsville camp meeting. I found a few saints here who are holding up the truth to all the light they have. They have never been in any meetings held by the saints or heard the evening light preached; but received the light through a brother passing through some time ago, and the reading of the *Gospel Trumpet* literature. I intend to hold a few meetings here and, the Lord willing, go on to Moundsville in time for camp meeting. I desire your intercessory prayers that God may have his way in all things, and use me to his glory, and cause the few here to be established in the present truth, and his cause built up in this place. Remember this request, making mention in your prayers. I remain your brother in the Lord, fully redeemed by two definite cleansings.[49]

At one point between June and September 25, 1900, M. N. Roark accompanied John Vance in holding meetings at Cincinnati. Roark, in a short notice in the *Trumpet*, mentions how in Cincinnati they "visited other holiness missions and distributed many *Gospel Trumpets* in that city." He adds, "Bro. Vance is talking of opening up a mission in Cincinnati....Any one desiring to correspond with him can address him at 106 East Court St., Cincinnati, Ohio."[50] Interestingly, the address that Roark gives for brother Vance is the home address of Rev. Robert Campbell, who had already opened a mission on Sixth Street.[51] Also, in the following issue of the *Trumpet*, John Vance mentions that prior to coming to Cincinnati many people's "prejudice was swept away and I think a better opening for the truth is in the future" for these towns.[52] Whether or not Seymour had contact with these people is not known, but this is probably the only "evening light" church in Cincinnati at this time. It is conceivable to think that Seymour went to the church on Sixth Street, visited Rev. Robert Campbell, or corresponded with John Vance at the 106 East Court Street address.

Seymour's Ordination in the Light?

Most scholars suggest that the Saints ordained Seymour while he was in Cincinnati.[53] Unfortunately, the primary sources for this are absent; this may be an "oral tradition" without direct documentation. Douglas Nelson places Seymour's "ordination" to ministry only after contracting smallpox while he was in Cincinnati.[54] Apparently, Seymour attributed meaning to his sickness, connecting it to God's judgment for his "disobedience to the divine call."[55] Nelson says that Seymour "accepted ordination with the Saints, who may have nursed him back to health."56 Unfortunately, no record exists of Seymour's ordination. Ordination lists do exist, although such lists are not all-inclusive of those ordained during that period.57 In fact, many traveling evangelists were not formally ordained; they simply felt the "divine calling" and started traveling and preaching.58

During the early Saints movement, "missionary homes" played an important role in developing ministerial candidates. In fact, according to Merle Strege, after 1892 the Saints planted approximately fifty homes in cities across the nation. These homes were "missions" which "undertook evangelistic work in the neighborhood and surrounding region."59 The *Gospel Trumpet* staff was an example of such a "missionary home" where "members lived in a genuinely communal arrangement."60 The staff lived together in a residence and received no salaries, but worked to provide for the needs of each other. Oftentimes these homes "served as hotels for traveling revivalists and missionaries."61 But most importantly, these homes "provided opportunities for inexperienced volunteers to validate and then develop their ministerial calling. The homes were magnets that drew young people, many of whom had 'seen the church' as it was described in the 'News From the Field' section of the *Gospel Trumpet*."62

Whether or not Seymour was ordained as an "Evening Light" minister we may never know; however, Seymour may have spent time in a "missionary home" as a volunteer developing his ministerial calling. Perhaps Seymour saw the "News From the Field" sections of the *Gospel Trumpet* in 1900 and sought refuge in the "missionary home" of Rev. Robert Campbell in Cincinnati. If so, Seymour's later Azusa Street Mission in Los Angeles would emulate the typical "missionary home" of the Saints where several individuals lived communally.63

"The Cleansing of the Sanctuary"

William Seymour's theology, as represented in the *Apostolic Faith* and in his book *The Doctrines and Disciplines of the Azusa Street Apostolic Faith Mission of Los Angeles, California,* reveals some important parallels to the "Evening Light" movement.64 Significantly, Seymour utilizes a central metaphor of the Saint's theology to propagate not only his doctrine of the baptism of the Holy Spirit, but his whole theological system. In fact, he utilizes the notions of the "the cleansing of the Sanctuary" metaphors used by Warner and Riggle in their book *The Cleansing of the Sanctuary* (1903) to provide a biblical vision of the true church.65

The diagram of "The Tabernacle" which Seymour provides in his book *The Doctrines and Disciplines of the Azusa Street Apostolic Faith Mission* (63) is the same diagram used in Warner and Riggle's book *The Cleansing of the Sanctuary* (99).[66] This diagram of the tabernacle foreshadows what Seymour calls "Full Salvation." The tabernacle typifies the progression of "full salvation" from (1) justification represented by the "Brazen Altar," (2) sanctification signified by the "Golden Altar," and (3) Baptism of the Holy Spirit signified by the "Holy of Holies." Warner and Riggle's diagram, from which Seymour seemingly copied, obviously advocates a "holiness" model of salvation, represented by two works of grace: justification typified by the "Golden Altar" and sanctification typified by the "Holy of Holies." For Warner and Riggle, the diagram represented Daniel 8:14, which says, "And he said unto me, unto 2,300 days; then shall the sanctuary be cleansed." The cleansing of the sanctuary was for Warner and Riggle to be fulfilled in their day. This verse, along with Zech. 14:7, acted as a prophetic self-understanding for the early Saint's movement which believed they were living in the last of the 2,300 days mentioned in Daniel. In fact, the "light" that shines in this "Evening Time" was thought to be the "cleansing" of the church, which God was doing through the Saints. For instance, Warner and Riggle affirm the following:

> The Work of cleansing the literal sanctuary, which Antiochus had defiled, which was accomplished by Judas Maccabeus at the completion of the 2,300 days of Daniel 8:14, was a perfect figure of the great work of cleansing the spiritual sanctuary, or church, which is now going on. Judas Maccabeus burned the heathen altars, set up the altars of the Lord, and reinstated the true worship of Jehovah according to the ancient custom. See 1 Macc. 4:36-55. So today, with the fire of holiness and truth, we burn the false religions of the earth, and restore the true worship of God as in days of old—as it existed in apostolic times.[67]

The Lord was thought to be using the Saints to cleanse the church of "sectism" and restore "true worship" as in apostolic times. For the Saints, restoring "full salvation" included justification and the subsequent work of sanctification. As mentioned above, "sin," according to the Saints, was the root problem of "denominations" and "sects"; "the only cure for this plague was a through-going experience of sanctification that would melt believers into a spiritual and physical union."[68] The very foundation of the Saint's vision for unity, therefore, was sanctification by Spirit baptism. The experience of sanctification was central to the message and vision of unity, for this experience was the perceived cleansing that God was doing to unify his church. The Saints envisioned a church free of race, gender, age, and sect discrimination, with all members unified in the Spirit.

William Seymour's theology emulates this same pattern, as typified in his diagram of the tabernacle.[69] His view of the progression of salvation is similar except for the added third-work of grace, the baptism of the Holy Spirit. Of course, Charles Parham's influence seems to be best illustrated here; however, Seymour wants to signify "Full Salvation" after the manner of his Saint's heritage.[70] Instead of the Saint's emphasis on sanctification," for William Seymour the terminology of the baptism of the Holy Spirit sets the foundation for Christian unity.[71]

Conclusion

William Seymour's association with the "Evening Light Saints" during his stay in Indianapolis and Cincinnati helped formed the theological-ecclesial convictions that remained a part of Seymour life and ministry. Perhaps Seymour developed his ministerial skills and learned of the Saint's teachings while visiting the "missionary home" of Rev. Robert Campbell in Cincinnati. In so doing, Seymour would have understood that the true church was "unified" by the Spirit of God, whose cleansing power was ridding the church of "denominations" and "sects" of every kind before Christ's soon return. Seymour's heritage of following the "evening light" produced a self-conscious identity that was rooted in temple imagery and biblical prophecy for the advocacy of Christian holiness and unity.

Notes

[1] One secondary source that deals with the "holiness" influences on William Seymour and the Azusa Street Mission in any detail is Charles Edwin Jones, "The 'Color Line' Washed Away in the Blood? In the Holiness Church, at Azusa Street, and Afterward," *Wesleyan Theological Journal* 34 (Fall, 1999). Jone's article highlights the influence of the Holiness Church of California on the Azusa Street Revival, particularly regarding racial reconciliation; however, Jones does not examine Seymour's holiness background with the "Evening Light Saints" which, in my opinion, potentially formed his holiness convictions about race, unity, and holiness.

2 The phrase "Evening Light Saints" has its roots in Daniel Warner's understanding of Zech 14:7. The "Evening Light," says Warner, "points to the holiness of the church in the 'time of the end.'" See D. S. Warner, *The Evening Light*

(Grand Junction, Mich.: Gospel Trumpet Publishing Co., 1895), 1.

³Douglas J. Nelson, *For Such a Time as This: The Story of William J. Seymour and the Azusa Street Revival* (Unpublished Dissertation, University of Birmingham, 1981), 151. See also, Rufus Gene William Sanders, *The Life of William Joseph Seymour: Black Father of the Twentieth Century Pentecostal Movement* (Unpublished Dissertation, Bowling Green University, 2000), 30. The Sanders dissertation presents much background and genealogical information about William Seymour's family as well as slave plantation ownership.

⁴Nelson, 152.

⁵Ibid., 154.

⁶Vinson Synan, *The Holiness-Pentecostal Tradition: Charismatic Movements in the Twentieth Century* (Grand Rapids, MI: Eerdmans Publishing Co., 1997), 93.

⁷Douglas M. Strom, *They Walked in the Spirit: Personal Faith and Social Action in America* (Louisville, KY: Westminster Knox Press, 1997), 36.

⁸Nelson, 159.

⁹Ibid. According to Nelson, the Indianapolis City Directories of 1896-1899 list Seymour living in Indianapolis. After 1899 his name does not appear and Nelson assumes that he moved to Cincinnati in 1900.

¹⁰Nelson, 160; Sanders, 62.

¹¹Nelson, 160; see also, Sanders, 63.

¹²Sanders, 63. Nelson never mentions that Seymour had contact with the "Saints" in Indianapolis. In fact, if it were not for Emma L. Cotton, no record would exist for Seymour's association with the Saints. Thanks to Cecil M. Robeck who brought this to my attention in an email exchange. Also, see Cecil M. Robeck, "Seymour, William Joseph," *The New International Dictionary of Pentecostal and Charismatic Movements*, ed. Stanley M. Burgess (Grand Rapids, MI: Zondervan, 2002), 1054.

¹³Nelson, 162; Sanders, 64.

¹⁴Sanders, 64.

¹⁵ *Indianapolis News and World*, Sept. 1, 1990, 390.

¹⁶Sanders, 64. Martin suggests that Seymour left Indianapolis for Chicago due to racial prejudice.

¹⁷Nelson never gives any sources or evidence of Seymour's stay in Cincinnati.

¹⁸Sanders, 64. Despite Sanders statement that Seymour never mentioned Cincinnati, C. W. Shumway says that Seymour contracted smallpox during his stay in Cincinnati. See C. W. Shumway, *A Study of "The Gift of Tongues"* (A.B. thesis, University of Southern California, 1914).

¹⁹The last time William Seymour's name appears in the Indianapolis City Directory is 1899. This is the year that is referred to by Nelson as the year he left Indianapolis. Larry Martin, *The Life and Ministry of William J. Seymour* (Joplin, MS: Christian Life Books, 1999), speaks of Seymour moving to Chicago in 1900; however, evidence for this move is nonexistent. We do not know where Seymour was in 1900.

20*Cincinnati City Directories* (Cincinnati, Ohio), 1901, 1902, 1904. In 1901 Seymour is listed as a waiter living in the rooms at 23 Longworth. In 1902 Seymour is listed as a waiter living in the rooms at 437 Carlisle Ave. and in 1904 he may have been listed as a laborer living in the rooms at 337 W. Front.

21James S. Tinney, "William J. Seymour: Father of Modern Day Pentecostalism" in *Black Apostles: Afro-American Clergy Confront the Twentieth Century*, eds. Randall K. Burkett and Richard Newman (Boston, Mass.; G. K. Hall & Co., 1978), 216.

22James Earl Massey, *An Introduction to the Negro Churches in the Church of God Reformation Movement* (New York: Shining Light Press, 1957), 17.

23 Ibid., 18.

24 Merle D. Strege, *I Saw the Church: The Life of the Church of God Told Theologically* (Anderson, IN: Warner Press, 2002), 145-147.

25Charles E. Brown, *When the Trumpet Sounded* (Anderson, IN: Warner Press, 1951), 156.

26W. J. Henry, "The Color Line" in *Gospel Trumpet* (December 20, 1906), 3.

27Tinney, 216.

28*Gospel Trumpet* (August 25, 1898), 5.

29*Gospel Trumpet* (April 26, 1900), 5.

30John W. V. Smith, *The Quest for Holiness and Unity: A Centennial History of the Church of God (Anderson, Indiana)* (Anderson, Indiana: Warner Press, 1980), 164. Jane Williams was a black woman who wrote several times to the *Gospel Trumpet* in hope of Warner or others holding meetings in Augusta, Georgia, to establish a congregation of the Church of God movement in that city. She had "dreams" for the Church of God to flourish in Augusta; however, racial prejudice inhibited her from such accomplishments. But, in due time many leaders such as A. J. Kilpatrick and W. Thomas Carter held meetings in Augusta. Her Church was the first property owned by Blacks in the Church of God movement.

31Barry L. Callen, *It's God's Church: The Life and Legacy of Daniel Sidney Warner* (Anderson, Ind.: Warner Press, 1995), 76.

32Much emphasis was put on 2 Corinthians 6:17 which says, "Come out...and be ye separate."

33See D. S. Warner, *Evening Light*, 1.

34John W. V. Smith, 97. Smith says, "In calling the faithful out of the bondage of sectarianism, they strongly insisted they were not asking the redeemed to join another sect but rather were inviting them to participate in the free fellowship of the Spirit."

35Strege, 21.

36Strege, 16; See also, John W. V. Smith, 88.

37Smith, 88.

38Barry L. Callen, *Contours of a Cause: The Theological Vision of the Church of God Movement* (Anderson, IN: Anderson University School of Theology, 1995), 191.

39"Full Salvation" was a phrase to indicate the Holiness Movement's message of "sanctification." Yet, in the case of the Saints, this would include the "unity" concept which was predicated on the experience of sanctification.

40Neither Douglas Nelson nor Rufus Sanders includes any source material for their assumption that Seymour was associated with the Saints in Cincinnati. However, we do know that Seymour stayed in Cincinnati during the years 1901, 1902, and possibly in 1904.

41Again, Nelson, Sanders, and Larry Martin offer no evidence or sources to suggest that Seymour went to God's Bible School.

42Perhaps Nelson categorically assumes that Knapp was a "Saint" because he was a "come-outer" and advocated similar doctrines such as racial inclusion, unity, and sanctification. However, in Knapp's publication, *Revivalist*, there are several articles from the *Gospel Trumpet* during the late 1890s. Some of these articles were written by G. Tufts, Jr., who belonged to the Saint's movement, but later was disfellowshipped because of associating with Knapp.

43"Deceptions and Counterfeits," *Gospel Trumpet* (August 22, 1901). Some of the "false doctrines" that Knapp's school was accused of were the following: denying the necessity of water baptism, teaching people "to stay in sectism among unbelievers," and ridiculing the idea of footwashing.

44I do not believe Tufts went to the School, but he did join the union and this, in fact, upset the Saints. Apparently, Tufts was writing articles for the *Revivalist* and sent these articles to various Saints in the region. In the articles Tufts said he was still a Saint and believed everything they endorsed ("full salvation" and "unity"), but apparently he "felt led" to "cooperate" with Knapp's people. The Saints were subtly warning Tufts about his ministry practices prior to these happenings (e.g., consistently preaching on the text about "owe no man anything" for which he had several outstanding debts; giving himself to a "streak of fanaticism prayer" [Tufts was locking himself in his room for days praying, for which the Saints said "God wants men of prayer, but he wants men of action—men who will believe what they pray and then put their belief into practice"]; however, Tufts was sympathetic with the Saints' discipline but did not show evidence of repentance. Despite Tufts' mistakes, his move to "associate" with Knapp's holiness union and Bible school obviously was the last draw for the Saints.

45In addition, during the year 1901 several articles were written in the *Revivalist* condemning the Saint's "anarchistical come-outism." Knapp's followers opposed the Saints by humorously poking fun at their "sect-cleansing," saying they were "sect-fighting sectarian[s]." See the following issues of the *Revivalist* (February 21, 1901; April 4, 1901; and September 12, 1901). In light of these articles alone, it would be inconceivable to think that any Saint would attend God's Bible School.

46Thanks to Paul Alexander, librarian for R. G. Flexon Library at God's Bible College, who assisted me in the archives at the Library. Of course, the various names of the Saint's I had living in Cincinnati around the years 1900–1904 were limited.

⁴⁷Montford L. Neal, *History of Southwest Ohio Churches of God (Anderson, Indiana, affiliation)*, compiled for the Church of God Centennial, 1980, 6-8. In 1904 Neal identifies a family by the name of Green who had connections with the early movement, but apparently they did not start a church. In 1907, however, Neal places a church led by a Mrs. Allender on "Sixth Street in the West End, and this became the first public services of the Church of God in Cincinnati." There appears to be evidence of the Saints' movement existing prior to this date in 1900, possibly meeting at this same Sixth Street location.

⁴⁸"Testimonies," *Gospel Trumpet* (April 12, 1900), 6. Prior to this date, however, on November 16, 1899, Louisa C. Adams writes to the *Gospel Trumpet* about how inspiring the *Trumpet* has been to her and contends, "I am here alone," suggesting she is the only Saint in Cincinnati.

⁴⁹"News from the Field," *Gospel Trumpet* (June 7, 1900), 5.

⁵⁰"News from the Field," *Gospel Trumpet* (October 4, 1900), 5.

⁵¹Perhaps both Vance and Campbell were collaborating together in establishing this mission.

⁵²"News from the Field," *Gospel Trumpet* (October 11, 1900), 5.

⁵³Martin, 80; Nelson, 165; Sanders, 69.

⁵⁴Nelson, 165.

⁵⁵Ibid.

⁵⁶Ibid.

⁵⁷Thanks to Douglas Welch, archivist at the Anderson University Library, for bringing this to my attention. In fact, early ordination lists do exist, but they are usually associated with those ministers who attended camp meetings. In James Massey's book, *An Introduction to the Negro Churches in the Church of God Reformation Movement*, he lists several African American ministers with the Church of God during this early period; however, Seymour does not appear on the list.

⁵⁸Strege, 82-83.

⁵⁹Ibid., 80-81. Some of these missions had specialized ministries to women and African Americans.

⁶⁰Ibid.

⁶¹Ibid., 81.

⁶²Ibid.

⁶³Along with William and Jennie Seymour, James Ross and Richard Asbery lived at 312 Azusa Street. See William J. Seymour, *The Doctrines and Disciplines of the Azusa Street Apostolic Faith Mission of Los Angeles, California*, ed., Larry Martin (Joplin, MS: Christian Life Books, 2000), 35.

⁶⁴For instance, the three ordinances of the church parallel the "Evening Light" movement: water baptism, foot washing, and Lord's Supper; see Seymour's *Doctrines and Disciplines*, 44-45. Another parallel with the Saint's theology was Seymour's insistence of Spirit Baptism with the evidence of love (42-43, 54), unity (41, 43), and holiness (25, 42, 64).

65Daniel S. Warner and H. M. Riggle, *The Cleansing of the Sanctuary* (Faith Publishing House, 1903, 1967).
66Seymour, 63; Warner and Riggle, 99.
67Warner and Riggle, 435.
68Strege, 21.
69Throughout *The Apostolic Faith* periodicals, this notion of tabernacle typology dominates Seymour's ideas of justification, sanctification, and Spirit baptism. For examples, see A. F., "The Way Into the Holiest" (October 2, 1906), 4; A. F., "Baptism with the Holy Ghost Foreshadowed" (Dec. 1906), 2; A. F., "Salvation According to the True Tabernacle" (Edition 10, 1907), 2. Also, see William J. Seymour, *Azusa Street Sermons*, ed. Larry Martin (Joplin, MS: Christian Life Books, 1999), where he advocates a "cleansing" motif in the last days within the church. Seymour states: "Those that will be permitted to enter in are those who are justified, sanctified and baptized with the Holy Ghost—sealed unto the day of redemption....The Holy Ghost is sifting out a people that are getting on the robes of righteousness and the seal in their foreheads" (44-45). Also, his sermon "Rebecca: Type of the Bride of Christ" shows a similar motif: "So God the Father has sent the Holy Spirit from the glory land down into this world and He, the Spirit of Truth, is convicting the world of sin, righteousness and judgment, and is selecting out of the body of Christ His bride. He is seeking among his kindred, the sanctified, and Jesus is baptizing them with the Holy Ghost and fire, preparing them for the great marriage supper of the Lamb" (57-58).

70Seymour's "later years (1915-1922)," during which he wrote his book, *Doctrines and Disciplines*, show strong evidence of Seymour reverting to his holiness heritage. Instead of advocating a Holy Spirit Baptism with the evidence of tongues, he suggests that "love" was the evidence of such baptism. This change of thought, however, was probably due to the dissatisfaction of his former teacher, Charles Parham, who was racially biased and questioned Seymour's credibility as a leader. Parham's consistent ridicule of Seymour during and after the years of the Azusa Revival led Seymour to respond with his book in 1915, *Doctrines and Disciplines*, thus denying Parham's "Annihilation Theory" and "evidential theory" of Spirit Baptism. See Cecil M. Robeck, Jr., "William J. Seymour and 'the Bible Evidence' in *Initial Evidence: Historical and Biblical Perspectives on the Pentecostal Doctrine of Spirit Baptism*, ed. Gary B. McGee (Peabody, Mass.: Hendrickson Publishers, 1991), 82-84. Robeck suggests that Seymour's "definition of what constitutes a Pentecostal would surely be a broader one than would be Parham's....It would remain more faithful to the Wesleyan-holiness tradition out of which the Pentecostal movement emerged, including a more profound commitment to the ethical dimension of the Christian faith" (89).

71See *The Apostolic Faith* (Jan. 1907), 1. For instance, "The Azusa Mission stands for the unity of God's people everywhere. God is uniting His people, baptizing them by one Spirit into one body." See also *The Apostolic Faith* (Sept. 1906), 1: "The Pentecostal movement is too large to be confined in any denomination or sect. It works outside, drawing all together in one bond of love, one church, one body of Christ." Also, see his emphasis of unity based upon the experience of the Spirit: "This meeting has been a melting time. The people are melted together...made one lump, one bread, all one body in Christ Jesus. There is no Jew or Gentile, bond or free, in the Azusa Street Mission....He is no respecter of persons or places" (in *Apostolic Faith*, Dec. 1906, 1). For further evidence of the Saint's theology of unity in Seymour's writings, see Seymour, *Azusa Street Sermons*, 108. There he illustrates Christian unity in the following way: "Apostolic faith doctrine means one accord, one soul, one heart. May God help every child of His to live in Jesus' prayer....O how my heart cries out to God these days that he would make every child of His see the necessity of living in the 7th chapter of John, that we may be one in the body of Christ, as Jesus has prayed." He continues by saying, "When we are sanctified through the truth, then we are one in Christ, and we can get into one accord for the gift or power of the Holy Ghost, and God will come in like a rushing mighty wind....O how I praise Him for this wonderful salvation that is spreading over this great earth. The baptism of the Holy Ghost brings the glory of God to our hearts."

Chapter 8

Women in Ministry: A Biblical Vision

by
Sharon Clark Pearson

There is a divide in the current "evangelical" Christian community over the issue of women in ministry. The Bible is used by many to restrict women to particular roles only. However, Sharon Clark Pearson argues persuasively that the more open and accepting stance of the Wesleyan/Holiness tradition, and of the Church of God movement (Anderson)) in particular, has definite biblical support. Although the early church also appears to have struggled with this issue, we find it inviting us to a vision of the new realities of God's kingdom—a freeing from standard human categories by the gracious power of the Spirit of God. Originally published in the Wesleyan Theological Journal *(31:1, Spring, 1996).*

Wesleyan theological tradition historically has held a "high view" of Scripture; that is a part of the ethos of our community. In a church tradition (with its community) that claims the integrity and authority of Scripture, questions of practice are taken seriously. The question of whether God ordains and blesses women in the practice of ministry (both in function and in office) is crucial to women because their personal and relational lives and their participation in the church have been defined and regulated by the interpretation of Scripture (as the lives of all of us should be). It is also a critical question for the church on many levels—if the church is serious about determining God's will, and then, by the grace of God, doing it!

In the church, answers given to the question of God's will concerning women seem to fall into three categories. Each of the three categories may be defined by their approach (perspective and procedures) to Biblical material. These distinctive approaches may be observed in the questions asked of Scripture, the principles exercised in the selection and evaluation (valuing) of biblical texts, the method applied in theological synthesis, and the subsequent proposed applications of conclusions. It may be further observed that the conclusions are significantly shaped by the "window" through which biblical texts are viewed.

Three Categories of Approach

One of these three approaches to the issue of women in ministry begins with a disclaimer. It either is inappropriate to address this question to the Biblical materials, argues this position, or these materials are inadequate for the task. The question of women in institutionalized ministry is seen as foreign to Scripture, and/or the instruction of Scripture is determined to be of limited value in the debate (irrelevant or impossibly culture bound). The "window" through which Scripture is observed is a presupposition about the value of Scripture itself, or about the hermeneutic that governs the way Scripture is used. In this category, theologians may proceed with general perspectives such as the equality of women and men in creation or broad principles of social justice and equality. Such an approach is focused on appeals to reason or general revelation (natural theology) or limited to a reductional existentialism. Those in the Wesleyan tradition may critique this approach as weak in that it abandons the special revelation Scripture does offer. The presupposition of this category of thought may be defined as a pluralist[1] view of the authority of Scripture; Scripture is only one of several authorities which may be appealed to as equally valid in the discussion.

The second and third approaches to the issue of the place of women in the church share the conviction that Scripture is a source of special revelation (revealed theology). Of these two approaches, one may be identified by the value it attaches to biblical statements of propriety and convention, such as those in the station codes and statements of restriction of female participation in the church (1 Cor. 14; 1 Tim. 2). These texts are made the starting place or "window" through which other biblical materials are perceived and interpreted. While this category appeals to the authority of Scripture (and so is committed to a self-consciously "high view" of Scripture), its approach is limited by a "mechanical literalism."

Methodologically, this category is inadequate in contextual investigation (literary and historical). Theologically, this approach is weakened by a restricted understanding of revelation as propositional statements. The presupposition of this category may be identified as a positivist view of Scripture (not logical positivism) in that it would interpret *sola scriptura* to mean that Scripture is the exclusive authority for theology.² In this paper, biblical positivism is defined as a position which takes the Bible itself to be the "given," the data or the evidence—and limited to that evidence alone as authority. In hermeneutical terms, this approach might be called monism and stands in contrast to the pluralism of the first approach.

The third category of approaches to the issue of women in ministry, precisely out of its commitment to Scriptural authority, attempts to incorporate the broad range of biblical evidence. The data considered to be important to the discussion includes such material as the biblical stories of the experience of the Jesus community and the early church. These stories are seen as reflections of the circumstances and the theologies of that church. The truly revolutionary practices of Jesus in relation to women, the participation of women alongside the apostle Paul in ministry, and the evidence of women's participation (leadership) in worship services are all accepted as contributing factors in the dialogue. The rationale for such a program is that this evidence reflects the theological perspectives of the biblical writers. For example, the Lucan and Pauline writings present theologies of a new aeon in which social and religious barriers are superseded. Texts such as Acts 2:16-21, Galatians 3:28, and Ephesians 2 (which helps define the Galatians passage) are the "window" through which the biblical materials are perceived.

This third category is also committed to standard research into broader references which are used as sources by biblical writers. So, creation accounts and the station codes are investigated for the purpose of identifying God's will as presented in the "whole council of Scripture." This category is not only serious about inductive study of Scripture as primary authority, it is sensitive to experience, reason (analysis), and church tradition, *norms which are reflected in the biblical materials themselves.* The presupposition that governs this approach may be described as the primacist view of Scripture in the question of authority, which also allows the evidence of reason, the appeal of experience, and the instruction of tradition. This position has been defined in Wesleyan circles as the Wesleyan Quadrilateral.³

The second and third categories reflect the tension inherent in Scripture, the tension drawn between eschatological vision (Joel) and arguments of social propriety.⁴ Arguments of hierarchy and dominance/subordination stand alongside stories of revolutionary attitudes and practice in Jesus' ministry and in the participation of women in the ministry of the early church.

The following presentation on the issue of women in ministry is necessarily brief, but demonstrates the method of the third approach to Scripture.[5] The synthesis derived from this work reflects the conviction that Scripture is relevant and does lend guidance and inspiration to practice in the church, in this case to the issue of women in ministry. The significance of this method is that it reflects the integrity of a Wesleyan approach to Scripture and a particular vision of the means of faithfulness to its authority.

The Case for Women in Ministry

All serious (and even not so serious) Bible students interpret Scripture according to some set of principles, even if they are tacit. When any question is asked of Scripture, certain principles are exercised in the selection, evaluation (valuing), theological synthesis, and proposed application of conclusions. All who read Scripture make choices between the instructions received therein. All decide what portion of the Scripture is timeless and always applicable and which passages are only cultural expressions of some larger question. For example, though many have read the stated requirement that women wear a head covering in public worship (1 Cor. 11:2-16), there is no concern expressed in our churches that this injunction is be obeyed by women today. It has been dismissed as circumstance-bound instruction that no longer applies (although the principle which governed the instruction should be interpreted and does apply). The question, then, is not whether to make such distinctions, which are in fact demanded by the nature of many of the texts in the New Testament—occasional letters—but where to draw the line in that process.

In making such a choice, two almost automatic instincts govern this writer. First, we are allowed to define an expression as limited to a particular circumstance (with a corresponding application) where we have a clearhr statement of such limits from that text or another. Second, an old dictum applies: Where the text speaks, we speak (without reservation). Where Scripture is silent, we speak only with a great deal of humility.

Another consideration in this discussion is that some of the questions we address to Scripture are foreign to it. These may be worked out only by implication. The question of women in ministry is not foreign to the New Testament, but is not answered explicitly therein. While it is clear that women participated in the ministry of the New Testament church, definition of the parameters of that participation is disputed. But, it must be remembered that interpreters all are working from the same limited evidence, and more, that the so-called "clear statements" limiting the participation of women are not clear at all. If they were, there would be no discussion.[6]

The method of this particular study is to begin by reviewing the information on women in general in the New Testament. That information was written, selected, and preserved in androcentric (man-centered) societies. It is remarkable that given the patriarchal worldview of the societies in which these documents were written, women were included in the story at all. There is enough evidence available in the various accounts of women in the New Testament to indicate that women were an integral part of the life and ministry of the early church. The story of the church could not be told without including the stories of women.

Women in the Gospels

It is shortsighted to consider the place of women in the church without recalling Jesus' attitude and actions toward the women around him. Women as well as men were attracted to Jesus in his three short years of ministry. Among Jesus' rugged band of followers were a number of women. Jeremias calls this event, the fact of women following a teacher or rabbi, "an unprecedented happening in history of that time" (374). We know about these women from a few short references (Mark 15:40, 41; Luke 8:1-3). These women supported Jesus and his disciples financially. They were women with means and so probably came from an upper echelon of society. The Marcan account paints the poignant picture of these women, along with other women from Jerusalem, at the scene of Jesus' crucifixion. The three women named in that portrait visit the burial site after Sabbath to anoint their Lord's body for burial. And then, in a society where a woman's word was not allowed in court, they were commissioned by Jesus to be the first to proclaim the resurrection. Nothing was more natural than their being among the 120 who waited in the Upper Room for the power that would give fire to their lives and witness. The church from its inception included women.

Who were the women who sought Jesus out and became a part of the Gospel story because of his impact on their lives? They are the three who became known as leaders among the group of women (Mary Magdalene, Mary the mother of Jesus, and Salome). They are Mary and Martha, who, contrary to social rules, invited Jesus into their home. They include the woman unclean with her feminine infirmity and the despised Samaritan woman at the well who was the first commissioned by Jesus to "spread the Word." They are the Syro-Phoenician (Gentile) woman who asked him for "the crumbs" for her demon-possessed daughter and the woman who, in a prophetic act, anointed Jesus.

A significant aspect of every story is that it was ever recorded and preserved. In a culture where women were property[7] and had no rights or privileges to call their own, these stories themselves would have opened the door of the church to criticism and even contempt. But what is most significant about these stories is that, in every case, Jesus crossed all lines of propriety—religious and social. His very actions were a challenge to the cherished traditions of his own people. He went so far as to commend women as examples of faith and spiritual vitality, women who no rabbi would teach, women who were not counted in the number of a synagogue, who were isolated to a separate court at the temple, and whose religious vows could be overturned by their husbands.

Along with stories of women who accompanied Jesus and his disciples is the story of Mary and Martha. Jesus teaches Mary as he would teach any man who would follow him—an unheard of breach of religious leadership. "Better to burn the Torah than to teach it to a woman."[8] Women were not educated in the Synagogue school nor at home. "He who teaches his daughter the law, teaches her lechery."[9] As if that were not enough, Jesus is recorded as having chided Martha for fulfilling her socially prescribed role instead of joining Mary (Luke 10:38-42).

The cumulative effect of such stories makes clear that Jesus broke custom in his championing of women as equally worthy of his concern and ministry. His evaluation of them far outstripped the most expansive and tolerant in his day and continually surprised even those who knew him well. The tone of his ministry was not to accept the status quo, but rather to model a new life and relationships to and for women. He challenged the sexist standards of his world—the lustful glance of an adulterous heart (Matthew 5:27-28.), the casual divorce, a male prerogative (Matthew 19:3-9),[10] and the threat of capital punishment applied unfairly—only to the adulterous woman (John 8:1-11). The popular attitude of the day was that women were responsible for all sexual temptation (and therefore sexual sin). None of these stories would be approved, much less applauded outside of the early church that preserved them. Yet, somehow, the gospel could not be told without them. Such events were so integral to the reality of the Jesus community that they comprised a part of the gospel itself.

An anticipated response to the above review of evidence regarding women in ministry is the popular objection that none of the women following Jesus became one of his twelve disciples/apostles. None were accorded equality. It is not necessary to argue cultural expediency here. It is enough to respond that no Gentile or slave was allowed that privilege either, but that was not and is not used to exclude these disadvantaged groups from the leadership and offices of the church.

Women in the Early Church

Clearly, women were an integral part of the Jesus community that awaited the empowerment of the Spirit (Acts 1:14-15). And just as clearly, these women were among those who received the Spirit in fulfillment of Joel's prophecy. The emphasis of Peter's sermon is the universality of the Spirit's work; those who previously were not candidates to share in proclamation—the young, the woman, the slave—were now anointed to prophesy as witnesses of the work of the Messiah (Acts 1:8, 2:1-4; Luke 24:44-49). It was incredible that women were included in the Gospel accounts; it is also a wonder that the participation of women in the early church was recorded in Acts and the Epistles. Against cultural expediency and propriety, these stories continued to be told. A brief perusal of the evidence of this participation can be listed in two categories: (1) brief references included in such incidental fashion as lists of women; and (2) epistolary discussions of women's participation in ministry. We also will note (3) the household codes, (4) the argument from creation accounts, and (5) the relevance of emphasis on the eschatological age of the Spirit.

1. **Lists of Women.** The incidental and therefore brief references to women identified as participating in various aspects of the ministry of the church are powerful evidence of apostolic recognition of women in ministry. Why? Because at least one agenda for listing these women was to elicit recognition and support of their ministry in the church. Furthermore, these texts not only assume the role of such women, they exhort support of those women, and precisely in their roles as ministers.

In the book of *Acts* Philip the evangelist is noted with a reference to his four daughters who had the gift of prophesy (21:9). The Apostle Paul places this spiritual gift at the top of his list as the most valuable gift for edification of the church (1 Cor. 14:1). Mentioned in several epistles in the New Testament, another character, Priscilla, evidently bore quite a reputation (Acts 18:2, 18, 26; 1 Cor. 16:19; Rom. 16:3-4; 2 Tim. 4:19). How many others were referred to as often or in such a variety of texts? Her distinction for the purposes of this study is that she, along with

Aquila, taught Apollos (Acts 18:26). Against Rabbinic tradition that identified women as "the wife" of the man who is named, the Apostle Paul recognized Priscilla as prominent enough not only to be listed along with her husband, but also to be referred to first in the pair more often than not (four of six times, one of these occurring in 1 Timothy, which indicates her prominence as teacher in the pair). By calling Priscilla a "fellow worker" in Christ Jesus, the Apostle Paul accorded Priscilla an equal place among other such workers as Timothy (Romans 16:21), Titus (2 Cor. 8:23), Luke (Philemon 24), Apollos, Paul (1 Cor. 3:9), and others.

This term applied to Priscilla, "fellow worker," was also applied to Euodia and Syntyche, leaders at Philippi. Phoebe is explicitly called a "minister" (a term historically translated as "servant" only in the case of Phoebe). The same term was applied to the leaders Apollos (1 Cor. 3:5), Timothy (1 Tim. 4:6), and Paul (1 Cor. 3:5). Along with the references to Phoebe and Prisca (Priscilla) in Paul's closing instructions to the Romans, four other women are listed as having "worked very hard" in the Lord: Mary, Tryophena, Tryphosa, and Persis. The Apostle Paul applied this same description to the ministry of other leaders in the church (1 Cor. 16:15-16; 1 Thess. 5:12; 1 Tim. 5:17). Finally, one of the two who Paul called "outstanding among the apostles" was a woman (Rom. 16:7). The name mentioned is Junias. David Scholer's review of the evidence is most helpful:

> Junias is a male name in English translations, but there is no evidence that such a male name existed in the first century A.D. Junia, a female name, was common, however. The Greek grammar of the sentence...means that the male and female forms of this name would be spelled identically....Since Junia is the name attested in the first century and since the great church father...of the fourth century, John Chrysostom (no friend of women in history), understood the reference to be to a woman Junia, we ought to see it that way as well. In fact, it was not until the thirteenth century that she was changed to Junias (12-13).

It is obvious from these informal, uncontrived lists, that women played a significant role in the early church as leaders. Their function in ministry is defined in these places by the same terms applied to the ministry of men, and no gender distinction is made in role or function in the lists. Yet, despite the power of this evidence, it is clear that the record of women in ministry was more limited than that of men. The heroes of the biblical records are almost always men. It is probable that opportu-

Women in Ministry: A Biblical Vision   139

nity for participation in ministry was more limited for women.

2. Evidence of Participation. One of the strongest evidences for the participation of women in the worshipping community comes from the brief discussion of 1 Corinthians 11:2-16. This text makes explicit reference to women prophesying and praying in services of worship. The reference is incidental; the practice is not commented on. That makes a strong case for inclusion of women in these ministries in services of worship. Such participation by women is evidently assumed under the wide rubric of spiritual gifts and ministries which have been designated to all (regardless of religious, social, or gender distinctions) for "the common good" (12:7). Several arguments are made in this text; a brief perusal is all that the confines of this study will allow.

First Corinthians 11:2-16 has been debated at length. The breadth of the arguments are best explained as arising out of what appears to be a contradiction in the text between vv. 4-7 and vv. 10-12.[11] Verses 4-7 require that women submit to the norms of their culture regarding head covering: "every woman who prays or prophesies with her *kephale* (head) uncovered (the word "veil" does not occur in this text) dishonors her head...let her keep her head covered."[12] Verses 10-12 are Paul's corrective; women may wear a covering over their heads or may not: "For this reason the woman ought to have *exousia* (power, right or freedom of choice, the ability to do something) over (covering) her head" (v. 10; cf. John 10:18, Acts 9:14, and Rev. 16:9 for the use of *exousia* with *echo*, and 1 Cor. 9 for *exousia*).[13] The Greek term *authority* should be translated as it is—that women should have "authority" over their heads. It should not to be translated as sign of *authority* or veil.[14]

In this context, *exousia* not only symbolizes woman's (wife's) glorification (vs. shame) of man (husband), but also her authority to play an active role in worship. "That is, her veil (sic.) represents the new authority given to women under the new dispensation to do things which formerly had not been permitted" (Barrett 255). Following this line of reasoning, such an interpretation is substantiated by the two verses following his statement. Having argued for natural differences between man and woman, Paul now lays down a new principle of mutuality and interdependence based also on creation (cf. 1 Cor. 7:3-5).

Prior to the argument of verses 4-7, a basic assertion is made which often is raised in the discussion of women in ministry: "Now, I want you to realize that the *kephale* of every man is Christ, and the *kephale* of the woman is man, and the *kephale* of Christ is God." The normal meaning of *kephale*, or *head*, in the New Testament is *source of being* or *origin;* the rarer meaning is *authority* or *dominion*. While it seems obvious that the argument is an appeal to some sort of order, the meaning and application of the statement is much less obvious. This statement is made in service of the argument about what women do with their *heads* in their exercise of ministry (public prayer and prophesy); to do so without a covering brings shame upon their heads.[15] Whatever Paul's statement does mean, it in no way functions in this text to limit the participation or leadership of women in public worship.

The translation *origin* or *source of being*, rather than *authority* or *dominion* makes quite a different statement; when translated as *authority/dominion*, and so *lord*, this passage has been used to promote a sort of idolatry of men by women; women owe men what men owe Christ. But, while the text appeals to the order of creation from Genesis 2:18-23, it does not go so far as a straight parallel would allow. It does not claim that woman is the "image" as well as glory of man (11:7). Woman shares the image of God (and therefore is not more removed from God than man); this is a concession to Genesis 1:27 and 5:2 (Barrett 248, 249). Verse 8 restates the concept of *origin* or *source* in the order of creation.[16]

A question is raised when we are encountered by the words of 1 Cor. 14:33b-36, which some have read only as a limitation of the role of women in worship—only three chapters after women are casually recognized for their participation and leadership. The apparent discontinuity between these two passages also has been explained in a variety of ways.[17] Here, the governing perspective offered is that chapter 14 is instruction to three groups of people: (1) the tongues-speakers (vv. 2, 5, 9-19, 27 ff.); (2) the prophets (vv. 3, 24, 29-32; and (3) the women (34f.). The regulations for each group are similar, including the explicit command to "be silent," and the basic corrective requirement of "order" (Fiorenza 230).

It is important to recognize Paul's use of the verb *lalein*, "speak," in 1 Corinthians 14:34. It should be translated *inspired speech* or argumentative and distracting *debate* or *questioning*. The term used is not Paul's usual term for preaching or prophesying, so there is no contradiction with the reference to women praying and prophesying in the eleventh chapter. No matter what final conclusion one places upon the instruction *to be silent*, it cannot be that women are not allowed to *pray* or *prophesy* in public worship. Ralph Martin's argument is basic: "Paul remains committed to social egalitarianism in the gospel (Gal. 3:28), and there is the undeniable evidence of the role he accorded women colleagues (Phoebe, Prisca [Priscilla], the women of Philippi [Phil. 4:3] and the several coworkers in Rom. 16). It is "prima facie" unlikely he should state categorically "Let your women keep silent" in worship (85).

One of the proposed pictures drawn to explain this text and the larger context of this epistle is that of women who aspired to be charismatic teachers, claiming special revelations in inspired speech which were above the usual corrections of the congregation and apostolic teaching. Their claims were so inflated that the Apostle is led to sarcasm: Did the word of God originate with you? Are you the only people it has reached? In this scenario, the heretical teaching going on in the Corinthian congregation was a gnostic sort of teaching (cf. chapters 7 and 15).[18] Whatever sociological history this text is mirroring, Paul's correctives were not aimed at the total restriction of women's participation and ministry in Corinth anymore than he forbade tongues (14:39) or the ministry of prophesy in general. Women functioned with the gift to which Paul accorded highest (and corrective) value in that community (14:1). The Corinthian evidence displays a community in which women were participating in leadership in the community, some of whom required correction, not of that function, but for abuse of the function.

The above discussions of the participation of women in public worship and lists of women who led in the early church all bear evidence to the fact that women did function in ministry in the early church. While there is no claim to "office" here, there is no question but that "function" occurred. Use of the lists of women in this discussion is an appeal to at least some of the tradition and experience of the early church. Such information should be considered alongside what are considered to be propositional instructions.

3. The Use of Household Codes. One significant aspect of the argument against women in ministry is the appeal to the household codes located in the New Testament. These household codes, with their hierarchical order, were not created by the New Testament authors but rather are quoted from the Graeco-Roman culture of that day.[19] The Greek philosopher Aristotle, who predated Christ by three and a half centuries, was the source of the formal arrangement of pairings based on this dominant/subordinate hierarchical model:

> The primary and smallest parts of the household are "master" and "slave," "husband" and "wife," "father" and "children"....Authority and subordination are conditions not only inevitable but also expedient....There is always found a ruling and a subject factor ...between the sexes, the male is by nature superior and the female inferior, the male ruler and the female subject.[20]

Aristotle expanded this household code to the realm of political life because in his thinking, "the household was a microcosm of the state."[21] He taught the authority/subordination model in the pairing of ruler/people. He promoted his social order as necessary to stability, harmony, and political security. Any threat to this Aristotelian value system was considered by the Roman Empire to be a threat to such stability and security. So, the Roman emperor Octavian instructed his soldiers to "allow no woman to make herself equal to a man" (Cassius 50.25.3, 28.3). What was the occasion for such an instruction? Antony and Cleopatra. David Balch reviews the problem as follows:

> If democratic equality between husband and wife as it existed in Egypt were allowed to influence Roman households, the government would degenerate into a democracy; and the Romans believed this changed form of government would be morally worse than the aristocracy or monarchy which had brought them to power. The Egyptian Cleopatra's goddess Isis, who "gave women the same power as men," was perceived as a threat to continued Roman rule (USQR 162-3).

The rights of the one in authority were assumed. Tyranny was not criticized as an expression of that authority in the dominant culture as directed by Aristotle's words: "For there is no such thing as injustice in the absolute sense towards what is one's own."[22] In the same writing Aristotle assumes that since the one owned is "as it were a part of oneself and no one chooses to harm himself; hence there can be no injustice towards them and nothing just or unjust in the political sense." He was advocating a benign tyranny based on inferior/superior natures. Yet, the Roman Stoic, Seneca, critiqued Roman treatment of slaves as "excessively haughty, cruel and insulting" (47.1 and 1).

This lengthy look back is necessary for us to recover the impact of the household codes as used in the New Testament. The impact is that the Roman household codes were not simply adopted. They were adapted, that is, qualified in the earlier New Testament texts (in chronological order—Col. 3:18-4:1; Eph. 5:21-6:9, 1 Pet. 2:13-3:7). They were not accepted as absolutes, but critiqued even as they were appealed to. For example, in Colossians 3:18-4:1, the traditional pairings are each followed by an unthinkable modification, which in fact, points to a higher code of ethics than the one encapsulated in the original codes:

>Wives be subject to husbands____husbands love wives.
>Children obey parents____fathers do not provoke children.
>Slaves obey masters____masters treat slaves justly.[23]

The injunctions of the code in Ephesians are filled with new meaning as they appear under the revolutionary paragraph heading "submit to one another," which is applied to all of the following discussion. The reason given there for submission is not an appeal to the superior or inferior nature of the other, but rather, reverence to Christ. It is impossible for the twentieth century student of the Bible to appreciate fully the newness of the relationship commanded of husbands and wives in Ephesians. Likewise, the command to Christian masters was full of the seeds of change: "treat your slaves in the same way" (i.e., by the same set of attitudes and conduct required of Christian slaves towards their masters). Such radical qualifications of the household codes are a class apart from any parallel in Greek philosophy, Stoicism, or Roman household codes (Balch 161). And the seeds of such thinking produced the fruit of the story of Paul, Onesimus, and Philemon.

First Peter also sets conditions on the household codes. In a setting of crisis, submission to human authority is for the Lord's sake. Christians were suffering "unjustly" at the hands of tyrannical masters (2:19-20), husbands (3:6), and local government officials (2:14, 3:14,17). The purpose of the code in 1 Peter is not to insist on conformity to traditional values, but pragmatically to steer a prudent line. The appeal is for Christian commitment even when it involves suffering.[24] There was no question of an "inferior nature" being advanced here, for all are called to live as "servants of God" (2:16). Christ as the "Suffering Servant of God' is the model to follow (2:21-24). In the specific address to slaves in chapter two, the terms used elsewhere in the codes for *servant (doulos)* and *master (kurios)* are not used here. Rather, the terms *household servants (oiketai)* and *despots (despotai)* are used. The reason for the shift from the traditional use of the code language is that the author has already used the term *servant* to refer to every Christian (2:16) and *master* (or *Lord*) for God (2:15).

Roman rulers might not judge "justly" as God has ordained that they should (2:13-14) and as God himself does (2:21-23), but are to be submitted to for the Lord's sake. Christian wives are to submit to pagan husbands for the purpose of evangelism (3:1-2) and are not to fear them (3:6). Christian husbands are called to a relationship with their wives quite different from the cultural norm. In fact, a most revolutionary concept appears here: the husband's spiritual vitality is dependent upon the way he treats his wife.

The most significant critique of the husband-wife pair of the household code in 1 Peter would be immediately obvious to the original hearers of that epistle. And yet, without historical and cultural background, readers today would all but miss it. The Christian women addressed in 1 Peter 3 were married to pagan husbands. And yet, despite the norms of the Roman (and, in fact, Jewish) culture of that time, these women were allowed the freedom of religious choice by 1 Peter. That instruction went against the typical Roman perspective such as is expressed by Plutarch:

> A wife should have no friends but those of her husband; and as the gods are the first of friends it is becoming for a wife to worship and know only the gods that her husband believes in, and to shut the door tight upon all queer rituals and outlandish superstitions. For with no god do stealthy and secret rites performed by a woman find favor (Plutarch 140D, 140DE).

Even while addressing women in this text by appealing to the social code of the day, 1 Peter assumes their religious independence from their pagan husbands (cf. 1:18, 4:3, 4). These women were encouraged to keep their faith and not to fear their husbands, who likely had been expressing extreme displeasure and concern at their wives' conversions. So, when those women heard this epistle in a service of worship, they heard a proclamation of freedom, religious responsibility, and increased value. Had their pagan husbands heard that same text, they would have heard insubordination and anarchy. And how would they have heard the words addressed to their wives, "Do not give way to fear"? Oh, how differently this text is read today!

Many scholars have recognized the difference in the way the household codes are used in the Pastoral Epistles. The predominant attitudes of the culture of that day seem to be expressed in the way the codes are used in these letters.[25] Here there is no leveling instruction to the dominant members of the pairs such as is found in the Colossians or Ephesians texts. And yet, the motivation for use of the code is telling. Why should women and slaves be subject? So that the church may win the acceptance of society. But, this is still not the Roman appeal to an inborn nature which is superior or inferior. It is a pragmatic appeal like the exhortation to prayer in 1 Timothy 2:1-3. The purpose for the instruction is "that we may live peaceful and quiet lives" which will provide the opportunity for the salvation of all.

First Timothy 2:11-15 is the text most often quoted by those who believe that Scripture teaches the restriction of women's ministry. In fact, it has been used by some as the defining text of the discussion of women's place in the church. It seems that the reason the passage is given such priority is that it is judged by some to be a clear statement of instruction. Yet, the complexity and difficulty of the passage is mirrored in the disagreement it evokes among even conservative scholars. The presupposition one begins with radically affects the way this text is valued and investigated. If the text is adopted as a propositional statement, as Paul's definitive (eternal and everywhere) word on restriction of the participation of women, then it follows that "I permit no woman to teach or to have authority over a man" (2:12) is taken as "clear instruction." However, the first level of investigation adopted here, literary and historical analysis, raises a number of serious challenges: the text is not at all "clear" in its meaning.

The first major challenge is that the interpretation of verse 12 depends on how one translates the verb *authentein* which is an *hapax legomenon* in the New Testament. The translator must rely on other sources to determine possible meanings; there are four and each one radically affects the sense of the whole passage.[26] This difficulty is increased by the fact that the verb *didaskein* in 1 Timothy is always used in conjunction with another verb which qualifies its meaning (e.g., 1:3-4, 4:11, 6:2-3). Therefore, in verse 12, *authentein* qualifies the teaching; it refers to the negative content of the teaching and not to the activity of teaching itself. The Kroegers have concluded:

> If the context of 1 Timothy 2:12 is neutral and refers only to the activity of teaching rather than to its positive or negative content, then it is the only time that didaskein is so used in the Pastorals....It is in keeping with the other uses of didaskein to find in this directive a condemnation of their heterodoxy (81).

This interpretation is strengthened by recognition that the grammar of the sentence allows at least two interpretations. One of these is that it is an indirect statement with a repeated negative, in which case the emphasis of the sentence would be on the content of the teaching and not on the function of teaching.

Further difficulties are presented in the verses surrounding verse 12. In verse 11, the term for *silence* is not the term used in 1 Corinthians 14 and has five possible meanings, none of which is as strong as the term used in that letter. The best interpretation of the term is *quietness* or *in a quiet demeanor* (Fee 72). That is its sense also in the instruction just verses earlier in 1 Timothy which exhorts prayers "so that we may lead a quiet and peaceable life." (1 Tim. 2:2; cf. 2 Thess. 3:12 and 1 Thess. 4:11). The term does not mean verbal silence but an attitude of reverence or a state of peacefulness. The phrase "I do not permit" is better understood if translated "I am not permitting," which suggests specific instruction for a particular circumstance (Fee 72).

For some, another problem in these verses is that Paul's usual term for "man" is not used in 2:8-15. In the Pauline letters, *aner* or *man* occurs fifty times, and *gyne* or *woman* occurs fifty-four times in eleven texts. In each case, the terms refer to husbands and wives, and not male and female. This complicates the interpretation of "full submission"; to whom exactly are women to be in full submission? Their husbands? Men in general? True Christian teachers? The grammar of the sentence does not make the answer easy. Once again, the passage is not "clear." Nevertheless, the best interpretation for the unit seems to be that these are general instructions directed to men and women. The conclusion selected here as best fitting the overall context is that women are to learn teaching quietly from true Christian teachers such as Timothy.

Finally, the relationship of verse 15 to the total passage is a puzzle; there is no consensus about the meaning of "she will be saved." Contextual and historical studies identify the passage as one of the several responses of the letter to the false teachers at Ephesus. The content of the false teaching included misunderstanding of the Old Testament, speculative Jewish myths (genealogies) and asceticism. That false teaching was particularly attractive to women and to younger widows who avoided remarriage and had opened their homes to those who taught false doctrines (2:9-15, 5:11-15, 2 Tim. 3:6-7). Such teaching has been identified as a "precursor to Gnosticism"[27] and as doctrines based upon "perversions of the Adam and Eve saga," with Eve as creator and spiritual illuminator of Adam and the serpent as offering "gnosis" to the world.[28] The influence of local goddess religions also is manifested in such teaching. All in all, the difficulties of this passage in 1 Timothy are best explained when the instruction is recognized as correction of false teaching and teachers at Ephesus.

Given just the few difficulties mentioned briefly above, it is remarkable and indefensible that verse 12, a difficult verse, and a single verse, would be given the status it has been given by some in the church. Even more, it is incredible that one single verse would be made the basis for any doctrine, especially one so critical in its impact on the church. Particularly if one counts the epistle as Pauline, these words must be weighed in light of the evidence that Paul allowed women in ministry, and further that he required submission to their leadership.[29]

The second level of investigation which affects the interpretation of

1 Timothy 2:11-15 is to study the passage in the broad context of the appeals for submission in the station codes as used in the New Testament. The major difference between 1 Timothy 2 and the earlier appeals to the codes is that there is no reciprocity in this instruction.[30] And yet, even here in the most conservative expression of the code in the New Testament, the reason given for submission is not the nature of the creation, but rather the story of the Fall. This appeal to woman's greater culpability in the Fall cannot be taken as a theological absolute. The Genesis account itself (Genesis 3) does not assign such a meaning to the woman's succumbing first to temptation (only the man who is defending himself appeals to any "priority" of guilt!); punishment is equally assigned. And the Apostle Paul, when referring to the Fall, talks about Adam's sin (Romans 5:12-14). In fact, the claim made in 1 Timothy 2:14 that "Adam was not the one deceived; it was the woman who was deceived and became a sinner" cannot be equated with the Genesis or Romans references to this event. It is much more like the rabbinical speculations of that time as expressed, for example, by Philo, the Apostle Paul's older-contemporary:

> ...the woman, being imperfect and deprived "by nature," made the beginning of sinning; but man, as being the more excellent and perfect nature, was the first to set the example of blushing and being ashamed, and indeed of every good feeling and action.[31]

Long ago, Adolph von Harnack presented his theory to explain the changes in social attitudes from Jesus' followers and the earliest expression of the church to Christianity as represented by the Pastoral epistles (1 Timothy and Titus). He observed the following progression: (1) the radical perspectives of Jesus, (2) unconventional freedom for women in the earliest congregations, (3) conditional appeals to the cultural norms by use of the household codes, and (4) uncritical acceptance of Graeco-Roman values. He called this progression an Hellenization process.[32] While Harnack's theory may be rightly critiqued for not allowing for the different trajectories in a complex early history, his observation may be redirected in recognition of the appeals to accommodation for the sake of evangelism or, in the case of the Pastorals, social conservatism in reaction to heresy.

This process of accommodation may be observed in an historical glance at a comparable social issue, slavery. In the Old Testament some laws reflected the concern that Jews were never to forget that they were once slaves. In fact, the central story of the Torah (first five books of the

Old Testament) is the Exodus. God freed the Hebrew slaves from their Egyptian lords. Therefore, slavery was conditioned with many protections in Israel. Slaves were to be freed after six years of service, were to be sent off with blessings and liberal provisions for livelihood (Exodus 21:1-6, Deuteronomy 15:12-18). Slavery was not to become a perpetual institution. There was no elitism involved. This was quite a different expression from Aristotle's concept of a natural hierarchy. Such an historical and literary history surely influenced the thinking of the early church, but the attitudes and values of the church through time have often followed (or, even led) arguments for cultural expediency and orthopraxy (or in the case of segregation of the church along racial lines, arguments for the effectiveness of evangelism).[33]

Careful study of the household or station codes reveals a very different usage in the New Testament than is claimed in some popular teaching of today. While the codes may be expressing a "reversion to convention"[34] the motivation demonstrated in the New Testament was pragmatic concern and was not based upon some concept of natural order by creation. The popular interpretation of these codes today is more Aristotelian than Christian and ignores the impact of the spiritual qualifications placed upon them by the New Testament writers and the motivation for their use.

4. Argument from Creation Accounts. In the above examination, arguments from the creation accounts have been referred to briefly. The creation account of Genesis 1 presents a creation in which male and female are together created in the image of God (cf. 5:1-2). The second creation account, which Paul appealed to (Gen. 2), includes two aspects which have been used to promote a hierarchical model of authority/submission. First, woman is created after man and from his rib. While it might be argued that 1 Corinthians 11 suggests an order of priority on the basis of this text, the original text does not support the development of a model of dominance/subordination. The "rib" is the symbol of correspondence between man and woman. The man and the woman belong to each other in a qualitatively different way than they belong to the animals: "The unique closeness of her relationship to the man is underlined above all through the fact that she is created, not from the earth but out of the rib from man himself" (Wolff 94). If anything, the woman is distinguished from the animals who are not suitable for relationship with the man, who are subordinate to him. The woman's superiority over the animals, not her inferiority in relationship to the man, is the point of the story.

The second aspect of the text used to support the dominance of man is that woman was created to be a *helper* for man (Genesis 2:20). Yet, this term *helper* is the same term used of God in his relationship with man (e.g., Exod. 18:4; Isa. 30:5; Psa. 146:5). With some humor, one might argue that since this term is used of the helping one who is superior (God), the woman who *helps* man, is the superior party. At the very least, there is no connotation of subordination with the use of the term; only that of correspondence. The term has been misapplied when it is interpreted to mean that woman was created to be servile to man.

The concept of subordination is only first referred to in Genesis 3:16 as a consequence of the Fall. Domination/subordination is presented as a new reality brought into being by sin and is represented as a part of what is broken in the marriage trust. Speculation on this text which envisages women as inferior or as properly subordinate is a late development in Judaism, occurring first in the second century before Christ. "The Old Testament [itself] does not emphasize the subordination of wives" (Balch 1986, 97). If the consequence of the Fall is the subordination of women, should that subordination be lifted up as the ideal? It seems obvious that it is a part of the fallen creation, the old order, which in the Apostle Paul's mind is passing away.

There is no doubt that the Jewish culture was patriarchal, especially in Jesus' day. Yet, women were generally accorded more value in the Jewish culture than in the Roman world. It is certain that misogynism (extreme devaluation of women) was a late rabbinical development which was adopted by some of the church "fathers" of the second and third centuries. Such attitudes are not careful reflections on the creation accounts of Scripture, but are adaptations of the Biblical message revealing the influence of Graeco-Roman culture.

5. The Eschatological Age of the Spirit. Another line of reasoning in the discussion of women in ministry is that which is developed along the lines of Peter's use of Joel's prophesy on the day of Pentecost as presented by Luke (Acts 2). The uniqueness of that event is explained as the universality of the pouring out of God's Spirit; the surprise of the crowd was that they all heard the gospel in their native languages. This prophesy proclaims the means behind the method in the book of Acts; the gospel will be proclaimed across many barriers (1:8) because the Spirit will be poured out "on all flesh," across all categories of the church: (1) age—young as well as old, (2) gender—female as well as male, (3) status—slave as well as free.[35] The sentiment of this prophecy is presented by the Apostle Paul in his teaching of the church (Gal. 3:28), the new creation, the new Adam (Romans 5), and a new Israel—all eschatological (end times) categories. In the line of such thinking, the Apostle Paul preaches a new time in which "we are no longer under the law." It is the time now in which "faith has come" (Gal. 3:25). In the same discussion, Paul speaks of the inception of that faith and baptism into Christ; in Christ (here in the corporate sense of the church): "There is neither Jew nor Greek, slave nor free, male nor female, for you are all one in Christ Jesus" (Gal. 3:28).

The threefold distinctions excluded in Paul's pronouncement "you are all one in Christ Jesus" correspond to popular formulas which maintained such distinctions. The morning prayer of the Jewish male included the thanksgiving that he was not created a Gentile, a slave, or a woman.[36] Against the Roman expression of distinction and division in the household codes and Jewish man's prayer, the Apostle Paul proclaims the positive dissolution of all such realities. The fact that Paul is presenting more than a visionary and "spiritual" ideal is proven in that it was precisely the human structures of these distinctions which were addressed in the life and practice of the early church.

For example, the vision of Peter in Acts 10 is lived out in Caesarea and then was the motivation for inclusion of the Gentiles in Acts 11. The unity Paul preaches is to be a reality in the social experience of the church (Eph. 2). Not only does Paul insist that the church live out such a vision, but he also attempts to model it himself. This vision is the basis of his confrontation with Peter. Paul also appeals to Philemon for the sake of Onesimus out of such convictions. And, his practice of including Christian women as partners in his ministry was the culminating expression of his conviction that "In Christ, all things are made new" (2 Cor. 5:17). Nevertheless, "whereas Paul's ban on discrimination on racial or social grounds has been fairly widely accepted...there has been a tendency to restrict the degree to which 'there is no male and female'" (Bruce 189). In the text of Galatians, the context may be limited to a discussion of baptism which is open to all (as opposed to circumcision which was the old sign of the law). "But the denial of discrimination which is sacramentally affirmed in baptism holds good for the new existence 'in Christ' in its entirety" (Bruce 190). F. F. Bruce's conclusion seems to be the best, given both content and context:

> No more restriction is implied in Paul's equalizing of the status of male and female in Christ than in his equalizing status of Jew and Gentile, of slave and free person. If in ordinary life existence in Christ is manifested

openly in church fellowship then, if a Gentile may exercise spiritual leadership in church as freely as a Jew, or a slave as freely as a citizen, why not a woman as freely as a man? (190).

Theological Synthesis

The evidence selected and analyzed above creates an argument which is cumulative in force; women should be included, not only in the life of the church, but also in the function of ministry (with appropriate office) in the church. The visionary expression of Jesus' life and ministry with women infers it. The practice and expressions of mutuality of the Apostle Paul indicate the same. The household codes are best thought of as cultural expressions appealed to for pragmatic concerns and in their very qualification indicate an open future. The appeals to "creation order" are not so conclusive as many would like us to believe and at any rate will not support the exclusion of women in ministry. Finally, the idealism of the eschatological age, the age of the Spirit, was certainly understood to have come into being at Pentecost. The implications of the "new creation" were gradually recognized and affirmed in the life and practice of the church. The record of the New Testament is the story of that process.

The question of degrees of implementation which the evidence implies has been argued by some along the lines of function versus office. This line of thinking is that women may function in ministry, but are not to be allowed the formal legitimacy of office. A derivation of this idea is that women be allowed in an office only where they would not be "over men." In this case, a woman always functions under the authority (and so supervision) of a man. Such a distinction seems artificial, especially given the history of distinctions between clergy and laity. Even the Catholic Biblical Association's committee on the Role of Women in Early Christianity makes the following observation:

> In the primitive Church...ministries were complex and in flux, and the different services later incorporated into the priestly ministry were performed by various members of the community....Thus, while Paul could speak of charisms as varying in importance...the New Testament evidence does not indicate that one group controlled or exercised all ministries in the earliest Church. Rather the responsibility for ministry, or service, was shared....The Christian priesthood as we know it began to be established no earlier than the end of the first or the beginning of the second century.

Therefore, the committee recognized that all of the members of the body were understood to have been gifted for up-building ministries (Eph. 4:12; cf. vv. 15-16; 1 Cor. 12:7, 12-31; Rom. 12:4-5). Women did perform ministry and exercise functions that were later defined by offices of ministry. Therefore, the committee concluded, *against* their own church traditions, that "the New Testament evidence, while not decisive by itself, points toward the admission of women to priestly ministry."37

It has already been noted that nowhere does the New Testament speak explicitly of women in church office. Only three discussions in the New Testament even touch on the participation of women in worship services. The basic concern of these texts is for proper conduct. First Corinthians 14 cannot mean that women are not to pray and prophesy (preach) in public assembly (cf. 1 Cor. 11:3-6). The prohibition in 1 Timothy (2:11-15) is unclear and the use of the household codes in 1 Timothy and Titus is the most conservative expression of the codes and runs counter to evidence of some other texts in the Scripture.

The household codes cannot be appealed to for the general supervision of all women functioning in ministry in the church. In their contexts they are applied most often to husbands and wives and are discussions of proper interpersonal relations in the family (and perhaps to that particular family in their experience in worship). If the Apostle Paul were applying his use of the household codes to ministerial function in the church, he never would have mentioned Priscilla's name first in the lists. He was already breaking tradition to mention her name at all, and more to list her as a teacher of Apollos.

While some New Testament texts portray (and react to) new-found freedom for women in Christian communities, other texts apparently restricted women in others along societal conventions. The impetus for change regarding the status of women was lively in the church just as it was for Gentiles and slaves. Participation of women in services of worship and their inclusion in ministry are evidence of that. Some of the early motivation given for teaching acceptance of one's present societal role or status was the conviction that Jesus was returning immediately (e.g., 1 Corinthians 7). In later texts, that motivation was replaced by the need for the tolerance of society and harmony in mixed-religion homes with the instruction about submission.

Despite the variety in the record of the experience of early Christian communities, there is much that leads us to see the early church, when it recognized women in ministry, as self-consciously wrestling with the new realities called into being in the kingdom of God, the messianic kingdom, the age of the Spirit. The best understanding of Scripture invites us to be so visionary today.

BIBLIOGRAPHY

Aburdene, Patricia and Naisbitt, John *Megatrends for Women.* New York: Villard Books, Random House, Inc., 1992.

Aristotle. *Nicomachean Ethics* 5. Translated by H. Rackham. Loeb Classical Library. Cambridge: Harvard University, 1956.

_____. *Politics* I. Translated by H. Rackham. Loeb Classical Library. New York: G. P. Putnam's Sons, 1932.

Balch, David L. "Early Christian Criticism of Patriarchal Authority: 1 Peter 2:11-3:12," *Union Seminary Quarterly Review* 39/3 (1984): 161-173.

_____. "Hellenization/Acculturation in 1 Peter." In *Perspectives on First Peter.* Edited by Charles H. Talbert. Macon, Georgia: Mercer University Press, 1986.

_____. *Let Wives Be Submissive: The Domestic Code in 1 Peter.* The Society of Biblical Literature Monograph Series, no. 26. Chicago: Scholars Press, 1981.

Barrett, C. K. *The First Epistle to the Corinthians.* Harpers New Testament Commentaries. New York: Harper & Row, Publ., 1968.

Bruce, F. F. *The Epistle to the Galatians.* The New International Greek Testament Commentary. Grand Rapids, Mich.: Wm. B. Eerdmans Publ. Co., 1982.

Cassius, Dio. *Roman History 50.* Translated by Earnest Cary. Loeb Classical Library. New York: G. P. Putnam's Sons, 1917.

Catholic Biblical Association's Committee on the Role of Women in Early Christianity, "Women and Priestly Ministry: The New Testament Evidence." *Catholic Biblical Quarterly* 41 (1979).

Elliott, John H. *A Home for the Homeless: A Sociological Exegesis of 1 Peter, Its Situation and Strategy.* Philadelphia: Fortress Press, 1981.

_____. "1 Peter, Its Situation and Strategy: A Discussion with David Balch." In *Perspectives on First Peter,* Edited by Charles H. Talbert. Macon, Georgia: Mercer University Press, 1986.

Fee, Gordon D. *1 and 2 Timothy, Titus* in the *New International Biblical Commentary.* Peabody, Massachusetts: Hendrickson, 1988.

Harkness, Georgia. *Women in Church and Society.* Nashville: Abingdon Press, 1972.

Harnack, Adolph von. *History of Dogma.* Translated by Neil Buchanan. New York: Russell & Russell, 1958.
_____. *The Mission and Expansion of Christianity in the First Three Centuries.* Translated by James Moffatt. New York: G. P. Putnam's Sons, 1908.
Hooker, Morna D. *New Testament Studies* X:410-416.
Jeremias, Joachim. *Jerusalem in the Time of Jesus.* Philadelphia: Fortress Press, 1949.
Jewett, Paul K. *Man as Male and Female.* Grand Rapids, Michigan: Wm. B. Eerdmans Publishing Company, 1975.
_____. *The Ordination of Women.* Grand Rapids, Michigan: Wm. B. Eerdmans Publishing Company, 1980.
Kroeger, Richard Clark and Catherine Clark. *I Suffer Not a Woman.* Grand Rapids, Michigan: Baker Book House, 1992.
Leonard, Juanita Evans, ed., *Called to Minister, Empowered to Serve.* Anderson, Indiana: Warner Press, Inc., 1989.
Martin, Ralph P. *The Spirit and the Congregation.* Grand Rapids, Michigan: Wm. B. Eerdmans Publ. Co., 1984.
Padgett, Alan. "The Pauline Rationale for Submission: Biblical Feminism and the *Hina* Clauses of Titus 2:1-10," *Evangelical Quarterly* 59 (1987).
_____. "Wealthy Women at Ephesus: 1 Timothy 2:8-15 in Social Context" in *Interpretation* 41(1989):19-31.
Pagels, Elaine H. "Paul and Women: A Response to Recent Discussion." *Journal of the American Academy of Religion* 42 (September, 1974): 538-549.
Plutarch. *Advice to Bride and Groom.* Translated by Frank Cole Babbitt. Loeb Classical Library. New York: G. P. Putnam's Sons, 1928.
Scholer, David M. "Women in Ministry." *The Covenant Companion* (December 1983, Febuary 1984).
Senaca. *Moral Epistles* 47. Translated by Richard M. Gummere. Loeb Classical Library. New York: G. P. Putnam's Sons, 1917.
Stendahl, Krister. *The Bible and the Role of Women.* Translated by Emilie T. Sander. Facet Books, Biblical Series 15. Philadelphia: Fortress Press, 1966.
Stern, Rabbi M., ed. *Daily Prayers.* New York: Hebrew Publishing Company, 1928.
Thorsen, Donald. *The Wesleyan Quadrilateral.* Grand Rapids, Michigan: Zondervan, 1990.
Williams, Donald. *The Apostle Paul & Women in the Church.* Regal Books. Ventura, California: GL Publications, 1977.
Wolff, Hans Walter. *Anthropology of the Old Testament.* Philadelphia:

Fortress Press, 1974.

Notes

[1] This article is dedicated to Dr. Marie Strong, my mentor and model, who passed into eternity January 18, 1995, and is now enjoying her reward. As a minister of the gospel for sixty years and as a Bible professor for over thirty years at Church of God (Anderson) colleges, "mother" Marie lived out her ministry in a church body (Church of God) that has sought to be an expression of the vision this article represents. I also take this opportunity to I thank Alan Padgett and Susie Stanley. Alan, in his insight, creativity, and kindness, helped to create the three "P" terms I use here. In the process, he helped me to sharpen my statements. Susie Stanley gave her time, intelligence, and heart in an initial discussion which helped to direct my focus.

[2] I am working from Hepburn's discussion of positivism and particularly from a specific statement made there: "The word 'positive' (probably deriving from a usage of Francis Bacon) is here contrasted with the conjectured: it is associated with the 'given', the data of the sciences" (*The Dictionary of Christian Theology*, 1969 ed., s.v. "Positivism" by R. W. Hepburn).

[3] The argument for the primacy of Scripture does not allow for any negation of Scripture as authority. Thorsen's summary is helpful in establishing this point: "Neither Wesley nor the quadrilateral controverts the primacy of scriptural authority. Those who use the Wesleyan quadrilateral to diminish the primary authority of Scripture misinterpret Wesley's belief and Outler's intention in coining the term 'quadrilateral.' But, while Scripture is viewed as primary, it should not be considered exclusive. Such an understanding would be inappropriate for Wesley as well as for Christian antiquity and the Protestant Reformation" (Don Thorsen, *The Wesleyan Quadrilateral*, Grand Rapids, Michigan: Zondervan Publishing House, 1990, 241).

[4] Those arguments are not simply for the sake of "propriety" however. In each case the purpose for the instruction has to do with a particular situation being addressed. See the following section on house or station codes.

[5] This presentation is a revision of my work "Biblical Precedents for Women in Ministry" in *Called to Minister, Empowered to Serve*, ed. Juanita Evans Leonard (Anderson, Indiana: Warner Press, Inc., 1989), 13-33.

[6] Some, voicing a "positivist" view of Scripture, would claim that no discussion is necessary, not only from the vantage point of Scripture, but also by appealing to church history. I was recently made aware that some think of the issue of women in ministry as a recent concern arising out of the social impulse to radicalism beginning in the 1960s. A knowledge of church history would correct such a misunderstanding, especially a history of the last 150 years. It is ironic that the issue arose primarily as a "low church" phenomenon in America, and as part of a reformation reaction to institutionalized and nominalized religion ("high church") from the 1860s through the turn of the century (with the

156   *The Church That God Intends*

Church of God, Anderson, Indiana, coming to the strongest practical expression of that phenomenon; in 1925—32% of its pastors were women). As these "low church" denominations gained identity and later a certain respectability, radical reform was less a concern, and institutional survival more important. What made such movements (pentecostal, holiness, etc.) suspect to established denominations was precisely such practices as women in ministry, racial integration of worship services, and other "social justice" expressions. But today it is the older denominations which ordain women, and many with a fundamentalist/evangelical perspective seek to distance themselves from such "liberal" practices. On the history of this in the Church of God movement, see "Women in Ministry" in *Centering on Ministry* (Winter 1980, 5:2): 1-2, published by the Center for Pastoral Studies of Anderson University.

[7]Women were listed as property along with cattle. See Georgia Harkness, *Women in Church and Society* (Nashville: Abingdon Press, 1972), 42-52. In general, women did not have the right to personal property; it belonged to husband or father. Exceptions to such mores would have been restricted to the elite. Samuel Terrien, *Till the Heart Sings* (Philadelphia: Fortress Press, 1985), 123.

[8]Rabbi Eliezer ben Hyrkanos, as quoted in Jeremias' *Jerusalem in the Time of Jesus*, 373.

[9]Ibid.

[10]"The right to divorce was exclusively the husband's" (Jeremias, *Jerusalem in the Time of Jesus*, 370). Jeremias adds that public stigma and the requirement that the financial agreement in the marriage contract be honored (that money be returned) acted as a deterrent for hasty divorce. Therefore, the Hillelite provision for capricious divorce was not necessarily fulfilled. This evidence does expose the attitudes of the day, however.

[11]Alan Padgett provides a logical presentation of the contradiction and offers the conclusion that vv. 3-7b are Paul's "description" of the Corinthian position, and vv. 7c-16 are Paul's correctives ("Paul on Women in the Church: The Contradictions of Coiffure in 1 Corinthians 11:2-16" in JSNT 20 [1984]: 69-86—hereafter cited as "Women in the Church"). This follows a pattern common in Paul's writings and certainly occurring in 1 Corinthians 6:12-17 and 8:4-13. Overviews of the debate on 1 Corinthians 11:2-16 are presented by Linda Mercandante in her *From Hierarchy to Equality: A Comparison of Past and Present Interpretations of 1 Cor. 11:2-16* (Vancouver: Regent College, G-M-H Books, 1978) and by Ralph N. Schutt in his "A History of the Interpretation of 1 Corinthians 11:2-16" (MA Thesis, Dallas Theological Seminary, 1978).

[12]Ibid. Veil or *kalymma* does not occur at all in this passage. See Padgett's summary of the evidence in "Women in the Church." Padgett points his readers to the original work in Jerome Murphy-O'Conner, "Sex and Logic in 1 Corinthians 11:2-16," *CBQ* 42 (1980): 483f. He also refers his readers to James B. Hurley, "Did Paul Require Veils or the Silence of Women?," *WJT* 35 (1972-73):190-220; Abel Isaksson, *Marriage and Ministry in the New Temple* (Lund:

Gleerup, 1965), 161-66; W. J. Martin, "1 Corinthians 11:2-16: An Interpretation," in W. W Gasque and R. P. Martin (eds.), *Apostolic History and the Gospel* (Grand Rapids: Eerdmans, 1970), 233.

13Padgett, loc. cit., 71-2. The translation "sign"/"symbol" of authority is disallowed syntactically and semantically, and does not fit the context, which makes an egalitarian appeal. See Padgett's article for in-depth and orderly discussion of this text and possible translations. The phrase *dia tous angelous* is more problematic, but could mean human messengers such as Pricilla who may have visited the church in Corinth. Padgett offers this suggestion with the judgment that "this interpretation...[is] at least as plausible as others," 81-82. *Exousia* was a watchword at Corinth. In response to the misguided grasping for "power" of the Corinthians (or at least of some significant group in the community), as is revealed throughout this correspondence, Paul makes the statement of his own *modus operandi*—his personal example in 1 Cor. 9.

14As many commentators have recognized, the term is Paul's normal word for "authority" and includes the sense of active exercise (and not passive reception of it as some have claimed). See Scholer, "Women in Ministry," 17. See also Barrett, *The First Epistle to the Corinthians*, 253-4 and M. D. Hooker, *New Testament Studies*, x, 410-416.

15*Head* may be a reference to the husband of the woman here. David W. J. Gill proposes that sociological factors of status and dress (including head coverings) are behind this text ("The Importance of Roman Portraiture for Headcoverings in 1 Corinthians 11:2-16," *Tyndale Bulletin* 41.2 [1990]: 245-260). See also R. Oster "When men wore veils to worship: the historical context of 1 Corinthians 11:4" *NTS* 34 (1988): 481-505 and C. L. Thompson "Hairstyles, Headcoverings, and St. Paul: Portraits from Roman Corinth," *Biblical Archaeologist* 51:2 (1989): 99-115.

16Padgett argues that the headship statement is a reference to the position of the Corinthians Paul is attempting to correct: "Thus the debate between Paul and the Corinthians can be seen as a debate over the meaning of 'head'" ("Women in the Church," 78-81). This fits the context; vv. 10-12 are egalitarian statements.

17The summary and critique by Ralph P. Martin of a number of these attempts to explain the apparent inconsistency is helpful. See *The Spirit and the Congregation* (Grand Rapids, Michigan: Wm. B. Eerdmans Co., 1984), 84-88. But some insist that the text is an interpolation and so need not be explained as Paul's instruction. It seems best to begin with the text as it appears and evaluate all possible options for making sense of the text before speculating about its insertion into the letter.

18These women could be sharing in a claim of "special knowledge" which included speculations that there was no actual resurrection of the body but that a spiritual "resurrection" had already occurred at baptism. Such teaching could have prompted Paul's extended reply, beginning with his question, "How can some of you say that there is no resurrection of the body?" (15:12). Their denial of the resurrection lay in the claim that they were raised in baptism—they were "angelic beings" (13:1) after a misapplication of the words of Jesus recorded in Luke 20:35-36. It is also apparent that Paul was responding to a belief in sacramental efficacy (11:17-34; 10:1-22). Such a concept lead to a confusion in the home; as resurrected beings they no longer participated in marriage obligations—they were attempting to live in a state of celibacy in marriage (7:3-5). These heretical teachers (women glossolalics) were to be kept "under control" as the "law" required (*nomos*, meaning *principle* and here referring to Paul's teaching; cf. vs. 37). The meaning of "asking their husbands at home" is a response to the challenge these women presented to their husbands in public assembly. The verb *eperotan,* inquire after, is used in the sense of interrogation, in the same way as they challenged apostolic authority. This interpretation, offered by Martin, fits the larger portrait drawn of the Corinthian church and is supported by a parallel circumstance in 1 Timothy 2:8-15 where arrogant women aspired to be teachers of "things they know not" (teaching gnostic perspectives and presuming the right understanding of the faith) (*The Spirit and the Congregation,* 84-88).

[19]The information about household codes is collected in the following two texts: John H. Elliott, *A Home for the Homeless: A Sociological Exegesis of 1 Peter, Its Situation and Strategy* (Philadelphia: Fortress Press, 1981) and David L. Balch *Let Wives be Submissive: The Domestic Code in 1 Peter* (The Society of Biblical Literature Monograph Series, 26, Chicago: Scholars Press, 1981). The articles most helpful for the argument developed here are by these same two scholars: John H. Elliott, "1 Peter, Its Situation and Strategy: A Discussion with David Balch" in *Perspectives on First Peter,* ed. Charles H. Talbert (Macon, Georgia: Mercer University Press, 1986), 61-78, and David L. Balch, "Hellenization/Acculturation in 1 Peter" in the same text, 79-102. I agree with Balch on the meaning of the "household codes" in the text of 1 Peter as I have presented it in this paper. Much of the following discussion comes from information collected by Balch in his article "Early Christian Criticism of Patriarchal Authority: 1 Peter 2:11-3:12," *Union Seminary Quarterly Review* 39/3 (1984): 161-173.

[20]Emphasis added. Aristotle, *Politics I,* 1253b 7-8; 1254a 22-23, 29-31; 1254b 13-21, trans. H. Rackham (New York: G. P. Putnam's Sons, 1932).

[21]See the discussion of Aristotelian political philosophy in David Balch's "Early Christian Criticism of Patriarchal Authority: 1 Peter 2:11-3:12" in *Union Seminary Quarterly Review,* 39:3 (1984): 161-3.

[22]Aristotle, *Nicomachean Ethics,* V, 1134b 9-18, trans. H. Rackham (LCL, Cambridge: Harvard University), 1956.

[23]This is David Balch's table expressing the household codes. This layout of the passage also reveals the qualification of each aspect of the code. See Balch, "Early Christian Criticism of Patriarchal Authority," 161.

[24]"Household codes" are better defined as "station codes" in 1 Peter. Submission to government is also enjoined.

Women in Ministry: A Biblical Vision   159

25It was not too much later that misogynism developed in full form both in Jewish and Christian literature. Plato's low evaluation of women is well documented and the Greek culture certainly influenced these times. The Jewish Law that a woman was unclean during menstruation (Leviticus 15:19ff.) and the rabbinical speculations on the special culpability of woman in the Fall were developed into negative doctrines and attitudes by some early Church Fathers.

26The technical study of the use of this verb is meticulously presented in *I Suffer Not a Woman* by Richard and Catherine Clark Kroeger (Grand Rapids, Michigan: Baker Book House, 1992), 79-104.

27Alan Padgett presents a compelling presentation for typology as the interpretive approach governing verses 11-15. Both Eve and the Ephesian women are deceived and "saved through childbirth" recalls Genesis 3:15. Eve bears the seed that is at enmity with the serpent. Eve then is made both positive and negative type: "She is an example of deception in verses 13-14 and an example of salvation through childbirth in verse 15," ("Wealthy Women at Ephesus," in *Interpretation* 41:1989, 19-31).

28Richard Clark Kroeger and Catherine Clark Kroeger present a lengthy study of the cultural and historical influences behind the false teaching which included pagan goddess religions and Jewish mythologies and genealogies or origins as gnostic developments. They then read this passage, along with Padgett and others, as a refutation of false teaching (*I Suffer Not a Woman*, 19-23, 62-66, 88-98, 103-177). See also Samuel Terrien, *Till the Heart Sings*, 191-193.

29For example, Phoebe is called a *prostatis* (overseer, guardian, Rom. 16:1-2) which is the term used to indicate elders who *preside* (1 Tim. 5:17), *rule* (Rom. 12:8) or *hold authority over* (1 Thess. 5:12), and which occurs in short instructions to respect and honor leaders or elders.

30The same is true of Titus 2:1-10. David Schroeder, *"Die Haustafeln des Neuen Testament"* (Diss., U. Hamburg, 1959) as summarized by Alan Padgett in "The Pauline Rationale for Submission: Biblical Feminism and the *hina* Clauses of Titus 2:1-10," *Evangelical Quarterly* 59(1987): 44. Padgett refers to the codes in the pastorals as "church codes" because they focus on relationships in the church (not the home).

31As quoted in Balch, 1981, 84.

32I am indebted also to Balch's summary of Harnack's work in "Early Christian Criticism" (Adolph von Harnack, *The Mission and Expansion of Christianity in the First Three Centuries*, trans. James Moffatt (New York: G. P. Putnam's Sons, 1908, I, 19, 31, 77, 314, and *History of Dogma*, trans. Neil Buchanan, New York: Russell and Russell, 1958, I, 45-57, 116-128; II, 169, 174).

33It was not so long ago that Paul's words in Ephesians 6:5-9, Colossians 3:22, and 1 Timothy 6:1-2 were used to support the institution of slavery in the United States of America and elsewhere, and that further, some church teaching included an Aristotelian philosophy of the natural inferiority of some peoples. Subordination to government has also been required by appeal to the station code texts. Martin Luther based his teaching on "Orders of Creation." This theory was behind the Lutheran support of the German state until the fall of the Hohenzollerns. As the Nazis gained power, German Christians justified the Nazi concept of the State by the same means. Karl Barth and other church leaders of the day critiqued such a use of Scripture to define a social order. See summary statement by Adam Miller in *The Role of Women in Today's World* (Anderson, IN: Commission on Social Concerns, 1978), 3-6.

[34]This language, created by Elaine H. Pagels, is an attempt to recognize the motivations for various teachings on women. See her article "Paul and Women: A Response to Recent Discussion," 546. This article comes from her talk at the AAR annual meeting in Chicago in 1973.

[35]Jews were more likely to have been disturbed by the inclusion of slaves as prophets than women. The Old Testament includes no stories of slaves as God's prophets. In contrast, there was a strong tradition of women as prophets (Miriam—Ex. 15:20; Deborah—Jg. 4:4; Huldah—2 Kg. 22:14; the wife of Isaiah—Is. 8:3. Rabbinical tradition refers to seven prophetesses—Sarah, Miriam, Deborah, Hannah, Abigail, Huldah, and Esther. This point is made by Knofel Staton in the paper he presented to the Open Forum of the Church of God and Christian Church (Independent) in Lexington, Kentucky on April 3, 1991, titled "The Teaching in Acts 2:17, 18 and Its Implications for Christian Unity," 7.

[36]The earliest record of this prayer identified thus far is in the work of Rabbi Judah ben Elai, c. A.D. 150. However, the formula itself can be traced back to the Greek Thales who was grateful that he was a man and not a beast, a man and not a woman and a Greek and not a barbarian (Diog. Laert., Vit. Phil. 1.33). Socrates and Plato said substantially the same thing and Aristotle adopts their thinking. As noted earlier, Aristotle's teachings where spread (process of Hellenization) by Alexander the Great in the 300s B. C. His empire covered much of what would later become the Roman empire. See expanded argument in F. F. Bruce, 188-191. It may be noted that the Jewish thanksgiving remains part of the orthodox Jewish expression. It occurs in the popular volume *Daily Prayers*, ed. Rabbi M. Stern (New York: Hebrew Publishing Co., 1928).

[37]"Women and Priestly Ministry: The New Testament Evidence," *Catholic Biblical Quarterly* 41 (1979):609, 613. The whole issue of church tradition must be reviewed given the explicit and astounding new evidence of participation of women in not only ministry, but also office. Against the standard presentations of the Catholic church, Mary Ann Rossi, translating the work of Giorgio Otranto, offers summaries of archaeological findings which portray women functioning as priests and bishops in the early catholic church: (1) fresco of a woman blessing the Eucharist in the Priscilla catacomb in Rome—possibly Priscilla; (2) inscriptions identifying four women by name as priests; (3) a Roman mosaic picturing one of four bishops as a woman, Theodora; and (4) ninth-century correspondence from Bishop Atto confirming that women served the early Church as priests and bishops, but were banned in the fourth century. Evidence such as this raises the question of official suppression of historical evidence of women's leadership in the church. Such evidence has been used for

a popular argument against the Catholic hierarchy by its appearance in *Megatrends for Wome*n by Patricia Aburdene and John Naisbitt (New York: Villard Books, Random House, Inc., 1992), 126.

Chapter 9

"Tell Me the Old, Old Story": An Analysis of Autobiographies by Holiness Women

by
Susie C. Stanley

Given the prominence of women in the early leadership of the Holiness Movement generally, and of Church of God movement (Anderson) in particular, it is crucial to understand certain things. One is the biblical support that exists for such prominence (see chapter 8 by Sharon Clark Pearson). Another is the pattern of social dynamics involved in their church leadership, dynamics quite different from what often is assumed. Such ministering women sometimes have been pictured as docile and unassertive, partly because holiness teaching supposedly worked against women's autonomy and self-reliance. But this study of Susie C. Stanley examines the writings of six of these women, including the ministry of early Church of God leader Mary Cole, and comes to a very different conclusion. Originally published in the Wesleyan Theological Journal (29:1, Spring/fall, 1994) under the title "Tell Me the Old, Old Story": An Analysis of Autobiographies by Holiness Women."

Autobiographies "draw us as surely as we are drawn to the pages of *People* magazine in the dentist's waiting room."[1] The person making this statement, however, apparently had not read some holiness autobiographies! Fortunately, another scholar observes: "There is less concern now with prescriptive definitions of a 'true' or 'good' autobiography."[2] Many holiness autobiographies would be disregarded if literary merit were the sole criterion for determining their value.

Autobiographical theory explores issues such as a psychological analysis of the self, the subversiveness of women's autobiographies, silences in and fictional dimensions of autobiography, and differences between autobiographies written by men and those written by women. This article focuses on the subversive nature of women's autobiographies by examining the writings of six women holiness preachers: Mary Still Adams, Mary Lee Cagle, Mary Cole, Sarah Cooke, Mary A. Glaser, and Alma White.

Another concern for readers of autobiographies is the argument over the death of the author, an argument being waged among literary theorists. Michel Foucault asks: "What matter who's speaking?"[3] Mary Still Adams seemed to be speaking of the death of the author long before this phrase entered the vocabulary of literary criticism. She wrote: "I have also prayed that the sketches and incidents be so clothed with the power of the Holy Ghost that the writer may be lost sight of in the things written."[4] While Foucault and others argue for anonymity, in this study the author must be identified because I am investigating women who challenged woman's sphere. Men were not and are not expected to conform to societal expectations which would confine them to the role of husband or father. The sex of the author is critical.

As the canon has expanded to include autobiographies of women, the tendency has been to establish an exclusive list of literary classics. Margo Culley advises scholars to "resist the temptation to establish a canon of 'great books' by women and to stop there."[5] Estelle Jelinek lists three prominent types of women autobiographers in the late nineteenth century: writers, pioneers who traveled West, and feminists and reformers.[6] Spiritual autobiography should be included as a fourth category. A preliminary bibliography of Wesleyan/Holiness women clergy lists over seventy-five autobiographies. The canon is incomplete without their inclusion. While many would not qualify based on literary merit, the books provide important information about women who rejected the confines of woman's sphere by preaching.

Phebe Davidson in her 1991 dissertation examines spiritual autobiographies written by women, including African American evangelists, but she is unaware of the writings of white women evangelists. She speculates: "Very probably the spiritual narratives of white women are buried somewhere—in odd attics and library archives that no one has gotten around to exploring."[7] This presentation represents an effort to bring some of these primary sources out of the attics or archives and add autobiographies of holiness women to the canon. Since stories by several nineteenth-century African American holiness women have been reprinted and incorporated into the canon, I have omitted them from this analysis.[8]

My purpose is two-fold: to introduce more holiness women's autobiographies into the canon of women's autobiography and to challenge Virginia Brereton's assertion that the doctrine of holiness mitigates against women's quest for equality and autonomy. Brereton claims in her book on women's conversions: "Nor is it difficult to comprehend the disgust which holiness teachings would elicit in those who have worked for and called for greater autonomy and self-reliance for women."[9]

Carolyn Heilbrun bemoans the fact that, contrary to the experience of men, women have no "alternative stories" to function as scripts for them to follow.[10] She argues that men have had access to stories told by other men that offer many possibilities for imitation. Holiness women are exceptions to Heilbrun's generalization in that they had alternative stories written by women such as Madam Guyon, Lady Maxwell, Hester Ann Rogers, and Mary Fletcher. The fact that Madam Guyon's and Hester Ann Rogers' autobiographies remain in print witnesses to their ongoing influence.[11] They continue to serve as alternative stories for holiness women.

Guyon (1648-1717) was a French mystic associated with Quietism. She emphasized a religion of the heart and engaged in an itinerant ministry, sharing with others her understanding of the holy life. John Wesley reprinted her autobiography.

Wesley instructed his followers to write journals, so it is not surprising that many of them left extensive journals, some of which were published after they died. Spiritual autobiography played an important role in Methodist class meetings and worship since exhorters centered on their religious quest, offering the opportunity to formulate an oral account of their lives.

Maxwell, Fletcher, and Rogers were contemporaries of John Wesley and worked with him in various capacities.[12] Lady Maxwell (c.1742-1810) founded a school, operated two Sunday schools, and counseled clergy. She also arranged public worship services, a duty generally conducted by men. Hester Ann Rogers (1756-1794), who was known for her piety, did not preach, but she did lead Methodist classes and bands and called on the sick. Mary Bosanquet Fletcher (1739-1815) was a school mistress who later performed a joint ministry with her husband at Madeley. Besides leading classes and bands, she also preached. She continued her ministries for thirty years after her husband died. Twenty editions of her journal had been printed by 1850.

The autobiographies of Madame Guyon and those women who worked with John Wesley provided alternative stories for holiness women, stories of women who engaged in public ministries. They also played an important role in their spiritual growth. Mary Cole mentioned reading the autobiographies of Mary Fletcher and Hester Ann Rogers, while Sarah Cooke was "wonderfully helped" by reading the lives of these two women.[13] Cooke also listed the life of Lady Maxwell among the books she had read and sprinkled her writing with quotations from Guyon.[14] She expressed dismay when her autobiographies of Fletcher and Guyon were among her possessions lost in the Chicago fire of 1871.[15]

Cooke highlighted the spiritual value of autobiographies: "In traveling, I often meet with Christians of deep experience who received their first religious light, especially on holiness, through the lives and writings of...Mrs. Fletcher, Mrs. H. A. Rogers and others....I know of no books, outside of the Bible, like these autobiographies."[16]

Glaser credited an unnamed autobiographer for spiritual guidance: "I had no one to instruct me in the way of holiness, but I had a book given me to read the experience of a good Christian woman, and while reading it, I was convinced I was living beneath my Christian privileges."[17]

Women were not defensive about writing their life stories because there were precedents within their religious tradition. They addressed an audience who fostered this activity and recognized the importance of autobiographies. Writers such as Adams did not attempt to justify their autobiographical work: "I have no apology to present for offering this sketch of my life-work to the people."[18] Adams appeared to be unaware of the subversive implications of her undertaking. She was not defensive because she was merely doing what others had done. Feminist scholars define women's autobiography as subversive activity which challenges the boundaries established by society to confine women's activities.[19] Cagle illustrated the subversive nature of her writing by adding her sermon "Woman's Right to Preach" at the end of her story.

In the following pages, I will focus briefly on the authors' spiritual journeys and their experience as women preachers, concentrating on their successful efforts to challenge the restrictive sphere that society sought to impose on them. The appendix includes a brief synopsis of the lives of the six women I am considering.

Conversion

Each woman provided an account of her conversion, often recording the conversation that occurred at the time. Their ages at conversion ranged from ten (Adams) to twenty-three (Cooke), with the other four being in their teens. Cole and Cooke were converted through the efforts of siblings while others experienced conversion in a church setting, either a regular service, a revival, or a camp meeting. Cole and White specified the date of their conversions, and two recorded the names of the revivalists under whose preaching they were converted. White is the only one of the six who chronicles a search of several years before experiencing conversion.

These women actively sought conversion, reflecting their Arminian heritage with its emphasis on the freedom of the individual to respond to God's call to salvation. This represents a shift from the spiritual narratives of Puritan women who played a passive part in their conversions, believing that God predestines the elect.[20]

Sanctification

Following conversion, the women pursued the possibility of sanctification, a second distinct work of grace. Like conversion, the quest for sanctification required the seeker to play an active role. Referring to her experience in the third person, Phoebe Palmer wrote: "she had been but a co-worker with God in this matter."[21] Basing their understanding of sanctification on Palmer's theology of holiness, Adams and Cooke used Palmer's "altar" terminology with reference to their own consecration preceding sanctification.[22] The person who counseled Adams shared Palmer's view of how sanctification could be achieved: "The altar sanctifies the gift, and if you have complied with God's requirements, God will and has done his part."[23] Cooke had read Palmer's *Entire Devotion* while Cole mentioned having read *Faith and Its Effects*, also by Palmer.[24]

Cole's account of her experience also follows Palmer's dual emphasis on consecration and faith: "I simply consecrated all a living sacrifice, and reckoned myself dead unto sin and alive unto God through our Lord Jesus Christ. I met the conditions and believed that the work was done."[25] While Cagle "at once sought and obtained the blessing" within three days after "she got the light on holiness,"[26] White spent at least ten years as a seeker before finally claiming the experience by faith. Like Palmer, White testified that no feeling initially accompanied her sanctification.[27] Along with consecration and faith, Cole followed Palmer's admonition to testify and shared her experience with others shortly after she had claimed it.[28]

Call to Preach

Several of the women related sanctification to their subsequent ability to preach. For White, sanctification enabled her to overcome her natural shyness and the "man-fearing spirit" which constrained her when she considered preaching before her sanctification.[29] Cagle's process of consecration included the willingness to preach. She had felt called to preach earlier in life, but with sanctification the call "was stronger than ever before."[30]

Likewise, in her examination of three African American holiness women preachers (Jarena Lee, Zilpha Elaw, and Julia Foote), Liz Stanley stresses the importance of sanctification in legitimizing their "entirely deviant and unwomanly behavior: public preaching and thus taking on a role preserved for a male church hierarchy."[31] Adams viewed sancti-fication as preparation for preaching. Equating the experience of Jesus' followers at Pentecost with sanctification, she quoted Acts 1:4: "And I did not want to go out without being wholly equipped for the warfare. Therefore I made up my mind to do as Christ had commanded his disciples to do, 'tarry at Jerusalem until endowed with power.'"[32] She received "the joy and power of the Holy Ghost" when she was sanctified.[33] Other women also spoke of the power of the Holy Spirit or the power of God which enabled them to preach.[34]

Glaser's preaching focused on her testimony of healing. She reported that her healing occurred on 22 August 1883 after sixteen months of illness; and that on "that memorable night" God spoke to her: "Yes, you are healed, you are to obey my voice in all things; you are to go where I command you, and speak what I give you to speak."[35] She believed God caused her sickness as the means of "crucifying me to become conformed to His own will."[36] Glaser reported: "But if I would shrink from duty, I soon began to lose strength of body."[37] She was convinced her continued good health depended on her willingness to tell others about her healing.

Churches in the holiness movement are among those that value a divine call to ministry. Cole experienced her call when she was about twenty-two. However, it was seven years before she began preaching.[38] As a child and young adult she was sickly. She reported being healed at age twenty-five but did not explain the four-year delay before she entered evangelistic work.

White believed she was called to preach within a week of her conversion, but she assumed her ministry would take place on the mission field.[39] It was not until after her sanctification that she inaugurated her public ministry, eventually founding the Pillar of Fire.

While Cagle professed that God had called her to ministry when she was a child, she initially expected, like White, that she would serve as a missionary since this was the only outlet for women's ministry in her church. In her early twenties, she was reclaimed for Christ, and at that time "the call came clear and plain," but it was a call to preach in the United States rather than a call to the foreign mission field. She preferred the missions option: "To go as a missionary would have been a summer vacation, compared to preaching the gospel at home, for all the people opposed it then."[40]

In the meantime, she married Robert L. Harris, an evangelist, and traveled with him. When her husband was on his deathbed, she bargained with God that she would preach if God healed him. "God seemed to speak back in thunderous tones. 'Whether I heal your husband or not, will you do what I want you to do?' And then came the most bloody battle of all her life—it raged hot and long."[41] She finally answered yes. Her husband subsequently died, and she became co-pastor of the church he had founded in Milan, Tennessee, before initiating her evangelistic ministry and founding numerous other churches.

God called Cooke to the ministry as she was walking across the Madison Street bridge in Chicago:

> The Lord in His tender compassion spoke to me in these never-forgotten words: "Lift up your voice like a trumpet, lift it up and be not afraid. Say unto the people, behold your God." No doubt, from that hour, has ever rested on me about woman's speaking in the churches; no doubt about my own call from His own Spirit to go forth in His name and preach the gospel.[42]

Like Cooke, Cagle and Glaser never doubted their call to ministry.[43] Adams, however, initially tested her call. If the call was valid, she asked that one person respond to her sermon. Six people came to the altar for salvation following her message, so for Adams the matter was settled.[44]

Opposition to Preaching

Each woman experienced opposition to her preaching. In some cases, family members raised objections. Cagle's brother-in-law said that if she preached his children would never call her Aunt again.[45] White's husband often opposed her preaching, but it was generally due to the content of her sermons rather than the act of preaching itself.[46]

Women spoke of opposition in general terms and also provided specific examples. The Methodist church in her hometown refused Cagle the use of its pulpit, so Missionary Baptists offered her their building. She reported that "as usual, she had to preach on 'Women's Right to Preach.'"[47] The phrase "as usual" reveals that this was a common sermon topic. Cole, too, encountered repeated disapproval of her preaching, at least in the early years of her evangelist work: "At nearly every meeting I had to explain the Scriptural teaching on this subject."[48] White also spoke frequently on women in ministry. Glaser reported finding prejudice everywhere. Her strategy was to "leave it all with the Lord as there is a day coming when these things will be made right."[49]

Women often faced hostility in churches where they preached. One Sunday morning, Adams filled Rev. Marshall's pulpit at his request. Entering the sanctuary, she discovered the Bible and a large hymnbook were on a small stand in front of the chancel instead of at their usual location on the pulpit. The church board had moved the books to indicate their displeasure at their pastor's choice of a woman supply preacher. Adams recorded her response to the incident:

> However, I being ignorant of the animosity to our sex, gathered up the ponderous books, and took my place in the pulpit. It was not an hour until I had delivered them my message, and the Lord had so blessed us they did not mind if I was a woman. I will add, if God did cause Aaron's rod to bud and bloom in the hand of Moses, he used me on that day to the opening of the eyes of the blind.[50]

Cooke spoke of one occasion where a man heckled her during her sermon at a soup kitchen in Chicago. Afterward, she passed him as she walked down from the platform and he spoke to her, judging her "a first-rate preacher."[51] He had changed his mind after hearing her preach.

Cagle and Cole encountered rumors intended to discredit their ministry. In Cagle's case, the male ministers in one city spread falsehoods seeking to terminate a revival she was leading. She claimed that "if one-hundredth part that was told on her had been true, she should have been in the penitentiary instead of preaching the gospel." In situations such as this one, she relied on the promise of Isaiah 54:17: "No weapon that is formed against thee shall prosper: and every tongue that shall rise against thee in judgment thou shalt condemn. This is the heritage of the servants of the Lord."[52] Rumors which circulated in Anson, Texas, spread the lie that she had robbed the United States mail, run a house of ill-fame and given away her four children.[53] Cagle reported that it would be impossible to give away her children since she was childless!

Regarding Cole, the rumor circulated that she was one of the James Boys, the famous outlaws, disguised as a woman.[54]

Challenging Woman's Sphere

The women were well aware of the fact that their preaching defied the prevailing attitude that woman's proper place was in the home. Their public activities undermined the social construction of gender based on essentialist claims that women either by "nature" or by "God's design" could not preach. Women preachers escaped the culturally-constructed sphere which had been designed to confine all women, including them, to the home. Several women attributed opposition to the devil. Cole claimed: "The devil tried to carry out his design to defeat the Lord's plan in regard to me."[55] White observed: "Meanwhile, the enemy kept busy in the churches. The pastors said it was a woman's place to stay at home and look after husband and children."[56] Adams recalled the diabolical temptation she faced when she left two children with their father while she went to a preaching engagement:

> The tempter came to me like a flood, saying, "what a fool you are to keep preaching against all odds;" there was not an argument in all his devilish mind which he did not use. He spoke of our poverty and of my leaving my children without a mother's care, suggesting that in all probability they would be dead upon my return home. The more he tempted me the more I looked through faith to God, who then and there turned into a present help in time of need, and filled my soul with power.[57]

God gave her power to combat the temptation to conform to woman's sphere and stay home.

When Adams received calls to preach, she did not stop to ask about leaving her seven children: "Oh! no, but I answered at once, 'here Lord I am, send me.'"[58] If a trustworthy person was not available to watch them, she took her children with her. They never disturbed anyone while she preached. In the fall of 1868 Adams' baby daughter Mattie was deathly ill. When a doctor arrived, Adams left her in his care and went to preach before a congregation of several thousand. After the sermon, she saw her husband in the audience holding the baby. Since he looked happy, she assumed, correctly, that the baby was out of danger.[59]

Glaser was understandably defensive about her situation. Her husband previously had abandoned her. Members of her church and others were unsympathetic when she was "called to leave her family to go to work for the Master."[60] Likewise, her children questioned her decision to leave home to carry out the work God had called her to do.[61] When her oldest daughter wrote that the youngest child, Ellie, who was twelve, was so homesick for her mother that she cried, Glaser's heart ached:

> All I could do was to take it to the Lord in prayer and lay my burden at his feet. I wrote to them as comfortingly as I could, and told them to be reconciled to the will of God. I prayed that they might see and understand that it was the Lord's will to leave them, to give all the honor and praise to Him. He did not answer my prayer.[62]

Along with the belief that her ministry was God's will, Glaser justified her long absences from home on the pragmatic grounds that God blessed her labors. She also argued that she was unable to perform housework due to ill health, but her physical problems disappeared when she engaged in ministry.[63]

While all the women challenged the notion of woman's sphere by preaching, White expanded the argument by contending that women should take an active role in the political arena as well as in the religious realm. She celebrated the passage of suffrage for women in 1920 and supported the Equal Rights Amendment when it was first introduced in Congress.[64] White defined "religious and political equality for the sexes" as part of her church's creed[65] and preached against the chains which kept women "in political and ecclesiastical bondage."[66] Sermon titles on this topic included "Emancipation of Woman" and "Woman's Place in Church and State."[67] She argued:

> Should not old traditions and customs be forgotten, and every effort put forth in this the dawning of a new era to place woman in her intended sphere, that she may help to start society on the upward grade? Women can never be made to feel their responsibility until they share in the ministry of God's Word, and take their places in the legislative bodies of the nations.[68]

Janet Wilson James has referred to several holiness women preachers, including White, as "traditionalists in their concept of woman's place."[69] White's explicit rejection of any ideology which seeks to limit women's activities disqualifies her as a traditionalist. Furthermore, their public speaking, in itself, counteracts the claim that other holiness women preachers were "traditionalists." Their preaching flagrantly challenged the traditional notion that woman's place was in the home.

Women vindicated their preaching by appropriating arguments based on Scripture. Cole and Cooke offered abbreviated versions while Cagle appended her standard sermon on the topic at the end of her autobiography.[70]

Holiness individuals previously had established the Scriptural basis for women preachers.[71] Women relied on this tradition. Defenses for the preaching of women listed Pentecost as the precedent for women's ministry.[72] The women tackled 1 Tim. 2:12 and 1 Cor. 14:34, verses often quoted by opponents of women preachers in their attempt to keep them from preaching.[73] Cole referred to one discussion where "the Lord helped me successfully drive these opposers out of their false positions and to show them they were misusing the Scriptures."[74]

Many leaders in the holiness movement endorsed women's preaching, so women did not face insurmountable barriers to preaching as did women in most mainline denominations. This supportive atmosphere played a positive role in making it possible for women to "hear" and respond to God's call to preach because they were in an environment which affirmed that God could call women to preach. Most holiness believers challenged the ideology of gender prevalent in their society. While they may have accepted the essentialist conceptions of gender which supported the view that differences between the sexes were "God-given" or "natural," they rejected the prevailing belief that because of those differences only men could preach.

Conclusion

Brereton acknowledges that God's authority competes with male authority, but she does not recognize the potential of God's authority effectively undermining male authority.[75] Glaser realized that potential when she asked: "Are we to obey man rather than God? I tell you nay."[76] Cole likewise contended: "But if you are certain of the leadings of the Lord, even if God does not make it plain to others, you may do as God bids you with certainty of success."[77]

Brereton claims that holiness teaching "has also accentuated the kinds of character traits that if embraced would keep women docile and yielding. The sanctified person—like the converted person, only more so—is supposed to be unassertive, selfless, serene, and slow to complain."[78] While some of the adjectives may be applicable to some sanctified women, docile and unassertive hardly describe the women I have examined. Cole's behavior at a camp meeting in Kansas is illustrative.

Rather than announcing who would preach ahead of time, all the preachers sat on the platform. Whoever felt led to preach would stand and walk to the pulpit at the appointed time. On this particular occasion, Cole noticed that another preacher whom she felt should not preach made a move toward the pulpit. She recalled that, at this point: "It came to my mind that if I wanted to obey the Lord and to keep my promise I must act quickly. I asked the Lord to exercise his control and to give me the needed opportunity to obey. He did, and I preached the sermon that day."[79] To do so, she had to race across the platform and beat the other pastor to the pulpit.

Brereton's description of the character traits of holiness teaching does not hold true for Cole or the other women in this study. They were not docile or unassertive. Likewise, these six women undermine her claim that holiness teachings work against women's autonomy and self-reliance. On the contrary, these women, empowered by the Holy Spirit, broke through the invisible barriers of woman's sphere and asserted authority in the public arena by preaching. For this reason, if for no other, they deserve to be added to the canon of women's autobiography.

Notes

[1]Margo Culley, "What a Piece of Work Is 'Woman'! An Introduction," in *American Women's Autobiography: Fea(s)ts of Memory*, ed. Margo Culley (Madison: University of Wisconsin Press, 1992), 3.

[2]Estelle C. Jelinek, *The Tradition of Women's Autobiography: From Antiquity to the Present* (Boston: Twayne Publishers, 1986), 4.

[3]Michel Foucault, *Language, Counter-Memory, Practice: Selected Essays and Interviews*, trans. Donald F. Bouchard and Sherry Simon (Ithaca: Cornell University Press, 1977), 138. He is quoting Samuel Beckett (*Texts for Nothing*, trans. Beckett [London: Calder & Boyars, 1974], 16) whom he cites on page 115. For a brief critique of the author's "death," see Liz Stanley, *The Auto/biographical I: The Theory and Practice of Feminist Auto/Biography* (Manchester: Manchester University Press, 1992), 16-17.

[4]Mary Still Adams, *Autobiography of Mary Still Adams or, "In God We Trust"* (Los Angeles: By the author, 1893), 4.

[5]Margo Culley, "Women's Vernacular Literature: Teaching the Mother Tongue," in *Women's Personal Narratives: Essays in Criticism and Pedagogy*, ed. Leonore Hoffman and Margo Culley (New York: Modern Language Association of America, 1985), 16.

[6]Jelinek, *Tradition of Women's Autobiography*, 97.

[7]Phebe Davidson, "Workings of the Spirit: Religious Impulse in Selected Autobiographies of American Women." Ph.D. diss. (Rutgers, The State University of New Jersey, 1991), 294.

[8]Several African American women's autobiographies have been reprinted. For instance, for the autobiographies of Jarena Lee, Zilpha Elaw and Julia Foote, see William L. Andrews, ed., *Sisters of the Spirit: Three Black Women's*

An Analysis of Autobiographies by Holiness Women 175

Autobiographies of the Nineteenth Century (Bloomington: Indiana University Press), 1986; *Spiritual Narrative: Maria W. Stewart, Jarena Lee, Julia Foote and Virginia W. Broughton* (New York: Oxford University Press, 1988); Frances Smith Foster, "Neither Auction Block nor Pedestal: The Life and Religious Experience of Jarena Lee, A Coloured Lady," in *The Female Autograph: Theory and Practice of Autobiography from the Tenth to the Twentieth Century,* ed. Domna C. Stanton (Chicago: University of Chicago Press, 1984), 126-151; and Amanda Smith, *An Autobiography: The Story of the Lord's Dealings with Mrs. Amanda Smith, The Colored Evangelist* (Chicago: Meyer & Brothers, Publishers, 1893; reprint, New York: Garland Publishing, 1987). Davidson considers Lee and Smith (Davidson, "Workings of the Spirit," 219-246, 251-292).

[9]Virginia Lieson Brereton, *From Sin to Salvation: Stories of Women's Conversions, 1800 to the Present* (Bloomington: Indiana University Press, 1991), 67.

[10]Carolyn G. Heilbrun, *Writing a Woman's Life* (New York: Ballantine Books, 1988), 39.

[11]Allegheny Publications (2161 Woodsdale Road, Salem, Ohio 44460) advertised *Autobiography of Mrs. Hester Ann Rogers* and *Madame Guyon-Autobiography* in its June 1993 catalog.

[12]Biographical information on Maxwell, Rogers, and Fletcher is from Earl Kent Brown's sketches of these women in *Women of Mr. Wesley's Methodism* (New York: Edwin Mellen Press, 1983), 116-154, 199-217.

[13]Mary Cole, *Trials and Triumphs of Faith* (Anderson, Ind.: Gospel Trumpet Company, 1914), 68; and Sarah A. Cooke, *The Handmaiden of the Lord, or Wayside Sketches* (Chicago: T. B. Arnold, Publisher, 1896), 37.

[14]Cooke, *Handmaiden of the Lord,* 49, 53, 65, 158, 197 and 284.

[15]Ibid., 45.

[16]Ibid., 108.

[17]Mary A. Glaser, *Wonderful Leadings* (Allenton, Pa.: By the author, 1893), 14.

[18]Adams, *Autobiography,* 3.

[19]Leah D. Hewill, *Autobiographical Tightropes* (Lincoln: University of Nebraska Press, 1990), 3; and Culley, "What a Piece of Work," 9.

[20]Narratives of Puritan women were generally edited by clergy and published after the women died. Ann Taves, "Self and God in the Early Published Memoirs of New England Women," in *American Women's Autobiography: Fea(s)ts of Memory,* 57.

[21]Phoebe Palmer, *The Way of Holiness with Notes by the Way: Being a Narrative of Religious Experience Resulting from a Determination To Be a Bible Christian* (New York: Lane and C. B. Tippett, 1845, 2nd ed.; reprint, Salem, Ohio: Schmul Publishing Co., 1988), 14.

[22]Adams, *Autobiography,* 67; and Cooke, *Handmaiden of the Lord,* 40, 259.

[23]Adams, *Autobiography,* 67.

[24]Cooke, *Handmaiden of the Lord,* 259; and Cole, *Trials and Triumphs,* 68.

[25]Cole, *Trials and Triumphs,* 41.

[26] Mary Lee Cagle, *Life and Work of Mary Lee Cagle: An Autobiography* (Kansas City, Mo.: Nazarene Publishing House, 1928), 21. For the most part, Cagle wrote in the third person.

[27] Alma White, *The Story of My Life and the Pillar of Fire*, 5 vols. (Zarephath, N.J.: Pillar of Fire, 1935-1943), 1:410, 2:206.

[28] Cole, *Trials and Triumphs*, 42.

[29] White, *Story of My Life*, 1:354.

[30] Cagle, *Life and Work*, 21.

[31] Liz Stanley, *Auto/biographical I*, 112; see also 113-114. Likewise, Andrews highlights the relationship between sanctification and preaching for these three women. They traced their self-reliance to their sanctification experience which, to them, offered "ample sanction for acts that many, especially men, would judge as rebelliously self-assertive and destructive of good order in the church" (Andrews, *Sisters of the Spirit*, 14).

[32] Adams, *Autobiography*, 66-67.

[33] Ibid., 5. Brereton speaks of power in the context of pentecostalism (Brereton, *From Sin to Salvation*, 95). However, she claims that power "is a word seldom emphasized in the narratives in connection with the experience of conversion or holiness" (70). For information on the relationship between sanctification and power, see Susie Stanley, "Empowered Foremothers: Wesleyan/Holiness Women Speak to Today's Christian Feminists," *Wesleyan Theological Journal* 24 (1989): 103-116; and Susie Stanley, "What Sanctification Means to Me: 'Holiness Is Power'" in *Sanctification: Discussion Papers in Preparation for the Fourth International Dialogue on Doctrinal Issues* (Anderson, Ind.: Anderson University School of Theology, 1989), 17-24.

[34] For instance, see Cooke, *Handmaiden of the Lord*, 22.

[35] Glaser, *Wonderful Leadings*, 54-55. For many women, the call to preach was related to personal illness. Examples include Margery Kempe, Jarena Lee, and Amanda Smith (Davidson, "Workings of the Spirit," 271).

[36] Glaser, *Wonderful Leadings*, 48. Glaser believed that "sin always lies at the root of sickness" (70). White believed that physical problems sometimes were a message from God trying to show her something (White, *Story of My Life*, 3:66).

[37] Glaser, *Wonderful Leadings*, 117.

[38] Cole, *Trials and Triumphs*, 50-52, 54.

[39] White, *Story of My Life*, 1:161.

[40] Cagle, *Life and Work*, 21.

[41] Ibid., 24.

[42] Cooke, *Handmaiden of the Lord*, 34.

[43] Cagle, *Life and Work*, 24; and Glaser, *Wonderful Leadings*, 143.

[44] Adams, *Autobiography*, 99.

[45] Cagle, *Life and Work*, 21.

[46] For two examples, see White, *Story of My Life*, 1:429, 2:64-65. Kent White questioned his wife's interpretation of Scripture.

[47] Cagle, *Life and Work*, 61.

⁴⁸Cole, *Trials and Triumphs*, 85.
⁴⁹Glaser, *Wonderful Leadings*, 145.
⁵⁰Adams, *Autobiography*, 147.
⁵¹Cooke, *Handmaiden of the Lord*, 129.
⁵²Cagle, *Life and Work*, 80.
⁵³Ibid., 72.
⁵⁴Cole, *Trials and Triumphs*, 106.
⁵⁵Ibid., 52.
⁵⁶White, *Story of My Life*, 2:30.
⁵⁷Adams, *Autobiography*, 133.
⁵⁸Ibid., 3.
⁵⁹Ibid., 150-151.
⁶⁰Glaser, *Wonderful Leadings*, 31. She recorded criticism in several other places (97-98, 105, 120-121, 139, 151).
⁶¹Ibid., 93, 120.
⁶²Ibid., 135.
⁶³Ibid., 138, 152.
⁶⁴White, *Story of My Life*, 4:236-237 and 5:329.
⁶⁵Ibid., 5:229.
⁶⁶Ibid., 5:276, 301.
⁶⁷Ibid., 5:32 and 5:86.
⁶⁸Ibid., 5:132-3; see also 5:144.
⁶⁹Janet Wilson James, "Women in American Religious History: An Overview," in *Women in American Religion*, ed. Janet Wilson James (Philadelphia: University of Pennsylvania Press, 1980), 21. Phoebe Palmer, Catherine Booth, Mary Cole and Amanda Smith were other holiness women whom Wilson James classified as "traditionalists."
⁷⁰Cole, *Trials and Triumphs*, 85-87; Cooke, *Handmaiden of the Lord*, 174-177; and Cagle, *Life and Work*, 160-176. White sprinkled references throughout her autobiography (White, *Story of My Life*, 2:237, 4:208, 5:125-128, 5:146, 5:277, and 5:284-5). Adams is the only woman in the sample who does not provide a Biblical defense for women preachers in her autobiography.
⁷¹Phoebe Palmer, *The Promise of the Father; or, A Neglected Specialty of the Last Days* (Boston: Henry V. Degen, 1859); reprint, Salem, Ohio: Schmul Publishers, n.d.; and Catherine Booth, *Female Ministry: Woman's Right to Preach the Gospel* (n.p., 1859; reprint, New York: Salvation Army Supplies Printing and Publishing Department, 1975).
⁷²Cooke, *Handmaiden of the Lord*, 174; Cole, *Trials and Triumphs*, 86; Cagle, *Life and Work*, 161, 169-171; White, *Story of My Life*, 3:236; and Glaser, *Wonderful Leadings*, 62. This was the only Scriptural defense that Glaser provided.
⁷³Cooke, *Handmaiden of the Lord*, 175-176; and Cagle, 174-175.
⁷⁴Cole, *Trials and Triumphs*, 85-86.
⁷⁵Brereton, *From Sin to Salvation*, 93.
⁷⁶Glaser, *Wonderful Leadings*, 104. The Biblical source for Glaser's position is:

"We must obey God rather than men" (Acts 5:29).
 [77]Cole, *Trials and Triumphs*, 191.
 [78]Brereton, *From Sin to Salvation*, 93.
 [79]Cole, *Trials and Triumphs*, 191.

Part III
Divided World; United Church

Chapter 10

A Wesleyan Perspective on Christian Unity

by
David L. Cubie

Several key theological perspectives of the Church of God movement (Anderson) were shaped in and by the American Wesleyan/Holiness tradition of the late nineteenth-century. In regard to the crucial subject of Christian unity, David L. Cubie, not associated with the Church of God movement, traces this doctrine in the Wesleyan/Holiness tradition and places the views of Daniel S. Warner (1842-1895) of the Church of God in this broad context. While nearly all holiness groups affirm or at least tolerate denominationalism, Warner and the movement that he helped pioneer championed a more radical anti-creedalism and anti-denominationalism. Originally appeared in the Wesleyan Theological Journal *(33:2, Fall, 1998).*

In the 1960s the evangelical conscience was awakened to its larger social responsibility and came to the conviction that in reacting against the social gospel it had rejected an essential part of its heritage. Another aspect which it now needs to re-evaluate is its ecumenical heritage. Conservative evangelical churches need to rethink their present stance and consider serious participation in the ecumenical dialogue among Christians. Ecumenism is a Christian heritage and mandate and in some form a constantly recurring practice, whether admitted or not. Today, the barriers are breaking down between the ancient churches of the East and West and between them and the Protestant churches. We are now seeing the possibility of the church being one again. The question is, What will be the shape of a united church? Conservative evangelicals have a contribution which is needed for the process. After all, evangelicals do confess, along with the rest of Christendom, "I believe in the holy catholic church."

Whatever one may think of the present state of the ecumenical movement, it must not be forgotten that its original impetus was evangelical and evangelistic. Within Protestantism, Pietism had nurtured an interdenominational evangelistic and missionary concern which transcended the rivalries of the seventeenth century. This was furthered by the interdenominational evangelism, first of Whitefield, Wesley, and Zinzendorf in the eighteenth century, and then of Charles G. Finney and Dwight L. Moody in the nineteenth. Its organizational roots include the Evangelical Alliance and the Student Volunteer Movement for Foreign Missions. Negatively, the Evangelical Alliance had in its first invitation in 1846 the call to combat "popery and Puseyism,"[1] a reference to the Anglo-Catholic movement which was then seeking to restore the Anglican Communion to its ancient Catholic relationships and discipline. More importantly, it was remarkable for the breadth of participation and spirit of unity among its participants. The Student Volunteer Movement for Foreign Missions, which was organized in 1886 by missionary statesman John R. Mott, originated at evangelist Dwight L. Moody's summer conference at Mt. Hermon, Massachusetts.[2]

Though generally not a part of the ecumenical movement as such, present evangelicalism is not without its ecumenical concerns. Two examples are the interconfessional National Association of Evangelicals and the more narrowly defined Christian Holiness Partnership, which is composed of those churches within the Wesleyan holiness heritage. Furthermore, who can overlook the contribution of Billy Graham in the latter half of this century to a broadly defined interdenominational evangelicalism, including his sponsorship of international and interdenominational conferences on evangelism. Nevertheless, though participating in interdenominational evangelism, contemporary conservative Protestantism is at best skeptical about wide ecumenical possibilities. Some are hostile even to such ventures as Billy Graham's crusades and the 1974 World Congress on Evangelism convened in Switzerland.

An Extensive Ecumenical Heritage

Within evangelicalism, the Wesleyan tradition has an extensive ecumenical heritage. It has a special perspective on Christian unity and a unique contribution to make. From its beginning in Wesley's time, it has combined both realism and optimism. It affirms both human sinfulness and perfectability, but the latter only by grace. Thus, however the church may be divided, the optimism of grace affirms that God can reunite it. This balance has not always been kept in mind. The proclamation of Christian unity which was frequently found in the nineteenth century holiness movement did not keep it from divisiveness; some, in the name of sanctification and unity, radically separated from existing churches.

This contrast of a search for unity with the experience of separation goes back to John Wesley who, while affirming loyalty to the Church of England, gradually created a distinct ecclesiastical structure. Wesley's United Societies developed out of the pragmatic need to find a way of preserving the fruits of the Evangelical Revival. The intent was that the United Societies should be a nurturing agency within the Church of England. Nevertheless, as early as 1755, because of the hostility of many Anglican clergy, many of Wesley's preachers, lay and clerical, urged him to form a Methodist Church of England. His brother Charles led the opposition to this move. As a result, John wrote his strong argument against separation, "Ought We to Separate From the Church of England?"[3] Throughout his life he looked for a dynamic *via media* in which separation and union could both operate in creative tension. The Methodist people were to be nurtured unto holiness and they in turn were to reform the church and nation. John Wesley's announced purpose was "to spread scriptural holiness throughout the land."

Wesley's ability to hold views of both union and separation was possible because for him the visible church existed under two formulationsóthe church composed of believers and the church composed of all those who profess faith; or, to restate the contrast, the church as nurturing and the church as sacramental community. The latter is the organizational church which contains those who profess to believe but who may not in fact be believers. This is the church "which is by law established" and which has prescribed doctrines, sacraments, and polity. Although Wesley himself at times blurs the distinction between the church of believers and that of those who profess to believe, his distinction must be kept in mind if one is to understand his teaching that the believer should separate from the wicked yet also receive the sacraments from an unworthy minister of a parish church.[4] Wesley held that the unworthy priest or church cannot interrupt the sacramental grace which is communicated by God through these ordained channels. He taught and practiced frequent communion. This practice, though not his reason for it, more than protected him legally from the accusation that he had separated from the church. Wesley reminded his opponents that, measured by the law which defined an Anglican as one who received communion at least once each year, he was more of an Anglican than they were.

The seeds of both division and non-sacramentalism were present. Although Wesley maintained that the sacraments should be administered by ordained clergy, the office of preaching was open to laypersons. What developed was a preaching order of ministry which was organized under Wesley's leadership and yet was independent of the sacramental and parish ministry. This independence was enhanced by his view that preaching and the nurturing community take primacy over the sacraments as a means toward salvation.[5] The primacy of preaching was indicated by his description of the prophet (or preacher) as one sent directly by God, while the priest is one whose office and ministries, although ordained by God, are commissioned by humanity.[6] He is not talking here of an ordained preaching ministry, but about his Methodist preachers. God calls whom he will, especially when the ordinary (the ordained) channels are befouled by the wicked and indifferent.

This organizational distinction was furthered also by Wesley's view of the church. The church exists in two overlapping but not necessarily identical forms—the church of believers and the church of those who profess to believe. Both the church of believers (the nurturing community) and the church composed of those who profess faith (the organized church) exist in parallel forms that are universal and particular. Thus, the church composed as "a congregation of believers"[7] includes: (1) At its outermost circle all those who fear God and work righteousness (Acts 10:36): "[He] *is accepted of Him*—Through Christ, though he knows him not." Just how inclusive this is Wesley makes clear. He continues, "The assertion is express, and admits of no exception. He is in the favour of God, whether enjoying his written word and ordinances or not."[8] (2) Within this wider kingdom is the church universal, defined as "all the persons in the universe whom God hath so called out of the world as to entitle them to the preceding character ['the saints,' 'the holy persons']; as to be 'one body,' united by 'one Spirit;' having 'one faith, one hope, one baptism; one God and Father of all.....'"[9] (3) Then follow the more particular forms: the true national Church "....those members, of the Universal Church who are inhabitants of England." This and this alone is the Church of England, according to....the Apostle,"[10] and at its most particular, the nurturing fellowship, including the Methodists.

The church of believers has all the characteristics of the church, being both catholic, existing since the beginning, and holy. As catholic, "their Teachers are the proper successors of those who have delivered down, through all generations, the faith once delivered to the saints; and their members have true spiritual communion with the 'one holy' society of true believers: Consequently, although they are not the whole 'people

A Wesleyan Perspective on Christian Unity   185

of God,' yet are they an undeniable part of his people."[11] The unity, character, and orthodoxy of this church of believers, whether in whole or in part, are kept inviolate because every member is holy: "And this church is....'ever holy;' for no unholy man can possibly be a member of it. It is ever orthodox;' so is every holy man, in all things necessary to salvation: 'Secured against error,' in things essential, 'by the perpetual presence of Christ; and ever directed by the Spirit of truth,' in the truth that is after godliness."[12] This holiness, though not final, is actual, "because every member thereof is holy, though in different degrees."[13]

Similarly, the church defined as "a congregation professing to believe" also exists from its general and inclusive to its most particular expressions, including the Methodists. One reason why Wesley opposed a new church organization was that he knew of no group that had separated to form a church that had retained the characteristics of a church of believers for very long. Wesley, although proud of his Methodists and the century-long revival, saw signs of decay among them. Thus, the church defined as "a congregation professing to believe" is for Wesley the "Church....taken, in a looser sense....."[14]

Wesley sometimes blurs the distinction between the church composed of believers and that composed of those who profess to believe, especially when he uses the definition of the church given in the Thirty-Nine Articles of the Church of England. From the latter he gained his way of referring to the true church as "a congregation of believers"[15] or "a company of faithful (or believing) people: *coetus credentium*."[16] Alhough he can say about the Nineteenth Article[17] that it is "a true logical definition, containing both the essence and the properties of a church,"[18] he was not completely happy with it. He observed, "I will not undertake to defend the accuracy of this definition."[19] His reason—it excluded the Church of Rome in which "neither is the pure word of God preached, nor the sacraments duly administered."[20] In this we see his ecumenical concern for the church as it is constituted in history.

For Wesley, "the Church of those who profess to believe," the church with its ordinances and ministry, whether Anglican or Roman, gains its validity from the true church within, rather than from apostolic succession or any other external sign. Even those who truly believe can have wrong opinions. Thus he says:

> Whoever they are that have "one Spirit, one hope, one Lord, one faith, one God and Father of all," I can easily bear with their holding wrong opinions, yea, and superstitious modes of worship: Nor would I, on these accounts, scruple still to include them within the pale of the catholic

Church; neither would I have any objection to receive them, if they desired it, as members of the Church of England.[21]

Though he would not anathematize any part of the church as it exists in history, he gave priority to that which was nurturing believers.

The priority which he gives to the converting and nurturing church rather than the sacramental community is further advanced by the term "congregation" used in the Thirty-Nine Articles. This is a term which is common to most of Protestantism. Luther's term was a *gemeinschaft* (a community). Thus, the church in its essential visible manifestation, rather than being the church universal, is a community. This *congregation* or *community* can be as broad as the Church of England or the Church of Rome, or as narrow as a local congregation. This concept of congregation is the ideological context by which Wesley gives priority to the nurturing community over against the universal or national church.

For Wesley, the nurturing community is the primary expression of the visible church. As he stated, "Be zealous for *the Church*; more especially for that particular branch thereof wherein your lot is cast."[22] The face-to-face characteristic of this "particular branch" he expressed by the clause, "that his [the Lord's] followers may….provoke one another to love, holy tempers, and good works….."[23] The terms "a congregation" and "a company" as nurturing societies can be and are extended to Wesley's United Societies. It is not a long step from this concept of congregation to what is later called a denomination. This development is evident in Wesley's reference in his later correspondence to the Methodists as "the Churches of God that are under my care."[24]

This primacy of the nurturing community is also evident in Wesley's defense in 1748 against the accusation of schism when he gathered his converts into societies. He answered, "That which never existed, cannot be destroyed."[25] He further asks, indicating the ideal character of that fellowship, "Who watched over them in love? Who marked their growth in grace? Who advised and exhorted them from time to time? Who prayed with them and for them, as they had need? This, and this alone, is Christian fellowship:…. are not the bulk of the parishioners a mere rope of sand?"[26] As he observed in 1754 in *Notes* on 1 Corinthians 11:18, "the indulging any temper contrary to this tender care of each other is the true Scriptural schism." Commenting on 1 Corinthians 12:25, he stated, "Schism here, means the want of this tender care for each other. It undoubtedly means an alienation of affection in any of them toward their brethren….."[27] This same definition is behind his rebuke of those who were dividing the societies in the name of Christian perfection:

"Beware of schism, of making a rent in the Church of Christ. That inward disunion, the members ceasing to have a reciprocal love for another, (1 Cor. xii.25,) is the very root of all contention, and every outward separation."[28]

Although schism may be defined as "causeless separation from a body of living Christians," Wesley states that this is only "in a remote sense" schism.[29] His preferred definition is that schism "is not a separation *from*....but a separation *in* a Church," that is, "destroying Christian fellowship" on the local level.[30] Separation "from a body of living Christians, with whom we were before united," he says, "is a grievous breach of the law of love."[31] Wesley's principle application of his opposition to schism was in regard to division within his societies. Thus he warns:

> .... if you would avoid schism, observe every rule of the Society, and of the Bands, for conscience' sake. Never omit meeting your Class or Band; never absent yourself from any public meeting. These are the very sinews of our Society; and whatever weakens, or tends to weaken, our regard for these, or our exactness in attending them, strikes at the very root of our community....[32]

Wesley's concern for the nurturing community does not imply that his concept of church government was congregational. His concept of government was that of a modified episcopacy through ordained presbyters. For most of Wesley's followers, the nurturing community was the United Societies under Wesley. Avoiding the term "church" for the societies through most of his life, preferring "the people called Methodists," in the 1780s he referred to them as "the Churches of God that are under my care."[33] The people responded by referring to him as their "dear father."[34] Although originally believing in apostolic succession, after reading Lord Peter King and Bishop Edward Stillingfleet in 1745,[35] Wesley came to the conviction that true succession and spiritual authority is through the church of believers, that is, through "a succession of Pastors and Teachers; men both divinely appointed, and divinely assisted; for they convert sinners to God...."[36] Prudentially valuing the episcopacy of the Church of England, he nonetheless insisted, "I firmly believe I am a scriptural *episcopos* as much as any man in England,"[37] a pragmatic concept, yet one that affirmed that he, too, along with his preacher-prophets, had an "extra-ordinary" calling.

Wesley's concept of the visible church being essentially manifest as congregations fit the realities of the church in the world. There were many factors other than human sinfulness which made organizational unity difficult, if not impossible. For one, evangelism cannot be limited to church structure. As he affirmed, "It is God alone who can cast out Satan [defined as bringing "sinners to repentance...from all evil to all good"].....And he sends whom he will send upon this great work...."[38] The "extra-ordinary" work of God transcends structure and results in some degree of pluralism within the church. Thus, "whensoever our Lord is pleased to send many labourers into his harvest, they cannot all act in subordination to, or connexion with, each other. Nay, they cannot all have personal acquaintance with, nor be so much as known to, one another."[39] Furthermore, he saw no evidence that people would ever think alike: they never had in the past, not even the apostles.[40] His Lockean concept of the mind led him to affirm, "I can no more think, than I can see or hear, as I will."[41] Thus in 1765, while in dialogue with his Calvinistic opponents, he asserted, "allow me liberty of conscience herein:....Allow me to use....["imputed righteousness....and the like expressions"] just as often as I judge it preferable to any other expression....."[42] He also saw that physical and temporal distance are obstacles. As he stated: "It is not easy for the same persons, when they speak of the same thing at a considerable distance of time, to use exactly the same expressions, even though they retain the same sentiments: How then can we be rigorous in requiring others to use just the same expressions with us?"[43]

That which distressed Wesley the most was that physical separation could end the practice of love. As he wrote in 1749 in his sermon "Catholic Spirit":

> ....although a difference in opinions or modes of worship may prevent an entire external union; yet need it prevent our union in affection? Though we cannot think alike, may we not love alike? May we not be of one heart, though we are not of one opinion? Without all doubt, we may. Herein all the children of God may unite, notwithstanding these smaller differences. These remaining as they are, they may forward one another in love and in good works.[44]

Earlier that year (July 18, 1749), in his "Letter to a Roman Catholic," he expressed the same sentiments:

> I hope to see you in heaven. And if I practise the religion above described, you dare not say I shall go to hell. You cannot think so. None can persuade you to it. Your own conscience tells you the contrary. Then, if we cannot as yet think alike in all things, at least we may love alike. Herein we cannot possibly do amiss. For of one point none can doubt a moment, "God is love; and he that dwelleth in love, dwelleth in God, and God in him."[45]

For Wesley, "catholic" love within the church transcends organizational distinctions, whether Roman or Anglican, or within the Anglican Church, whether parish church, Lady Huntingdon's Calvinistic societies, or his own Arminian societies. The concept of congregation permitted pluralism within unity.

In the Holiness Movement in America, the visible expression of the church was also essentially that of a congregation or community. Within American Methodism the idea continued that the particular church or denomination is in some sense a congregation. A term commonly used to describe the particular denomination was "connection."[46] This term was used in part in reaction to the tight ecclesiastical discipline imposed by Asbury and his successors in the Methodist episcopacy. Asbury had a somewhat restorationist concept that the Methodist Episcopal Church was the re-founding of a primitive episcopacy. In his organization of Methodism, he left little room for local autonomy. For him, "the apostolic order of things" was a church called and disciplined under a hierarchy of itinerant bishops, who appointed itinerant presiding elders, who in turn appointed the stationing of itinerant preachers, who then formed and gave order to a local congregation.[47] For Asbury, justification for the establishment of the Methodist Episcopal Church of America was that he was restoring the primitive order of things, which he contrasts with the English hierarchy (and by implication all other resident territorial practices of episcopacy) which is "a settled, man made, worldly ministry under no discipline...."[48] Asbury was far more episcopal than Wesley, for whom the method of government was a prudential, practical judgment. For Asbury, episcopacy was primitive and apostolic.

In response, whether as reaction or out of fundamental conviction, those groups who broke away from Methodism from the division led by James O'Kelly of 1792 to those of the modern Holiness Movement affirmed the concept that the primary visible expression of the church of God in history was that of the congregation, especially the local congregation. Thus, in 1801 O'Kelly led his followers quickly from their first name, the Republican Methodist Church, to the name Christian Church, which eventually became part of the Congregational Christian Churches, and now part of the United Church of Christ. Congregational concepts were also adopted by the Methodist Protestants in their separation in 1820. Thus it was that when the Wesleyan Methodist Connection, now named the Wesleyan Church, came into existence in 1843 over the Methodist Episcopal Church's attempt to silence the abolitionists, they chose a congregational polity. The Wesleyans saw themselves as a connection of local congregations. According to one of the original leaders, Luther Lee, the designation "connection" was consciously chosen. Lee asserts:

> The term "connection" was approved by all, as it expresses a principle. Single Christian congregations are held to be Churches, in a New Testament sense, and that all these Christian congregations, collectively, are not a Church. All the Wesleyan Methodist churches in America are not a Church, but being connected by a central organization, they are a connection of Churches, hence we call ourselves "The Wesleyan Methodist Connection of America."[49]

After the Civil War, when the leaders sought to unite the movement with the Methodist Protestants and failed, this congregational polity made it possible for about half of the local congregations to unite with the Methodist Protestants or return to the Methodist Episcopal Church. Luther Lee himself, though having argued so strongly for congregational principles, returned to the Methodist Episcopal Church.[50] More recently, when the Wesleyan Methodists united with the Pilgrim Holiness Church (1966) to form the Wesleyan Church, the Allegheny Conference, one of the original conferences, chose to remain out of the union in order, among other reasons, to protect these congregational principles.[51]

The connectional concept was not limited to the Wesleyans. Samuel Wakefield, a theologian of the Methodist Episcopal Church, in his *Christian Theology* published in 1858, describes the emerging government of the primitive Christian Church as existing "in that form which, in modern times, we should call a religious connection, subject to a common government."[52] John Miley, quoting from the Methodist Articles (Article XIII), applies the term "congregation" more directly to the idea of denomination. About the statement, "The visible Church of Christ is a congregation of faithful men," he comments, "This is properly the definition of a local church, but, so far as the more vital facts are concerned, may be accepted as the definition of a denominational church, however numerous the local churches which it comprises."[53] Thus we can see that, from the perspective of these nineteenth-century Methodists, denominations, instead of being divisions within the Christian church, are connections of local churches or a congregating within the larger church. Thus the nineteenth century Methodist concept of the visible church is not essentially different from that of the Baptist or Congregational churches, only that for continuity, conservation, protection, and evangelism the connection was made a little tighter.

At the close of the nineteenth century, when the holiness revival within Methodism began to wane and the Methodist hierarchy began to discipline the proponents of entire sanctification, many of those disciplined opted for varied forms of congregational polity. The variety of church concepts within the Wesleyan-Holiness tradition ranged from the radical anti-creedalism and anti-denominationalism of Daniel S. Warner, who, though never a Methodist, had adopted the Methodist doctrine of sanctification,[54] to the modified Methodism of Phineas F. Bresee, a former Methodist pastor and presiding elder. Possibly the only exception to this choice of congregational polity were the Free Methodists (1860), who retained the Methodist Episcopal discipline, its method of assigning pastors, and eventually even gave the title of Bishop to their General Superintendents. Warner's ecclesiology was derived from the Church of God, General Eldership, founded by John Winebrenner, of which Warner had been a minister. Warner was disciplined by this group for preaching the Methodist doctrine of entire sanctification.

Existing concurrently throughout the nineteenth century with the congregational and connectional concept was a widespread concern for Christian unity. While separating from the churches of their origin, those who departed, whether as "forced-outers" or "come-outers," affirmed a call to Christian unity. In fact, their discipline by the parent body was often in relationship to some interdenominational activity which they then sought to defend. As Barton W. Stone was disciplined in 1804 by the Lexington Presbytery for his Methodist theology and participation in the Kentucky revival, a spontaneous and widespread cooperative effort by Presbyterians and Methodists, so also the abolitionists and the participants in the later holiness revival were disciplined because their cooperative life with others was seen as a threat to Methodist unity and discipline. The very furtherance of the message across denominational lines created independent agencies beyond denominational control, which became objects of suspicion. Those opposing their activities slowly but surely managed to enable the denominational machinery to curtail them and reduce their influence. Some in Methodism, after building large congregations, were ostracized to small parishes by unfriendly bishops. It should be noted, though, that part of this ostracism reflected tension within the episcopacy. Holiness bishops such as Bishop Willard F. Mallalieu placed holiness advocates in positions of influence only to have them removed, as was Bresee by Bishop John H. Vincent, who opposed the message. The reaction to denominational control was also expressed by a radical interdenominationalism. Thus B. W. Huckabee, editor of the *Pentecostal Advocate*, in 1907 called for a radical "interdenominationalism." On the one hand, he could write in an editorial entitled "Inter-denominationalism Essential to Christian Unity": "Inter-denominationalism is one of the most prominent ideas in the tho't of the Christian world to-day, and as the churches become more spiritual, this idea becomes more prominent. The spirit of strict and exclusive denominationalism always indicates a falling temperature in the church."[55] On the other hand:

> We would most emphatically declare that denominationalism (with accent on the "ism,") has ever tended toward exclusiveness and away from unity. What is known as the Church Federation movement offers but little hope of immediate, or even ultimate success. This movement is like a body without life, a form without power. The movement is dominated by the ministry, the hardest of all men to unite. It is not now and never will be but little more than a semblance of unity. What the courtesies of social life are to the social life, the Church Federation is to the church—mostly gush.[56]

Huckabee was not thinking narrowly. Among the interdenominational figures whom he mentions with admiration are Henry Ward Beecher, DeWitt Talmage, Charles H. Spurgeon, and D. L. Moody. These and others "in thought and service and sentiment belong to nothing short of a whole race."[57]

As with Wesley, although in a variety of different ways, the founders of the Holiness Movement advocated the unity of the church and expressed abhorrence for division while even they were separating from Methodism. Part of the reason for this is that the doctrine of Christian perfection has both separatist and unitive themes in it; the separation of holiness—"...come out from them, and be separate from them...." (2 Cor. 6:17, RSV)—and the unity of love—"...put on love, which binds everything together in perfect harmony" (Col. 3:14, RSV). Wesley unites sanctification and love and defines and redefines sanctification as love. As he states in his sermon "On Patience" (1784), "Love is the sum of Christian sanctification."[58] Divine perfection and the heavenly kingdom are also defined as love. Commenting on 1 John 4:8, Wesley wrote:

> *God is love.* This little sentence brought St. John more sweetness, even in the time he was writing it, than the whole world can bring. God is often styled holy, righteous, wise: but not holiness, righteousness, or wisdom in the abstract: as he is said to be love: intimating that this is his darling, his reigning attribute; the attribute that sheds an amiable glory on all his other perfections.[59]

Because love so consistently defines sanctification for Wesley, we need to examine its influence on the issue of separation versus unity. Actually, the problems of separation and unity are faced and systematized in a complex concept of love formulated by Augustine and expanded by the medieval church. In his doctrine of the church, Wesley uses no less than six different terms of love: (1) *Storge*: love or loyalty to family and nation; (2) Benevolence or beneficence: an equal compassion and care for all; (3) Complacence, delight: love for the saints; (4) Reciprocal love: the *Koinonia* fellowship love which is the opposite of schism; (5) Catholic love: a comprehensive love which includes all the preceding, plus an ecumenical concern for the whole church; (6) Zeal: love aflame, but prioritized according to the degree of value in its object.[60] It is by the interlay of these concepts that Wesley explains and defends his relationship to the Church of England. Complacence, the delight love reserved for the saints, for those who are worthy objects of love, is that which most tended toward separation from the unworthy. Though Wesley refused to accept the deduction from this that one ought to separate from the church, he did teach that one ought to separate from wicked persons in the church and only "converse with them, First, on business...; Secondly, when courtesy requires it....Thirdly, when we have a reasonable hope of doing them good."[61]

In his sermon, "In What Sense We Are to Leave the World" (1784), which is an exposition of Paul's words, "...come out from among them, and be ye separate, saith the Lord, and touch not the unclean thing" (2 Cor. 6:17, RSV), Wesley wrote against "conversing with ungodly ["unholy"] men when there is no necessity...."[62] His reason is that "As Christ can have *no concord* with Belial; so a believer in him can have no concord with an unbeliever. It is absurd to imagine that any true union or concord should be between two persons, while one of them remains in the darkness, and the other walks in the light."[63] Wesley limits the application to unholy individuals and denies that it means separation from the church. To apply this scripture to the church, Wesley says, "is totally foreign to the design of the Apostle....[To have] done so....would have been a flat contradiction both to the example and precept of their Master. For although the Jewish Church was then full as *unclean*, as unholy both inwardly and outwardly, as any Christian Church now upon earth, yet our Lord constantly attended the service of it."[64]

Despite Wesley's reference to some leaders in the church as "mitered infidels," he never went so far as some nineteenth century holiness advocates, such as D. S. Warner, as to refer to any church as Babylon, even though he could say that in them "the kingdoms of Christ and of the world, were so strangely and unnaturally blended together...."[65]

Despite this possibility that complacence love might require some degree of distance, Wesley's overwhelming emphasis in love is toward unity. Thus, *storge*-love argued for loyalty to the national church; benevolence-love required compassion for the sinners within the church, including ungodly clergy, and Catholic love required not only complacence toward "the saints....and upon such as excel in virtue"[66] but also equal mercy to all mankind. Beyond the varied concepts of love used by Wesley, central to Wesley's thought was his conviction that "It is the nature of love to unite us together...."[67] The sermon "On Schism" (1786) is in part a defense of the emerging separation of the Methodists from the national church, but it also has the other thrust of seeking to keep the Methodists in that church. That which argues against division is that a principle purpose of the church is to develop love. Unity works love and love naturally seeks unity. Thus he wrote in his sermon "On Zeal" (1781) "that his followers may the more effectually provoke one another to love, holy tempers, and good works, our blessed Lord has united them together in one body, the Church, dispersed all over the earth...."[68] He was especially concerned for unity among the evangelical clergy in the Church of England, whether Calvinistic or Arminian in theology, despite indifference and open opposition to the idea by many who were Calvinistic. As he wrote in 1761 to George Downing, chaplain to the Earl of Dartmouth, the friend of Lady Huntingdon, "For many years [twenty] I have been labouring after this—labouring to unite, not scatter, the messengers of God. Not that I want anything from them....But I want all to be helpful to each other, and all the world to know we are so. Let them know who is on the Lord's side."[69] His efforts increased during that decade, even seeking to establish a basis of union. He records in his Journal for March 16, 1764: "I met several serious Clergymen. I have long desired that there might be an open, avowed union between all who preach those fundamental truths, Original Sin, and Justification by Faith, producing inward and outward holiness...."[70] He was even willing to push aside differences over "absolute decrees on the one hand, and perfection on the other."[71] What he wanted was an active expression of "Catholic love." To this end he proposed that they

- Remove hindrances out of the way? Not judge one another ....
- Love as brethren? Think well of and honour one another?...
- Speak respectfully, honourably, kindly of each other...?
- This is the union which I have long sought after....[72]

This union never materialized. Instead, division increased. Near the end of the century, when the number of Calvinistic clergy in the Church of England were increasing, those who spoke against Christian perfection were included with the Arians, those Anglican clergy that Methodists ought not to have to hear if they were persuaded that hearing them would be spiritually damaging.[73]

Holiness Movement Views of Christian Unity

The nineteenth-century holiness advocate who expressed the most radical disparity between concepts of separation and unity was Daniel S. Warner, the primary pioneer of the Church of God (Anderson, Indiana). While affirming love-unity and often using the term sanctification in this context, he also called for a radical separation. He blamed divisiveness on denominationalism and called for a new unity outside of and separated from the denominations. Despite this emphasis on separatism, for Warner entire sanctification automatically removes divisiveness and brings unity. As he could sing,

> How sweet this bond of perfectness,
> The wondrous love of Jesus!
> A pure foretaste of heaven's bliss,
> O fellowship so precious!
>
> O brethren, how this perfect love
> Unites us all in Jesus!
> One heart, and soul, and mind we prove
> The union heaven gave us.[74]

Just as jubilant is his celebration of the saints' separation from denominational Babylon and Babel and their return to the church of God:

> Lo! The ransomed are returning,
> Robed in shining crystal white,
> Leaping, shouting home to Zion,
> Happy in the ev'ning light.
>
> Free from Babel, in the Spirit
> Free to worship God aright,
> Joy and gladness we're receiving,
> Oh, how sweet this ev'ning light.[75]

For him, sanctification "makes God's children one" and ends sectarian relationships:

> The chief object of God's ministers is to "perfect the saints." And when perfected in love and holiness, they come into the "unity of the faith once delivered unto the saints"....The pure in heart have perfect fellowship....There is therefore no real cause of division but sin ....
>
> To know the truth is our privilege, to teach the truth, our duty. But to have fellowship with the pure and upright of heart is an involuntary and spontaneous fact. Sects are the result of carnality; nothing but perfect holiness destroys carnality and thus removes both sectism and its cause. The fire of God's love saves the soul, harmonizes all hearts that receive it, leads them into perfect and uniform obedience to all truth, and drives afar all who refuse to pass through its purging fire and gain the plan of holy fellowship.[76]

Observe that last clause—"and drives afar all who refuse to pass through its purging fire and gain the plan of holy fellowship." The church in which Warner most frequently mentions holding holiness crusades and then dividing the sanctified from "sect Babylon" is the United Brethren (now part of the United Methodist Church), a church which at that time was very open to the holiness message.[77]

In 1907, Andrew L. Byers, also of the Church of God movement, described a sectarian holiness which is preached to attempt to keep the true holiness people in the denominations. As he recollects:

> A kind of sectarian holiness arose. In many instances of God's people leaving the Protestant denominations, the sectarian ministers immediately began to preach holiness, thinking to retain those who were leaving. It is evident, of course, that sectarian holiness is not the genuine, for the latter is certainly destructive of sectarian elements. Holiness associations were formed in which members could still retain membership in their respective denominations. False holiness became more plentiful than the true.[78]

Not all within the denominations were denounced as false professors. As Byers added, "The idea of leaving the churches (so called) began to be strongly denounced by many who had themselves accepted holiness."[79] Thus Byers follows his affirmation that "Entire sanctification makes God's people one, in accordance with the prayer of our Saviour....'Sanctify them through thy truth...that they all may be one.'"[80]

In all fairness, it must be stated that Warner's radicalism against denominational holiness was spurred by his rejection by those organizing interdenominational holiness associations. He records:

We had supposed that fellowship and cooperation should not exclude any person or truth that is in Christ Jesus....We were positively denied membership on the ground of not adhering to any sect."[81]

In part because of his teaching that unity is an essential characteristic of the church, the Church of God (Anderson) has developed an ecumenical concern. It is officially represented on the Faith and Order Commission of the National Council of Churches. Ecclesiologically, its doctrine of unity is based on a radical congregational concept of the visible church, but its vision takes in the entire church.[82]

All other major components of the Holiness Movement affirm or at least tolerate denominationalism. Unity among them is more usually defined in terms of fraternal relationships. Though they may be, as Donald Dayton describes them, "fiercely ecumenical within their own circle,"[83] there is no theological drive toward unity. Attuned to the congregational concept of the visible church, they yet affirm the practical necessity of organization, both nationally and internationally. From this perspective, denominations are not schisms, but a gathering of God's people. Phineas F. Bresee, a founder of the Church of the Nazarene, likens the denominations to regiments within the armed forces.[84] Those thrust out of the older churches could gather and become a regiment of God's army, loyalty to which would not be radically different from the *esprit de corps* of the Marines, Air Force, Navy, or Army. Similarly, Bresee uses the analogy of families: "As a community may be one with many families, so the Church may be one with many altars and many organizations, not against each other, but all—in their divinely led way—getting men saved and filling the world with the light of God. Those who follow not us may yet do miracles in his name."[85]

Though affirming, as does Warner, that "the carnal nature...the 'old man' must be destroyed in order that there may be Christly unity in any form,"[86] Bresee argues that "Any other general union than that of the Spirit is impracticable and undesirable. Denominationalism is, no doubt, a providential condition of the Church."[87] Furthermore, possibly in opposition to the ideas of Warner, he states that "Those who fill the air with their cry of 'Church unity' are usually, as far as we have been able to observe, not those who have the spirit of unity with anybody but themselves, whose hand is against every man, who would tear down every instituted thing which God has been and is using to bring forward some vague notion of their own."[88] To Bresee, divisiveness was not expressed by any new denominational organization of the church.

In one of his last addresses to the students at what is now Point Loma Nazarene College, Bresee advocated "a strong, pure, healthy denom-i--na-tionalism," and added, "We have no sympathy with the twaddle which attempts to express the desire that all people be of one denomination. We believe that such is neither providential nor desirable. We are lovingly, earnestly, intensely denominational. If any one wishes to criticize his own denomination, this is a poor place for him to do it."[89] Olin Alfred Curtis, a Methodist theologian at the beginning of the twentieth century, took the same view: "I am out of sympathy with every effort to crush out the denominational churches in the name of Christian unity."[90] Bresee further affirmed in the context of "healthy denominationalism" that "Any students...will, we trust, find no effort here to proselyte, but to help each of them to be 'a man of God, perfect, throughly furnished unto every good work.'"[91]

Of all of the founders of the Church of the Nazarene, Bresee probably spent the least time outside of a denominational structure, and that only briefly in the Peniel Mission from which he was shut out by the proprietors. Nevertheless, as he notes, he had no intention of starting a denomination. Instead, what he planned was to start a "center of holy fire," a center where the poor would not only be evangelized, but nurtured. What he gave as his goal for the Peniel Mission was applied to the Church of the Nazarene: that "those that are being gathered in, who have no church affiliation, who need care and fellowship, and a place to find a home and work"[92] would have a church home. This practical view was also arrived at by William Booth, founder of the Salvation Army, who wrote:

> My first idea...was simply to get people saved, and send them to the churches. This proved at the outset impracticable. 1st.. They would not go when sent. 2nd. They were not wanted. And 3rd. We wanted some of them ourselves, to help us in the business of saving others. We were thus driven to providing for the converts ourselves.[93]

This gathering in and creating a home implies that the fundamental expression of the visible church is the local church. Bresee stated: "The unity of the whole church is of the spirit and not necessarily of organization, but local organization, in the Spirit, and under the providence of God is a necessity."[94] His view of the church was essentially congregational. Though not using the term congregation as broadly as Wesley, the extension of congregation is present in his concept of denomination. The Church of the Nazarene began as a single church in 1895, but in 1899 Bresee wrote, "...it is something more than a single church, having several churches."[95] To those who opposed his "organization of new Churches," Bresee answered: "this is a painful exhibition of ecclesiasticism. Are there to be no new centers of spiritual power? Must the Holy Ghost be put into the leading strings of any dead or half dead organization? Are we to put ourselves over against the coming of the Spirit of God and raising up in these days as in the past new agencies to save and bless men?"[96] In essence, then, a denomination is a connection of local churches which are gathered together for evangelism and Christian nurture. Through evangelism other congregations are added to that connection.

The language of apostasy was used against the Methodist Church. Bresee himself does not use the "language of Babylon" against it, but one of Bresee's colleagues, F. E. Hill, in 1899, used apocalyptic language to denounce "The iron heel of this monster ecclesiasticism." He added, "Soon, if not already, will the many thousands who are yet under the power of the lion begin to lose courage; rent and torn by the ravages of the beast, their carcasses will be strewn by the way, and within a very few years will be numbered in the valley of the dry bones, within the castle yard of ecclesiasticism. It is coming! O, it is coming!"[97] Between 1899-1901 Bresee frequently referred to the Methodist Church as that "ecclesiasticism." His strongest words refer to it as a "hating church." He asks, "Why does not the [Methodist] church love the holiness people? Is it not to 'spread scriptural holiness' that the [Methodist] church has been raised up? It now dislikes holiness people because it has become worldly....To have souls converted that they might be made holy would only increase the hatred of this hating church."[98]

More typical of Bresee's thought is the need of new bottles for new wine. He asks, "Why the Salvation Army?... Why the Keswick movement?... Why the organization...of Holiness Associations...[and] why the Church of the Nazarene?" He answers:

> Simply because of the failure of Methodism to continue to preach the pure Pauline doctrines of entire sanctification, by a second definite work of grace. Simply because Methodism will not brook holiness revivals, and be an agency for the distinctive work of entire sanctification. It is no child's play to go out under the blue sky, without means and agencies and try to create them. Anybody would prefer to work through and in connection with those already formed.[99]

J. B. Chapman, Nazarene General Superintendent between 1928 and 1944, continued Bresee's vision of the church. He equated denominations with districts in a church:

As to denominations, these are justified on just the same ground that district organizations are justified within the bounds of a denomination, and on the same ground that separate organizations of the same districts are set up to meet the needs of the people and to utilize the forces of the Church for the propagation of the gospel....Denominations or local churches which separate from their fellows without due reason are a hindrance to the unity of the Church, and as such are to be bewailed. When the separation is caused by someone's desire for the "pre-eminence" or by some other personal and narrow consideration, it becomes a faction and is injurious to the work of God. But when the grounds of separation are justifiable, separation and organization serve to preserve and promote the work of God in the world. This has been abundantly proved by experience, as well as by the precepts and examples of the early apostles and disciples (Acts 15:36-41).[100]

To such founding fathers of the Holiness Movement as William Booth, Luther Lee, Daniel S. Warner, Phineas F. Bresee, Seth Rees, and Martin Wells Knapp, Christian unity was very important. But this was not the only option. A pedestrian denominationalism expressed by the term "the Church of his choice," an expression used in the General Conference Proceedings of 1915 of the Wesleyan Methodist Church, was also evident.[101] Bresee, though expressing voluntarism, had a different emphasis. He wrote, "...you can....find your providential place."[102]

What is the solution to division within the Christian church, at least for those who take Jesus' prayer seriously—"that they may be one"? We have seen Bresee's: that true unity is of the Spirit, and that denominations can be and ought to become healthy manifestations of that church in which "when each part is working properly, makes bodily growth and upbuilds itself in love" (Eph. 4:16, RSV). Bresee himself, though, was not adverse to inviting other holiness bodies to unite. The pages of *The Nazarene Messenger* advocate the union of like-minded denominations and local churches into a national holiness church.[103]

Nevertheless, because unity is of the Spirit, there is no sense of ought, that working toward universal Christian unity is our obligation. In fact, the history of the denominational idea includes not only the ideal that we are all one, but also the disturbing reality of divisiveness and hostility. As in the armed services, *esprit de corps* has too frequently included an unhealthy rivalry. The danger of denominationalism is that the prayer of Christ—"that they may be one"—is not taken seriously. The inner life of a local church or a denomination or even an association of churches may devolve into sectarianism.

These conditions were not unanticipated. Criticisms of sectarianism were given and teachings advanced both to avoid division and to heal those divisions existing. Wesley expresses his criticism in the poem "Primitive Christianity" (c. 1743):

> Ye different sects, who all declare
> "Lo! Here is Christ!" or "Christ is there!"
> Your stronger proofs divinely give,
> And show me where the Christians live.
>
> Your claim, alas! Ye cannot prove;
> Ye want the genuine mark of love:
> Thou only, Lord, thine own canst show,
> For sure thou hast a church below.[104]

Throughout the nineteenth century denominational rivalries both existed and were criticized. D. S. Warner combined Methodist pietism with radical denominationalism and attacked what he called "sectism," not, of course, recognizing that his radical come-outism was itself sectarian. During the same period (c. 1875) A. C. Northcutt, a Methodist minister and son of one who participated in the great Kentucky revival of 1805, suggested that denominational rivalry interferes with evangelism. As he wrote, "It is strange that the Churches did not realize that God had a controversy with them for their own uncharitable bearing toward each other. I have no doubt but that he was waiting for them to lay aside their wicked prejudices, that he might consistently honor and bless them in the work of saving men."[105] Northcutt was convinced that the revival of 1805 was a result of Presbyterians and Methodists laying aside their differences for the purpose of evangelism.

Principles from the Wesleyan/Holiness Tradition

Though denominations of the Wesleyan tradition are, like others, usually content with separation, there has existed within that tradition a vision that unity ought to be the reality among Christians. This is evident in the eschatological vision of the church present in Wesley and which was to reappear at different times. For Wesley, the future was to be a restoration of the church at Pentecost, when Christians held all things in common and "were all of one heart and soul." Thus he wrote:

Then shall "the times of universal refreshment come from the presence of the Lord." The grand "Pentecost" shall "fully come," and "devout men in every nation under heaven," however distant in place from each other, shall "all be filled with the Holy Ghost;" and they will "continue steadfast in the Apostles' doctrine, and in the fellowship, and in the breaking of bread, and in prayers;" they will "eat their meat"...."with gladness and singleness of heart..." and they will be "all of one heart and of one soul." The natural, necessary consequence of this will be the same as it was in the beginning of the Christian Church: "None of them will say, that aught of the things which he possesses is his own; but they will have all things common."[106]

A similar eschatological hope was expressed by Francis Asbury. On August 19, 1806, after the united effort of Methodists and Presbyterians to evangelize had come to an end, he wrote: "Friendship and good fellowship seem to be done away between the Methodists and Presbyterians; few of the latter will attend our meetings now; well, let them feed their flocks apart; and let not Judah vex Ephraim, or Ephraim, Judah; and may it thus remain, until the two sticks become one in the Lord's hands."[107] John Fletcher, vicar of Madeley, whom Wesley had designated his successor, similarly looked for God to raise "a pentecostal Church again in the earth."[108]

Eschatological hopes were also high at the turn of the twentieth century. The interdenominational holiness revival encouraged a widespread expectation that denominations would disappear in a mighty outpouring of the Spirit. This expectation occurred among both pre- and post-millenialists and included H. B. Huckabee, early editor of the *Pentecostal Advocate*, a paper that later merged into the *Herald of Holiness*, the official magazine of The Church of the Nazarene. Huckabee prescribed an interdenominationalism in which denominations would disappear, in which "creeds will be forgotten in the common zeal for souls....Unity will be the common aim...and the heated discussions on dogma and cult will be antiquated by common consent."[109] Others who were also captured by this eschatological vision were A. M. Hills of The Church of the Nazarene[110] and Martin Wells Knapp and Seth Rees, fathers of the Pilgrim Holiness Church, which in 1966 united with the Wesleyan Methodists.[111] As noted, Bresee saw the promoters of unity as being divisive and was wary of them.

Can present-day Wesleyan evangelicals make a contribution toward the future which God is planning? If so, they must not lay aside those discoveries of grace which have come out of their own traditions. There are some principles from the Wesleyan evangelical tradition which would need to be affirmed if dialogue is to be meaningful.

First: An essential Protestant principle, held by Wesley and most of his followers, is that the fundamental visible expression of the Church of Christ, the Holy Catholic Church, is the congregation. But at present, the concept of unity seems to be working from the concept of episcopacy and hierarchy. An evangelical entrance into the dialogue should of necessity involve a re-evaluation of the congregational principle, both in its local and extended senses.

Second: Unity to be unity must be pursued within the context of spiritual renewal. The emphasis on Pentecost in this tradition coordinates unity with the coming of the Holy Spirit: "they were all together in one place" (Acts 2:1, RSV), reminders that unity must be of the Spirit who brings unity, is present in it, and prepares each of us for it by inward cleansing.

Third: A principle that has largely been lost by the present holiness denominations, except for the Church of God (Anderson), is that the unity of the church is an essential part of eschatological hope. For Wesley, it is a keystone in his attempt to develop his Methodists into an evangelizing and nurturing society within the Church of England without separation from it. His hope was that they would stay in the church for its reformation. Though he saw separation as in some sense inevitable, it was never to be the last word.

Fourth: Wesley's catholic love and eschatological vision bring into focus an essentially Pauline concept regarding the restoration of apostate churches. If apostate Israel can be restored, so also can apostate churches (see Rom. 11:23, 28). We must have a profound hope for one another and for reconciliation. This is an affirmation of God's sanctifying grace within his church, which is to be purified and made one (Eph. 5:27, 31-32). Apostate must always be seen as an adverb and not as an adjective, as a description of action rather than a description of kind or nature. Thus every church, however it may have strayed from gospel principles, is still "beloved for the sake of their forefathers." God is able "to graft them in again" (Rom. 11:28, 23, RSV). The future must include reconciliation, both with God and with each other.

Fifth: Any concept of unity, including unity as an eschatological concept, must include room for departure and return. Either the sins of the church or God's call to repentance may result in separation. As Wesley and Bresee remind us, "God can send by whom He will send," and God can raise up "new centers of holy fire." Paul's call to "come out from among them, and be separate from them" (2 Cor. 6:17, RSV) is in tension with his call to unity (Eph. 4:1-16) because it affirms that some divisions may be necessary. Though Anglo-Catholics may affirm that the Reformation was a mistake, can evangelicals? Can black Christians ever deny their ancestral exodus from the white churches which were so filled with hostility and paternalism? Both the Reformation and the post-Civil War exodus were necessary within the context of the church of their times. Departure may be necessary for the evangelizing and nurturing of God's sheep. In any unity there may be the oppressed or neglected other sheep of God. With Wesley, we must affirm the priority of love, and in that context the priority of evangelism and nurture.[112] People are more than structure. To paraphrase Jesus' words, religious structure was made for man, not man for structure (Mark 2:27).

It should be recognized that, as long as time lasts or our Lord delays his return, division will continue. Man by nature is hostile and divisive. Evangelism, whether of children within the church or pagans from without, brings injured people who defend themselves by identification with a group. Though Christians are called away from a party spirit, they are called away from that which inevitably is there. John 17 and Ephesians 2 and 4 suggest that sanctification is in part a process of moving from innate hostility to the unity of love. The Corinthian church provides an interesting study of division and reconciliation. According to the witness of the Epistle of Clement, the Corinthians had overcome the divisiveness described in Paul's letters, a division between Paul, Apollos, and Cephas, and had become notable for their righteousness. But a new generation found a new occasion for division. This time it was between those siding with young leaders against the elders, reminding us that each generation must be transformed from hostility to unity.[113]

Yet return must take place. The greatest tragedy is not the fact of division, but that we tend to justify and perpetuate it. We need some of Wesley's vision which saw beyond the difficulties of the present to God's future. Wesley taught an eschatology of return. Thus in 1783, just the year before he ordained Coke for the superintendency of the church in America, he saw even separation as the beginning of God's general renewal. Thus, out of what to him was a necessary division, he envisioned God's sanctifying restoration of his church: "he will never intermit this blessed work of his Spirit, until he has fulfilled all his promises...."[114]

Sixth: I would affirm the importance of the doctrine of Christian perfection in the quest for unity. Realized eschatology, whatever others may mean by that term, is essentially a perfectionist concept. It affirms that God is able to accomplish in the human situation, whether personal, ecclesiastical, or in the world, that which is impossible to "mere man." Perfection is a grace term which affirms that what God has promised will be brought to pass. God may need to bring these promises to pass over and over again. Nevertheless, the church must exist within the context of God's restoration and renewal and both aspire to and claim this promise of unity. The church, which is constantly reborn with every generation and even with every individual who is "added daily to the church," must always aspire to and work toward Christian unity.

Seventh: Finally, I would affirm that the unity of the church must first of all be understood as a unity of love. The structures which contribute to unity may well vary from time to time, but structure must never be allowed to limit love. The nature of love, according to Paul, is that it "binds everything together in perfect harmony" (Col. 3:14, RSV). It is inclusive rather than exclusive. It does not require a loyalty which keeps others out. The molecules of the body of Christ cannot be bound together by coercion. Denominations ought to never make exclusive claims on local congregations united with it for mission and discipline. Love requires a network of relationships, not only in corporate structures but also in free relationships with other churches. Perfect love cannot be exclusive, but must be catholic in its relationship. Love to be love must have the liberty of sovereignty. Love is "the royal law" and "the law of liberty" (Jas. 2:8, 1:25, RSV). Unity, then, must not be seen exclusively in structural terms, but in the networking of God's people in loving relationships for the evangelism of the lost for the nurture of God's people and for the advancement of God's kingdom.

Christian unity is the ongoing work of God in the church. Young men and women, as well as fathers and mothers in Christ (1 John 2:12-14), will need to become incarnate in the human divisiveness, not to advance division, but to bring the church and the world out of sectarianism to the perfection of unity in Christ. The Christian church exists both to be one and to participate in God's work of making all one.

Notes

[1] Ernest R. Sandeen, "The Distinctiveness of American Denominationalism: A Case Study of the 1846 Evangelical Alliance," *Church History*, 45 (June 1976):223.

[2] Williston Walker and Richard A. Norris, et al., *A History of the Christian*

Church, 4th ed. (New York: Charles Scribner's Sons, 1985), 687.

³Frank Baker, *John Wesley and the Church of England* (Nashville: Abingdon Press, 1970), Appendix, 326-40.

⁴John Wesley, Sermons: "In What Sense We Are to Leave the World" (1784) and "On Attending the Church Service" (1788), *The Works of Rev. John Wesley, A.M.*, ed. Thomas Jackson, 14 vols. (London: Wesleyan Methodist Book Room, 1829; rpt. 5th ed. Wesleyan Conference Office, London, 1872), 6:464-75 and 7:174-85. Hereinafter referred to as *Works*.

⁵Sermon, "The Ministerial office," (Bicentennial Edition, "Prophets and Priests") (1789 or 1790), 11, 17-18; *Works*, 7:273-81.

⁶Ibid., 6.

⁷Sermon, "Of the Church" (1786), 16; *Works*, 6:396.

⁸John Wesley, *Explanatory Notes Upon the New Testament*, 1754 (Naperville, IL: Alec R. Allenson, Inc., rpt. 1958). Hereinafter referred to as *Notes*.

⁹Sermon, "Of the Church" (1786), 14; *Works*, 6:395-96; see also 7, 394.

¹⁰Ibid., 17, 397.

¹¹Letter, "To the Editor of the London Chronicle" (Feb. 19, 1761), *Works*, 3:42.

¹²Ibid.

¹³Sermon, "Of the Church" (1786), 28; *Works*, 6:400.

¹⁴"Minutes of Some Late Conversations," Conversation I (1744); June 27, Q. 1; *Works*, 8:280.

¹⁵Sermon, "Of the Church" (1786), 16: *Works*, 6:392-401.

¹⁶"An Earnest Appeal...." (1743), 76; *The Works of John Wesley*, vol. 11, ed. Gerald R. Cragg (Oxford: Oxford University Press, 1975), 77. Hereinafter referred to as *Works*, Bicentennial ed. Cragg notes that Wesley's memory was imprecise in this place. The original Latin was *coetus fidelium*; 77, n. 1.

¹⁷Wesley refers to this article as "our Twentieth Article" in his letter to his brother Charles, *Works*, 13:254; see also *The Letters of the Rev. John Wesley, A.M.*, ed. John Telford, 8 vols. (London: The Epworth Press, 1931), 7:285. Hereinafter referred to as Telford, *Letters*.

¹⁸Letter, "To Charles Wesley" (Aug. 19, 1785), *Works*, 13:254; see also Telford, *Letters*, 7:285.

¹⁹Sermon, "Of the Church" (1786), 19, *Works*, 6:397.

²⁰Ibid.

²¹Ibid.

²²Sermon, "On Zeal" (1781; 1758 Smith), 3.9, *Works*, 7:65.

²³*Works*, 8:251.

²⁴Letters, "To Jonathan Crowther" (May 10, 1789), *Letters, 8:136;* "To Richard Whatcoat" (Nov. 1790), ibid., 249. See Baker, *John Wesley and the Church of England*, 284-85, for discussion.

²⁵Ibid. See also Telford, *Letters*, "To Vincent Perronet" (1748), 2:295.

²⁶*Works*, 8:251.

²⁷Sermon, "On Schism" (1786), I.7, *Works*, 6:405.

28"Cautions and Directions...." (1762); "A Plain Account of Christian Perfection," 25, Q.37; *Works*, 11:433.
29 Ibid.; Sermon, "On Schism," I.10, *Works*, 6:406.
30 Ibid., I.l, 402; "A Plain Account of the People Called Methodists" (1748), I.11, *Works*, 8:251.
31Ibid., I.11, 406.
32"Cautions and Directions...." (1762); "A Plain Account of Christian Perfection," 25, Q. 37, *Works*, 11:433.
33Letter, "To Jonathan Crowther" (May 10, 1789), Telford, *Letters*, 8:136. Similarly, he refers to "the Church of God throughout our Connexion in these kingdoms," Letter, "To Richard Whatcoat" (Nov., 1790), Ibid., 249. See Baker, *John Wesley and the Church of England*, 284-85, for discussion.
34Francis Asbury, Letter, "To Joseph Benson" (Jan. 15, 1816), *The Journal and Letters of Francis Asbury*, 3 vols., ed. J. Manning Potts, et. al. (Nashville: Abing-don Press, 1958), 3:545.
35Baker, *John Wesley and the Church of England*, 145-50.
36Letter, "To the Editor of the London Chronicle" (Feb. 19, 1761), *Works*, 3:42.
37Letter, "To Charles Wesley," Aug. 19, 1785, Telford, *Letters*, 7:284.
38Sermon, "A Caution Against Bigotry" (1749), I.13-14, *Works*, 5:483.
39Ibid., II.1, 484.
40Ibid., II.3, 484.
41Sermon, "Catholic Spirit" (1749), II.1, *Works*, 5:499.
42Sermon, "The Lord Our Righteousness" (1758; pub. 1766), II.20, *Works*, 5:245.
43Ibid., II.2, 238.
44Sermon, "Catholic Spirit" (1749), 4, *Works*, 5:493.
45Letter, "To a Roman Catholic" (July 18, 1749), 16, Telford, *Letters*, III.13. See also *Works*, 10:85.
46Wakefield, *Christian Theology* (1869), 544, as quoted by A. M. Hills, *Fundamental Christian Theology: A Systematic Theology*, 2 vols. (Pasadena: C. J. Kinne, Pasadena College, 1931), 2:289.
47See his "Valedictory Address" written to "William McKendree, Bishop of the Methodist Episcopal Church" (Aug. 5, 1813), *The Journal and Letters of Francis Asbury*, 3:475-92.
48Asbury, Letter, "To George Roberts" (Feb. 11, 1797), Ibid., 160.
49Luther Lee, *Wesleyan Manual: A Defense of the Organization of the Wesleyan Methodist Connection* (Syracuse: Samuel Lee, 1862), 155-56. As quoted by Ira Ford McLeister and Roy Stephen Nicholson in *Conscience and Commitment: The History of the Wesleyan Methodist Church of America*, 4th rev. ed., eds. Lee M. Hains, Jr., and Melvin E. Dieter (Marion, IN: The Wesley Press, 1976), 33-34.
50McLeister and Nicholson, 76-78.
51Ibid., 294-95, et seq.
52Hills, *Fundamental Christian Theology*, 2:289, citing Wakefield, *Christian*

Theology, 2:544.

⁵³John Miley, *Systematic Theology*, Library of Biblical and Theological Literature, eds. George R. Crooks and John F. Hurst. vol. 6, *Systematic Theology* (New York: Eaton & Mains, 1894), 2:387.

⁵⁴See Barry L. Callen, *It's God's Church: Life and Legacy of Daniel Sydney Warner* (Anderson, IN: Warner Press, 1995).

⁵⁵B. W. Huckabee, "Inter-denominationalism Essential to Christian Unity," *Pentecostal Advocate*, Jan. 24, 1907 (Peniel, TX: Advocate Publishing Company), 8.

⁵⁶Ibid., 9.

⁵⁷Ibid., 8.

⁵⁸Sermon, "On Patience" (1784; 1761 Smith), 10, *Works*, 6:488.

⁵⁹*Notes*, 1 John 4:8.

⁶⁰In relation to Nygren's motif analysis, "benevolence" is the term Wesley uses to express *agape*. His other terms are influenced by the *caritas* tradition. See my dissertation, *Wesley's Concept of Perfect Love: A Motif Analysis*.

⁶¹Sermon, "On Friendship with the World" (1786), 10; *Works*, 6:456.

⁶²Sermon, "In What Sense We Are to Leave the World" (1784), 6; *Works*, 6:466.

⁶³Ibid., 8, 467.

⁶⁴Ibid., 2, 464.

⁶⁵Sermon, "Of Former Times" (1787), 16, *Works*, 7:164.

⁶⁶Sermon, "Catholic Spirit" (1749), 2, *Works*, 5:492.

⁶⁷Sermon, "On Schism" (1786), 11, *Works*, 6:406.

⁶⁸Sermon, "On Zeal" (1781), 2, *Works*, 6:150.

⁶⁹Letter, "To George Downing" (Apr. 6, 1761), Telford, *Letters*, 4:146.

⁷⁰Journal (Mar. 16, 1764), *Works*, 3:161.

⁷¹Ibid. (Apr. 19, 1764), 170.

⁷²Ibid., 170-71.

⁷³Sermon, "Of Separation from the Church" (July 22, 1786), *Works*, 13:257.

⁷⁴Daniel S. Warner, "The Bond of Perfectness," quoted by Barry L. Callen, ed., *The First Century*, 2 vols. (Anderson, IN:Warner Press, Inc., 1979), 1:269.

⁷⁵Warner, "The Evening Light," in Callen, *The First Century.*, 271.

⁷⁶Warner, "The Experience of Oneness," excerpted from *The Church of God, or What the Church Is and What It Is Not*" (Gospel Trumpet Company, 1885), ibid., 1:255-57.

⁷⁷Callen, *The First Century*, 1:68, 76, 151, 152, 217.

⁷⁸Andrew L. Byers, "The Origins of the Movement," excerpted from *The Gospel Trumpet Publishing Work Described and Illustrated* (Anderson, Ind.: Gospel Trumpet Company, 1907), Callen, ed., *The First Century*, 1:55-56.

⁷⁹Ibid., 1:56.

⁸⁰Ibid., 1:55.

⁸¹Warner, "We Forever Withdraw!" excerpted from Andrew L. Byers, *Birth of a Reformation* (Anderson, Ind.: Gospel Trumpet Company, 1921), in Callen, ed.,

The First Century, 1:49.

⁸²See Barry Callen and James North, *Coming Together In Christ: Pioneering A New Testament Way To Christian Unity* (Joplin, MO: College Press, 1997).

⁸³Donald Dayton, *The American Holiness Movement: A Bibliographic Introduction* (Wilmore, KY: The B. L. Fisher Library, Asbury Theological Seminary, 1971), 52.

⁸⁴Phineas F. Bresee, "To the Nazarenes," *The Nazarene Messenger*, July 18, 1901 (Los Angeles: Nazarene Publishing Co.), 6.

⁸⁵Bresee, "The Church," editorial in *The Nazarene Messenger*, Jan. 31, 1901 (Los Angeles: Nazarene Publishing House), 4.

⁸⁶Ibid.

⁸⁷Ibid.

⁸⁸Ibid.

⁸⁹E. A. Girvin, *Phineas F. Bresee: A Prince in Israel* (Kansas City, MO: Nazarene Publishing House, 1916), 440-41.

⁹⁰Olin Alfred Curtis, *The Christian Faith* (New York: Eaton & Mains, 1905), 424. Curtis, Professor of Systematic Theology at Drew Theological Seminary, is of interest here. He was one of the last theologians at an official Methodist seminary to profess and teach entire sanctification. His *The Christian Faith* is a futuristic personal vision; yet in it he states the following: "*Christian Unity.* At this point I cannot speak an effective word; for I am out of sympathy with every effort to crush out the denominational churches in the name of Christian unity. I believe in uniting all those churches where the fundamental interpretation of the Christian faith is the same; but I do not believe in asking any church to yield any real conviction. In the present state of things there is more Christian vitality in these denominational convictions than in all the superficial combinations of forced external conformity. Solidarity is the ultimate, is the Christian ideal; but real Christian solidarity cannot come by sacrificing personality to machinery. I fully appreciate the dreadful fact of waste; but a waste of life is better than any artificial economy."

⁹¹Girvin, *Phineas F. Bresee*, 440.

⁹²Timothy L. Smith, *Called Unto Holiness: The Story of the Nazarenes: The Formative Years* (Kansas City, MO: Nazarene Publishing House, 1962), 51. Smith is quoting from the *Peniel Herald*, vol. 1, no. 3, Dec. 1894.

⁹³As quoted by St. John Ervine, *God's Soldier: General William Booth* (New York: The Macmillan Company, 1935), 1:471; William Booth, in his preface to George Scott Railton's *Twenty-One Years' Salvation Army*. Railton was Booth's principle assistant commissioner.

⁹⁴"A Church," editorial in *The Nazarene Messenger*, Feb. 22, 1900 (Los Angeles: Nazarene Publishing House), 4.

⁹⁵"People's United Church," editorial in *The Nazarene [Messenger]*, Feb. 1, 1900/1899 (Los Angeles: Nazarene Publishing House), 4.

⁹⁶"Holiness Churches," editorial in *The Nazarene [Messenger]*, Jan. 24, 1901 (Los Angeles: Nazarene Publishing House), 4.

97F. E. Hill, "The Holiness Movement and Its Opposition," *The Nazarene Messenger*, July 20, 1899 (Los Angeles: Nazarene Publishing House), 5.

98"Slipped a Cog," editorial in *The Nazarene Messenger*, Aug. 2, 1900 (Los Angeles: Nazarene Publishing House), 1.

99"A Serious Question," editorial in *The Nazarene [Messenger]*, June 28, 1900 (Los Angeles: Nazarene Publishing House), 4.

100J. B. Chapman, *Nazarene Primer* (Kansas City, MO: Nazarene Publishing House, 1949), 48.

101McLeister and Nicholson, *Conscience and Commitment*, 143; see also 168.

102Phineas F. Bresee, Sermon, "The Passion That Absorbs," *Sermons on Isaiah* (Kansas City, MO: Nazarene Publishing House, 1926), 164.

103See especially *Nazarene Messenger, Church Union Number*, July 4, 1907 (Los Angeles: Nazarene Publishing Co.).

104John or Charles Wesley, "Primitive Christianity," stanzas 9 and 10. Included in the second edition of "An Earnest Appeal to Men of Reason and Religion" (1743), *Works*, Bicentennial ed.; 2:91. See Cragg's discussion of the dating, 90, n. 4, and Appendix, 543.

105H. C. Northcott, *Biography of Rev. Benjamin Northcott: A Pioneer Local Preacher of the Methodist Episcopal Church in Kentucky* (Cincinnati: Western Methodist Book Concern, 1875), 31.

106Sermon, "The General Spread of the Gospel," (1783), 20, *Works*, 6:284.

107Journal, Aug. 19, 1806. Asbury, *Journal and Letters*, 2:515.

108Letter, "To Miss Perronet," Jan. 19, 1777; Fletcher, *Works*, 4:351.

109"The Year of 1907," editorial in Pentecostal Advocate, Jan. 10, 1907 (Peniel, TX: Advocate Publishing Company), 9. See his continued discussion of this theme in his editorials entitled "Inter-denominationalism Essential to Christian Unity," in both Jan. 24 and Jan. 31 issues of 1907.

110See Smith, *Called Unto Holiness*, 217.

111Paul Westphal Thomas and Paul William Thomas, *The Days of Our Pilgrimage: The History of the Pilgrim Holiness Church* (Marion, IN: The Wesley Press, 1976), 13-17.

112Sermon, "On Zeal" (1758, Smith), III.9-12, *Works*, 7:65-67. This entire sermon is what Wesley calls an exercise in "comparative divinity," *Works*, 5; 7:60.

113First Clement II, 5; III, 1; XLVIII, 1, and XLIX, 1.

114Sermon, "The General Spread of the Gospel" (1783), 27, *Works*, 6:288.

Chapter 11

An Ecumenical Vocation for the Wesleyan/Holiness Tradition?

by

Elizabeth H. Mellen

Christian unity is both gift and task, a gift of God and the work of God's people. Ecumenical leader Elizabeth Mellen, an Episcopalian with a Wesleyan heritage, recalls numerous efforts toward Christian unity made by the Wesleyan Theological Society, certain of its members, and the holiness bodies with which they are affiliated. She highlights organizations, dialogues between church bodies, and individual ecumenical efforts. The Church of God movement (Anderson) receives particular attention, including its ecumenical leaders John W. V. Smith, Barry L. Callen, James Earl Massey, Gilbert W. Stafford, and Susie Stanley. Also noted with appreciation is the movement's multi-year dialogue with the Christian Churches/Churches of Christ (chronicled by co-author Barry L. Callen in the 1997 book Coming Together in Christ). *Originally published in the* Wesleyan Theological Journal *(34:1, Spring, 1999).*

The ecumenical movement has long understood Christian unity as something that confronts us as both "gift and task." This is a Biblically grounded thought which has been expressed helpfully and quite eloquently by two holiness writers, James Earl Massey and Barry L. Callen, both of the Church of God (Anderson). Massey wrote, "Unity is given, but our experience of it must be gained."[1] Callen put it that "While Christian unity is a gift from God through the Spirit, it is realized only as Christians intentionally open themselves to be in community with other believers." I have discovered that Christians in the American-born

Wesleyan/Holiness tradition have been gaining significant and fairly extensive experience of Christian unity through "intentionally opening themselves to be in community with other believers."[2] This paper seeks to tell the story of this explicit reaching out by Holiness people to other Christians within and beyond their own circles, certainly to make it more widely known and appreciated, but also to make it possible to look at this experience, to study and assess it, and reflect on its meaning and implications for the future direction of Wesleyan/Holiness interaction and on behalf of Christian unity itself.

Some key questions are: Does the Wesleyan/Holiness tradition actually have a calling along these lines—something that could be called an ecumenical vocation? Does such a vocation come naturally to the tradition? That is, is there an imperative to be found, or at least strong grounds for such a vocation in the Wesleyan/Holiness theological heritage and understanding of Christian faith and church mission—a kind of orientation which has been grounding its moves all the while? Most important, could and should such relational work—the reaching for the experience of Christian unity—be taken on more consciously as a Christian calling by those in the tradition? It is interesting to speculate— if the tradition can be said to have this calling, and those within it are willing to take responsibility for it—about the shape that calling might take. Three factors would seem likely to influence the shape and character of things to come: (1) the experience of Christian unity already gained in Wesleyan/Holiness circles (now actually a tradition to build upon, if the story here counts for evidence); (2) the degree to which an ecumenical vocation is seen as organic to the tradition, theologically, missionally, and morally; and finally, (3) the particular location of the Wesleyan/Holiness churches both in their immediate context and in the wider ecclesial terrain.

I have engaged with this question of the ecumenical experience and calling of Holiness people as a fellow Christian in another tradition, and also as a member of the staff of the Graymoor Ecumenical and Interreligious Institute, where my assignment at the Desk for Evangelical and Free Churches is relations with churches not self-defined as part of the "ecumenical movement," and with Anabaptists and other Believers Church traditions, whether or not they fall under this first rubric.[3] I came to the Institute from work as Associate in the Faith and Order Studies office of the NCC.

This paper has engaged me in a special way because, although I am now an Episcopalian, I had the good fortune to have been raised in the

Wesleyan tradition. My father's parents, active at the turn of the century in student YMCA and YWCA work at the University of Kansas, served as Methodist (M. E.) missionaries in China for 50 years. My father himself was ordained a Methodist elder and served as a missionary abroad and as a pastor in the U. S. The families of both of my mother's parents were interwoven with the life of Lecompton, Kansas, where from 1870-1900 the United Brethren were the dominant church, and the small college they established there the town's chief enterprise. The decision taken by the United Brethren in York, Pennsylvania, in 1889 to revise its constitution and thus allow participation in "secret societies" (e.g., Masonic groups), and the subsequent split in the denomination had aftershocks in Lecompton which affected these families deeply. Radicals all—as they had been for the abolitionist cause a generation before—they walked out of the church and became the backbone in that place of the new Old Constitution United Brethren Church, although later my grandparents moved back to the regular United Brethren Church. I value my Wesleyan heritage. I have loved coming to annual meetings of the Wesleyan Theological Society, both to learn from its fresh scholarly explorations of the Wesleyan/Holiness tradition and of American religious history and to deepen my grasp of the heritage generally. This article expresses both my appreciation for the fellowship and my hope for serious engagement on the part of WTS scholars with the question of the unity of the church.

Organizational Means of Building Christian Community

The Christian Holiness Partnership in its early form as the National Camp Meeting Association for the Promotion of Holiness was organized in 1867 as a means for bringing together those of like holiness persuasion, activity and purpose. It has persisted as a fellowship and serves today as the chief organizational expression of the Wesleyan/Holiness interest in building and keeping community with other believers beyond the denominational level. It is a venerable fellowship of denominations and related schools, missionary agencies, camp meeting associations, and individuals for whom the Wesleyan/Holiness tradition is a living and lived heritage.[4] A recent change of name from Christian Holiness "Association" to "Partnership" was made to show even more clearly the cooperative relations and collective intent of its member denominations and organizations. The opening speaker at a recent annual meeting of the CHP (April 1997), which I visited, sounded this note: Sanctification is about breathing in grace and breathing out love. In a later address, David Gyertson, President of Asbury College, applied this understanding of the practice of holiness ecumenically—that is, to church relations. He testified to having met many Spirit-filled Christians outside of Holiness circles, feeling discomfited because of their ignorance of the Holiness tradition, yet being more affected by their not requiring him "to embrace all they believed and practiced in order to be embraced by them." He said he was concerned about "an increased spirit of separatism and animosity towards those outside our tradition....a holding on to our holiness distinctives...[and] unprecedented erosion of the theology of sanctification." He was critical of a Holiness "fortress mentality" and the use of "sarcasm and put-down humor." He lifted up the "cornerstone of fellowship wrapped up in Mr. Wesley's words, "If your heart is warm, give me your hand!" and spoke of the need for "a fresh baptism of the ability to speak the truth in love."[5] This note connecting holiness to relationality, love and reconciliation held through the whole CHP meeting.

The Wesleyan Theological Society (WTS) is not a free-floating academic or intellectual society, but an ecclesially grounded one. It came into being in the CHP matrix, and it keeps faith and fellowship with it as an active Commission of the Partnership.[6] At the same time, the Society opens its membership to individual United Methodists, Pentecostals, Adventists, and others who claim the Wesleyan/Holiness heritage but whose own churches do not belong to CHP. In addition, a recent change permits other Christians who may not wish to subscribe to the Holiness-specific doctrinal basis to be affiliate members. Solidly grounded in its tradition, and organizationally tied to holiness churches, the WTS stance is hospitable and relational.

That the majority of Holiness churches and church people continue in close association through the Christian Holiness Partnership raises an interesting question. Various confessional movements in the latter part of the nineteenth century sought to bring churches in the same theological tradition into fellowship internationally. The Seventh Day Adventists held a world conference in 1863; the first Lambeth Conference (Anglican) was in 1867; the World Alliance of Reformed Churches was started 1875; the World Methodist Council convened in an early form in 1881; the Baptist World Alliance met in 1905; Lutherans began consulting in 1923. There are now nineteen self-identified "Christian World Communions" which include the Salvation Army, the Catholic Church (since 1968), and most recently the Pentecostal World Fellowship. The secretaries of these diverse bodies have met annually since 1957. Although independent of it, the "world communions" do confer with the World Council of Churches (WCC) about their role in the quest for unity. In addition, they have themselves become avenues for international interconfessional dialogues. There is now quite a significant network and record of bi-lateral conversations.[7]

The early and continuing CHP fellowship "for the Promoting of Holiness" could certainly be thought of in terms of a confessional movement. During a sabbatical exploration at WCC offices in Geneva, Donald Dayton learned about the Christian World Communions and asked, "Where is the Christian Holiness Association?" He learned that this body "apparently qualified but that no one had ever heard of it." Then he asked members of the CHP Board of Administration "why we are not represented and was told that no one had heard of World Christian Communions." No action was taken by the Board, but Dayton found the members open to the idea of such representation.[8]

Each of these world communions brings Christians together. One of the them, the World Methodist Council (WMC), counts the Wesleyan Church, the Free Methodist Church, and the Church of the Nazarene among participants in the heritage it represents.[9] Two holiness bodies, the Wesleyan Church and the Free Methodist Church of North America, are actually members of the WMC; the Nazarenes and Salvation Army participate in WMC activities.[10] Among Nazarenes there is some current interest in joining. Clearly the historic relationship to Methodism needs to be claimed publicly and such common interests as Wesley studies owned—this has been taking place.[11] It remains to be seen, however, whether the CHP will take its place among this world family of traditions and there represent the nineteenth-century Wesleyan/Holiness movement, now spread worldwide, in a more precise and inclusive way than the World Methodist Council has, and in a fuller and broader way than the Salvationists can do alone.[12] If it does so, it may also consider initiating theological dialogue at the international level, thus introducing its Christian testimony and heritage into this wide ecumenical arena.

Beyond the CHP, the most significant expression of the desire to relate organizationally is the membership of over half the Christian Holiness Partnership churches (13 out of 20, including five of the six largest) in the National Association of Evangelicals. The Church of God (Anderson) is a notable exception.[13] These Holiness bodies participate in the fellowship and opportunities for broad consultation and common endeavor which that organization, in its commitment to Christian unity, provides.[14]

Generally speaking, Holiness denominations have not connected with the conciliar movement and instead have kept an intentional distance from the expressions and instruments of the "Ecumenical Movement," a stance they share with others involved in the twentieth-century neo-evangelical movement and church culture. Interestingly, examples can be found nonetheless of involvement on the part of Holiness denominations with one or more aspects of National Council church work in the U. S. (e.g., mission and stewardship education, religious liberty, religious statistics, and communications.)[15] In addition, Holiness congregations can quite often be found as members of local councils of churches (as distinct from ministerial associations).

Relating Through Dialogue

Beyond these organizational means one also finds the Wesleyan/ Holiness tradition gaining experience in Christian unity through theological conversation with Christians in other traditions. One of the more important arenas historically for multi-lateral scholarly work on issues of Christian division and unity is the Faith and Order movement, which pre-dates the World Council of Churches. While it became an integral part of the World Council in 1948, it is open to and has always included the participation of representatives of churches or traditions which are not WCC members and so retains its distinctive "movement" character.

Although the Wesleyan/Holiness tradition was represented at the Fifth World Conference on Faith and Order in 1993 by a WTS scholar, it has not otherwise been active in international Faith and Order studies.[16] It has been very active, however, in the U. S. Faith and Order work carried on under the auspices of the NCCC/USA. The Church of God (Anderson) has been represented ever since 1957, when the inaugural "North American Conference on Faith and Order" was convened at Oberlin, Ohio. John W. V. Smith attended from Anderson University School of Theology and came thereafter to the ongoing meetings until his death in 1984; Gilbert W. Stafford has attended since 1984. His recent interpretive essay, "The Faith and Order Movement: Holiness Church Participation" offers an introduction to Faith and Order work for a Wesleyan/Holiness (or a general evangelical) audience, touching on its aims and methodology. Stafford provides some little-known history of

Holiness involvement, an account of his own experience in Faith and Order meetings, and the benefits to be gained through participation.[17] The Wesleyan Theological Society itself decided in the early 1980s to choose and send not one but two of its scholars to the twice yearly meetings.[18] David Cubie, Donald Dayton, and Paul Bassett have served as faithful, able, and imaginative contributors.

The 1980s and early 1990s were a creative time for U. S. Faith and Order studies. It was "the special contribution of its director Jeff Gros during this period to make this [Faith and Order] working group one of the most diverse and representative theological arenas in the ecumenical world."[19] American church scholars, from the oldest of traditions to the newest, from Orthodox to Pentecostal, with roots in other parts of the world or of American origin, committed themselves to making a "distinctive contribution" to ecumenical studies precisely out of the eclectic North American ecclesial context. They hoped to move beyond what seemed at times, as WTS representative Donald Dayton put it, to have "become something of a pale, North American imitation of the work being coordinated out of Geneva."[20] The histories and critical questions that representatives of Holiness, Pentecostal, Adventist, American Restorationist, Southern Baptist, and African American church traditions brought to the mix enabled fresh considerations of how to live into our unity as Christians. In 1982 the WCC's Commission on Faith and Order initiated the study program "Towards the Common Expression of the Apostolic Faith Today."[21] The amazing proliferation of new churches in North America from the nineteenth century forward could be viewed with dismay "as a final playing out of the unfortunate Protestant tendency to endless splitting and fragmentation," and a betrayal of any notion of a common apostolic faith, or as "an amazing flowering of new forms of Christianity that deserve sympathetic exploration for the insights that they might bring to ecumenical discussion."[22] The American Faith and Order Commission chose, at the risk of further complicating an already complex ecumenical discussion, to see it as a flowering. Noting that all churches explain and understand themselves as "apostolic," it recognized each tradition as having emerged from its own struggle to achieve a lived fidelity in continuity with the faith of the apostles, and each as showing forth "dimensions" of the Apostolic Faith.[23]

In this spirit, a number of specific studies and consultations went forward, involving an array of traditions in different ways. A persistent interest throughout was in challenging the witness of church history to reveal more fully the catholicity of the church, and pressing for the expansion of the ecumenical imagination into a less limited version of the ecumenical task.[24] Although papers from the "American Born Churches Consultation" held in Texas in 1991, where Donald Dayton (Wesleyan Church), Paul Bassett (Church of the Nazarene), and Russell Staples (Seventh Day Adventist) of the WTS were presenters, were not finally published, the work done there is surfacing in other contexts. The strong contribution of Wesleyan/Holiness scholars—there were always three represented—in conceptualizing and carrying out these U. S. ecumenical studies can hardly be overemphasized.[25]

John W. V. Smith played a pivotal role in productively involving an array of American churches in Faith and Order work. His own Church of God (Anderson) is a movement which, along with its holiness heritage, has a foundational understanding that baptism properly follows a decisional response of faith. It has been a strong participant in the series of Believers Church Conferences from their beginning in the U. S. in 1967. When the WCC's Faith and Order Commission initiated the Apostolic Faith Study, it also concluded a long study by the churches of the issues of Baptism, Eucharist, and Ministry, published the famous BEM document,[26] and began the process of eliciting responses to it from hundreds of churches around the world. John Howard Yoder noted later that it was Smith who saw the pertinence to the Believers Church Conferences of the WCC Faith and Order Commission's BEM statement.[27] It was his initiative that led to the addressing of the three concerns of the convergence document in three separate Believers Church Conferences (1984, 1987 and 1994), each involving not only Believers traditions, but also Faith and Order spokespersons and participants from other church traditions. The first, on Baptism, was held at Anderson, Indiana; the collection of papers from it, which Smith had been editing when he died, was dedicated to his memory.[28]

One more Wesleyan/Holiness contribution to Faith and Order work should be mentioned. In the U. S., a Faith and Order study group explored resources in various traditions for developing an approach for Christians to use in facing religious pluralism and interfaith relations. Floyd T. Cunningham (Church of the Nazarene) made a valuable contribution in his look at the Wesleyan heritage; his insights and conclusions were remarkably close to those of a Methodist who also presented.[29]

Since the early 1980s the WTS has made itself into an arena for dialogue, through presentations at its meetings by persons from beyond the Wesleyan/Holiness circle (Anabaptist, United Methodist, Anglican,

Adventist, and Dispensationalist), many by special invitation.[30] Recently, the WTS became an agency for of dialogue in another way, as the partner in planning an historic joint meeting with the Society for Pentecostal Studies held March, 1998, in Cleveland, Tennessee. The proposal came in 1993 from Cheryl Bridges Johns (Church of God/Cleveland) and Susie Stanley (Church of God/Anderson), then presidents respectively of the SPS and WTS, who had become acquainted that year at the Fifth World Conference on Faith and Order in Spain.[31] But earlier developments had prepared the way for the formal proposal. Groundbreaking work by Vinson Synan and Donald Dayton had shown the close relationship between the Wesleyan/Holiness churches and Pentecostalism, "to the great discomfort of both groups," as David Bundy put it.[32] The related question about whether Wesley and early Methodism made use of pneumatological (Pentecostal) language in relation to entire sanctification or whether that was a 19th-century development was widely researched and debated in the WTS from 1973-1980.[33] With the recognition of the theological and historical ties connecting the two movements, the way was open to ask whether the historic tensions between the two, which included official positions taken by some Holiness bodies against Pentecostalism, might redemptively be revisited.[34] In 1987, the year his significant monograph *The Theological Roots of Pentecostalism* was published,[35] Donald Dayton was vice president and program chair of the Society for Pentecostal Studies. He arranged for that Society to meet on the campus of Asbury Theological Seminary. The program included exchange with Wesleyan/Holiness scholars.[36] These Holiness–Pentecostal relations, developed first in a tentative way, but now are becoming a solid reality with great promise for on-going fellowship and shared reflection of a sort that few could have anticipated.

The Work of Individuals

There are more than a few individual Wesleyan/Holiness leaders and scholars whose work would need to be lifted up in any comprehensive study of developing Wesleyan/Holiness ecumenical interest and activity. Only three will receive attention here. The first is Barry L. Callen, who has explored at length the special legacy of concern for Christian unity in the Church of God (Anderson) tradition, following its primary pioneer, Daniel S. Warner (1842-1895). Warner understood holiness to apply not only to an experience of individual believers but also to the church itself and so joined together "the passion for Christian holiness, the dream of [visible] Christian unity, and the belief that the first enables the second."[37] Callen demonstrated the theological link between Warner's passionate conviction about visible unity and his "come outer" activity and has provided a valuable listing of works by other scholars on this heritage and its relevance to the larger church's quest for Christian unity today.[38]

More recently, Callen of the Church of God (Anderson) has co-authored *Coming Together in Christ: Pioneering a New Testament Way to Christian Unity* with James North of the Christian Churches/Churches of Christ tradition,[39] a work documenting a ground-breaking dialogue between their traditions, both of which, from their founding days, have had a strong calling in relation to Christian unity.[40] In 1988, the Independent Christian Churches were convicted by ecumenical scholar Michael Kinnamon (Christian Church/Disciples) of the sin of doing little or nothing of substance about that calling.[41] Largely as a result of this, a dialogue relationship was sought with the Anderson church, a tradition also known to be restorationist in theology and tending to stand apart from rather than affiliate with others, out of a particular ecclesiological understanding.[42] The authors report in moving fashion the ensuing process of the two bodies' intentionally getting acquainted over several years, how they engaged in mutual study and reflection, what the two traditions (one Holiness, one not) have learned together about themselves and each other, and finally some recent steps taken toward practical cooperation in the mission of the church.

A strength of the volume is the authors' putting this dialogue in wider historical context, situating it in three ways: within their own traditions' histories and theological self-understandings,[43] within the on-going concern for unity in the long history of the Christian church, and within 20th-century developments—the ecumenical movement and the movement for greater unity among evangelicals who often stand apart from the formalized ecumenical movement. Their hope is to encourage other conservative churches to address the unity issue seriously. The book and the dialogue reports are animated by the scriptural understanding that being "in Christ" (Eph. 1:3-14) means to be caught up in God's larger purpose of bringing all things together and becoming part of "a unique and visible togetherness of all who are His...a divinely enabled togetherness...the church, the new community brought into being by the received grace of Christ," intended as "a hopeful witness to a divided world."[44]

Another and potentially divisive perspective, however, is also present. This may be because the Christian Churches/Churches of Christ separated from the Christian Churches (Disciples of Christ) in 1926, during and in relation to the fundamentalist-modernist controversy (though other issues were involved), and are concerned with issues related to that historic impasse in Christian relations—though that concern is hardly limited to them! Whatever the reason, the authors early on report with care the existence in evangelical circles of sentiments against the ecumenical movement—the generally suspicious and negative depictions, the typical accusations—with apt quotes from various writers past and present to illustrate. These are always spoken of as what evangelicals or conservatives think, not necessarily as the authors' own sentiments.[45] Yet because the authors do not clearly take issue with them, even in the case of the most flagrantly irresponsible statements, the stance seems ultimately to be that the authors are in some sympathy with them. Indeed, they posit a distance-keeping premise that there are two worlds of church—"evangelical," and "liberal" (the historically "ecumenical" belonging to the latter)—one of which is safe and takes truth seriously and one which does not.

In the chapter "Testing the Evangelical Alternative," Callen and North aver that their multi-year dialogue "has been rooted in a commitment that the Scriptures are authoritative and should guide all approaches to doctrinal issues and Christian unity efforts," whereas "religious 'liberals' can carry on ecumenical dialogues with a greater sense of negotiability." Denominations may reflect together in dialogue on their traditions, as they themselves have done, yet:

> ...if the presupposition is that such traditions are conditioned only by history and circumstances, then there is considerable flexibility when it comes to harmonizing differing views. But conservatives generally choose against this broad kind of flexibility. There is thought to be no room for negotiating what is judged to be truly divine revelation. Understanding Scriptural teaching may change, but in the final analysis changes in belief between dialoguing groups should occur only when all involved believers are convinced that the teaching perspective in question is in harmony with Scripture. This understanding of biblical boundaries is crucial and places some restrictions on "conservative" doctrinal dialogues that religious liberals do not normally worry about.[46]

Thus Callen and North seek an "evangelical alternative" to dialogue where more "flexible" standards prevail, hoping their dialogue can represent an emerging "conservative paradigm," allaying evangelical fears about dialogue and serving as "a challenge to other conservative/evangelical groups" to join the larger discussion, since "ecumenical endeavors need not be the private preserve of the liberal denominations."[47]

Certainly the ecumenical movement is broader than and not to be equated with any particular ecumenical effort, instrument, organization, or dialogue, which has recognized and seeks to serve the unity of the church, and ecumenical concern/activity is certainly not a private preserve. To suggest, however, that there can be segregated (quarantined?) dialogue arenas seems not to follow. Nor is the idea supportable if there is only one Lord, one faith, and one baptism. No such understanding informed either John W. V. Smith or Gilbert W. Stafford of the Church of God (Anderson) as they entered conversations in multilateral settings.

The authors could assess the quality of other bi-lateral dialogues—not one was cited—to establish for themselves just who pursues a "liberal" line: Eastern Orthodox in conversation with Roman Catholics? Roman Catholics with Lutherans? Moravians with Anglicans? Pentecostals with Reformed churches in a developing new international dialogue? And who fails to treat Scripture as authoritative, or abandons beliefs for the sake of "harmonizing" because they see them as conditioned by history and circumstance. They would discover, I think, that their dialogue, with its skillful, sensitive delineation of theological differences in the two traditions and an agreement reached on baptism, does not differ in kind, and is neither more nor less faithful to the faith once delivered to the saints than other Christian dialogues pursued in the quest for deepened fellowship; and that the joy and refreshment they found in the process has been shared by many others.[48]

Proceeding into ecumenical exploration, yet with this deference and healthy respect for that particularly intimidating chasm of division that is our inheritance from the fundamentalist-modernist controversies, Callen and North remind us that those tensions are there and that there are particular risks involved in reaching in some directions to deepen that fellowship given us in Christ. The happy implication of their firm faith that we are brought together in Christ, however, is that even this divide must be understood as a brokenness not beyond the reach of God's reconciling power in Christ.

Coming Together In Christ is a significant volume. The experience gained in the COG-CC/CC dialogue, the theological vision which undergirds it, including understandings of the nature of Christian truth and its pursuit, and its understanding of the movement of the Spirit and depiction of the church as "divinely enabled togetherness" are important. The book and the dialogue involving a prominent Holiness church are milestones in a developing reflection by Wesleyan/Holiness scholars on the unity of the church.

Nazarene historian and theologian David Cubie is another major thinker in relation to the Wesleyan/Holiness ecumenical calling. Stimulated by participation in the Faith and Order arena in the 1980s, he wrote papers now recently gathered and published under the title "A Wesleyan Perspective on Christian Unity."[49] Cubie looks at John Wesley's writings on the unity of the church and on the central importance of realizing the fellowship offered and made possible in Christ, and seeks to relate these to Wesley's understanding of the gospel, the role of love, his own mission and that of the "Methodists" in general— who both served and later pulled away from the Church of England. Cubie brings to light some rich tendencies-in-tension, especially regarding the nature of the church and therefore of church unity. There are passages showing that Wesley saw the unity of the church expressed as much in the quality of the fellowship and Christian life within the church as in a state of formal undividedness, with this implication: that an undivided church might appropriately be designated "sectarian" if it were not the Spirit-filled communion it was intended to be.

Cubie then investigates the history of the Holiness denominations in the U. S. emerging in various ways and times out of Methodism, examining pivotal events, written evidence of leaders' convictions and thinking, and the patterns of institutional change within individual Holiness denominations which reveal Wesleyan/Holiness understandings of church division and church unity. Among his findings is a decisive tendency in Holiness denominations toward a congregational understanding of the church which does not preclude concern for the church universal. Cubie concludes by laying out principles drawn from this Wesleyan evangelical tradition which in his view must be the basis for authentic Wesleyan/Holiness participation in dialogue. With special eloquence he explicates the last, that "the unity of the Church must first of all be understood as a unity of love." One anticipates thoughtful response by other scholars in the tradition to this foundational study, and Cubie's own affirmation: "The Christian church exists both to be one and to participate in God's work of making all one."

Finally, no survey of ways Wesleyan/Holiness people have opened themselves to community with other believers can omit mention of the contribution of Donald Dayton of the Wesleyan Church. A collector and bibliographer of a wide range of English-language materials documenting developments in 19th and 20th-century popular Christianity, Dayton has helped build a basis for a more catholic appreciation of the church today. As historical theologian, he has contributed to new understanding of the relationship of Holiness and Pentecostal traditions[50] and challenged characterizations of evangelical Christianity which in his view defy the historical record.[51] As part of a scholarly debate, he has taken the position that the various ecclesial/theological traditions within "the evangelical big tent" are the basic carriers of Christian faith, and that their shape and logic and sense of church must ultimately be more determinative in people's faith lives than their "evangelicalism."[52] Along with others, Dayton has encouraged creative debate in the WTS, much of it in the interest of and with implications for inter-church relations. He has been a significant participant in U. S. Faith and Order work. Ecumenical emissary as well as thinker, he plays a remarkable role as a Wesleyan/Holiness ecclesial visitor and ecumenical explorer and apologist. A compelling account of this work, combined with careful reflection on the question of Wesleyan/Holiness churches and their relationship to the ecumenical movement, can be found in his "The Holiness Witness in the Ecumenical Church," presented to the WTS in 1987.[53]

This overview, concluding with a look at three ecumenically minded individual scholars, indicates that there is a strong, serviceable record of Wesleyan/Holiness interest in the intentional deepening of Christian fellowship in a variety of directions and a maturing theological reflection drawn from the Wesleyan/Holiness tradition accompanying the activity. There almost seems to be an ecumenical calling already recognized that is being attended to, and certainly a developing ecumenical praxis. The primary question, then, may be: To what extent will Wesleyan/Holiness church people own this vocation even more self-consciously and more corporately in the context and terms of their ecclesial situation and theological tradition? That is a question, of course, not for Wesleyan/Holiness church people only, but worthy of address by churches and church people in all traditions.

Location as Vocation

The biblical witness concerning the unity of the church comes not as a worked out theory, rule or guideline, but largely in the form of exhortations and challenges addressed to early Christian communities whose internal unity and bonds of fellowship were strained or threatened. We also have the creeds—the Apostles and the Nicene—but even the assertions here about the nature of the church (as one and holy, catholic and apostolic) were evolved in the thick of lived Christian life and problems, and are an application and distillation of Scriptural wisdom in later situations where the nature and quality of Christian fellowship needed to

An Ecumenical Vocation for the Wesleyan/Holiness Tradition? 225

be lifted up. In a similar way, our own calls to work for reconciliation and the unity or deeper fellowship of the church come in our particular personal, social, national, and ecclesial contexts, and require of us some serious thought about the strained places in those given relations. In his "The Holiness Witness in the Ecumenical Church" Donald Dayton takes such a contextual, historical approach, assuming that the relations and connections integrally a part of Wesleyan/Holiness history and institutional terrain are the appropriate place to begin in thinking about a Wesleyan/Holiness ecumenical agenda.[54]

Following that approach here, we can think about Wesleyan/Holiness relationship seeking efforts—both those already undertaken and those that could be—from the perspective of the various places the tradition is located. Ecumenical attention could thus continue in relation to or could intentionally be given: (1) to those in the immediate vicinity, that is, to other Wesleyan/Holiness bodies, both those which have sought each other out in the Christian Holiness Partnership and the more conservative (or more radical) who out of conviction have declined that fellowship[55] (2) to the Methodist family (matrix of the Holiness movement) and specifically in the U. S. to the historic Black Methodist bodies and to the United Methodists;[56] (3) to Pentecostalism, Holiness offspring and/or sibling; (4) to other 19th-century revivalist movement churches and traditions; (5) to the on-going opportunities for dialogue available in Faith and Order studies in North America and internationally; (6) to the neo-evangelical Christian community and culture (the "evangelical big tent"); (7) to the ecumenical community—those who have understood themselves to be part of the ecumenical movement, and the instruments of the movement, e.g., conciliar agencies; and (8) to other traditions within the Christian church. Bi-lateral conversations, of which the dialogue of the Church of God (Anderson) with the Christian Churches/Churches of Christ, and the burgeoning WTS academic exchange with the Society for Pentecostal Studies, and the various discussions among Holiness denominations regarding mergers (achieved or not), are interesting and varied examples that can be an important means of relating in any of the context. They could be explored with other traditions nationally or internationally and either by individual Holiness denominations or by the Christian Holiness Partnership/WTS. The tradition is well poised to do constructive relational work in many directions.

In closing, we will take special note of the distinctive and creative role this tradition is already playing in relation to the evangelical and ecumenical arenas, looked at together as one area of common tension and historic Christian division. In the late 1980s ecumenist Alan Falconer, reflecting on the situation in Northern Ireland in an essay titled "From Theologies-in-Opposition Towards a Theology-of-Interdependence,"[57] asserted that "the role of religion in the shaping of the identity of the different communities has been fundamental." He suggested that the ecclesial traditions themselves, Catholic and Protestant, have contributed to the cohesion of the separated communities by countenancing the development of "theologies-in-opposition," theological frameworks bolstering the differentiation in identity of the two communities, thus helping the churches to play "chaplain" to continuing division. These clarify the identity of each community as a community-in-opposition, providing theological support for continually reiterated versions of history that keep them differentiated and their hostility alive. The "theologies-in-opposition" are exquisitely interdependent: "Your" identity has been phrased in terms of "our" actions; "our" identity has been cast in terms of "your" actions.

Though our context is quite different, I have wondered about the applicability of Falconer's analysis to the U. S. situation, a church environment still affected and shaped by the fundamentalist-modernist debate that reached a nationally politicized fever pitch seventy years ago, pulled Protestant Christians in the U. S. apart, and still provides terms for our thinking and behavior.[58] Developing opposing characterizations of each other, were we also caught up in a system of theologies-in-opposition? Have we been serving in our church communities as chaplains to division?

This thought shed light on the stubborn operative negativity I discovered in myself when I set out eagerly on my ecumenical assignment to relate to evangelicals. I had a kind of supercilious attitude deposited in my own thinking that was difficult to let go. Falconer's essay suggested to me that I was wrestling with the compelling, even coercive power that mutually interdependent patterns of negative categorizing can have when internalized as part of our self-understanding *as Christians* and inherited as part of our faith identity, so that to abandon them is to risk being unfaithful, or disloyal, in our own eyes.

We know in my sector of the church world that as ecumenically identified Protestants we are ecumenical, relational, and open and these others have always stirred up trouble and been divisive. It would be a virtual heresy—since we are so tied to the understanding that we are not like them—to imagine that our community may have been caught up in the creation and may now be a perpetuator of a mutually dependent hostility-in-opposition. It is hard to recognize that our judgmental dismissal of or our applying the blobby category "fundamentalism" to some group of people out there, culturally despicable, irritating, even dangerous,[59] is hostile language towards real people and fellow Christians with whom we have a common heritage and hope. But in doing this, mainline church people in "ecumenical" churches match the equally tragic lack of concern or interest in and the stereotyping of ecumenical churches on the part of many evangelicals.

Falconer, of course, has a "resource" to suggest to the Irish churches—the possibility through God's grace and the power of the Holy Spirit of remembering Jesus of Nazareth, "the discoverer of the role of forgiveness in human affairs,"[60] and of repenting, forgiving, and re-membering themselves as members one of another. It is our resource, too. We can assume responsibility for our part in this status quo and be brought to a place beyond the knee-jerk responses of Christian "parties" mired in dysfunctional interdependence, and, as Christians, pursue closer acquaintance and interdependence in the constructive sense. At the least, we could acknowledge that we may be wed more deeply and more "religiously" than we know to a well constructed mutual antipathy.

In their own way, from the evangelical side, Wesleyan/Holiness Christians have been challenging this state of tension and some of its premises. With a ripple effect, careful questions they raise about their own identity generate questions in and for the wider arena. For example, the tradition has noted at least three ways in which it does not fit the standard profile of evangelicalism.

First, the Anglican/Wesleyan/Holiness theological heritage has been in implicit dialogue with the 18th-century common sense Scottish enlightenment views of Scripture which have largely defined neo-evangelicalism. It brings an understanding (and large but understated claim) regarding the Scriptures' sufficiency in matters pertaining to salvation which does not require an additional faith stance about the "inerrant" authority of the Bible in all matters, including those scientific and historical.[61] At least as important, and perhaps more so, when that dialogue has become explicit, the Wesleyan/Holiness tradition has shown a capacity to negotiate stormy waters of debate about inerrancy in deft, gentle, and civil ways rather than confrontationally and to divisive effect; and also, when the dialogue is implicit, the tradition has shown a capacity to forbear and live with some ambiguity. Note Paul Bassett's account of a discussion and its outcome among the Nazarenes[62] and the story of the WTS itself moving away from the inerrancy language of its first faith statement. Of the latter, Leo Cox recalls how "After some rather heated discussions...during those early years, Dr. Ralph Thompson, in his report...in 1969 gave this conciliatory appeal:

> Considerable discussion has taken place on the subject of Biblical inerrancy. Those who know me best know I tend to take a stand in favor of the doctrine....Many of my brethren do not see the matter as I do; yet they appear to believe as strongly as I do in the inspiration and authority of the Scriptures....I wonder if a position we hold but cannot prove should debar from membership in this Society those whose minds do not operate exactly as ours. Let us be exceedingly careful lest we take any step that will weaken our position with respect to the inspiration and authority of the Scriptures. But if a change in the wording in our doctrinal statement could be made that would protect our position and at the same time respect that of our brethren whose intellectual honesty will not allow them to subscribe to our statement, I recommend that such action be taken.[63]

Second, as Wesleyan/Holiness scholars have been at pains to point out, the Holiness Movement and the precipitation of new denominations primarily from Methodism which followed occurred earlier and around different issues than those of the fundamentalist-modernist clash which tore at the Presbyterian and Baptist fellowships. Thus, even though some of its key alliances and affiliations were developed in the context of the fundamentalist/modernist controversy and even more so in the post World War II neo-evangelical movement, it carries within itself another logic and memory.

Third, a piece of the self-understanding of Holiness Movement churches was and is that it is right and good to confer ministerial orders on women with a recognized call to ministry.[64] Insofar as evangelicalism is associated with patriarchal norms and claims, the Wesleyan/Holiness tradition provides a telling contrast. In this way again it suggests the desirability and the possibility of developing a more complex notion of evangelicalism than has served in the past.

In addition, the stated basis for fellowship among evangelicals has been assent to the "fundamentals." Differences among traditions who may be "free" (i.e., Baptist, Mennonite, Wesleyan/Holiness, Pentecostal, etc.) are generously tolerated as "distinctives" for the sake of evangelical unity, fellowship, and the making of common cause within the big tent. Along with others, the Wesleyan/Holiness tradition raises questions about whether such tolerance does justice to significant theological difference and whether presumed or apparent agreement around fundamentals represents a philosophic/theological methodology or commitment of only some voices/traditions within the evangelical big tent.[65] In due course, thanks to the Wesleyan/Holiness presence, these questions may be raised within the National Association of Evangelicals itself.

Holiness denominations are part of the evangelical culture and fellowship. They come, pay, agree to the terms, participate and contribute significant leadership within the National Association of Evangelicals fellowship and in associated networks and agencies (e.g., the Coalition for Christian Colleges and Universities where the Holiness schools are an important component). It is unlikely that the ecumenical calling of the Wesleyan/Holiness tradition will be played out apart from these developed relationships of accountability and ties of affection within evangelicalism generally. Indeed, it is in this context, I would suggest, that its special ecumenical genius may be discovered and played out. Its "differing" in some matters with other evangelicals is likely to be done in a transformative rather than in a divisive way, so as to open up discourse rather than close off conversation, even as it continues to be interested in fellowship beyond evangelical circles. Raising questions while keeping and building fellowship, Wesleyan/Holiness leaders may quietly and creatively decline to play the role of chaplain to division in the body of Christ, keeping as their focus the holiness which "is about breathing in grace and breathing out love."

Notes

[1]James Earl Massey, *Concerning Christian Unity* (Anderson, Ind.: Warner Press, 1979), 11.

[2]Barry L. Callen, Appendix F, "Excerpt from *Contours of a Cause: The Theological Vision of the Church of God Movement (Anderson)* in Barry L. Callen and James B. North, *Coming Together in Christ: Pioneering a New Testament Way to Christian Unity* (Joplin, MO: College Press, 1997). The Biblical understanding eloquently expressed here is foundational in the ecumenical movement.

[3]The Institute is a ministry of the Franciscan Friars of the Atonement, an American Roman Catholic order with a charism for work toward Christian unity. The experience of participating in a National Council of Churches' consultation with Pentecostals held at Fuller Theological Seminary in 1987 may have been what inspired its Director, Fr. Elias Mallon, to develop this desk.

[4]The CHP has twenty member denominations, many of them relatively small. The five largest are the Church of God (Anderson), Free Methodist Church of North America, Church of the Nazarene, Salvation Army (USA and Canada/ Bermuda), and the Wesleyan Church. Some others are the Methodist

Evangelical Church, Evangelical Friends, Brethren in Christ, and Missionary Church (north central district).

⁵David J. Gyertson, "The Practice of Holiness: Testing God's Worth." The address was published in *Ecumenical Trends* 27:4 (April 1998), 49-56.

⁶See "Purpose and Doctrinal Basis" from the Wesleyan Theological Society Bylaws, printed in the *Wesleyan Theological Journal*, and William Kostlevy, "An Historical Overview" and Leo Cox, "The First Decade" in "Thirtieth Anniversary of the Wesleyan Theological Society," *WTJ* 30:1 (Spring 1995), 212-221.

⁷See "Christian World Communions" in *Dictionary of the Ecumenical Movement* (Geneva: WCC, 1991); *World Council of Churches Yearbook 1997* (Geneva: WCC). Among the better known dialogues are: the long term Lutheran-Roman Catholic dialogue with its recent "Joint Declaration on the Doctrine of Justification"; Lutheran-Anglican dialogue, discovering such deep consensus that in many regions of the world the two churches are declaring themselves to be "in full communion," i.e., clergy permitted to serve congregations of the other church and closer collaboration in mission and witness.

⁸Donald W. Dayton, "The Holiness Witness in the Ecumenical Church," *Wesleyan Theological Journal* 23:1-2 (1988), 102.

⁹Cf. *World Parish* (International Organ of the World Methodist Council), 36:1 (January/February 1996). The issue looked forward to the first WMC meeting to be held in Latin America and lifted up the number of "Methodists" in each Latin American country. The number was the sum of Methodists, Free Methodists, Wesleyans, and Nazarenes in each place, with a note that all were WMC members.

¹⁰*World Methodist Council Handbook of Information 1997-2000* (Lake Junaluska, NC: WMC); conversation with WMC staff, Lake Junaluska, November, 1997.

¹¹Howard Snyder, "Wesleyan Theological Society: The Third Decade (1985-1984)," in "Thirtieth Anniversary of the Wesleyan Theological Society," *Wesleyan Theological Journal* 30:1 (Spring 1995), 228-229; Donald W. Dayton, "The Holiness Witness in the Ecumenical Church," *WTJ* 23:12 (1988), 104-105. Both of these call attention to Holiness scholars' participation in the WMC-sponsored Oxford Institute of Methodist Theological Studies.

¹²Donald Dayton has suggested it ("The Holiness Witness," 102), and, aside from possible monetary constraints, thought there could be no objections.

¹³This body has not been a "joiner," but nonetheless carries a strong burden for Christian unity. Certain of its leaders are very active ecumenically—Edward Foggs with the National Association of Evangelicals, Gilbert Stafford with the Faith and Order movement, and Barry Callen as Editor of the *Wesleyan Theological Journal*. In 1975, its General Assembly in North America formed a "Commission on Christian Unity" because "the need and responsibility for unity and cooperative work among Christians is so strategic to Christian witness and world evangelism and the Church of God continues to need a representative group to make contacts, hold conversations, and develop lines of cooperation

An Ecumenical Vocation for the Wesleyan/Holiness Tradition? 231

with other church bodies of similar spirit and concern" (as in Barry L. Callen, compiler and editor, *Journeying Together: A Documentary History of the Corporate Life of the Church of God Movement [Anderson]* (Anderson, IN: The Leadership Council of the Church of God, 1996, 27). *Editor's note:* Dr. Stafford's involvement with Faith and Order has been through appointment by this Commission on Christian Unity.

[14]*National Evangelical Directory, 1997-1998* (Carol Stream, IL: National Association of Evangelicals).

[15]Conversations with Sarah Vilanculu of the NCCC/USA Office of Communications and with David Cubie, Mount Vernon (Ohio) Nazarene College.

[16]During his 1986 sabbatical at the WCC, Donald Dayton was placed as informal consultant with its Commission on World Mission and Evangelism; he had assumed that as a theologian he would be assigned to Faith and Order. WCC General Secretary Emilio Castro had an interest at that time in introducing WCC member churches to some non-member churches. Articles were written anonymously by members of the latter churches, and published with the approval of their respective bodies in *Ecumenical Review*: some in 19:1 (January 1967); some in 23:3 (July 1971), including Church of God (Anderson) and the Church of the Nazarene; still others in 24:2 (April 1972); and the last in 28:4 (October 1976), including the Wesleyan Church—the latter by Dayton.

[17]Gilbert W. Stafford, "The Faith and Order Movement: Holiness Church Participation," *Wesleyan Theological Journal* 32:1 (Spring 1997); also published as Appendix H in Barry L. Callen and James B. North, *Coming Together in Christ: Pioneering a New Testament Way to Christian Unity* (Joplin, MO: College Press, 1997). Stafford's own contributions to Faith and Order work are listed here as well.

[18]The story of this development and his judgment that "this decision was one of the most visionary and important that we have ever undertaken as a society" is related in Dayton, "The Holiness Witness," 93.

[19]Donald W. Dayton, "Introduction: American-Born Churches Consultation" (written for Faith and Order NCCC/USA consultation held in Dallas, TX, March 13-14, 1991, unpublished).

[20]Donald W. Dayton, "The Holiness Witness in the Ecumenical Church," *Wesleyan Theological Journal* 23:1-2 (1988), 103.

[21]A common understanding and confession of faith, the mutual recognition of baptism, eucharist and ministry, and common processes for decision making and teaching have for some time been recognized as at least three basic marks of a true fellowship of churches, marks that would make their unity visible. These studies relate to the first of these. Cf. Hans-Georg Link, ed., *The Apostolic Faith Today*, Faith and Order Paper No. 124 (Geneva: WCC, 1985); Hans-Georg Link, ed., *The Roots of Our Common Faith: Faith in the Scriptures and in the Early Church*, Faith and Order Paper No. 119 (Geneva: WCC, 1984); *Confessing the One Faith: An ecumenical explication of the apostolic faith as it is confessed in the*

Nicene-Constantinopolitan Creed, Faith and Order Paper no. 153 (Geneva: WCC, 1996); George Vandervelde, "The Meaning of 'Apostolic Faith' in World Council of Churches' Documents," in Thaddeus D. Horgan, ed., *Apostolic Faith in America* (Grand Rapids, MI: Eerdmans, 1988).

[22]Donald Dayton, "Introduction: American-Born Churches Consultation."

[23]Thaddeus D. Horgan, ed., *Apostolic Faith in America* (Grand Rapids, MI: Eerdmans, 1988).

[24]Timothy J. Wengert and Charles W. Brockwell, Jr., *Telling the Churches' Stories: Ecumenical Perspectives on Writing Christian History* (Grand Rapids, MI: Eerdmans, 1995) is the fine volume that came out of this concern.

[25]Two published U. S. Faith and Order papers by Donald Dayton not cited above: "Reflections on Apostolicity in the North American Context" in Horgan, ed., *Apostolic Faith in America*; and "Pneumatological Issues in the Holiness Movement," in Theodore Stylianopoulos and S. Mark Heim, eds., *Spirit of Truth: Ecumenical Perspectives on the Holy Spirit* (Brookline, MA: Holy Cross Orthodox Press, 1986).

[26]*Baptism, Eucharist and Ministry*, Faith and Order Paper 111 (Geneva: World Council of Churches, 1982).

[27]John Howard Yoder, Introduction to Merle D. Strege, ed., *Baptism and Church: A Believers' Church Vision* [papers on the theme "Believers' Baptism and the Meaning of Church Membership: Concepts and Practices in an Ecumenical Context" presented at the 7th Conference on the Believers Church," Anderson, Indiana, June 1984] (Grand Rapids, MI: Sagamore Books, 1986), 6.

[28]The two besides *Baptism and Church* were: David B. Eller, ed., *Servants of the Word: Ministry in the Believers' Church* [papers from the 8th Believers Church Conference, Bethany Theological Seminary, Oak Brook, IL, September 1987] (Elgin, IL: Brethren Press, 1990); Dale R. Stoffer, ed., *The Lord's Supper: Believers Church Perspectives* [papers from the 11th Believers Church Conference, Ashland Theological Seminary, Ashland, OH, June 1994] (Scottdale, Pa.: Herald Press, 1997).

[29]Floyd T. Cunningham, "Interreligious Dialogue: A Wesleyan Holiness Perspective," in Mark Heim, ed., *Grounds for Discussion: Ecumenical Resources for Responses to Religious Pluralism* (Grand Rapids, MI: Eerdmans, 1998). The writer takes credit for Cunningham's participation. They met at a World Evangelical Fellowship/Theological Commission meeting in the Philippines and again at a WTS meeting.

[30]William Kostlevy, "An Historical Overview," in "Thirtieth Anniversary of the Wesleyan Theological Society," *WTJ* 30:1 (Spring 1995), 214; John G. Merritt, "Fellowship in Ferment: A History of the Wesleyan Theological Society, 1965-1984," *WTJ* 21:1-2 (1986), 185-203.

[31]Susie Stanley was the delegate from the Wesleyan Theological Society; Johns was sent by her denomination.

[32]David Bundy, "The Historiography of the Wesleyan/Holiness Tradition," *Wesleyan Theological Journal* 30:1 (Spring 1995), 63, 67.

³³John G. Merritt, "Fellowship in Ferment: a History of the Wesleyan Theological Society, 1965-1984," *Wesleyan Theological Journal* 21:1-2 (1986), 197-199. *Editor's note*: This subject was reopened in the March 1998 joint meeting of WTS/SPS by the provocative paper of Laurence Wood that is published in this journal issue.

³⁴Work along this line is seen in various sources: Melvin E. Dieter, "The Development of Nineteenth Century Holiness Theology," *Wesleyan Theological Journal* 20:1 (Spring 1985), 61-77; Howard A. Snyder with Daniel V. Runyon, *The Divided Flame* (Grand Rapids, MI: Francis Asbury Press, 1986); and Dieter review in *WTJ* 22:2 (1987), 126-7; Melvin E. Dieter, review of W. T. Purkiser, *Called Unto Holiness*, Vol. 2, *The Story of the Nazarenes, the Second Twenty-Five Years, 1933-1958* (Kansas City, MO: Nazarene Publishing House, 1983), in *WTJ* 20:1 (1985), 155-161.

³⁵Grand Rapids, MI: Zondervan (Francis Asbury Press), 1987.

³⁶Donald W. Dayton, "The Holiness Witness in the Ecumenical Church," *Wesleyan Theological Journal* 23:1-2 (1988), 105-106.

³⁷Barry L. Callen, "Daniel Snyder Warner: Joining Holiness and All Truth," *WTJ* 30:1 (Spring 1995) 92-110. Quote, p. 103. On p. 98 Callen notes and quotes Melvin Dieter's earlier recognition of this theological insight of Warner's (in *The Holiness Revival of the Nineteenth Century*, Metuchen, NJ: Scarecrow Press, 1980).

³⁸Callen, "Daniel Snyder Warner," 108.

³⁹One of the three major groupings of churches in the Stone-Campbell Restorationist tradition.

⁴⁰Barry L. Callen and James B. North, *Coming Together in Christ: Pioneering a New Testament Way to Christian Unity* (Joplin, MO: College Press, 1997).

⁴¹Kinnamon's address appears as Appendix D in the Callen/North volume.

⁴²Between 1987 and 1994, the Church of God (Anderson) invited critique of its own "stand apart" history. Among those who addressed its General Assembly were three leaders in Christian Holiness Partnership churches. See Callen and North, 106-111.

⁴³An illuminating selection of excerpts of writings, historic and current, from both of these traditions appears in the appendices to the book.

⁴⁴Callen and North, 9-10. Callen's own convictions and their grounding in the Anderson Church of God tradition are apparent here. Cf. Appendix F, excerpted from Callen's *Contours of a Cause: The Theological Vision of the Church of God Movement (Anderson)*.

⁴⁵Cf. Callen and North, 26 and elsewhere.

⁴⁶Callen and North, 90.

⁴⁷Callen and North, 101. Cf. all of chapter 5, "Doctrine: Testing the Evangelical Alternative" and chapter 6, "Joining the Larger Discussion."

⁴⁸Callen and North, 101. If and when other dialogues are or appear to be less faithful to the truth, we should take heed; we should after all "normally worry" about the same things, if that truth is one. If we don't, we should ques-

tion each other about our ways of proceeding, our warrants and methodologies and address differences forthrightly and together, taking others' claims seriously and allowing ourselves to be questioned critically, but yielding no understanding or conviction that grounds us.

[49]David L. Cubie, "A Wesleyan Perspective on Christian Unity," *Wesleyan Theological Journal* 33:2 (Fall 1998), 198-229.

[50]See report and notes above on the Holiness-Pentecostal rapprochement.

[51]He did this to greatest effect in evangelical circles with his *Discovering an Evangelical Heritage* (Peabody, MA: Hendrickson, c1976, 1988, reprinted with new preface), which countered the prevailing conservative account of what was evangelically correct behavior with a tradition of evangelical social concern. In his "Yet Another Layer of the Onion; Or Opening the Ecumenical Door to Let the Riffraff In" (*Ecumenical Review* 40:1, 1988, 87-110) he raises broader questions of historiography.

[52]Donald W. Dayton and Robert K. Johnston, eds., *The Variety of American Evangelicalism* (Downers Grove, IL: InterVarsity Press, 1991).

[53]Donald W. Dayton, "The Holiness Witness in the Ecumenical Church," *Wesleyan Theological Journal* 23:1-2 (1988).

[54]Dayton, "The Holiness Witness."

[55]Dayton, "The Holiness Witness," 104; Wallace Thornton, Jr., "Sweet Radical Holiness": Behavioral Standards, Embourgeoisement, and the Formation of the Conservative Holiness Movement," *Wesleyan Theological Journal* 33:2 (Fall 1998), 172-197.

[56]There has been little official communication between United Methodists and the descendants of Holiness groups who arose in and left the Methodist Episcopal Church, despite some important linking occurring within the World Methodist Council. Many if not most Methodists know little or nothing about Holiness denominations, and/or do not take them in as part of Methodist history and so as "relatives." Connections have been severed too completely for too long. Methodist interest in dialogue has been focused elsewhere. It would seem obvious to start a process of becoming acquainted today and reconnecting with a history that WTS scholars are helping to recover.

[57]Alan D. Falconer, "From Theologies-in-Opposition Towards a Theology-of-Interdependence," *Life and Peace Review*, vol. 4, 1990. Falconer is current Director of Faith and Order studies, World Council of Churches. A Scotsman and Presbyterian, his thoughts about Christian unity were honed during years of work in Ireland. See Falconer, ed., *Reconciling Memories* (Dublin: Columba Press, 1988) for an elaboration of the theme. Also Falconer, "Towards Unity through Diversity: Bilateral and Multilateral Dialogues," *One in Christ* 29:4 (1993), 279-287.

[58]Cf. Martin E. Marty, *Modern American Religion: The Irony of It All, 1893-1919* (Chicago: University of Chicago, 1986); George M. Marsden, *Fundamentalism and American Culture: The Shaping of Twentieth-Century Evangelicalism, 1870-1925*

(NY: Oxford, 1980).

⁵⁹A recent example is Episcopalian Bruce Bawer's *Stealing Jesus: How Fundamentalism Betrays Christianity* (New York: Crown Publishers, 1997). Bawer has done some research and learned some facts and history, but, as he operates within a basic oppositional construct, it is difficult to class his work as real inquiry or exploration.

⁶⁰Falconer cites Hannah Arendt, *The Human Condition* (University of Chicago Press, 1958), 236-247, and quotes Donald Shriver: "To remember Jesus of Nazareth is to participate in 'realized forgiveness'" (in "Justice and Reconciliation: Forgiveness and the American Blacks," *Studies* 78(3), 89 no. 310, pp. 136-150).

⁶¹Paul Merritt Bassett, "The Theological Identity of the North American Holiness Movement: Its Understanding of the Nature and Role of the Bible," in *The Variety of Evangelicalism* (Downers Grove, IL: InterVarsity Press, 1991).

⁶²Paul Merritt Bassett, "The Fundamentalist Leavening of the Holiness Move-ment: 1914- 1940," *Wesleyan Theological Journal* 13 (1978), 65-91.

⁶³As quoted in Leo Cox, "Wesleyan Theological Society: The First Decade," *Wesleyan Theological Journal* 30:1 (Spring 1995), 220-221.

⁶⁴The celebration and strengthening of this heritage by the hundreds of women in attendance at the recent Wesleyan/Holiness Women Clergy conferences (1994, 1996 and 1998), developed by clergy women with the support of Christian Holiness Partnership denominations, means that it is less likely ever again to be as undercelebrated as it was in the period of "fundamentalist leavening."

⁶⁵Baconian/Scottish enlightenment thought has been a pervasive presence in American religious thought and played a part in the development of 19th-century Holiness theology. Cf. Paul Merritt Bassett, "The Theological Identity of the North American Holiness Movement" and Al Truesdale, "Reification of the Experience of Entire Sanctification," *Wesleyan Theological Journal* 31:2 (Fall 1996), 95-119. It is not inherently "fundamentalist." We are speaking here of the concern of some in evangelical circles that this approach should have such preponderant and constraining authority.

Chapter 12

Practicing the Unity Being Preached

by
Merle D. Strege

The teaching history of the Church of God movement (Anderson) is clear. Christian unity is God's intention and a prominent aspect of the church's need for radical reform. Historian Merle D. Strege recounts this burden of the movement and focuses on how it has sought to practice what it has preached. He cites the roles of Barry L. Callen with the Wesleyan Theological Society, Edward L. Foggs with the National Association of Evangelicals, and the prophetic ministries of Samuel G. Hines and Cheryl J. Sanders in Washington, D.C. The church is to stand united against the perverted power arrangements of this world. The goal is the actual visibility of the unity of all Christians so that the world may know that God was in Christ, bringing salvation and genuinely new life and community for all people. Originally published in the Wesleyan Theological Journal *(42:2, Fall, 2007) under the title "The Doctrinal Practice of Christian Unity in the Church of God (Anderson)."*

More than twenty-five years ago, John W. V. Smith rightly described the Church of God movement as a people on a quest for holiness and unity, a phrase that captures the heart of the movement's mission.[1] Early Church of God people fervently believed that God had called the movement into being to witness to the world of its need for salvation *and* to witness to the divided body of Christ on behalf of the crucial need of unity. Moreover, they saw this mission as two sides of one coin: to remove or diminish either was to render the accomplishment of its partner much more difficult. Unity without evangelism is to no purpose; evangelism without unity is highly problematic.

The Church of God is a non-creedal tradition. Three implications of this statement deserve special emphasis. First, to say that we are non-creedal means not that we have no convictions, but that we have "no creed but the Bible," and thus prefer to test doctrinal practice directly against the Scriptures. However, unless we are content to be a collection of ecclesiological cowboys, this conviction commits the church to careful, communal biblical study. Second, that we are non-creedal does not necessarily imply theological disagreement with the contents of Christendom's great doctrinal statements—e.g., the Apostles and the Nicene Creeds. Indeed, writers from Charles E. Brown to Gilbert W. Stafford have observed that the Church of God does not teach or practice a doctrine alien to these statements. Third, our non-creedal position commits us to a practical approach to Christian doctrine, i. e., practice trumps belief statements. Thus, the Bible is certainly a book to be believed, but, even more, it is to be performed, practiced, lived. Life is acting as well as being.

Within the theological perspective of the Church of God, dialogical life aims to address the questions: (1) What kind of people is God calling us to be? and (2) How are we to be and act in the world and toward Christendom with respect to the practice of Christian unity? In ecclesial traditions like the Church of God, formal beliefs must be practiced, and the latter is the proof of the former. In a real sense, the practice is the doctrine. So, we aim at more than propositional understanding; we hope to form the church's practice.

To gain a purchase on this task, we must first attend to two formative influences on our common life. At the outset we must consider our narratives, consulting our ancestors' and contemporaries' ideas and practices about Christian unity. This is a consultation, not a search for preemptive or definitive statements. To grasp the presumed definitive would be to lend to it the kind of creedal stature that our forefathers and foremothers opposed. Rather, we will consult our formative narratives by respectfully listening to the living faith of the dead, and so let them cast a vote on answers to our question. Secondly, not in order of theological importance but only in sequence, we will consult some salient biblical texts.

Concerning the topic of unity, early Church of God preachers frequently resorted to John 17, and so will we. Lena Shofner's sermon on Ephesians 2:14-22 proved a memorable extension of the practice of unity, and Galatians 3:28-29 is another oft-quoted text. What are the implications of these passages for the contemporary doctrinal practice of Christian unity in the Church of God movement? After working with the biblical text in light of our narratives, hopefully we will finally come to a proposal for our own ecclesial life.

An Historical Overview of Theological Statements and Practice

It could be said of the Church of God reformation movement that it is an extended practice of the church. Historically, a particular vision of the church as one body has gripped our attention. Scratch the surface of many theological debates and you will find that what we are really discussing is the church. For example, although Herbert M. Riggle wrote several books attacking premillennialist eschatology, the theological issue fundamentally at stake was the doctrine of the church. If premillennialist interpretation of the Book of Revelation was correct, then Riggle and other early church-historical interpreters were wrong; and if that were so, much if not all of what they taught about the church would necessarily be thrown into question. The doctrine of the church and, derivatively, Christian unity, is at the heart of the life and thought of the Church of God movement, and we can think of the movement as an extended discussion—sometimes a debate or even an argument—about what it means to be the church.

Daniel S. Warner (1842-1895) inaugurated a discussion and practice of the church that attempted to restore her to the model found in the New Testament. This is a form of Christian primitivism, a mindset that finds norms or patterns in the ancient Christian past and urges believers to restore or return to those norms. Other primitivist traditions include the Christian Churches and the early Friends, as illustrated in George Fox's slogan: "Primitive Christianity revived." Warner discussed his theology of the church in a small pamphlet entitled *The Church of God: What the Church of God is and What it is Not*. The booklet covers a range of topics, including the subjects of Christian unity and the problems associated with what Warner called "sectism."

Scholars in religion often use the term "sect" to refer to voluntary Christian bodies over against the established church, but Warner used the term in a much more pejorative sense. He defined sect from the Latin meaning "to cut," and from which we get such English words as "section" or "dissect." According to Warner, all the churches of Christendom (in the United States they are called denominations) were nothing other than sects because they divide or cut up the body of Christ. However, the church must contain all the redeemed, and from this premise Warner concluded, "No sect contains all of the body of Christ, therefore no sect is the church of God. Then, as honest men, who expect to be judged by the Word of God, let us never call anything the church but the body of Christ; i. e., all the saved, either universally or in any given locality."[2] That the sects were not the true church was also evidenced by their use of creeds, formal rules of membership, and bureaucratic forms of organization or "man-rule." Warner asserted that the true church trusted only in the Bible, was comprised of all the saved, and was governed by Christ through the gifts of the Holy Spirit.

Warner's theology of the church and his criticism of American Christianity's denominational structure pressed him to a strong appeal for unity. Christ, the one head of the church, could have but one body, even as her bridegroom could have but one bride.[3] Warner and other early preachers offered several New Testament texts in support of this claim, but none was cited more frequently than Jesus' explicit plea for his disciples' unity in John 17. Galatians 3:28 declares that all are one in Christ, and Ephesians 2:14-22 refers to the collapse of the dividing wall of hostility through his work. But John 17 records Jesus' prayer for his disciples in the hours just before his Passion began. The moment's sheer drama would be enough to lend his words heightened significance, but the prayer also specifies the means by which Jesus' disciples will be united. Jesus prays here that his disciples and all who might believe through their witness "may be sanctified in truth…that they all may be one."[4] Obviously, the union of all Christians could not be achieved through any form of bureaucratic organization. Warner concluded from John 17 that only through the work of the sanctifying Spirit could Christian unity be accomplished. The chorus of his gospel song "The Bond of Perfectness" expressed this insight in its chorus:

> Oh brethren! How this perfect love
> Unites us all in Jesus;
> One heart and mind and soul we prove
> The union heaven gave us.

The phrase "perfect love" is, of course, a synonym for Christian perfection, the experience of entire sanctification, or Christian holiness. In the late 1870s, Warner had adopted this theology through his connection with the Holiness Movement that emphasized entire sanctification as a second work of grace. Wesleyan soteriology thought of salvation as a "double cure." As Charles Wesley had written, Christ "breaks the power of canceled sin." On this view, salvation comprised first of all *justification*—what God does in us—or the cancellation of sin, and secondly *sanctification*—what God does in us—namely, breaking sin's hold over the believer. Camp meeting revivalism was the natural home of holiness preachers, and in that context the instantaneous reception of sanctification after justification became the standard view. To this view Warner was no exception. However, to use his phrase, "Bible salvation" brought more than freedom from sin. It also bound the redeemed and sanctified together in all-sufficient love.

Warner thus articulated an experience of harmony often the subject of testimonies from those who attended holiness camp meetings even before 1880. The experience of unity to which they testified Warner explained theologically, and it became a fundamental rallying point for the little group gathered about the *Gospel Trumpet* publication of the young Church of God movement. No creeds, rules of fellowship, or other artificial tests were required among those who lived on the plane of Bible holiness. As the true foundation of Christian unity, as in Warner's ecclesiology, holiness yielded a pervasive harmony in fellowship, worship, and ethical life; the early Church of God movement attempted to practice this understanding of the true church and its unity.

Through the Church of God movement's first fifty years, the message of Christian unity through the sanctification of believers remained fairly constant. Herbert M. Riggle's 1913 work *The Christian Church, Its Rise and Progress*[5] illustrates this consistency. Riggle (1872-1952) explicitly extended the primitivist conception of the church implicit in Warner's earlier work. However, during the years between Warner's pamphlet and Riggle's book, the church-historical interpretation of biblical apocalyptic writing had emerged first in the work of W. G. Schell and later with F. G. Smith.[6] The full title of Schell's work illustrates the connection to ecclesiology established by church-historical exegetes: *The Biblical Trace of the Church, from her Birth to the End of Time: Showing the Origin and Termination of Sectism and Proving We are Near the End of the World*. Riggle himself had helped to establish this connection, having edited and completed Warner's unfinished typological reading of Daniel and the Revelation, *The Cleansing of the Sanctuary*.[7] Thus, he opened his study of the church with this description:

> As we stand on the summit of the present truth and point our telescope back over the mists and clouds that move along at our feet, and over the twelve hundred and sixty years of utter darkness that extend far beyond, even into the third century, we behold, on the mountains of God's own holiness, the temple of God, resplendent with the morning light of his own glory. With admiration we view her and behold, she is "fair as the moon, clear as the sun, and terrible as an army with banners." She is "all fair," the city of the great king. That golden city is the primitive church.[8]

Riggle's explicit primitivism meant that the "golden city" of the ancient New Testament church provided the standard by which the authenticity of all subsequent churches was to be assessed. Among the distinguishing criteria of the New Testament church were oneness and unity. Riggle repeated the logic that required one body for the church's one head, Christ. Never one to mince words, Riggle sharpened the rhetoric used to describe "the sects," asserting that the call to join one of these various bodies "must proceed from antichrist."[9]

As the primitive church, so also the latter-day restored church must exhibit a complete unity that replicates the New Testament model. Accordingly, the saved members of this church must: (1) not be of this world but shun its "popular amusements and abominations; (2) abide in Christ alone and refuse to join any human substitute for the church; (3) take for themselves the only New Testament name for the church and abjure any and all modifiers; (4) accept the one and only proper discipline for the church, the Bible; and (5) be sanctified, for "sanctifying grace removes all carnality, which is the cause of division, and the all-pervading love of God, shed abroad in the heart by the Holy Spirit, brings all hearts into the same harmony that reigns in heaven, into perfect unity, as the Father and Son are one."[10]

H. M. Riggle and the second generation of Church of God leadership generally repeated Warner's connection between holiness and unity. However, the church-historical exegesis sharpened these themes and gave them a harder edge. To name some Christians "daughters of Babylon the great harlot" gave new force to the call to come out of sectism. In point of fact, ever since Warner (d. 1895), Church of God people had been urging believers to quit the false churches of the denominations and enter the true New Testament body of Christ. Nevertheless, the apocalyptically grounded self-understanding of Schell, Smith, the early Riggle, and those they influenced deepened the gulf separating the Church of God from other believers. If the essence of the sectarian mentality is to refuse legitimacy to any other groups, then, despite protestations to the contrary, the Church of God shaped by the church-historical exegesis threatened to make of itself the very thing it had originally opposed—a divisive sect. Thus, by the decade of the 1920s, the Church of God may very well have been more isolated from other Christians than at any other time in its history.

Not all members of the Church of God subscribed to the apocalyptically grounded view of the church. During the 1920s, opponents of this view began to express themselves in published statements and sermons.

In their view, the church-historical exegesis and insistence that others "come out of Babylon" was closing the movement off from fellowship with other believers. Even before 1920, George P. Tasker challenged Smith's apocalyticism and practiced a Christian unity that took him into YMCA lecture halls and Presbyterian pulpits in Lahore, India, where Tasker served as a missionary of the Church of God. By the end of the decade, E. A. Reardon and Russell Byrum had publicly repudiated the narrow sectarianism into which they believed the Church of God was descending. The details of their opposition are well known.[11] Reardon was voted off many of his board assignments. Tasker was deprived of his missionary appointment; Byrum resigned his faculty position. These developments illustrate the intellectual honesty of the three, as well as the strength of the apocalyptic mindset's influence on much of the Church of God ministry at the time.

Into this highly charged atmosphere stepped Charles E. Brown (1883-1971), newly ratified as Editor in Chief of the Gospel Trumpet Company in 1930. While many knew his reputation as a thinking minister, few could have predicted the ecclesiological revolution that would flow from this man's prolific typewriter. Brown possessed a knowledge of Christian history more comprehensive than any of his predecessors or contemporaries, and this broad knowledge served as a basis by which Brown assessed the life and thought of Christians in other times and places. This historical awareness and knowledge also steered him away from the apocalypticism of the preceding Editor, F. G. Smith. At the same time, these intellectual characteristics moved Brown toward embracing what he termed, in one of his book titles, *A New Approach to Christian Unity*.[12]

Within a year of succeeding Smith, Brown had developed a new position on Christian unity even as he perpetuated some of the previous generation's ideals. On one hand, Brown continued the earlier judgment that divisions within Christianity constituted both a problem and a reproach on those content to live in disunity. In so doing, he also disputed a widespread notion that Christians enjoyed a spiritual unity that transcended denominational walls. Spiritual unity was important, wrote Brown, but Christ also prayed for "organic unity."[13] Like Warner, Riggle, and Smith, Brown took the primitive church of the New Testament as the standard for contemporary church life. Eschewing apocalyptic language, however, he preferred to describe ideal Christian life and thought as "radical" in the sense of getting to the root of the matter. While he agreed that the post-New Testament church had lost its radical nature and pursued ineffective means of unity, Brown did not reach that conclusion by employing church-historical exegesis. He remained consistent with the ideals of earlier Church of God primitivism; however, his proposal for a return to the unity of the New Testament church departed from earlier discussions.

Brown believed that the apostolic church enjoyed a profound unity and that it was incumbent on the contemporary church to recover that relationship. He proposed three steps to this recovery in a program he labeled "spiritual disarmament." The first step was to "drop all official creeds insofar as they are official and authoritative definitions of denominational belief."[14] Brown was not demonizing creeds or those who use them. Quite the contrary, he regarded creeds as useful for theological students, and for him any reasonably founded belief in a creed was unobjectionable. Nevertheless, he also appreciated the divisive role that creeds have played in separating Christians.[15] Such divisiveness is a characteristic that he applied to unwritten creeds as well. Written or unwritten, Brown regarded as a pernicious evil creeds that exclude some faithful Christians from the fellowship of other believers. However, ideally speaking, an unwritten creed possesses the virtue of a vitality that renders it "capable of responding to the divine guidance of the living Christ in the church. It can broaden with the increase of knowledge."[16]

Brown's second step to the recovery of New Testament unity was the abolition of all formal denominational structures. He proposed not merger but abolition. Here we see at work Brown's appreciation for radical Christianity. He reminded his readers that, in the long view of Christian history, denominations were a fairly recent phenomenon. In what today may be considered a moment of astute prescience, Brown declared, "All signs point to their eventual abolition and the gathering of God's people once again into the blessed peace and unity of the ancient church."[17] It should be noted that Brown saw in most denominations positive qualities that they would contribute to this church beyond division, e.g., Quaker "inner light," Baptist democracy, Presbyterian fidelity to the truth, and Methodist evangelistic fervor.

Third and most important, Christians of today can recover their lost visible unity only by committing themselves to Christ, the Lord of the church. Here Brown gave expression to the Pietist heritage of the Church of God movement:

> Doctrine is very important; but more important it is to get back to the supreme Person, who is the source of all true doctrine. He has said, "I am the WAY, the TRUTH, and the LIFE." When all Christendom gets

back to him it will be one. There will be plenty of time to compare and study doctrines, when the clamor of debate has given place to the silence of the humble and earnest pupils in the school of Christ.[18]

Ultimately, the unity of the church rests, not on loyalty to a creed, nor even to a book, but to a Person. From this position, Brown concluded that all who are saved in Christ are already members of the body of Christ regardless of their denominational affiliation. This view could not but legitimize any church where faithful disciples were found. Once such legitimacy was granted, the sectarian posture and mindset of the Church of God movement had to begin eroding. No longer could the movement be so determined in its withdrawal to the isolation from which it called others to come out of Babylon. The view that all who are saved in Christ are members of the "church of God" is thus a crucial step in the development of the movement's doctrinal practice of Christian unity. More than any other single voice, it was C. E. Brown who articulated the ecclesiology and vision of unity that permitted, even encouraged the Church of God to cross- denominational borders formerly regarded as sealed. By the early 1940s, a growing number of ministers were critical of "come-outism," contending that functionally it underwrote the unity only of the movement and not all Christians.[19]

The History of a Doctrinal Practice

Earlier I stated that, for non-creedal groups like the Church of God doctrine is better conceived as a set of practices than a collection of propositions or a belief statement.[20] One may conveniently refer to published theological statements as a way of getting a handle on "doctrine," but it is more important to ask, "How were Church of God people practicing the church and, specifically, Christian unity?" I have already identified "come-outism" as a pervasive doctrinal practice of unity in the Church of God in the years before 1930. What other versions, if any, of Christian unity were also in practice?

The twentieth century was the great age of ecumenism. The Federal Council of Churches was founded in America in 1908 and the World Council of Churches in 1948. Church of God people were either aware of or attended each of the latter's two great precursors. In 1925 C. J. Blewitt of the New York missionary home attended the Universal Christian Conference on Life and Work in Stockholm, Sweden. Blewitt approvingly described "so many great men and women showing such humility and earnestly seeking to get the world to understand the meaning of love in domestic and public relations."[21] Two years later the other parent of the World Council of Churches, the World Conference on Faith and Order, convened in Lausanne, Switzerland. The Church of God sent no official observers to this meeting, but R. L. Berry, Managing Editor of the *Gospel Trumpet,* kept a watchful eye on its proceedings. More skeptical than Blewitt, Berry expected the conference to fail because it pursued what he supposed to be the path of federated unity. He concluded that the devil would likely be in attendance. However, Berry added, "But God will also be there if any of his people are, and we cannot doubt that. So we believe God will be there to inspire his people to real unity such as the Bible demands and inspires."[22]

Even before Blewitt and Berry offered their observations about world ecumenism, Church of God folk had joined cooperative Christian ventures in the United States. In 1918 the Missionary Board affiliated with the Foreign Missions Conference. Shortly afterward, the Board of Christian Education and the Gospel Trumpet Company adopted the use of International Sunday School Outlines for the preparation of Church of God curriculum. Christian educators reached across conventional lines more than others. In 1928 they joined the International Council of Christian Education; a few years later they joined the World Council of Christian Education, as well as committees responsible for the preparation of Sunday school lesson outlines.

As a body, the Church of God did not join the American Council of Churches or its successor, the National Council. However, individuals from the Church of God have participated with or served as members of individual program units. The first Executive Secretary of the Executive Council, C. W. Hatch, was a longstanding member of the Federal Council's Commission on Stewardship, serving as chairperson for a term. Otto F. Linn joined a sub-committee working on the National Council's translation project, *The Revised Standard Version* of the Bible. Church of God youth programs, the women's organization, and the Board of Church Extension associated with cooperative Christian ventures as early as 1930.

One clear ecumenical example is the fact that Barry L. Callen has functioned as Editor of the *Wesleyan Theological Journal* since the early 1990s, guiding this scholarly forum for the exploration of doctrine and practice in many denominations with which the Church of God movement has much natural affinity. Perhaps the most striking example of commitment to an ecumenical approach to Christian unity has been the movement's membership on the Commission on Faith and Order of the National Council. Through the participation of John W. V. Smith and

Gilbert W. Stafford, the Church of God has enjoyed uninterrupted membership in Faith and Order since its inception in 1957. Stafford in particular has proved an eloquent and longstanding spokesperson for Christian unity. Never an advocate of merger or formalized unions, he has exemplified the dialogical approach to Christian unity characteristic of the American conciliar movement.[23] These examples illustrate that at least one alternate practice of unity was alive and well alongside the apocalyptic mindset of "come-outism."

More recently, under the auspices of the former Executive Council and now the Ministries Council of the Church of God, people of the Church of God have engaged in bi- or multi-lateral conversations with representatives of other Christian communions. In the 1960s the movement entered into a series of discussions with representatives from the Churches of God of North America, the Church of the Brethren, and the Brethren Church. In 1968 the Church of God joined the Evangelical Covenant Church in a similar series of bi-lateral discussions. Although feared by some, formal church unions were never the goal of any of these conversations. They were advanced in the warm ecumenical atmosphere that enveloped American Christianity during that decade and were committed simply to an honest search for points of commonality.[24]

The spirit of honest searching has also characterized the longest running bi-lateral conversation, a series of meetings with the Independent Christian Churches/Churches of Christ beginning in 1989. In a forum held that year at Trader's Point Christian Church at Indianapolis, representatives of both groups met to discuss theological topics ranging from history and theology to church practice and the ordinances. Participants from both groups recognized many points of commonality, and there has ensued a series of occasional meetings, the most recent of which occurred in the spring of 2006. The enduring discussion topic of these meetings has been, "In what ways can these two movements join in common work for the advancement of the kingdom of God on earth?"[25]

In conversations bi-lateral or quadrilateral, in associations with cooperative Christian ventures to assist and enrich the ongoing life of the church, and in the memberships of boards or individuals in program units of ecumenical bodies, people of the Church of God have practiced forms of Christian unity different from the isolationist posture of the apocalyptic self-understanding. These alternate practices have not gone un-noticed or without occasional rebuke. In 1985 the General Assembly adopted a resolution encouraging efforts "to seek intentional inter-church relationships through which its own ministries are enriched and which provide opportunity for the Church of God reformation movement to live out its message of Christian unity through enriching the entire Body of Christ."[26] However, in 1987 both the National and World Councils of Churches received stinging criticism from the floor of the Assembly, and questions were raised concerning the propriety of agency membership in program units of either body. At the same time, former Executive-Secretaries Paul Tanner and Edward Foggs have served in leadership positions within the National Association of Evangelicals without strong vocal criticism, all of which serves to illustrate the diversity of the movement's practice of unity.

In this connection, it is perhaps worth noting the fate of the Commission on Christian Unity, a program unit within the movement that was born in the midst of this diverse practice. It took the Church of God some eighty-four years to officially create this commission, whose purpose was the advancement of one of the movement's cardinal doctrines. Scarcely more than a generation later, the General Assembly overwhelmingly adopted a restructuring plan that called for the elimination of all divisions and commissions—including the Commission on Christian Unity. This was not a move against cooperation unity, but restructuring for purposes of organizational efficiency and dollar savings.

The apocalyptic self-understanding of come-outism and what might be broadly termed the practice of ecumenical cooperation share an important feature. Although widely variant practices, both think of Christian unity in theological terms; both approach the subject ecclesiologically. Christian unity so conceived addresses the topic as the problem of Christians who are separated individually and by group. In the 1970s and 1980s new voices in the movement raised questions about the nature of Christian unity that were constructed in very different terms.

Given the strident call for the racial integration of American society in the 1950s and 1960s it was unavoidable that African-American clergy would raise questions concerning the practice of Christian unity. They cast the movement's earlier rhetoric in a new light. Where Galatians 3:28 had once been quoted to reinforce a call to *church* unity, now the same text was applied to the racism that divided even a movement that historically has declared unity to be its reason for being. In 1970 the Caucus of Black Churchmen in the Church of God met in Cleveland, Ohio, to "share the burden of the Black church and to share the concerns it feels under God to be imperative if the church is to be the salt of the earth."²⁷ The Caucus exposed a raw wound in that part of the body of Christ known as the Church of God. The ministers gathered in Cleveland asserted that racism was an ugly fact calling into question the movement's commitment to Christian unity.

No person challenged racism more than the late Samuel G. Hines, native of Jamaica and long-term pastor of Third Street Church of God in Washington, D. C. Hines was fond of saying that the Church of God deserved an "A" for its message of unity, but an "F" for its practice. He and the Rev. Louis Evans, pastor of National Presbyterian Church, overcame this tendency by forging a friendship that brought their two congregations into close bonds of Christian fellowship. Hines understood doctrine to be a set of practices that must be lived out in the church's life. If the Church of God was to faithfully live out its call as a movement of Christian unity, racial reconciliation had to be more than a claim; it had to be at the heart of the movement's doctrinal practice.

Hines' theological and pastoral legacy has been extended at Third Street church by Cheryl Sanders, also a professor at Howard University. Sanders has pointedly connected the issue of racial reconciliation to what she calls an ethic of holiness and unity. In an essay contributed to an anthology titled *Called to Ministry, Empowered to Serve*,²⁸ she developed a foundation for Church of God ethics on which she built a connection between sanctification and social change. In Sanders' view, the call to holiness necessarily involves the dismantling of division based on race or sex.²⁹ The movement's traditional theological theme that holiness brings unity was thus applied to aspects of the movement's internal life; Christian unity was no longer merely a matter concerning the many churches. By the 1980s, people in the Church of God were increasingly reflecting on the practice of unity *within* the movement as social and theological fissures either were exposed or opened wide enough so as not to be ignored. What had begun as a criticism of and concern for a divided Christendom had also become an instrument for self-examination and critique.³⁰

Consulting Scripture on the Topic of Unity

H. M. Riggle believed that no sincere Christian could ignore or otherwise set aside Jesus' prayer in John 17. A scriptural consideration of Christian unity appropriately begins with and rests upon the text to which Church of God preachers and writers have referred so often in the course of 125 years.

Jesus' prayer for his disciples is part of a lengthy section of John's gospel beginning at chapter 13 and focusing around the Last Supper. Jesus has already washed the feet of his disciples, shared the meal with them, and identified Judas as his betrayer. Chapters 14 through 16 comprise a lengthy discourse followed by 17:1, "These things Jesus spoke; and lifting his eyes to heaven he said. . . ." For our purposes, the relevant verses are vv. 16-21:

> They are not of the world, even as I am not of the world. Sanctify them in the truth; Thy word is truth. As Thou didst send Me into the world, I have also sent them into the world. And for their sakes I sanctify Myself, that they may also be sanctified in truth. I do not ask in behalf of these alone, but for those also who believe in Me through their word; that they all may be one; even as Thou, Father, art in Me, and I in Thee, that they also may be in Us; that the world may believe that Thou didst send me. (NASB)

Three elements and their interrelationship in this text are noteworthy. Jesus prays for the *sanctification* of his followers, their *unity*, and the *fruitful evangelism* of the world. Neither the disciples' unity nor holiness is an end in itself, nor is it likely that the world will recognize Jesus as God's Christ in the face of a divided body of believers. Holiness leads to unity, and unity encourages the world's belief in Jesus. How are we to interpret this text, at once so simple and yet so profoundly demanding of the church?

To be holy is to be sanctified. The Greek *hagiazo*, "sanctify," carries the dual understanding of being purified and being set apart. Ben Witherington opts for the latter interpretation, citing Jer. 1:5 and Exod. 28:41 as precedents: "The disciples are to be set aside in the truth, just as Jesus sets himself apart, or consecrates himself in the truth."[31] Otto F. Linn concurs, "Holiness is not always thought of as the opposite of impurity, but often, as here, it is a dedication to a sacred purpose over against the common use of life for selfish ends....Holiness in this sense demands an inward conformity of heart and will to the will and purpose of God."[32]

On the other hand, Rudolf Bultmann does not think that purity is a notion to be ruled out of the interpretation of this text, and in fact makes it central to the dynamic separating church and world:

> If it is true that the existence of the community depends upon maintaining its purity, i. e., on receiving and preserving its raison d'etre and nature not from the world but from beyond it, then unity is an essential part of that nature. Accordingly, the prayer for the oneness of the community is joined to the prayer for the preservation of purity. . . ."[33]

Purity here is not to be narrowly defined with the holiness codes of nineteenth and early twentieth-century American Protestantism. Rather, to be holy, in the sense Bultmann takes, is to be marked off from the world, which we may take in John for a symbol for anything that refuses to acknowledge Yahweh and his way. Such a view aligns with the idea of sanctification as separation. To be set apart for the service of God, to be conformed to the will and purpose of God, is to be set over against the world and thus, in Bultmann's sense, to be pure.

Sanctification in the word of truth is the means by which the disciples will be made one. They are made one through their sanctification by God. The church is joined to Christ and through their sanctification share Christ's complete devotion to the world's redemption. Thus, the union of the church rests in its union with Christ and Christ with God.[34] The implications of this unity are world-annulling and commit the church to a counter-cultural way of life. Commenting on John 17 more than a decade before *Brown v. Board of Education*, Otto Linn wrote, "There can be no racial, social, economic, or intellectual differences great enough to justify separation between those who have experienced the unity of the divine life through faith in Christ."[35]

Commentators agree that the unity of the church is the work of God and not the product of their own making. Several also agree that the rejection of creeds and other human institutions is not *ipso facto* grounds for unity. It cannot be achieved either through the use or rejection of creeds or other human inventions:

> But such unity has the unity of the Father and Son as its basis. Jesus is the Revealer by reason of this unity of Father and Son; and the oneness of the community is to be based on this fact. That means it is not founded on natural or purely historical data; nor can it be manufactured by organisation, institutions, dogma; these can at best only bear witness to the real unity, as on the other hand they can also give a false impression of unity. And even if the proclamation of the word in the world requires institutions and dogmas, these cannot guarantee the unity of true proclamation. On the other hand, the actual disunion of the church, which is, in passing, precisely the result of its institutions and dogmas, does not necessarily frustrate the unity of the proclamation. The word can resound authentically, wherever the tradition is maintained.[36]

The word may resound authentically, but the disciples' unity renders its proclamation more effective. According to John 17:21, it is through the disciples' unity that the world will know that God sent Christ into the world. Such unity may be evidenced through the fellowship of worship and/or service. In the hour of prayer, differences melt before God. Christians joining together on Habitat for Humanity construction sites and in cooperation for disaster relief projects from Hurricane Katrina to the Indian Ocean tsunami manifest the church's unity. Such moments are crucial to the church's witness to the world, for in them the world is made aware that it is the world and not the church. None other than one of the favorite whipping boys of the Church of God, John Calvin, saw this connection:

> [John] again lays down the end of our happiness as consisting in unity, and justly; for the ruin of the human race is, that, having been alienated from God, it is also broken and scattered in itself. The restoration of it, therefore, on the contrary, consists in its being properly united in one body, as Paul declares the perfection of the Church to consist in believers joined together in one spirit....Wherefore, whenever Christ speaks about unity, let us remember how basely and shockingly, when separated from him, the world is scattered; and, next, let us learn that the commencement of a blessed life is, that we all be governed, and that we all live, by the Spirit of Christ alone.[37]

The church is sanctified through the word of truth, in John's gospel Christ, and made one with him and the Father. This unity transcends and overcomes all of the categories and differences the world customarily uses to rank and divide people, and by which we often polarize ourselves. Paul's declaration, "There is neither Jew nor Greek, there is neither slave nor free man, there is neither male nor female" (Gal. 3:28a, NASB) does not describe a church built on mutual respect for fundamental differences or an agreement to disagree. No, "You are all one in Christ Jesus" (3:28b, NASB). We are not all alike, but that is not the issue, for uniformity is not Christian unity. Says Bultmann, "It is not personal sympathies or common aims that constitute the unity, but the word that is alive in them all and that gives the community its foundation; and each member represents the demand and gift of the word over against his fellow believer, in that he is for him."[38]

The Church as the Restoration of Babel

In some senses, discussions of Christian unity today may seem a joke. Denominational loyalty in the United States is declining rapidly, and, although most precipitous among mainline Protestant groups, this decline is experienced by a wide range of evangelicals. Religious special interest groups compete with established traditions for the time and dollars of faithful disciples of Jesus. Alternatives to conventional denominational affiliation such as the new monasticism and the emergent church also are attracting the attention of earnest Christians. Even more broadly, the growing preference for spirituality over against religion, where religion is often misunderstood as church rules and regulations, also poses serious questions for the future of conventional church life in the Unites States.[39] In the face of so many alternatives, why do we bother to continue discussing this particular topic?

The simplest answer to this question is that we aim to be conformed to Scripture. The New Testament cannot envision Christian faith and discipleship apart from the church. The church is, as Cyprian declared, the sole ark of salvation, at least in the sense that all the redeemed are her passengers, but also because our characters are in the process of being made whole as we are joined to our brothers and sisters in Christ. Most of them are not much like us, and thank God for that! The church is a company of strangers, rightly described by Bill and Gloria Gaither as a family. Unlike friends, we do not get to choose our family members; we are stuck with them. But, because blood is thicker than water, we find a way to go on. Likewise, we do not get to choose the membership of the church; all of us are thrown in with each other, but here too blood is thicker than water—only it is not our own blood that joins us. Cyprian may not have meant it precisely in this way, but the church is crucial to the moral formation of individual Christians. *Extra ecclesiam nulla salus,* "there is no salvation outside the church." The continuing doctrinal practice of Christian unity is part of the lifeblood of any individual congregation, denomination, or movement, and, because the New Testament envisions cooperation among far-flung congregations and different cultures, ultimately it is the ideal for all who take the name of Christ. Speaking parochially for those of us associated with the Church of God movement, unless we believe God has released us from our original reason for being, we have no choice but to continue thinking, talking, and practicing Christian unity.

Viewed though the lens of church-historical exegesis, the terms "Babel" and "Babylon" held powerful symbolic value in the Church of God. The former was taken to refer to religious confusion, from the linguistic confusion sown among Nimrod and his subjects. The latter was taken as a symbol of the confusion of competing and contradictory denominational voices. Religious confusion would eventually be overcome "as the evening light doth shine." I suggest that the church remains the answer to the problem of confusion and disunity, but that Babel and Babylon should be interpreted more broadly.

The story of the Tower of Babel is an aetiological narrative that explains the emergence of different languages and ultimately people groups. Linguistic and cultural barriers, with their resultant misunderstandings and tension, have ever since threatened the possibility of peace among the peoples of the world. Babel is a problem, but it is larger than religious division and confusion. Historical-critical scholars like Otto Linn take Babylon in Book of Revelation more commonly to refer to the Roman Empire than to denominations or Roman Catholicism, and I follow their lead. Rome boasted that she was the "Eternal City," but Christians believed otherwise. In this sense, Babylon is an apocalyptic symbol that refers to any worldly powers of sufficient arrogance and self-absorption as to usurp the place of God. Such empires have troubled the people of God from the Assyrians to Babylonians to Persians to the Selucids to Romans, etc.

Old Testament scholar Walter Brueggemann has noted the threat that empire poses for the people of God.[40] The books of Daniel and Isaiah both address the empire's invitation to settle down and become comfortably domesticated and accept an empire that is not and cannot ever be home. Thus, in Brueggemann's view, the church, like the Israelites living in Babylon, must decide between accommodating to the culture and continuing to understand that they are exiles. "'Exile' is not simply a geographical fact, but also a theological decision."[41] Like Babel, therefore, "Babylon" also remains a problem, but its scope is larger than divided Christendom.

Acts 2 narrates the story of Pentecost, which is not the revival of the church but the account of its birth. Filled with the Spirit, the soul of the church and the source of its bond of union, the disciples testified in their own Galilean-accented Aramaic. Much to everyone's amazement, people in the large crowd—Egyptians, Parthians, Medes, Mesopotamians, Libyans, Cyrenes, Romans, Arabs and many others, each heard the disciples speaking Aramaic, but understood in their own respective language. What had been done at Babel was undone in Jerusalem at Pentecost. In this view, the church is, as Stanley Hauerwas observes, "God's new language."[42] But this language aims at more than the unity of all Christians; unity is not the goal of the Spirit's sanctifying work.

Although not particularly cognizant of Church of God ecclesiology, Hauerwas helps us understand more completely the implications of our theology of the church: "Salvation cannot be limited to changed self-understanding or to insuring meaningful existence for the individual. Salvation is God's creation of a new society which invites each person to become part of a time that the nations cannot provide."⁴³ The name of that society is "church." Since 1881, Church of God people have stated that salvation makes one a member of the church, but we have not been as clear in our understanding of the church's purpose. Of course, we understand that the church is to witness to the world and to the broken body of Christ. But the church itself, in its daily practice, also has a function.

The church stands and properly lives as God's alternative to the world, the world out of which Jesus' disciples are called. Through the sanctifying Spirit, all disciples are purified of worldly ways of doing business, worldly arrangements of power, worldly patterns of division and segregation. Pentecost and the formation of the church thus overturn Babel and Babylonian pretensions of power. The church stands as God's alternative to human confusion and power arrangements. If the world is to understand that its orders can bring neither peace nor salvation, then the unity of all Christians cannot be simply an ongoing discussion topic, but a key practice in the life of a church through which the world comes to believe that God has sent Christ to be its savior.

Notes

¹John W. V. Smith, *The Quest for Holiness and Unity* (Anderson, Ind.: Warner Press, 1980).

²*The Church of God: What the Church of God is and What it is Not*, reprint edition (Guthrie, Oklahoma: Faith Publishing House, n. d.), 1.

³Early Church of God writers and preachers often employed the latter notion in a piece of rough and ready logic against a divided church. If denominations were each a church, Christ would necessarily be the husband of more than one bride. The suggestion of a morally compromised Christ as bigamist or worse was offered as proof positive that multiple churches or denominations could not possibly be the true church.

⁴John 17:17-21, *passim.*

⁵Anderson, Ind.: The Gospel Trumpet Company, 1913.

⁶W. G. Schell, *The Biblical Trace of the Church* (Grand Junction, Mich.: Gospel Trumpet Publishing Company, 1893); F. G. Smith, *The Revelation Explained* (Anderson: Gospel Trumpet Company, 1908).

⁷Moundsville, W.V.: Gospel Trumpet Publishing Company, 1903.

⁸Riggle, *loc cit.,* 33; Riggle's emphasis.

⁹*Ibid.,* 44.

¹⁰*Ibid.,* 69-84; quotation, 84.

¹¹For an extended discussion, see Robert H. Reardon, *The Early Morning Light* (Anderson, Ind.: Warner Press, 1979), and my *I Saw the Church* (Anderson,

Ind.: Warner Press, 2002), especially chapter 9, "Challenging the Apocalyptic Identity." Cf. also excerpts from E. A. Reardon's 1929 Anderson Camp Meeting sermon, in Barry L. Callen, ed., *Following the Light* (Anderson, Ind.: Warner Press, 134-136; see also Russell Byrum's 1929 paper read to the Indiana State Ministers' Meeting, *ibid.*, 127-133.

[12]Anderson: The Warner Press, 1931.
[13]*Ibid.*, 27.
[14]*Ibid.*, 149.
[15]*Ibid.* One of Brown's favorite examples of the divisive effects of creeds was the *filioque* controversy that played an instrumental role in opening a ninth-century doctrinal schism that contributed to the eventual division of Christendom into the Eastern Orthodox and Roman Catholic churches in 1054.
[16]*Ibid.*, 151.
[17]*Ibid.*, 163.
[18]*Ibid.*, 170.
[19]The views of some of these ministers are reported in Robert H. Reardon's unpublished S. T. M. thesis, Oberlin Graduate School of Theology, 1943.
[20]I tried to establish this position in *I Saw the Church*, x-xiv. For supportive viewpoints, see James W. McClendon, Jr., *Systematic Theology*, Vol. I, *Ethics* (Nashville: Abingdon Press, 1986), Dorothy Bass, *Practicing Our Faith* (San Francisco: Jossey-Bass, 1997), and Alasdair MacIntyre, *After Virtue*, 2nd edition (Notre Dame: University of Notre Dame Press, 1984), 187.
[21]*Gospel Trumpet*, September 24, 1925, 4-5.
[22]*Gospel Trumpet*, July 14, 1927, inside front cover.
[23]In this connection, see the volume recently edited by Stafford, Ted A. Campbell, and Ann K. Riggs, *Ancient Faith and American Born Churches: Dialogues Between Christian Traditions*, Faith and Order Commission Theological Series (Mahwah, N.J.: Paulist Press, 2006). Stafford's dialogues with Catholic and Orthodox scholars on holiness and worship, respectively, illumine what is described as a dialogical approach.
[24]For a summary of these conversations, see *Christian Unity and Ecumenical Trends* (Anderson, Ind.: Executive Council of the Church of God, n. d.).
[25]The question is quoted from a comprehensive summary of this conversation through 1997, Barry Callen and James North, *Coming Together in Christ* (Joplin, Missouri: College Press Publishing Company, 1997).
[26] Callen, ed., *Following the Light*, 187.
[27]*The Church of God in Black Perspective* (n. p., n. d.), i.
[28]"Ethics of Holiness and Unity in the Church of God," in Juanita Evans Leonard, ed., *Called to Ministry, Empowered to Serve: Women in Ministry* (Anderson, Ind.: Warner Press, 1989).
[29]*Ibid.*, 145.
[30]In response to issues raised by the Anderson College controversy in 1980, the Board of Directors of the Executive Council convened two dialogues in 1981 under the theme of "internal unity." The first dialogue (January) consid-

ered biblical, structural, and relationship issues. The second (December) discussed leadership development in higher education, the priesthood of believers, and movement stances on world affairs. Cf. Barry L. Callen, ed., *Following the Light*, 291-295.

[31] Ben Witherington, III, *John's Wisdom: A Commentary on the Fourth Gospel* (Louisville, KY: Westminster John Knox Press, 1995), 270.

[32] Otto F. Linn, *The Gospel of John* (Anderson, Ind.: The Gospel Trumpet Company, 1942), 133.

[33] Rudolf Bultmann, *The Gospel of John: A Commentary*, trans. by G. R. Beasley-Murray (Oxford: Basil Blackwell, 1971), 503.

[34] Linn, *loc cit.*, 134; Witherington, *loc cit*, 270-271.

[35] Linn, *ibid.*

[36] Bultmann, *loc cit*, 513.

[37] John Calvin, *Commentary on the Gospel According to John*, vol. II, trans. by William Pringle (Grand Rapids: William B. Eerdmans Publishing Company, 1949), 183.

[38] Bultmann, *loc cit.*, 513.

[39] Researcher George Barna predicted that by 2025 no more than 30-35% of Americans would experience and/or express their faith through affiliation with a local church, a figure which would be down from 70% in 2000. Cf. *Revolution* (Carol Stream, Ill.: Tyndale House Publishers, 2005), 49.

[40] Cf. *Hopeful Imagination: Prophetic Voices in Exile* (Philadelphia: Fortress Press, 1986), esp. 89-130.

[41] Ibid., 93.

[42] "The Church as God's New Language," in *Christian Existence Today: Essays on Church, World, and Living In Between* (Durham, N.C.: Labyrinth Press, 1988), 47-65.

[43] Ibid., 48.

Chapter 13

Holiness Church Participation in the Larger Church

by
Gilbert W. Stafford

Prominent representatives of the Wesleyan Theological Society, like Paul Bassett, Donald Dayton, Susie Stanley, and Don Thorsen, have been active ecumenical leaders. Gilbert W. Stafford (1938-2008) was a passionate Christian theologian and ecumenicist who represented the Church of God movement (Anderson) for many years in the Faith and Order work of the National Council of Churches (U.S.A.). He believed that bodies associated with the holiness tradition increasingly should involve themselves in the conversations and ministries of this prominent ecumenical body. Stafford recalls the history of this commission and identifies nine reasons why there should be more holiness participation in the life of the larger church. Citing appreciatively John Wesley's sermon "The Catholic Spirit," Stafford judges that ecumenical activity, particularly with substantial holiness involvement, may be one way to bring an answer to the unity prayer of Jesus (John 17:21-22). Originally published in the Wesleyan Theological Journal *(32:1, Spring, 1997) under the title "The Faith and Order Movement: Holiness Church Participation."*

The phrases "holiness movement," "ecumenical movement," and "charismatic movement" are widely used in general conversation. They evoke responses of allegiance and/or concern. The "faith and order movement," however, is a term not widely used in general conversation and therefore may evoke little more than a blank stare. It is a movement of significance to contemporary Christianity and one to which bodies associated with the "holiness" tradition should give increasing attention.

The Genesis and History of Faith and Order

The genesis of the Faith and Order movement can be traced to an event that took place at the 1910 World Missionary Conference held in Edinburgh, Scotland. There, for the first time since the rise of denominational Christianity, a world conference was held with participants who were not simply those interested in the subject matter, but persons officially chosen by denominations and missionary societies. Those at Edinburgh had the responsibility of representing the positions and concerns of their ecclesial sponsors. This put a different stamp on the character of this conference. It was first and foremost an officially representative gathering.

In the course of the conference it became apparent, at least to some, that the identities imposed on emerging churches around the world were the result of theological and doctrinal disagreements having historical roots and social contexts that were foreign to the newer churches. These various denominational identities, therefore, did not reflect their own wrestling with faith issues. This was of such great concern to Bishop Charles H. Brent of the Protestant Episcopal Church in the United States-at the time Bishop of the Philippine Islands-that near the end of the Edinburgh meeting he pled for the churches in the future to convene for the purpose of addressing not only missionary concerns but doctrinal concerns as well.

After Edinburgh, Brent did what he could in his own church to bring this about. In October of that year—on the day prior to the convening of the General Convention of the Protestant Episcopal Church in Cincinnati, Ohio-Brent addressed a mass meeting of Episcopalians. He shared his passionate concern that the churches begin addressing doctrinal issues-i.e., matters of faith and order-in formalized discussions between persons officially chosen by their respective communions to represent them. On October 19, 1910, the Episcopal church responded by passing unanimously the following resolution:

> That a Joint Commission be appointed to bring about a Conference for the consideration of questions touching Faith and Order, and that all Christian Communions throughout the world which confess Our Lord Jesus Christ as God and Saviour be asked to unite with us in arranging for and conducting such a Conference.[1]

The vision was caught by other churches and in 1911 the proposal for such a conference was communicated in a letter to Christian communions around the world. While the response was positive, the intricacies of planning such a gathering and the turmoil associated with World War I slowed down the process. Finally, though, the first World Conference on Faith and Order was held in Lausanne, Switzerland, in 1927 with 394 delegates representing 108 churches from around the world.[2] Subsequent conferences were held in Edinburgh (1937),[3] Lund, Sweden (1952),[4] Montreal, Canada (1963),[5] and Santiago de Compostela, Spain (1993).[6]

Besides the Missionary Conference movement and the Faith and Order movement, a third development, called the Life and Work movement, also emerged. Bishop Nathan Söderblom of Sweden was convinced that contemporary international and societal issues could be addressed adequately only by a Christian church united for social witness. The view held was that, whereas doctrine inevitably divides, social witness can be an opportunity for a united Christianity. On the basis of these strong convictions, the Universal Christian Conference on Life and Work was convened in Stockholm, Sweden, in 1925, and the second conference was held in Oxford, England, in 1937.

By this time, however, there was a growing realization that life-and-work was inevitably theological, and, consequently, could not be kept in isolation from faith-and-order considerations. In 1937, with Life and Work meeting in Scotland, and Faith and Order meeting in England, it was convenient for the two to consider working as one unit. The decision was made to formalize the union of the two movements, to be known jointly as the World Council of Churches. The chaos of World War II, however, kept this process from coming to culmination until 1948 when the WCC held its founding Assembly in Amsterdam, Holland.[7]

With the union of Faith and Order and Life and Work, the latter ceased to exist as a separate entity whereas Faith and Order continued as a distinctive movement which, while now sponsored by the WCC, continued to be wider than WCC membership.

The Holiness Presence in Faith and Order

No representative from an American holiness church was present at Lausanne, Edinburgh, or Lund. The first holiness participation was at Montreal in 1963 with a delegate (Gene W. Newberry) and two observers (Louis Meyer and John W. V. Smith) from the Church of God (Anderson),[8] and with two U.S.A. delegates from the Salvation Army (Commissioner S. Hepburn and Lt-Col. P. S. Kaiser).[9] At Santiago de Compostela in 1993, holiness representatives included Cheryl Bridges-Johns of the Church of God (Cleveland)[10] and Susie C. Stanley of the Church of God (Anderson).[11]

In 1957 Faith and Order sponsored a conference particularly for the church in the United States and Canada. Called the North American Conference on Faith and Order, it was held September 3-10 of that year in Oberlin, Ohio. Regarding holiness participation, the Salvation Army was a full member with two representatives. One was a member of the study section on "Authority and Freedom in Church Government," and the other in the section on "Racial and Economic Stratification."[12] In addition to this, the holiness movement was indirectly represented by James Royster of the Church of God (Anderson) who was a youth delegate from the Interseminary Movement.[13] Consultants from churches that were not members of the World Council included Donald Demaray from the Free Methodist Church, who worked in the section on "Baptism Into Christ,"[14] and John W. V. Smith from the Church of God (Anderson) who worked in the section on "Doctrinal Consensus and Conflict."[15] In addition, observers a category for those who, while not official delegates of the sending churches, could nevertheless participate- included three from the Church of God (Anderson): Clarence W. Hatch who worked in the study section on "Authority and Freedom in Church Government,"[16] Gene W. Newberry who worked in the section on "The Life of the Congregation"[17] and Harold Phillips in the section on "Imperatives and Motivations."[18]

Ever since Oberlin the Church of God (Anderson) has continued to participate. Serving as commissioner until his death in 1984 was John W. V. Smith, and for a short time in 1983-84 Juanita Lewis, and since 1984, Gilbert W. Stafford. The only other holiness church (though also pentecostal) that currently participates is the Church of God (Cleveland) represented by Cheryl Bridges-Johns. Two additional holiness churches participate indirectly by virtue of the Wesleyan Theological Society's appointment of Paul Bassett of the Church of the Nazarene and Donald Dayton of the Wesleyan Church. WTS participation began in 1985 with the appointment of Dayton and David Cubie of the Church of the Nazarene. Bassett followed Cubie in 1988. The Church of God (Anderson) is, therefore, the only non-pentecostal holiness church that participates officially as a church.

Faith and Order work in the United States is now sponsored by the National Council of the Churches of Christ in the U.S.A. (NCCC). In keeping with the long-standing tradition of including churches that are not members of the NCCC, present membership encompasses a wide range of non-NCCC churches, including Roman Catholic, Church of God (Cleveland, TN), Church of God in Christ, Mennonite, Friends General Conference, International Evangelical Church, Lutheran Church-Missouri Synod, Independent Christian Churches, Assemblies of God, Christian Reformed, Cooperative Baptist Fellowship, Korean Presbyterian, Churches of Christ (non-instrumental), and the Church of God (Anderson).

The Ongoing Vision of Faith and Order

In my years of Faith and Order work, I have found that the original purposes of the movement are still in place:

> ...to proclaim the essential oneness of the Church of Christ and to keep prominently before...the churches the obligation to manifest that unity and its urgency for the work of evangelism.

> ...to study questions of faith, order, and worship with the relevant social, cultural, political, racial and other factors in their bearing on the unity of the Church. . . .

> ...to study matters in the present relationships of the churches to one another which cause difficulties and need theological clarification. . . .[19]

What Samuel McCrea Cavert said in 1970 about Faith and Order is still true:

> The Faith and Order movement, in both its worldwide and its national aspects, has consistently adhered to the policy of making its contribution through study and dialogue. It has carefully refrained from presenting any particular plan of union, regarding this as necessarily the responsibility of the ecclesiastical bodies themselves.[20]

The inaugural report of the 1996-1999 quadrennium of study states the current vision of Faith and Order in North America:

> To further the longstanding work of Faith and Order on theological issues that are church-dividing and church-uniting by engaging more fully and directly the faithful people of the churches of Christ in ecclesial settings of ongoing worship and witness, with renewed commitment to engagement with churches in wide ranging ecclesial traditions, and

thereby to nurture the NCCC's commitment to fuller ecclesial fellowship.[21]

The Benefits of Participating in Faith and Order

What, then, are the benefits of a church's participation in Faith and Order? I list the following.

1. Participation is **an opportunity to learn *about* other traditions in a dialogical setting.** One of the more rewarding intellectual experiences of my life was my sub-group's discussion in an earlier triennium (as it was then) of our several understandings of apostolic faith. The fact that each Christian tradition makes claims of being apostolic in its faith provided a basis for vigorous discussion. In our extended deliberations we learned enough about each other's traditions to be able to identify points both of agreement and of divergence. We came to appreciate that all of us agree that being a church of apostolic faith includes at least these basic components: the confession that Jesus Christ is God and Savior; the guidance and inspiration of the Holy Spirit; the authoritative witness of the Scriptures; and the church as the community of faithful worship, witness, and service in the world. But we differ when it comes to other characteristics of what it means to be apostolic. Some traditions emphasize normative creedal and confessional statements; others emphasize normative teaching offices and polities; and others emphasize normative experiences of conversion, sanctification, holiness, and liberation.[22]

2. Faith and Order is an opportunity **to learn *from* other traditions.** Other traditions of the faith ask questions about one's own tradition that insiders tend not to ask. Once in a discussion about creeds, I explained that traditionally my own church (Church of God, Anderson) has been anti-creedalistic and that we even have a song one stanza of which begins: "The day of sects and creeds for us forevermore is past."[23] "What!" an Orthodox priest exclaimed, "how can you be Christian if you don't believe something?" He asked the right question and pressed the right issues for a tradition that has perhaps been too unreflective in its anti-creed rhetoric.

3. Faith and Order provides **an arena of discussion with a wide spectrum of Christian traditions.** This arena is wider than any other I know. Obviously, wide spectrums can be found in seminaries, theological forums, the academy, and in informal conversations. That which makes Faith and Order distinct from these, however, is that its members are, for the most part, chosen in some official way to represent their respective churches or organizations. In my case, I am elected by the Commission on Christian Unity of the Church of God, a commission made up both of representatives from our several national agencies and persons elected by the General Assembly of the Church of God.

The role of a participant is not that of setting forth his or her own personal theological positions, but those of the church being represented. Faith and Order participants are, in a sense, personifications of the differing traditions of Christian faith. For instance, when in my own sub-group Samuel Nafzger of the Lutheran Church-Missouri Synod speaks, we want him to give voice to the Missouri Synod. The assignment is not "Tell us what you personally think about this issue," but "Tell us, to the best of your ability, what you believe your church tradition holds concerning this matter." That goes even for the most overtly independent participants. When Doug Foster, a member of the Churches of Christ (non-instrumental), speaks, he, true to his tradition, makes it clear that he speaks only as Doug Foster, but we push him to represent to us, to the best of his ability, the Church of Christ tradition, not the Doug Foster view.

Where else can one find such a wide spectrum of thought being expressed by those who seek earnestly to speak for the respective traditions out of which they come? In my sub-group this quadrennium are representatives from churches as diverse as United Methodist, Orthodox, Roman Catholic, Churches of Christ (non-instrumental), Quaker, Evangelical Lutheran, Reformed Church in America, Assemblies of God, Presbyterian, United Church of Christ, National Baptist, and Church of God (Anderson).

4. Faith and Order provides each participant the opportunity **to teach other traditions about one's own tradition.** It is as though each tradition has the opportunity to bring other Christian traditions into its classroom for a short while for the purpose of teaching something about the Christian faith which it believes God has entrusted to it. Over the course of several years, for example, I have had the opportunity to present to my colleagues in Faith and Order several short papers: two on "The Apostolic Faith" as understood by the Church of God (Anderson), another titled "The Holy Spirit and the Experience of Church," and two papers on authority: "Authority in the Church of God (Anderson . . .)" and "Authorities for Making Decisions in the Church of God. . . ." Also, I prepared a paper in answer to the question: "What would be the prerequisites for the Church of God (Anderson) to become a part of a

Christian organization which is inclusive of Christian faith in its widest possible spectrum?" Another paper was prepared under the title, "Visioning for Koinonia in the Life of the Church." All of these were opportunities to teach others about matters which my church believes are crucial if the church at large is to be in health.

More recently, my papers have centered especially on our identification as a holiness church. I presented a paper titled: "The Nineteenth Century Holiness Movement and Christian Unity." At the time of this writing, I am working with two other colleagues on presentations for an upcoming meeting in New Orleans. The first project has to do with "The Unitive Power of Holiness." The sub-group will consider my paper from the holiness perspective and that of Father Kevin McMorrow, editor of *Ecumenical Trends*, from the Roman Catholic perspective. Upon exchanging papers, each of us will write a response that will include three components: points of resonance with each other, differences, and points at which we simply do not understand the other. These four papers, then, will be presented to our sub-group for discussion.

The second project will use the same dialogical method on the subject of "The Hermeneutics of Reconciliation in Worship." My partner is John Erickson, professor of theology at St. Vladimir's Orthodox Theological Seminary in Crestwood, New York. In preparation for this assignment, Professor Erickson told me that since he had never worshipped in a holiness church, he would like to have that experience. I put him in touch with a Church of God congregation which, without my knowing it, turned out to be close to St. Vladimir's. He has already worshipped there and has invited the Church of God to be guests at St. Vladimir's. In New Orleans, he and I will present our papers to the plenary, which we hope will be enriched both by holiness and orthodox insights.

5. Faith and Order work is the opportunity for one's own tradition to **recognize in other traditions dimensions of the apostolic faith which lie dormant in one's own.** While for one Christian tradition verbal confession about the person and work of Christ may be very much alive, an emphasis on the converting ministry of Christ in the here and now may lie dormant. In another tradition the enlivening presence of the Holy Spirit may be very much front and center, but the hard sayings about Kingdom life may lie dormant. For still another tradition an emphasis on personal conversion may be alive, but communal confession of the faith may be dormant. And for another tradition Kingdom teachings may be considered with great seriousness, but the joy of the risen Christ may be dormant. Faith and Order provides an ecclesial opportunity for each tradition of the faith to feed into the bloodstream of other traditions. It is in this kind of setting that the emphasis on personal sanctification, which holiness churches are convinced is part and parcel of the apostolic faith, can be fed into the bloodstream of a wide spectrum of other Christian traditions.

An example of how this happens is reflected in the following segment of the summary report of the last quadrennium:

> At Newark the Episcopal representative was inspired by what the Church of God (Anderson) representative had said about...join[ing] his church. When asked how people become members, he replied: "The process would be similar to the acceptance around this table. None of us has been formally 'checked out.' We sense some basic assumptions as we talk with each other. We share. It's not legalistic. . . ." As the representative of the Church of God (Cleveland) said in response to the information about the lack of formal joining in the Church of God (Anderson): "You are probably providing a model for the future, where things aren't so sharply defined as [they are] by organizational entities."[24]

Whether one agrees with the subject mentioned in this excerpt is not the point. It is simply an illustration of how one tradition can feed into the bloodstream of other traditions. In this instance an anabaptist-holiness tradition, a pentecostal-holiness tradition, and a mainline-anglican tradition were engaged in conversation about a new paradigm never before considered by some.

I cherish the possibility of the Church of the Nazarene, the Wesleyan Church, the Free Methodist Church, the Salvation Army, and others, as *churches*, taking advantage of the Faith and Order opportunity to feed their own rich understandings of the apostolic faith into the bloodstream of the wider church.

6. Faith and Order is the opportunity **to develop a deeper understanding and appreciation of one's own tradition**. It is both refreshing and challenging to explain one's tradition to those who may be learning about it for the first time. As we are pressed to explain the meaning of a particular aspect of our tradition, we are required to rethink the dynamics of it. That which within the circles of the tradition itself is dealt with in a shorthand way has to be written out in longhand, so to speak, for those unacquainted with it. The end result is that one's understanding of one's own tradition matures.

7. Faith and Order work is the opportunity for churches **to guard against becoming root bound** within their own narrower tradition. Just as root-bound plants eventually die, so do Christian traditions that limit themselves to their own little bit of Christian soil. Doctrinal development in controlled theological hot houses may lead to only superficially healthy churches. In order to be in health, all churches need to develop in the open spaces of doctrinal discussions in the church at large.

8. Faith and Order is the **opportunity for a wide spectrum of ecclesial bodies to work together** in theological endeavors. In 1982 at a Faith and Order meeting in Lima, Peru, over one hundred theologians unanimously agreed to present a statement for common study by and official responses from any and all churches willing to do so. Published under the title "Baptism, Eucharist and Ministry" (BEM), it is the product of some fifty years of study and consultation representing Orthodox, Catholic, Lutheran, Anglican, Reformed, Methodist, Disciples, Methodist, Adventist, and Pentecostal traditions. BEM has become one of the more widely discussed theological documents in the church's history.

In 1984, the Believers Church Conference (consisting of churches that stress believer baptism) was hosted by Anderson School of Theology for the purpose of discussing the baptism section of BEM. Participants included Brethren, Mennonite, Church of God (Anderson), Adventist, Churches of Christ, Disciples, and Baptist theologians and church historians. But also present were scholars from infant baptism churches, including the associate director of Faith and Order (NCCC), Brother Jeffrey Gros, a Roman Catholic. On the basis of four days of papers and discussion, the conference affirmed eight points of agreement with BEM on baptism, stated six points of disagreement, listed two consequences that so-called believers churches can draw from BEM for their relationships and dialogues with other churches, and stated four contributions that BEM can make to them as believer baptism churches. The report concludes by giving three suggestions for the ongoing work of Faith and Order, which included the view of some in the conference that "Scripture...[should] be regarded as the sole source and criterion of Christian belief, standing as the authoritative corrective to our various traditions."[25]

My only reason for lifting up this last issue is not to emphasize the "Bible only" position, but to use it as an illustration of the opportunity that Faith and Order both provides and promotes for a wide spectrum of ecclesial traditions to be heard as they work together in theological endeavors.

One of John Wesley's well-known sermons is on the "Catholic Spirit." His text is 2 Kings 10:15, "Is thine heart right, as my heart is with thy heart: And Jehonadab answered, It is. If it be, give me thine hand." In the sermon, Wesley spells out what he has in mind by one's heart being right: it is right with God; it believes in the Lord Jesus Christ; it is "filled with the energy of love"; it is doing the will of God; it serves the Lord with reverence; it is right toward one's neighbor; and it shows love by what it does.

This "catholic spirit" is to be expressed both towards those outside the faith and within. Regarding those outside the faith, Wesley says that the person with a catholic spirit "embraces with strong and cordial affection neighbors and strangers, friends and enemies. This is catholic or universal love. And he that has this is of a catholic spirit. For love alone gives the title to this character: catholic love is a catholic spirit" (III.4).

Following this consideration, Wesley then deals with the catholic spirit in relation to fellow believers. He refers to love for all "whatever opinion or worship or congregation, who believe in the Lord Jesus Christ, who love God and man, who, rejoicing to please and fearing to offend God, are careful to abstain from evil and zealous of good works." Continuing, Wesley says that the one who is of a truly catholic spirit, "having an unspeakable tenderness for their persons and longing for their welfare, does not cease to commend them to God in prayer as well as to plead their cause before men; who speaks comfortably to them and labours by all his words to strengthen their hands in God. He assists them to the uttermost of his power in all things, spiritual and temporal. He is ready 'to spend and be spent for them' [cf. 2 Cor. 12:15], yea, 'to lay down his life for' their sake [Jn. 15:13]" [III.5].[26]

9. Faith and Order provides the opportunity for us to become **interpreters of other traditions at points where they may be misunderstood.** A personal example of this is Cecil Robeck's information about the traditional pentecostal understanding regarding the distinction between tongues as the initial evidence of baptism in the Holy Spirit and the gift of tongues. Robeck, professor at Fuller and a representative of the Assemblies of God, taught all of us in that particular discussion that the classical pentecostal position is not, as some non-pentecostals think, that all Spirit-baptized persons have the gift of tongues. Rather, tongues speaking is simply an initial evidence of the baptism. Consequently, a person baptized in the Holy Spirit may initially speak in tongues but never again do so because they do not have the gift.

As a result of that Faith and Order "lecture," I, as a non-pentecostal, have been able to teach others about a pentecostal understanding and to correct a widespread misunderstanding in my own church that pentecostals believe that all should have the gift of tongues. Many among us point to 1 Corinthians 12:30 which asks rhetorically, "Do all speak in tongues?" and has the implied answer that not all do. Why, then, they want to know, can't pentecostal people see the error of their ways? But that is to misunderstand the pentecostal position. Robeck has helped me as a seminary teacher, preacher, and writer to fulfill an important role of clarifying the pentecostal position among my own people, not so that they will become pentecostals, but so that they will relate to others of "like precious faith" on the basis of accurate information instead of misinformation. Christian charity demands no less. In like manner, would it not be helpful to have more people in non-holiness churches *clarifying* for those traditions holiness terminology such as Christian perfection and entire sanctification?

Faith and Order is certainly no panacea for the dividedness of Christ's church, but it is an opportunity for that dividedness to be addressed within the context of a broad spectrum of Christian faith traditions. Many have been the times when I have been thoroughly frustrated in the meetings and by the process. There have been times when I have wondered whether it was worthwhile. But the benefits far outweigh the liabilities.

At Faith and Order meetings (twice a year), I often desire the participation of more of my holiness colleagues in the faith. By participating, a church has much to gain. Not only may it feed into the bloodstream of the wider Christian community its own treasures of the apostolic faith, but also it can be immeasurably enriched by the treasures of the same faith which others feed into the bloodstream. But of greatest importance is this: Faith and Order is one additional small step toward the fulfillment of our Lord's prayer in John 17:21-22 that we "may all be one," to the end "that the world may believe." It is one additional feeble attempt toward responding positively to Paul's plea in Ephesians 4:1-3 for us "to lead a life worthy of the calling to which [we]...have been called...making every effort to maintain the unity of the Spirit in the bond of peace."

Notes

[1] Tissington Tatlow, "The World Conference on Faith and Order," *A History of the Ecumenical Movement 1517-1948*, Fourth Edition, ed. Ruth Rouse and

Stephen C. Neill, Vol. I of *A History of the Ecumenical Movement 1517-1968* (Geneva: World Council of Churches, 1993), 407.
[2]Ibid., 420. For conference papers, proceedings, decisions, and membership, see H. N. Bate (ed.). *Faith and Order: Proceedings of the World Conference, Lausanne, August 3-21, 1927.* New York: Doran, 1927.
[3]See Leonard Hodgson (ed.), London *The Second World Conference on Faith and Order Held at Edinburgh, August 3-18, 1937*: Student Christian Movement Press, 1938.
[4]See Oliver S. Tomkins (ed.), *The Third Conference on Faith and Order Held at Lund, August 15th to 28th, 1952.* London: SCM, 1953.
[5]See P. C. Rodger and Lukas Vischer (ed.), The *Fourth World Conference on Faith and Order, Montreal 1963.* New York: Association, 1964.
[6]See Thomas F. Best and Günther Gassmann (ed.), Official Report of the Fifth World Conference on Faith and Order: On the Way to Fuller Koinonia. Geneva: WCC Publications, 1994. Also, Günther Gassmann (ed.), *Documentary History of Faith and Order, 1963-1993.* Geneva: WCC Publications, 1993.
[7]All three streams finally came together when in 1961 the International Missionary Council merged with the WCC at New Delhi, India.
[8]Rodger and Vischer, op. cit., 107.
[9]Ibid., 115.
[10]Best and Gassmann, op. cit., xx.
[11]Ibid., xxii.
[12]Paul S. Minear (ed.), *The Nature of the Unity We Seek: Official Report of the North American Conference on Faith and Order, September 3-10, 1957, Oberlin, Ohio* (St. Louis: Bethany, 1958), 295.
[13]Ibid., 296.
[14]Ibid., 297.
[15]Ibid., 298.
[16]Ibid., 299.
[17]Ibid., 300.
[18]Ibid.
[19]Quoted from the original constitution of Faith and Order in Minear, op. cit., 13.
[20]Samuel McCrea Cavert, *Church Cooperation and Unity in America* (New York: Friendship, 1970), 336 f.
[21]"Conspectus of Study, 1996-1999," Faith and Order, The National Council of the Churches of Christ in the U.S.A. (distributed at Pasadena, CA.: Fuller Theological Seminary, March 15-16), 2.
[22]See Thaddeus D. Horgan (ed.), *Apostolic Faith in America* (Grand Rapids: Eerdmans, 1988), 60-66.
[23]Charles W. Naylor, "The Church's Jubilee," *Worship the Lord: Hymnal of the Church of God* (Anderson: Warner, 1989), No. 312.
[24]O. C. Edwards in "Faith and Order Reports 1992-1995" (New York: The National Council of the Churches of Christ in the U.S.A, 1995), 21.

[25] Merle Strege (ed.), *Baptism and Church: A Believers' Church Vision* (Grand Rapids: Sagamore, 1986), 201.

[26] See John Wesley, ed. Albert C. Outler (New York: Oxford University Press, 1964), 91-104.

ns; the Church's Challenge
Part IV
God's Intentions; the Church's Challenge

Chapter 14

Reconciliation: The Biblical Imperative

by
James Earl Massey

The mission of the church is to share the good news of Jesus Christ. This news announces God's redemptive activity on behalf of all humans and sends those who gratefully receive the news into the world as reconcilers of God's behalf. The Church of God movement (Anderson) has always been biblically oriented, evangelistic in focus, and deeply concerned about reconciliation in its several dimensions. In view have been both peace between individuals and God, among individuals, and among groups of Christians (the divisive denominations). James Earl Massey has modeled the ministry of reconciliation in exemplary ways, always representing well the movement he has been part of all his life. Originally appeared in the Wesleyan Theological Journal *(37:1, Spring, 2002).*[1]

The topic of reconciliation is strategic and timely because everywhere one looks, whether at life within America or at life across our world, conflicts between persons and groups are playing themselves out, with publicized, prolonged, and uncivil struggling over differences—differences in values and ethics, differences in religious views, differences over land claims, territorial rights, political ends, and a host of other fractious debates. All of them are deepened by the drama of power and its abuse. Conflict holds center stage in our time and in all places, and voices of wisdom addressed to those involved in the fray—or the number of persons of good will to help quell the conflicts—are all too few. I applaud and join the Wesleyan Theological Society in its concern to become more effective agents of our Lord as we face the issues and handle the living of these days as God's people.

Addressing this august assemblage is both a joy and a challenge: a joy because as "people of the Book" we have a deep respect for what the Christian Scriptures have to say on the subject of reconciliation, as well as on all other subjects; while the challenge includes us all because of the task that awaits us along the path we must take, a path that stretches out into territory fraught with the conflicts that occur when people meet. These conflicts we are called and sent to address in the name and power of the One who is our peace. In preparing for this keynote address, I took comfort in the fact that I would be among treasured friends and esteemed colleagues, all of you persons who, because of your training as well as your work, form what James Barr has referred to as "an instructed theological public."[2]

Reconciliation: The New Testament Teachings

As we begin, I invite you to join me in re-exploring the four major biblical terms regarding reconciliation, giving due attention to the contexts within which these terms were used and the meanings and guidance to which we are heirs because of these terms.

Term One: *Diallasso*. The first reconciliation passage to which I call attention is found among the ethical instructions from our Lord, and it is located in Matthew's account of the Sermon on the Mount, Matthew 5:21-26. It is the section that contains the first of those six bold antithetic imperatives from our Lord that reflect his authority as not only Moses' successor but Moses' superior. These six antitheses carry us to the very center of what constitutes a truly righteous heart response in human experience; they tell us how the new life under the lordship of Christ surpasses life under the old laws of Moses, which explains the construction that is found in these teachings: "You have heard that it was said...but I say to you."

This section from Matthew 5 deals with anger, that strong human feeling of displeasure that at a belligerently wrathful stage can result in murder. Jesus here instructs his followers on how to handle anger before that stage of belligerency is reached. He also tells how anger can block a relationship with God. Note that the speaking of rash, insulting words to others, all selfish speaking out of intense feelings that are full of human wrath, even if these feelings have been provoked by someone's prior selfish action, is viewed by Jesus as not only a selfish response to the offending person but as a sinful deed in God's sight as well. Hostility is an activity of the heart, and those who wish to be accepted in peace by God must be serious about remaining at peace with humans.

True worship is blocked whenever and as long as hostility rages within the heart against another human. As vss. 23-24 state, reconciliation between the aggrieved parties must take place before God will accept our worship. The instruction is "be reconciled," meaning that the one who seeks to please God must take the initiative to remove whatever blocks a right relation with the other person. The verb used here is *diallagethi* [aorist imperative passive of *diallasso*], a word that appears only here in the New Testament. It is one of four terms used by the New Testament to teach the need to restore or bring back into agreement or harmony a relation that has been broken or at least is at odds.

Term Two: *Sunallasso*. The second passage I call to your attention is found in Acts 7. The entire chapter reports Stephen the Deacon's defensive speech to the Sanhedrin as its members sat in council against him and he witnessed about Jesus. As he engaged in historical retrospect, seeking to show that the history of the Hebrew people pointed to the very happenings to which he was giving witness, Stephen recalled the life and times of Moses, the nation's great lawgiver, and how Moses had been readied for his role by growing up as a prince in Egypt, the place of the first and longest confinement of the Jews. Then comes that section in the narrative which includes verse 7:26: "The next day he came to some of them as they were quarreling and tried to reconcile [*sunellassen*] them, saying, 'Men, you are brothers; why do you wrong each other?'" It is not necessary to say anything more about that passage except to point out that the word used in vs. 26 for "reconcile" is *sunallasso*, a second term used in the New Testament. The imperfect form of the verb, *sunallassen*, is used here in the report to indicate that Moses "tried to reconcile" the two recalcitrant brawling Hebrews.

Term Three: *Katallasso*. A third passage that mentions reconciliation, using *katallasso*, a third term, is found in 1 Corinthians 7, and the passage is part of some instruction from Paul about the need to restore a lost or problem-threatened spousal relationship. Interestingly, this instruction will show an immediate dependence by Paul upon the sayings of Jesus about marriage. The ethics Paul taught actually reflects exact parallels at many points with the teachings of Jesus, and even when no parallel is evident his judgments and recommendations to believers are understandably at one with the spirit of those teachings.

In the instruction Paul gives in 1 Corinthians 7:10-11, it is quite clear that he has appropriated a known teaching of the Lord and passes it on in the interest of restoring a broken or fragmenting marriage relationship. It is possible that Paul appealed here to some fixed written record that he possessed, some form of sayings-collection that had been gathered because of controversies, questions about moral matters, and the meaning of certain passages from the Hebrew Bible (in its Septuagint translation) that were important for instructing the believers. While that is possible and would explain so much, I cannot state that it was indeed the case, but the very fact that he could write "To the married I give this command—not I but the Lord" shows a strict knowledge about the Lord's words on the matter of spousal relations. Thus, Paul was not inventing new directions when he counseled: "To the married I give this command—not I but the Lord—that the wife should not separate [*me choristhenai*] from her husband, but if she does separate [*choristhe*], let her remain unmarried or else be reconciled [*katallageto*] to her husband, and that the husband should not divorce his wife" (7:10-11).

Paul here addresses a Christian couple whose married life has for some reason become problematic and irksome or broken. His charge to them is based on the Lord's own teaching on the matter: do not divorce one another. The traditional teaching as reported in Matthew 5:32 and 19:9 and in Mark 10:11 is reflected here. The family should remain in solidarity; if the wife insists upon leaving the marriage, she must remain single [*meneto agamos*], and the husband must not marry someone else during the separation. This command of Jesus that Paul quotes and applies regards the bond that marriage involves, and he reminds the couple that reconciliation should be their proper concern if that bond is placed under severe strain and they separate.

Katallasso, the word Paul used here, is the most regularly used word in the New Testament for reconciliation, and its basic meaning is "to change, or exchange; to effect a change." This word is used exclusively by Paul among the New Testament writers, and always to help express and explain to his readers some of the meaning and effects of Christ's deed of dying for us on a cross. In the uses of this term on Paul's part, we are being instructed about the Atonement, which in the words of Vincent Taylor, is "the work of God in Christ for man's salvation and renewal."[3]

The word *katallasso* denotes a relation, a relation that has undergone a change for the better. It is one word among many in a family of images that set forth to us the meaning of a changed relation. The changed relation is made possible by someone acting toward someone else with concern to effect that change. The image in the word shows something having been set aside [**kata**]: an attitude, a grievance, a position, a deed, a distance, a result, in order to induce or bring about a change for the better. A new disposition is exhibited, a new stance is assumed, a new framework is established granting a rich togetherness where enmity and distance previously were the order. Paul used the noun "reconciliation" [*katallage*] to report something proffered to us by God (Romans 5:8-11) and something experienced by us on the basis of the sacrificial death Jesus Christ underwent on our behalf (2 Corinthians 5:17ff).

Term Four: *Apokatallasso*. The fourth term used in the New Testament for reconciliation is the word *apokatallasso,* found at Eph. 2:16 and Col. 1:20, 22. It also is a part of Paul's same theological message about the meaning and effects of the death and resurrection of Jesus for those who believe on him. I will return to this word and the cited verses in which it appears, but first I want to examine 2 Corinthians 5 where one finds that classic passage regarding reconciliation.

In 2 Corinthians 5:16-21, Paul makes a personal statement and an advisory claim. Having entered upon a new life-course through his converting contact with the Risen Christ, and having undergone a full change of world-view thereby, Paul here states his reasons for the ministry at which he has long been engaged now: (a) He is part of a "new creation" inaugurated by being "in Christ" (=inhabiting a new sphere of reality); and (b) He has received a commission to announce to all people the reconciling action of God in Christ by which that newness became possible.

It is helpful to point out that this statement on Paul's part is in defense of his ministry that had been the subject under attack by some of his critics (see 2:14-7:4). The attitude of those critics toward him was not just suspicious but hostile and defiant (see 2:5-11; 7:12). Paul was no longer the Moses-follower (3:1-18), like his critics, but a Christ-follower; Paul knew that the promised New Age had already dawned, and he knew himself called by God to announce that fact and expound upon its results and effects for all who believe.

Paul wrote as he did because he was concerned about two things: to keep trusting believers rightly informed about his ministry; and to become reconciled with those who were his detractors. Paul wanted his critics to be compatriots in Christ, to be in right relation with him again. As he sought to inform, influence, and win them, he became poetic, and his lyrical bent comes through in the hymnic statement we find in this great passage. Viewing the whole of life and humanity now through eyes touched by the Risen Christ, Paul wanted his readers to be fully oriented to a new way of viewing him and all others as well. As he states it:

> 5:16 From now on, therefore, we regard no one from a human point of view; even though we once knew Christ from a human point of view, we know him no longer in that way.

5:17 So if anyone is in Christ, there is a new creation: everything old has passed away; see, everything has become new!

5:18 All this is from God, who reconciled [*katallazontos*] us to himself through Christ, and has given us the ministry of reconciliation [*katallage*];

5:19 that is, in Christ God was reconciling [*katallasson*] the world to himself, not counting their trespasses against them, and entrusting the message of reconciliation [*katallages*] to us.

5:20 So we are ambassadors for Christ, since God is making his appeal through us; we entreat you on behalf of Christ, be reconciled [*katallagete*] to God.

Paul explains that God is the reconciler, God took the initiative, while the world, i.e., humankind, is the object of God's reconciling action. Christ is God's agent of reconciliation, and through Christ alone was that reconciliation made possible. ". . . in Christ God was reconciling the world to himself," Paul declares, and he urged his believing readers to join him in being reconciled in full: "be reconciled [*katallagete*, aorist imperative passive] to God." What God initiated through grace and has proffered in love we can experience through an accepting faith and continuing obedience. Romans 5:10-11 repeats the statement about what has been proffered and experienced:

5:10 For if while we were enemies, we were reconciled [*katellagemen*, aorist passive] to God through the death of his Son, much more surely, having been reconciled [*katallagentes*, aorist participle passive], will we be saved by his life.

5:11 But more than that, we even boast in God through our Lord Jesus Christ, through whom we have received reconciliation [*katallage*].

Let us turn back now to the two passages I mentioned, Ephesians 2:16 and Colossians 1:20 and 22. In Eph. 2:16 we see Paul's discussion of reconciliation as it relates to the removal of the previous division that existed between Jews and Gentiles, a division based upon not just one but several separating factors: religious differences, legal differences, cultural differences, racial and social differences. In a bold and declarative announcement, Paul states that God's reconciling deed in Christ has changed that division altogether and has made the two groups one in his sight: "He has abolished the law with its commandments and ordinances, that he might create in himself one new humanity in place of the two, thus making peace, and might reconcile [*apokatallaze*, aorist subjunctive] both groups to God in one body through the cross, thus putting to death that hostility through it" (2:15-16).

Then follows that grand teaching about the believing Gentiles' privileged participation, on equal footing, with believing Jews in God's "household," the church. Here we see a wider communal interest to God's reconciling deed in Christ, a wider social application of the effects of reconciliation. The God-ordained relationship between Christian believers, of whatever previous backgrounds, is not just one of harmony but a oneness where neither group is dominant nor subservient anymore. The fence that once stood between them is now down. Because believers are reconciled to God, they are also related to each other. A new set of criteria obtains now for human relations in the church. In church life social distance must no longer be the order, and a sense of oneness and equality must prevail when previously-honored differences seek to intrude themselves.

The last reference text is Col. 1:20, 22, where that fourth term for reconciliation, *apokatallasso*, is used again. Let us read it in context:

1:19 For in him all the fullness of God was pleased to dwell,

1:20 and through him God was pleased to reconcile [*apokatallazai*, aorist infinitive] to himself all things, whether on earth or in heaven, by making peace through the blood of his cross.

1:21 And you who were once estranged and hostile in mind, doing evil deeds,

1:22 he has now reconciled [*apokatellazen*, aorist] in his fleshly body through death, so as to present you holy and blameless and irreproachable before him—

1:23 provided that you continue securely established and steadfast in the faith, without shifting from the hope promised by the gospel that you heard. . . .

The universal and cosmic significance of God's work through Christ is in view where the passage speaks about "all things" being reconciled, "whether on earth or in heaven." Reconciliation, then, will finally involve the universe as a whole and not just believing humans; the time will come when the universe will no longer be subjected to decay or dissolution but will reflect the harmony that God originally intended for all that was created.

The actual work of reconciling requires a distinct focus and distinctive frame of reference: it requires a focus on the other person as someone of value, whatever the facts that make that person different or difficult or distant, and it requires an attitude of forgiveness and inclusiveness that can claim or reclaim that person for relation and closeness. The attitude of forgiveness motivates one to set aside that which causes distance, and the spirit of inclusiveness exhibits openness by which togetherness can begin and achieve development. According to several of the texts we have examined, in Christ God has acted kindly toward us in this way, proffering forgiveness for sins, restored harmony after a life of disobedience, and peaceful relations after our selfish waywardness that displeased God. Christ acted on our behalf as God's reconciling agent. Paul explains that, having received reconciliation, he had been given a ministry as a reconciler. This means that he had to learn to see other people as God sees them, he had to be open to relate to people with a view to their God-given worth, their human potential, and their deepest human need.

This framework and focus is the basis for evangelism in depth and human community in full. As Howard Thurman once voiced it, "One person, standing in his [or her] own place, penetrates deeply into the life of another in a manner that makes possible an ingathering within that other life, and thus the wildness is gentled out of a personality at war with itself."[4] We too can develop this ability, this way of relating to another, provided there is, first, a deep gratitude to God for having reconciled us, and second, an intentional concern to be a reconciling person. God has been open to us. We can learn to be open to others. It begins with a simple interest in learning to be open, with a concern for people's deepest need, and it deepens through a continuing gratitude to God for accepting us as He has so graciously done. This is how, like Paul, we become "ambassadors for Christ," and work among people with "God making his appeal through us." Paul must have been seeking to underscore the importance of this when, in concluding that classic passage in 2 Corinthians about reconciliation, he quickly and rightly advised his readers, "we urge you also not to accept the grace of God in vain" (2 Cor. 6:1).

Reconciliation: Aspects of Our Task

Our re-examination of the biblical statements about reconciliation has highlighted four Greek terms and has yielded at least three results: (1) It has reminded us about what reconciliation means in the vocabulary of faith; (2) It has refreshed our understanding about God's reconciling work through Christ Jesus, thus deepening our gratitude for received grace, which in turn can stir us to worship God more attentively; and (3) It has brought into sharper focus our task as reconciling agents, a task which in the press of our times calls for greater attention and more strategic action on our part.

The first and second of these results from our study are in the vertical category of our Christian experience since God and the self are related by a personal faith. The third result involves the horizontal dimension of our Christian experience since it requires interacting with other humans. The longer we consider this, the greater the awareness becomes that personal faith in Christ—the vertical dimension—and the obedient outworking of that faith in dealing with others—the horizontal dimension—*always form a cross*. This must be remembered as we go about our work in the world because reconciliation is always a costly matter. It was by cost to Jesus Christ that we were reconciled to God, and we cannot be reconciling agents in his name without undergoing some demands that will press upon us.

Before I extend this line of thought, here is a short list of some books which treat the theological aspects of reconciliation in greater detail than I can do here, and with it a still shorter list of two books which can give further guidance regarding the social aspects of reconciliation. As for the theology of reconciliation, the following four books can both widen one's perspective and also deepen one's devotion:

Leon Morris, *The Apostolic Preaching of the Cross* (Grand Rapids: William B. Eerdmans Publishing Co., 1956);

Vincent Taylor, *The Cross of Christ: Eight Public Lectures* (London: Macmillan & Co., Ltd., 1957);

Vincent Taylor, *Forgiveness and Reconciliation: A Study in New Testament Theology* (London: Macmillan & Co., Ltd., 1960);

Ralph P. Martin, *Reconciliation: A Study of Paul's Theology* (London: Marshall, 1981).

These are but four books selected from among many other studies which treat the theology of reconciliation, but I believe you will find these four both readily available, intellectually arresting, and theologically astute.

For insights on the social outworking of the reconciliation concern, these two books, despite the many others now available, are the two that I rate at the top of the list:

Howard Thurman, *Disciplines of the Spirit* (New York and Evanston: Harper & Row, Publishers, 1963);

Curtiss Paul DeYoung, *Reconciliation: Our Greatest Challenge—Our Only Hope* (Valley Forge: Judson Press, 1997).

Howard Thurman (1899-1981), an African-American, was a noted minister, educator, and author who in his preaching, teaching and writings delineated, in my judgment, the most thoroughly analytical, scholarly, and practical account of how the Christian faith can inform the American democratic tradition for its fullest development. His insights were addressed to healing the deep-seated social ills of this nation, and the final chapter in his book on *Disciplines of the Spirit* offers his counsel, derived from a fresh examination of the Christian faith allied with proofs from his own experiences, about how to become and develop as a reconciling person. Thurman delineated with clarity how and why it is that "the discipline of reconciliation for the religious [person] cannot be separated from the discipline of religious experience"[5] itself. Influenced by the account we have examined in Matthew 5:24, Thurman explained that: "What a man knows as his birthright in his experience before God he must accept and affirm as his necessity in his relations with his fellows." He further explained: "This is why the way of reconciliation and the way of love finally are one way."[6] Thurman's discussion about the discipline that *agape*-love provides in the life of someone who *wills* and *works* for reconciliation is the best that I have ever read.

Curtiss Paul DeYoung, author of *Reconciliation: Our Greatest Challenge—Our Only Hope*, is Caucasian, a former student of mine, and presently serves as president of TURN Leadership Foundation, a metro-wide ministry network based in Minneapolis that serves as a catalyst for reconciliation and social justice in Minneapolis and St. Paul, Minnesota. DeYoung is one of those voices of goodwill speaking out to offer guidance and give help to persons and cities experiencing social conflict. His book is his attempt to share wisdom, a wisdom that is biblical and tested in his own life struggles. This book is a logical and planned sequel to his earlier book entitled *Coming Together: The Bible's Message in an Age of Diversity*, which discussed the Bible as, in part, a record of a culturally diverse people seeking God's will, and how the person Jesus, "an Afro-Asiastic Galilean Jew," became a universal Christ who liberates, shapes a new and inclusive community, and empowers his followers to be agents of reconciliation. The book *Coming Together* ends with a call for reconciliation, and DeYoung's treatment in the book *Reconciliation* offers counsel on the process one must understand and follow in developing a reconciliation mind-set, entering into meaningful relationships, and taking responsibility for the polarization that exists. There are places where DeYoung calls attention to how he came to experience what he has written about, and he has written about it all with a responsible and contagious bearing. His is a holistic approach, with an accent on the discipline and cost of being a reconciler. Knowing him as I do, and knowing some of the risks he has had to take and some of what he has had to undergo as a believing, teaching, active practitioner of *agape*-love, I strongly recommend DeYoung's books on reconciliation. Based in a vital Christian faith, they offer sound guidance, a guidance that is never past tense but contemporary, focused, creative, and practical.

I have called attention to Thurman's work and DeYoung's treatment of reconciliation because both deal necessarily, forthrightly, and helpfully with the discipline demanded for those who would work as agents of reconciliation. It is a discipline that demands realism in the face of divisive walls, hostility, and hate; a discipline that refuses to cower before the barriers that block harmony; a discipline that properly and steadily informs, encourages, and energizes one to engage in the divine process of reconciliation, that readies one to take responsibility, and, understanding the necessity for forgiveness, seeks to effect it by touching the soul, repairing the wrong that injured, and establishing the needed relationship. This discipline demands an active love, a healthy self-image, willingness to risk oneself, and a sense of being companioned in the task by God.

A word is in order about the part forgiveness plays in becoming reconciled, both the seeking of forgiveness and granting it. Forgiveness is that ability and active willingness to pardon someone and thus "wipe out," as it were, the reason for the discord and separation. Forgiveness demands the letting go of grudges and attitudes that block being related. Some months ago, while reading an issue of *The Chronicle of Higher Education* (July 17, 1998, A18-A20), I was delightfully surprised to learn from one of its articles about some research currently underway in several universities dealing with "Forgiveness Studies." In view of marital discord, families in disarray, and nations wracked by ethnic, tribal and religious divisions, social psychologists have become increasingly concerned about the effects of anger, resentment, and the desire for revenge, among other attitudes and feelings, on mind-body connections, and how forgiveness can improve physical as well as mental health. At the time the article appeared there were twenty-nine projects underway in universities on forgiveness research, with the John Templeton Foundation having underwritten most of the support cost. The scholars are at work conducting studies, developing inventory checklists to assess whether and how persons learn to forgive and what they forgive. They have been busy administering tests, collecting data, organizing conferences, bringing researchers into contact with each other, and publishing preliminary reports and articles about their still embryonic science. They are concerned to define the meaning and parameters of forgiveness, the need for forgiveness, as well as the effects of forgiveness. Although most people equate this subject with religion and not science, some of the scientists have shown concern about finding common ground between the two approaches to forgiveness. The current research is aimed at determining what forgiveness is, how it works, in which cases, and what its effects are at the level of mind-body connections.

From the standpoint of religious experience, we know that true forgiveness can and does happen in the human heart, and that emotional and behavioral changes take place in both the forgiving person and the person who is forgiven because of the creative and healing power of love. Those persons who are deeply aware that God loves and has forgiven them seem to deal with their hurt feelings more quickly and forgive more readily. We humans can be trained to forgive, and reconciling agents must help people learn and choose to do so. The bottom line is always that the wounded person must willingly turn away from the history of the happening, refuse to harbor resentment raised by the happening, and choose to forgive those responsible for wronging them. This is easier to achieve when the offending action is in the past and the offender or offenders have offered a sincere apology, but even when this has not happened a reasonably thinking person can be predisposed in spirit to forgive. A serious believer will surely be so predisposed, instructed by the example of Jesus as he hung on his cross: "Father, forgive them; for they do not know what they are doing" (Luke 23:34a).

As church leaders, we will all readily agree that the church has a potential and mandated role to bring people together, to help people experience forgiveness, both the forgiveness God grants and the forgiveness needed from other people. We must remain mindful of our Lord's encouraging pronouncement: "Blessed are the peacemakers, for they will be called children of God" (Matt. 5:9). This beatitude is preserved only in Matthew's account of the Sermon on the Mount and seems addressed to those who have a heart for helping others to become reconciled. In the setting of that day, it could as well have been a word of caution to those in the listening crowd who were of a zealotic bent, those listeners who were sympathetic to militaristic attempts to remove the yoke of Roman rule from the Jewish nation's neck. Was this a warning word from Jesus that the only holy crusades are crusades for peace? The political environment of our Lord's ministry should never be overlooked in studying what he taught and how he taught.[7] In this beatitude Jesus tells us all that God's kingdom is not promoted by human violence, that peacemaking is the way to shape the best future, and that those who do this work of effecting reconciliation are God's true children.

In light of this, it is important to reflect on how often this emphasis on being peaceful or on making peace appears in the New Testament. Interestingly, the exhortation "be at peace with one another" (Mark 9:50b) is linked in that verse with the instruction of Jesus that we are to be like salt in the world. Here is the full saying: "Salt is good, but if salt has lost its saltiness, how can you restore its saltiness? Have salt in yourselves, and be at peace with one another" (Mark 9:50). There are two passages in Romans with a similar emphasis: "If it is possible, so far as it depends on you, live peaceably with all" (Rom. 12:18); and "Let us pursue what makes for peace and for mutual upbuilding" (Rom. 14:19). In 2 Corinthians 13:11 we are told: ". . . agree with one another, live in peace, and the God of love and peace will be with you." First Thessalonians 5:13*b* exhorts us, "Be at peace among yourselves." Hebrews 12:14 offers the same directive, with a reminder about right living: "Pursue peace with everyone, and the holiness without which no one will see the Lord." Then there is that illuminating statement in James 3:18, part of a set of pointed instructions to a group of believers fractured by religious, economic, and social differences: "And a harvest of righteousness [or: the fruit of justice] is sown in peace for those who make peace." The message in the image is that righteousness makes its presence known and felt through peace. This line in James 3:18 is like the teaching of Jesus in the seventh beatitude, and it simply reports that peacemaking is the highest activity and the greatest deed. The truly righteous person promotes peace.

We recall the well-publicized news received in June of 1995 after the Southern Baptist Convention, the largest Protestant denomination in the

United States, at its annual meeting passed a resolution of repentance for the denomination's involvement in and support of slavery, one of the contributing causes for founding the Convention one hundred and fifty years earlier. A public apology was made to African Americans, whose ancestors suffered under that pernicious system. The Convention sought forgiveness for justifying the slavery system, for involvement in the segregating system that followed slavery, and for its part in the history that shaped the racist climate that still afflicts this nation. The concern was reconciliation, and forgiveness was being sought in order to experience this benefit and need.

There were critics who viewed the Convention resolution with suspicion, coming so late as it did in the group's history, but I viewed the apology as responsible and honest. It is never too late to right a wrong, however long-standing, and the delegates were attempting to do so. That resolution of apology would never have happened apart from an announced "change of heart." Over time, the Southern Baptist Convention was readied for reconciliation, and it took more than one influencing factor: it took the impact of a more enlightened public, the legal overthrow of segregation, and a heightened moral and social conscience, among other things, but I must also highlight the critical influence upon the Convention's members of a more informed and humane reading of the Scriptures and the steady ministry of the Spirit of God who works always to effect reconciliation.

Our Lord's mandate that we evangelize (Matthew 28:18-20) is at one with our assignment to be reconcilers (2 Cor. 5:19-20). Both service roles have been entrusted to us, and both are strategically related in two ways: first, the same message that brings salvation is the basis for reconciliation not only with God but with other persons; and second, the same *agape*-love that motivates us to evangelize also motivates us to be reconciling agents. These two ministries might well be described as two sides of one coin since they are so closely conjoined for believers.

The ministry of evangelizing and the ministry of reconciling both call for a knowledgeable, earnest, patient, persistent, and unselfish spirit of caring about people. The caring must be strong and steady because evil forces do not yield their control without a fight, and destructive hostilities and entrenched angers are never scared off by just a Christian presence, however right our cause. We must be armed with meanings that matter, use apt methods to share those meanings, and we must care deeply enough for people in order to deal effectively with the attitudes, feelings, and other fall-out from the deep consciousness people have of personal offenses suffered and the threats people fear because of color differences and cultural diversities. I say this because these problems continue to be more determinative when people meet each other than the more reasonable goal of finding a common ground for relating peacefully and fruitfully. Remembered injuries and differences in color and culture continue to predispose people to negate, exclude, or fight rather than seek peace. Our mandate to evangelize and our mission to reconcile authorize and empower us to break through the walls that block people from the harmony we so sorely need in this world.

We have noted earlier that reconciliation cannot be achieved without an active willingness to seek forgiveness and to forgive. As reconcilers, we can help persons reach and act out that willingness. In addition, and in the interest of maintaining harmony, we must help persons recognize, admit, and overcome their prejudices and learn to discipline their preferences. I will spare you further talk about *prejudices*, about which we often hear, but something more must be said here about *preferences*, since these can also block right relations between people.

The dictionary defines a *preference* as "a greater liking; a first choice; a giving of priority or advantage to someone or something." We all know what it means to put one thing ahead of something else, as when choosing a car, a certain kind and size of house, a college or university to attend, to name a few instances. We exercised a preference when dating, which led to courtship and marriage. Preferences are very personal matters, daily concerns in the business of living and relating. We know what it is to enjoy having and doing what we prefer, and we know what it is to endure not having our likes and chosen priorities fulfilled. Preferences are part of our personality system, and their roots extend deep into the soil that nurtured our personal growth. Preferences must be understood and valued for what they are and for what they enable us to be and do. But preferences must also be scrutinized because they bias us, they slant us within, so that our interests, concerns, attitudes, and judgments about things will lean in a certain direction. Preferences must be measured and tested by something higher than our "likes," "dislikes," and "personal priorities" lest we find ourselves living really by prejudices. Unexamined preferences can be socially problematic. They can influence us, unwittingly, to act unwisely in some matter, or to give priority to some concern that does not promote peace but discord. A preference must be honored when it is just and unselfish, but it should be changed when it makes one selfishly judgmental, racist, and socially prohibitive.

So much goes into the molding of our lives, and that molding produces consequences in us that we follow mostly without thinking—until we are stirred by something that forces us to think about those consequences.[8] Growing up, as we did, in some specific national, ethnic, racial, cultural, geographical, and denominational settings, we all tend to honor and prefer these settings and we tend to judge all else and all others by what our settings mean to us. But the time comes when we are stirred by something to think more deeply about what conditioned us and we find it necessary to alter our view about some matter or resist some influence that conditioned us improperly against responding openly, peacefully, and helpfully in the places where we now find ourselves. The conditioning is there inside us, and it stays there, steadily influencing us, until we see it for what it is and deal with it and ourselves, affirming what we should and altering what we must. Reconciliation is achieved only when we are no longer limited to or bound by what conditioned us against relating to others. And the fruits of reconciliation can only grow when we are disciplined and kept under management by a strong ethic for staying in relation.

I have quoted much from Paul and with understood reasons. As I conclude, I want to do so by highlighting Paul's declaration about how he handled his prior conditioning as a Hebrew as he dealt with the wider world of differing groups in the Roman Empire. His is a declaration about the principle that disciplined his preferences and kept him open as a relational and reconciling person. The declaration is found in 1 Corinthians 9:19-23:

> 9:19 For though I am free with respect to all, I have made myself a slave to all, so that I might win more of them.
>
> 9:20 To the Jews I became as a Jew, in order to win Jews. To those under the law I became as one under the law (though I myself am not under the law) so that I might win those under the law.
>
> 9:21 To those outside the law I became as one outside the law (though I am not free from God's law but am under Christ's law) that I might win those outside the law.
>
> 9:22 To the weak I became weak, that I might win the weak. I have become all things to all people, that I might by all means save some.

9:23 I do it all for the sake of the gospel, so that I may share in its blessings.

Such was Paul's approach to handling his preferences; he kept those preferences ordered and informed by the higher principle of the relational imperative of *agape*-love. This kind of caring-sharing love does not concern itself with social expediency but with spiritual necessity and the best human future. So, it was truly the case with Paul, as he confessed to his Corinthian readers:

> From now on, therefore, we regard no one from a human point of view; even though we once knew Christ from a human point of view, we know him no longer that way. So if anyone is in Christ, there is a new creation: everything old has passed away; see, everything has become new! All this is from God, who reconciled us to himself through Christ, and has given us the ministry of reconciliation; that is, in Christ God was reconciling the world to himself, not counting their trespasses against them, and entrusting the message of reconciliation to us. So we are ambassadors for Christ, since God is making his appeal through us...(2 Cor. 5:16-20a).

May this be the case with us as well.

Notes

[1] This article was the keynote presentation at the 2001 annual meeting of the Wesleyan Theological Society. Portions were previously published in substantially the same form as a chapter in Timothy George and Robert Smith, Jr., eds., *A Mighty Long Journey* (Broadman & Holman Publishers, 2000), 199-222. Used here by permission.

[2] James Barr, *The Semantics of Biblical Language* (Oxford University Press, 1961), vii.

[3] Vincent Taylor, The Cross of Christ (London: Macmillan and Co., Ltd., 1957), 87. For some additional treatments of reconciliation as related to the church's teaching on atonement, see also Vincent Taylor, Forgiveness and Reconciliation: A Study in New Testament Theology (London: Macmillan and Co., Ltd., 1960), esp. 70-108; Leon Morris, The Apostolic Preaching of the Cross (Grand Rapids: William B. Eerdmans Publishing Co., 1956); Ralph P. Martin, Reconciliation: A Study of Paul's Theology (London: Marshall, 1981).

[4] Howard Thurman, *Disciplines of the Spirit* (New York: Harper & Row, Publishers, 1963), 108.

[5] Ibid., 121.

[6] Ibid., 122.

[7] On this, see especially Howard Thurman, *Jesus and the Disinherited* (Nashville: Abingdon Press, 1949); Alan Richardson, *The Political Christ*

(Philadelphia: The Westminster Press, 1973).

⁸ For more on this, see H. Richard Niebuhr, *The Responsible Self* (New York: Harper & Row, Publishers, 1963), esp. 42-68.

Chapter 15

Becoming a Community of the Spirit

by
James W. Lewis

The words of James W. Lewis of the Church of God movement (Anderson) are direct: "All Christians should sense the moral indictment inherent in speaking more confidently about unity than actually living it.... Christian unity should be seen as synonymous with the notion of a 'reconciled community of the Spirit'." Lewis sees the wedding of holiness and unity as positioning the Church of God movement to have an important voice today. However, even this movement must meet a critical challenge. Viewing the church as God's special community with a "radical" character, Lewis reviews the reality of power in this world and insists that, for there to be real communities of the Spirit, the Church of God movement and other Christian communities must break free of some prevailing cultural assumptions and be reoriented to the Spirit's power to create new communities. The radical church serves the radical Jesus in his radical ways—and thus functions as a community of the Spirit of Jesus. Originally published in the Wesleyan Theological Journal *(37:1, Spring, 2002).*

On Race Relations Sunday or in other community-wide worship celebrations, Christians see preachers engaging in pulpit exchanges with black, white, hispanic[1] and other Christians, coming together in one place. The place pulsates with an air of expectancy, if for no other reason than a sense of the novelty of it all. Important things may happen, but soon all go their separate ways, deferring Christian unity to some unknown future. The rhetoric of Christian unity, while valuable, falls agonizingly short of truthful practice. While I celebrate all efforts to live in the spirit of Christian unity, all Christians should sense the moral indictment inherent in speaking more confidently about unity than actually living it. Rhetoric is fundamentally what we say and how we say it.[2] Therefore, living "between" rhetoric and practice is equivalent to a "pursuit." Such pursuit then captures both the reality of the church's ambivalent existence [division] and its assent that God does call us to live in unity with each other.

Christian unity should be seen as synonymous with the notion of a "reconciled community of the Spirit." It is a fundamental belief of Scripture that those who follow Jesus constitute a community. John Wesley believed that Christianity is not intended to be lived in isolation from others: "Christianity is essentially a social religion; and...to turn it into a solitary one is to destroy it."[3] What contributes to the dissonance between rhetoric and practice is an often distorted view of community. It is not just any kind of community to which the church should aspire.[4] God's call is to a "reconciled" community of the Spirit.

The Church of God movement (Anderson) has much to contribute to contemporary discussions about Christian unity.[5] This movement's twin distinctives of Christian unity and biblical holiness position it to help other Christians experience the unity of all believers. But there are some factors, even in this movement, that impede an experiencing of reconciled communities of the Spirit. What follows identifies these factors and some implications that might help communities of faith to experience afresh the reconciling Spirit and the truthful practices of God's new community. Inter-ethnic or racial reconciliation is a key moral issue with important ecclesial implications. But first, we need clarity about the Church of God movement.

No contemporary movement should be so presumptuous as to claim that it is the sole voice on issues of Christian unity. The early first-century Christian communities certainly can lay claim to identifying Christian unity as integral to the gospel. Any contemporary reflection on Christian unity must be in conversation with the living tradition(s) of the Christian past. A long and broad view of history is necessary. Some attention should be given to this history as a way to provide critical perspective on the nature of the church as a new and reconciled community of the Spirit. Gerhard Lohfink provides a compelling account of God's actions in history.[6] This is the kind of account that is biblically faithful, theologically imaginative, and truthfully compelling. This account of God's dealings in history extends in a faithful way the more limited renderings of the biblical story articulated by many denominational historians and theologians. It is my belief that to recapture a passion for reconciled communities of the Spirit requires a view such as Lohfink's.

A Theological (Normative) Narrative of the Reconciled Community of the Spirit

Gerhard Lohfink has produced an exceptional work on God and history, specifically God's purposes through Israel and the church. For many North American Christians who require that the worship of God be entertaining and spontaneous, this kind of God may be a bit too tame and boring. However, Lohfink does not succumb to the excesses of the common cultural entrapment by values alien to God's reign. The Trinitarian God *needs* the church because God wills the world's salvation only in the context of human freedom and continual growth. While God desires the salvation of all nations, this desire would remain amorphous and abstract if it found no place to land. Lohfink's argument consistently unfolds in the direction of a radical particularity, from God's election of Israel in the Old Testament to God's election of the church through Jesus Christ in the New Testament. Lohfink says, "For Jesus, the reign of God is also tangible and visible. It does not simply exist in human hearts, nor is it hidden somewhere beyond history. It can be seen already, touched, acquired, traded. For that very reason it can fascinate people and move them to give up everything for the sake of this new thing without thereby losing their freedom" (47).

For contemporary Christians who lament the church's disunity, Lohfink's provocative reading of salvation history gives us reason to hope that the Spirit can act powerfully today. The not-yetness of God's reign does not necessarily mean its deferral to some future time. According to him, in Mark 1:15, "'the kingdom has come near' cannot mean that the time of fulfillment has not really come yet. It is true that 'has come near' contains an element of 'not yet,' but that has to do not with God's action but with Israel's response. At this moment Israel has not yet repented....Jesus' hearers would prefer to put everything off to some future time, and the story comes to no good end. The time is indeed fulfilled, but God's *basileia* is not accepted. The 'today' God offers is disputed, and so that 'already' becomes 'not yet'" (135, 136).

Lohfink's poignant discussion of salvation in the New Testament maintains the emphasis on both God's sovereign election and Israel's human freedom. The "already-not yet" of the kingdom of God is the resistance of the "not-yet" from the human side against the superabundant "already" of fulfillment from God's side (139). Jesus and the new society—the eschatological new society (the emerging church)—growing up around him embodies the limitless generosity of God (153). God's overflowing fullness is manifest, according to Lohfink, in none other than the reality of the church's concrete existence. Jesus' bodily resurrection possesses consequences for the church (207). The church is also a "body." "It is visible, palpable, tangible. It is socially organized" (207). The church cannot exist invisibly or reside only in the hearts of the faithful. It is a tangible reality. To be "in Christ" cannot be construed as only an individual transaction with God through Jesus. It is to be inextricably in community, with real brothers and sisters, being the foretaste of God's eschatological new people. They practice a new lifestyle in a reconciled community.

For Lohfink, the *ecclesia*, the called-out assembly, is the gathering of no less than the *people of God*. Gathering is a fundamental feature of the church (218). As the book of Acts summarizes the history, this assembly lives publicly in the world, living its life as God's just society and sustained by its desire for consensus discovered through the praise, prayer, and power of the Holy Spirit. According to Lohfink, the "public" nature of the *ecclesia* indicated that "they did not see themselves as a group of like-minded friends and also not as a group of people...joined together because of particular interests" (218). Instead they were created by God and had an interest in all things. The assembly's very nature was construed as a public assembly of the *whole*. Although conflicts arose in the community, they did not resort to violence, but rather to finding solutions by consensus.[7] Lohfink defines unanimity as "allowing oneself to be placed by God on a new footing, what Paul in Philippians 2:1-5 calls 'sharing in the Spirit' and 'being in Christ.' This new basis is made possible by Jesus' surrender of his own life, which Paul speaks about...in Philippians 2:6-11" (236). The church is understood to live through and in its concrete gatherings where unity of the whole church is preserved.

These concrete and continuous assemblies would not constitute the church just by their gathering. "Among the Church's most precious possessions is the knowledge that of itself it is incapable of bringing about even something *resembling* a community, and that when it attempts to do so in spite of that knowledge the effort yields nothing but dead-end rivalries....The center that sustains everything and that it cannot make of itself...is a gift: the Spirit of Jesus. Only from this center can it find unanimity, and that unanimity is then its entire strength" (222-23). Lohfink believes that it is in such assemblies where "the community can ask, again and again, what its way is to be, what is its next step, what is God's concrete will for it" (235). In such a practice of public unanimity, construed against the notion of "democratically organized church," is God's hope for gathering the separated from all nations. The tension of the "already-not yet" of God's kingdom is still experienced even among the baptized.

The Pauline form of the *people of God* is the *body of Christ*. In opposition to religious individualism, Christian salvation involves incorporation into the church as a social body.[8] One can have communion with Christ *only and always* in communion with others" (255, emphasis mine).[9] In Paul's indictment of the Eucharist practiced by the Corinthian congregation, he identifies the fundamental principle of community: "that each esteems the other above himself or herself (Phil. 2:3)" (259).

The unity of the body of Christ is not achieved by humanistic appeals to solidarity or brotherhood or sisterhood, since rivalries between individuals, families, groups, and nations are much too strong. Rather, the community lives from "the dying and rising of Jesus" (260). Christian unity does not obliterate differences. The body of Christ, therefore, must rest on that which preserves the "virtues" of difference, without destroying society. It rests entirely on freedom, voluntariness, and on the belief that differences are a means to mutual enrichment (261).[10] *Agape* binds together that which otherwise would drive to disunion. The gift of the divine Spirit released through Jesus' surrender of his life makes possible what is impossible through human agency alone. The church's *wholeness* is its undivided, exclusive worship and obedience to the God of Abraham and Jesus of Nazareth. In the gospels and the Pauline letters, this theme of wholeness is promoted as central to the unity of the body of Christ. This wholeness refers not only to local communities existing currently, but also to those throughout the history of the tradition. Furthermore, it speaks to the universality of the church's mission since salvation and the lordship of Jesus over the universe occurs *through the Church* (cf. Ephesians; Lohfink, 282-290). The reconciling power of the Spirit and the presence of peace exist where Jesus is head, including in the church.[11]

This extended summary of Lohfink's theology provides a compelling vision of the church. In locating unity in the worship of the Triune God–the God who creates the world and yearns for its redemption, the church trumpets the ongoing importance of Christian unity as intrinsic to its life and witness. Several church groups have recognized the centrality of unity as indispensable to the witness of God in the world. As Barry Callen says, "The Stone-Campbell movement (the Disciples)…from early in the nineteenth century had perceived most of the same dilemmas and proposed some of the same solutions that later would characterize the Church of God movement."[12] However, what is it about the Church of God (Anderson) that positions it to offer substantive insights to the wider church's pursuit of Christian unity—the reconciled community of the Spirit?

The Church of God Reformation Movement: Wedding of Holiness and Unity

Daniel S. Warner is accorded the status of the principal (human) founder of the Church of God movement (Anderson, Indiana). Although many church groups go by the name "Church of God," Warner intended the name to convey his belief that the church belongs to God and not to any cadre of humans and their institutions. My purpose in this section is not to re-tell the story of its birth and growth, for that would move us far afield. There are several sources that can orient the interested reader.[13] I will focus primarily on the movement's "distinguishing" doctrines of biblical holiness and Christian unity. From its inception, the movement's intent has been "to give priority to the presence and governing power of the Holy Spirit."[14] Warner did not warm initially to holiness teachings. He bristled at what he saw as disturbing hypocrisy in many of the holiness devotees he knew. However, being ever receptive to the Spirit's leading in his life, Warner appeared to bring together in his person the long-held convictions about church divisions and heart holiness.[15] There was "an urgency about a God-ordained mission in the 'last days.' The themes of unity, holiness, and biblical prophecy blended and were conveyed powerfully by the preaching skill of Daniel Warner."[16] Warner's life and early struggle to "reform" his own Indiana Holiness Association is akin to a "principled search" to recapture authentic Christian unity and biblical holiness.

A. Holiness. Many church groups who take Scripture seriously will affirm holiness to some degree. However, the Church of God movement has "a stronger emphasis and a sharper focus on the doctrine and practice of holy living than is true in most church groups."[17] One cannot fully appreciate the Church of God at its best without realizing its commitment to utter dependence on the Bible truths as personally experienced through the Spirit.[18]

The scriptural admonitions to be "perfect" are often translated as to be "mature" or "fully grown." Being mature carries the notion of "responsible adulthood, a readiness to fulfill the purposes for which one is created."[19] For John Smith, the New Testament writers mean by "perfection" a spiritual maturity, perfect love, heart purity, victory over any intentional wrongdoing.[20] Absolute perfection was not intended, but rather a release from the reigning power of sin. This victory over the power of sin is not a human achievement, but an empowerment of the Holy Spirit. Smith further elaborates:

> Receiving the Holy Spirit into one's life as a "helper" is a way of describing the experience of sanctification that has been so strongly emphasized in the Church of God and in other holiness groups....Living a life under the direction of the Holy Spirit means living with victory over sinful desires and temptations.[21]

The Church of God movement does not view the doctrine of holiness as an abstract theological concept. It is to be expressed in actions, attitudes, and aspirations. Biblical holiness is to encompass the purity of all life. A holy lifestyle by definition could not be truncated to simply an inward piety, although that dimension is certainly present. Holiness then is sustained in community. This community of the sanctifying and cleansing Spirit is a holy community called church. One verse of a well-loved heritage hymn of the Church of God says: "Oh Church of God, one body is. One Spirit dwells within. And all her members are redeemed and triumph over sin." The Church as the holy, transformed community fundamentally evokes the idea of the church's essential unity.

B. Christian Unity. The early leaders of the Church of God (and many today) often spoke of "seeing" the church. The church they saw was a vision of God's great plan for his people "as a mighty company made up of all redeemed persons on the earth."[22] The church they saw crossed all human barriers, whether of race, color, nationality, caste, clan, class, sex, educational level, temperament, or culture.[23] Such a church bore witness to God's love for all humankind.

While the church partakes of human characteristics, it is fundamentally a divine institution. It is an institution that is Jesus' "primary continuing living presence in the world."[24] It is also divine in that the Holy Spirit rules and governs the church.[25] The Church of God movement owes much of its origin to revivalistic Wesleyanism and experiential pietism; its view of the church is that of a dynamic organism. The church was and is more than a collection of individuals desiring only the satisfaction of their own needs and desires. The church is seen as "God's people in community with one another."[26] It is a community of holy people, governed and equipped by the Spirit, and witnessing to the world through the spiritual agency of reconciled believers saved across all human barriers. Hence, the church is a *visible* community of persons redeemed by God's grace. The Church of God movement attests to God's ownership by insisting that only "persons who had experienced the new birth were already members of the Church."[27] This visible community of believers is indeed a reconciled community. It is a community of the Spirit who gifts the community with unity. The earliest Church of God reformers believed that God was calling them to proclaim and model the visible earthly expression of the one, holy, catholic church. God does not have church*es*, but *a* church.[28]

Jesus' prayer in John 17 serves as a pivotal passage for the call to Christian unity: "That they all might be one." The Church of God reformation holds, in the face of pervasive divisions in the church, that God wills the unity of all God's people. It is to be a unity (community) created by Jesus through the power of the Holy Spirit. Warner affirmed that holiness and unity are inseparably linked, with unity being the beautiful fruit of perfected holiness. As a result, the Church of God reformers shunned any organization, seeing all such attempts as the human promotion of "sectarianism." History reveals, however, the continuing struggles of the Church of God to live up to its ideal of Christian unity. Forthright assessment of its struggles is a necessary activity of moral vigilance.

C. How is This Movement Doing? The Church of God (Anderson) possesses a biblically defensible and theologically grounded doctrine of unity and holiness. Like most church groups, however, it has experienced the gnawing discrepancy between fundamental teaching and concrete actions. There is much to commend the movement. It is linked with the wider church tradition, especially with the Radical or Believers' Church tradition.[29] Historically, it has been one of the more inclusive church bodies. While the early reformers may not have spoken explicitly much of the time about racial issues, they faithfully heralded the message of holiness and Christian unity. Many blacks heard the message and embraced the hope of the message and the commitment of its messengers. Is rhetoric important? Yes, there is no need to dismiss the message. But there still is a problem.

The problem is a shared one with Christendom as a whole. It is a problem characterized by the continuing, persistent, and embarrassing deficit created by the distance between our rhetoric of unity and our practice of it. On a macro-level, the moral problem is disunity in the global church. On a micro-level, the moral problem often gets described as sins within congregational life. The Church of God (Anderson), on a macro-level, experiences a somewhat unified national and global structures. However, there is a great deal of diversity [oftentimes division] among various groups in the movement. The Church of God has experienced some separation in its history. It is amazing that the movement has remained together, despite broad differences. For example, there is the great diversity among believers in non-Western societies, as well as the strong influences coming from the National Association of the Church of God (a predominantly African-American constituency in the United States), the North American ministries center in Anderson, Indiana, a fellowship of pastors and congregations in the lower Midwest, and the ever-growing Spanish Concilio. Unity is a complex challenge. Disunity is a pervasive reality.

D. Does Race Still Matter? While our nation has established an annual celebration of Black History month and many celebrate the strides made in race relations, these great strides are still insufficient. This is particularly true in reference to the church. "Racial fatigue" and chronic denial still plague the collective psyche of both Christians and non-Christians. To quote an often used cliché that still happens to be true: The 11:00 hour is still the most segregated hour in America.[30] The problem appears virtually intractable, so that we are goaded into believing that we should not expect too much in this present life.

Barry Callen's insightful overview essay in a recent publication is titled "Realizing the Ideal." It captures for the Church of God its rather ambivalent responses to its own vision and existence.[31] It has championed unity, but been dogged by incidents of disunity and cultural accommodation. Its General Assembly in North America has passed several resolutions over the years pertaining to race and race relations, all biblically informed and culturally relevant. Yet the movement's polity, more autonomous than interdependent, mitigates against any sustained optimism that such resolutions might temporarily inspire within us. This is illustrated by the length of time for some separate state assemblies (black and white) to merge into one. There still exist in many states separate assemblies. Also, there are some states where the separate Ministerial Fellowships have merged, but the state assemblies embodying the congregations remain separate. Even the Women of the Church of God, who have often led the way on many social issues, have experienced recalcitrance in a few states in the call for them to unify their racially separate womens' groups. This is a moral problem that hits at the heart of the gospel of Jesus Christ!

As a member of the wider church, and living out my life in the group of people known as the Church of God (Anderson), I am blessed to be a part of these people as we worship the Trinitarian God on behalf of the whole church. Yet I am saddened by the continuing presence of the vestiges of racism in the life of the Church of God. This grief is especially wrenching given the historic message, heralded for over a century, of unity of all God's children and holiness of lifestyle.

Thus, I argue that the rhetoric of Christian unity in the Church of God (Anderson) is the right one, but the practice of unity is frustratingly inconsistent. The reason for the inconsistency is not simply because people are human or live between the times. Rather, the inconsistency is nurtured by forces that array themselves against the working of the Spirit to empower the church's effort to maintain the unity of the faith in the bond of peace. Proclamation fails to produce its intended purpose when the church does not serve the Spirit's goal of orchestrating *concrete* practices of unity within God's new community. Believers should embrace the articulation of Christian unity from ecclesial traditions like the Church of God (Anderson), but go beyond rhetoric to practice for a radical assent to the demands of the Spirit to be one. We must seek to overcome the glaring schism between rhetoric and practice through a radical re-appropriation of the power of the Spirit. We cannot be content to assume that God is going to make everything come out right in the end. To be passive is to legitimate divisions among believers. Gerhard Lohfink gives this scathing denunciation of the passive posture:

> There are theologians who make a virtue of the painful fact of division and assert that the many churches and confessions reflect, like a thousand facets, the richness of the Christian reality. There is certainly an element of truth in that: all the churches that have gone their separate ways have brought to light elements of faith that were affirmed onesidedly, obscured, or covered over in the Catholic Church. Even all the serious sects have reminded the Church unmercifully that faith demands…the genuine community of the faithful.

And yet, the thesis that all separations simply be explained and even transfigured

> …as the "richness of variety" not only contains a highly dangerous element; it is also unbiblical. The condition of Christianity at the present time is nothing like a colorful field in which wheat is growing and poppies and cornflowers are blooming; it is rather like a broken mirror that distorts the image of Christ. In light of the New Testament the splintering of the people of God cannot be regarded in any other way. There

the question of divisions within the communities and within the Church as a whole was already present, and the answer given by New Testament theology is unequivocal.[32]

In our contemporary racist society in North America, Christians must be at least "bilingual"—good theologians and acute cultural critics. Without both the church is more easily captured by the logic and practices of a dominant culture than by the practices of an alternative culture called "church." Here are some impediments that mitigate against the church's witness of authentic unity and holiness.

Docetic Christians

William J. Jennings describes the theological and practical problem for Christians as a docetism that haunts us in relation to race, culture, and the problem of racism. How often do we hear these responses from well-meaning Christians regarding race? "I don't see anyone as black or white, just my sister or brother in Christ. There is no such thing as race, we are all one in Christ." Or we say, "we just need to learn how to forgive, respect and live together and go on to the future." Or we say, "where I was raised there were no black people; therefore race was and is not an issue for me." Jennings characterizes all such statements as docetic. This quote by Jennings indicates what docetism means in relation to our views on racism:

> Our docetism in matters of race surfaces in our articulation of a social redemption [rhetoric] that is beyond the actual realities and operations of our humanity [practice]. Our docetic tendency is not merely our inability to deal with human "differences." Our docetism in matters of race comes to light in our desire to see racial harmony and peace [rhetoric] without the actual transformation of identity rooted in the real conversion of our forms of social existence and community [practice].
>
> These kinds of statements [those listed above] commonly found in the mouths of Christians exhibit the worst kind of theological deception. Here we claim a commitment to a changed perspective [rhetoric] without the requirement of any significant display of that commitment [practice]. Such ways of speaking and thinking exhibit the total denial of any Christological mediation that would shape the way we live and that would demand a way of life that indicates the seriousness of Christian transformation. Here we exhibit the foolishness of Western individualism as it deceives us into thinking that a changed heart means a changed world.[33]

This keen observation is particularly astute. It seeks to unmask the power of the deception inherent in particular construals of the faith. Holiness and other groups who endorse a more inward piety or individualistic approach to the Christian life are especially encouraged to heed the warning of docetic tendencies. A personal appropriation of faith is not the same as a private faith. I lament the great disconnect between an individual's personal convictions (or beliefs) and the social embodiment of those convictions in faithful practices. There is a serious moral problem inherent in the passionate preaching and testifying of many Christians, especially white Christians, when it is not mirrored in correlative relationships and institutions.[34]

The early pioneers of the Church of God movement rightly saw the church as a "visible" reality of Christian unity. But the movement's revivalistic and experiential focus has tended to marginalize in reality what has been vigorously embraced rhetorically. The church appears to be an appendage to what many now see as the most fundamental spiritual reality—*the salvation of individual souls*. This mode of discourse opens any movement to the seductive logic of Western individualism that centers the individual and de-centers the community. We then become, on Jennings' terms, more "docetic." This "virtue" of western society encourages the church's captivity to alien powers embedded in the dominant culture. The community of believers is in danger of being seduced.[35]

Rodney Clapp ventures the view that the "heresy of white Christians" may result in destroying the faith of others. He says that

> ...if white, racist Christians have rarely denounced the doctrine of the Trinity or Christ as Savior, they have often embodied and practiced their faith in such a way that others, whom they subjugated in the name of that faith, could not themselves come to affirm orthodox doctrines. The heresy of white Christianity, then, is one of distorting and deviating from truth in such a way that even if it does not destroy your own faith confession, it effectively prevents or destroys the faith confessions of others.[36]

The experience of the reconciled community of the Spirit is impeded by a distorted view of power. When we say "power of the Holy Spirit," what do we intend?

The Power of the World vs. the Power of the Holy Spirit

The Church of God reformation, along with other Wesleyan/Holiness traditions, promote a thoroughly biblical view of the Holy Spirit. The sanctifying work of the Holy Spirit can transform the heart and empower us to love. The problem, however, is subsequently acting in ways consistent with the will and purpose of the Trinitarian God. The Church of God movement has promoted a doctrine of the Holy Spirit that features the call to continued growth and transformation in holy living. This maturing and empowering function of the Holy Spirit often is impeded by perverted surrender to certain cultural realities.

Academic theologians enjoy a certain amount of power made possible by the separation of the academy from the church. A power of analysis that emerges from the perceived hegemony of objective and detached analysis is always tempting. The problem becomes the subtle ways in which reflections are shielded from the churchly practices that authorize them. Worshippers in local congregations can be held captive to ways of thinking that insulate them from the truthful demands of the gospel. Theologians and biblical scholars should dare to help Christians tell the truth about their temporal existence. An urgently needed truth involves facing the divided Church and feuding Christians with the sin in their communal and individual lives.[37]

I agree with Barry Callen's affirmation of the Believers Church tradition. In comparing this tradition with "liberation theologies" and contemporary evangelicalism, he properly critiques "liberation" theologies for their "optimistic world view." Their "[focus] on the power of God and the potential of the *transformation of this present world by concerted Christian action* (emphasis mine)" fuel this optimism. While I do not argue with his conclusion, I hope that the reader might also have an appreciation for the positive contribution of liberation theologies. A strength of such theologies is their potential to critique oppression, affirm the humanity of the oppressed, and evaluate the experience of the oppressed as a source and criterion for truth. Therefore, any premature dismissing of liberation theologies may lead to an unintended marginalization of those who lack power—the poor, the widow, the children, minorities, and women. Cheryl Sanders holds to the benefits of black liberation theology as "an invaluable starting point for discussion of the past plight and future prospects of the African American people." She goes beyond the limits of black liberation theology in order to address its limitation.[38]

The ability to discern the experiences of others often is missing in our church communities, and it is especially necessary in a world where we are increasingly rendered incapable of "seeing rightly" and "acting justly." Christians can be rendered morally blind even as they wax eloquent theologically. In the most "powerful" society on the face of the earth by most accounts, the language of national power often serves as the paradigm for the church's language of power. In the wide-ranging field of Christian advertising and marketing, our view of power in the Christian life often is a Jesus very at home on Wall Street, in the Pentagon, or in the Oval Office. A case can be made for the tragedy of the church's tendency to equate the power of the Holy Spirit with the power of the world.

To the extent we do not acknowledge this mutation of divine power, we align ourselves with the limited agendas of worldly powers and authorities. Does the kingdom of God really require intimate partnership with the Republican or Democratic parties? Does it really necessitate the literal enthronement of kingdom servants on secular thrones? While I am not suggesting that the church have no interactions with the world, I am suggesting that the form such actions take should be "Christian."

Why speak in this way when there are competing visions in the gospels of Jesus' identity? It is because the church in America too often defers to the image of John's Jesus of glory rather than the image of Mark's suffering Messiah. Jesus is presented as powerful, but Scripture affirms in a clear voice his marginal status, his powerlessness, his servant's heart, his active though nonviolent engagement with the world's powers, his penchant for self-sacrifice, even to death on a Roman cross. These descriptions do not exhaust who Jesus is. Yet they make the point that the contemporary church's view of Jesus is a woeful caricature of the Jesus of Nazareth revealed in the gospels. The power Jesus displays is imperialistic power turned on its head. Kenneson provides an excellent description of this radical Jesus who, in a culture of hubris and aggression, embodied the character of gentleness:

> When John...looks for the conquering Lion who can open the scroll and its seven seals, he sees instead a Lamb. The Lion is the Lamb, and the way of the Lamb is the way of the cross.... When we look for a king born of royalty, we find instead a baby wrapped in strips of cloth lying in a manger, born to a peasant girl of no account.... When we look for Jesus to take the world by storm, to win over those who have power, influence and prestige in order to advance his kingdom more efficiently, we find instead an itinerant preacher and healer who spends much of his time with the weak and outcast of society: children, lepers, prostitutes and tax-collectors. When we see Jesus rejected by the Samaritans, we look for him to do what his disciples wanted done—to rain down fire upon them—but instead he rebukes *us*. When we look for the conquering hero to make his move, to enter into the royal city on his white charger to sig-

nal to the people that the time has come to establish his kingdom, we find instead a Jesus who enters into Jerusalem astride a humble donkey....When we look for a deliverer who will crush the opposition by superior force, we find instead a servant-messiah who allows himself to be crushed and bruised for us. What kind of God is this?[39]

The power of the Spirit is the real presence and mediation of the life and character of this Jesus. The docetic captivity of much of Christianity and distorted notions of power impede our experiencing the reconciled community of the Spirit.

Recapturing the Radical Dimension

Ecclesiology is central to my constructive proposals. The view of the church espoused here is its radical Christian character. The racial divide in the United States represents one of the most insidious social and spiritual problems facing the American church. Therefore, the Church of God (Anderson) and other Christian groups must passionately desire to exhibit to the world an alternative vision. The church is to be a sign of God's eschatological reconciliation of the world, and therefore a community in which "there is no longer Jew or Greek" (Gal. 3:28; cf. Eph. 2:11-22). Through the cross one new community (humanity) is created (cf. Eph. 3:9-10; 4:3). According to Richard Hays:

> Insofar as the church lives the reality of this vision, it has a powerful effect in society; insofar as it fails to live this reality, it compromises the truth of the gospel....The continuing racial separation of America's churches in the 1990s is a disturbing sign of unfaithfulness that can only reinforce the racial tensions abroad in our culture.[40]

Racism is a heresy that issues the church a very pragmatic task. The task is to form communities that seek reconciliation across ethnic and racial lines.[41] Barry Callen says that the Believers Church "calls for rigorous discipleship, experience with the Holy Spirit's power, biblical critique of contemporary culture, and the strategy of a new-community model of the church as a fundamental aspect of a holistic witness to Christ in the world."[42] In a nutshell, Callen captures the nature of the kind of community in view here. The strength of this view is that it is biblically inspired and theologically faithful.

Embodying the Church's Alternative Narrative

Racist assumptions are bolstered by (pseudo)science and racist hermeneutics. The church and Christians in North America have accepted ways of seeing the world and its inhabitants from the perspective of a normative gaze—the gaze of Eurocentric privilege. A truthful telling of history in the United States reminds us of the church's complicity in legitimating racist and exclusivistic social orders. The wedding of the church and its mission to the universal claims to power of nation-states is always problematic. Hence, Rodney Clapp is correct to argue that now "[it] is the community called 'Church' that teaches people the language and culture that enables them to know Jesus as Lord. And it is the Church in the fullness of its life—not primarily its arguments—that draws others to consider the Christian faith."[43] He insists that if we quit foundationalist rhetoric we can claim the specifics of the Christian tradition and forthrightly speak the name of Christ in any public forum. A necessary focus on the radical nature of the church, Jesus, and discipleship can position Christians to identify and counteract practices sustained by other [racist] narratives.

Re-Visioning Holiness

A re-visioning of holiness along the lines proposed by Stanley Hauerwas might provide just the perspective that would permit authentic transformation within a transformed community. The church in the United States often mirrors the polity of the nation-state. It reflects the radical individualism and broad liberties characterizing our social order. While a notion of the "common good" certainly is valued, it is not considered prior to the dominance of the free individual. The church in the United States also reflects the rationality inherent in a national polity that encourages us to forget the particularities of our histories and the traditions that birthed us. Consequently, such ways of thinking render any notion of "community" as essentially a collection of self-interested individuals. In a society that honors radical individualism, the experienced reality of being the "people" of God is minimized.

Racism depends on notions of power that inscribe the logic of superiority-inferiority on the collective psyche. It is the kind of logic and practices that cater to radical individualism and group loyalties sustained by worldly power. Thus, Hauerwas's proposal offers an alternative to this entrenched individualism and rationalism.[44] The community or "body" of Christ is to be a sanctified community of the Spirit where old "selves" are transformed into a new body. In this new body, the church, racism is illogical because it has no place within the bounds of a sanctified body. This view of the "body of Christ" not only permits but requires a reversal of the worldly (racist) logic of superiority-inferiority.

The church's view of itself must be changed. Viewing the body of Christ as constituting a mathematical collection of individual bodies is biblically and theologically unacceptable. The racist rhetoric and ideology is supported by Holiness people who view the "physical" body and its external characteristics as determinative for naming the identity of other people and groups. The hegemony of racism is broken as both its rhetoric and corresponding practices are transformed by the presence of Jesus through the gift of the Holy Spirit. Since racism requires communal legitimation on some level, its eradication requires an alternative legitimation within a *new* community—a reconciled community of the Spirit. When the body of Christ norms our individual bodies—bodies that respond to liberal individualism, then we learn the reality of each person being a member one of another. The "over againstness" assumed in racist ideology is rendered illogical and thereby is stripped of its power. Hierarchical structures no longer are inevitable, but rather structures based more on the mutuality of relationships intrinsic to the body of Christ. In this communal context, there lies the eschatological hope for our individual transformation in relation to God and the other. This view is wholly consistent with the biblical vision of unity given in Ephesians 2:11-22 and Galatians 3:28.

Taking Seriously the Notion of Power within Relationships

The church cannot escape the notion of "power" in its varied dimensions. It is rather what kind of power is intrinsic to the Christian community. James McClendon reminds the church that "Christian obedience is challenged by a world of power as surely as it is framed in a world of nature."[45] According to John Howard Yoder, "the faithful Christian 'community' will not ask whether to enter or to escape the realm of power; rather it must ask, 'What kinds of power are in conformity with the victory of the Lamb?'"[46] The power of the "Lamb" is the form of power that is more truthful to the story of faith. There are other forms of power that are antithetical to the gospel.[47] There are many forms of power in the world and the church is not immune from being dominated by them. Therefore, the church must exercise moral responsibility in its relations with others and must be sensitive to the ways in which persons are ordered in relation to the goods of a community.

Power and knowledge are intimately related. At this point, caution is required even in the rhetoric we use. The rhetoric of unity and racial reconciliation can be linked to forms of power that mitigate or obscure any truth it promotes. Communal practices can be "powerful" or "corrupt" practices. Joel Shuman says that "the most significant characteristic of knowing in modernity is the role given to the subject, the ostensibly detached observer."[48] Further, the object of thought, whether another person, thing, or God, "always maintains an element of strangeness and is never brought fully within the conceptual boundaries maintained by the thinker."[49] The subject seeks always to manipulate the object of thought to conform to the subject's conceptual boundaries. Human "knowing" becomes power or a type of power. The church is cautioned to discover the ways in which our articulation of "truth" and "doctrine" serves to mask our will to exert power on others in both conscious and unconscious ways—all in the name of Jesus the Reconciler. The church is called to an openness to subjugated knowledge, which may be just the kind of humility required to set the Spirit free among the community of faith.

If this analysis bears any truth, then power is embedded in relationships among peoples and their contexts. A battle for the truth may be the offshoot of a strategy of struggle. Christians who truly desire authentic reconciliation within our contemporary contexts should be conscious of such power dynamics that order relationships and create knowledge that energizes it. Like Yoder and others, Shuman interprets Foucault as saying that "it is not a matter…of emancipating truth from every system of power (for truth is already a power) but of detaching the power of truth from the forms of hegemony, social, economic, and cultural, within which it operates at the present time."[50]

Walter Wink argues that many Christians have been rendered passive, cowardly, or complicit in the face of injustice because of their wrong sense that Jesus' commands are impractical idealisms.[51] Many Bible translations have followed the lead of the King James interpreters by inbreeding passivity, subordination, and monarchical absolutism (entrenchment of the status quo) into Jesus' commands found in the Sermon on the Mount. Wink concludes, *contra* many other biblical interpreters, that "Jesus abhors [both] passivity and violence as responses to evil."[52] For Wink, Jesus' response is a "creative moral response"—a third way—that empowers the powerless and disarms the powerful. This third way is the opposition to evil without mirroring evil.[53] Wink's approach to violence might be useful in identifying creative approaches to the expressions of power that challenge Christian unity. He clearly addresses and analyzes power and frees Jesus from captivity to human agendas.

Conclusion

The Church of God (Anderson) holds a view of Christian holiness and unity that potentially can contribute meaningfully to the unity of the church. Yet, in its current state of relative captivity to certain impeding cultural assumptions, there must be a reorientation to the Spirit's power to create new communities. The church must recapture its status as a radical church, serving a radical Jesus in radical ways.[54] Our skills of discernment must be enhanced so that we might be emancipated from the power of sin and corrupt practices it engenders, individual and collective, cultural and systemic.

This conversation must continue. Life in a reconciled community is buoyed by Christian hope, but not by denial. Our conversation must be real and truthful, or else we remain in the tentacles of demonic powers. Let us be bold in our convictions, humble in our spirits, and gracious in our actions and words. Let us also embody the virtue of truthfulness, the command for justice, and the practice of forgiveness, which we are commanded to extend to others willingly as it is extended to us by grace. Note Willie Jennings' challenge to the church—for those whose passion is that we all be one:

> We need a church made up of people who refuse to live out racial politics, who refuse to participate in the racial realities of this nation, who refuse the power and privileges of whiteness, who reject the stereotypes of blackness, who claim a new way of life born at the cross and the resurrection, who will not be known even by family, tribe, friends or nation after the flesh, but who would know themselves only through the power of resurrection and the call of the cross of Christ.[55]

Notes

[1] This author is aware that the term "Hispanic" is inclusive of many groups and may not include "Mexicans" or some other people groups. I use the term "Hispanic" in a generic sense.

[2] There is much written about the nature of rhetoric, both ancient and contemporary. I am addressing the most basic dimension of "what we are saying about a subject" that should logically unfold into practices which correspond to it, but does not. Hence, rhetoric finds no place to land within the concrete contexts of human experiences.

[3] From *Sermons I*: 381f; Wesley as quoted by Manfred Marquardt, *John Wesley's Social Ethics: Praxis and Principles*, translated by W. Stephen Gunter (Nashville: Abingdon Press, 1992), footnote 2, 184. According to Marquardt,

"Wesley explicitly rejected the religious self-satisfaction of the believer and any restriction to a personal I-God connection; this was one of [Wesley's] essential objections to mysticism" (121).

⁴The increasing globalization of the world and its manifestation within the United States certainly require the inclusion of other ethnic groups in our discussion. However, the scope of this paper centers on the historic black-white paradigm, since it represents a continuing dilemma and an unfinished agenda.

⁵This is not new in that the Church of God Reformation Movement has been in conversations with the Christian Church. I want to affirm this, but I am arguing for more than a coming together that leaves each group essentially unchanged.

⁶Gerhard Lohfink, *Does God Need the Church? Toward a Theology of the People of God*. Translated by Linda M. Maloney (Collegeville, MN.: The Liturgical Press, 1999). All page numbers included in the text.

⁷These conflicts in the book of Acts arise both from within and outside the communities of faith. If consensus was not reached, the decision was postponed.

⁸Lohfink juxtaposes the distinct social reality of the church against the religious individualism fostered by the mystery cults of the Greco-Roman world, especially the worship of Eleusis. While "salvation" was promised and given directly to the initiate, it had no corresponding social consequences (234).

⁹Strict proponents of western individualism will find this claim a bit too strong for their taste. However, the church construed on this basis has succumbed to the logic that its existence is like a fraternal society of those who *already* believe—apart from the church (Lohfink, 254).

10 Unanimity does not mean uniformity. Uniformity can be achieved, if at all, only through coercion and violence. To insist on uniformity requires the subordination of difference under some totalizing discourse that promotes deception and hypocrisy.

¹¹It is important to affirm the lordship of Jesus over heaven and earth (cf. Matthew 28:19). The Church is to acknowledge and embody the lordship of Christ as a witness to the worldly powers that their status as would-be "rulers" is absolutely false and coming to a certain end.

¹²Barry L. Callen, *Contours of a Cause: The Theological Vision of the Church of God Movement (Anderson)* (Anderson, Ind.: Anderson University School of Theology, 1995), 22. See also Barry Callen and James North, *Coming Together In Christ* (Joplin, MO: College Press Publishing, 1997).

¹³Two of the classic historical accounts are: Charles Ewing Brown, *When the Trumpet Sounded: A History of the Church of God Reformation Movement* (Anderson, Ind.: The Warner Press [Gospel Trumpet Company], 1951; John W. V. Smith, *The Quest for Holiness and Unity: A Centennial History of the Church of God* (Anderson, Ind.: Warner Press, 1980). More recent contributions are from Barry L. Callen: *It's God's Church! The Life and Legacy of Daniel Sidney Warner* (Anderson, Ind.: Warner Press, 1995; *Following the Light: Teachings, Testimonies,*

Trials and Triumphs of the Church of God Movement, Anderson (Anderson, Ind.: Warner Press, 2000).

It is important to acknowledge that the Church of God movement is not distinctive in highlighting holiness and unity. These themes, in conjunction with others, help to define a peculiar consciousness within which these become distinctive. For example, John W. V. Smith highlights eight doctrines characterized as "distinguishing" for this movement. For Smith, all these eight doctrines are thoroughly Christian and Scripture-based. [John W. V. Smith, *I Will Build My Church: Biblical Insights on Distinguishing Doctrines of the Church of God* (Anderson, Ind.: Warner Press, 1985), 2-4.

[14] Barry L. Callen, *It's God's Church!*, 10.
[15] Ibid., 137.
[16] Ibid.
[17] John W. V. Smith, *I Will Build My Church*, 80.
[18] The last stanza of D. Otis Teasley's 1901 song *Back to the Blessed Old Bible* says:

> Back to the blessed old Bible, Back to the Master's call,
> Back to the words of our Savior, Loving, obeying them all.
> Never in sects to be scattered, Never again to do wrong.
> *Unity, holiness*, heaven, Ever shall be our song. [emphasis added.]

[19] John W. V. Smith, *I Will Build My Church*, 82.
[20] Ibid., 83.
[21] Ibid., 85.
[22] Smith, *I Will Build My Church*, 91.
[23] Ibid.
[24] Ibid., 93.
[25] Ibid., 97.
[26] Ibid., 99.
[27] Ibid., 100.
[28] James Earl Massey rightly reminds us, however, that "while some critics are still saying that we must look for the Church beyond the churches, it must also be reported that some have seen the Church because of the churches" (*Concerning Christian Unity: A Study of the Relational Imperative of Agape Love*, Anderson, Indiana: Warner Press, 1979), 91.) If Massey is responding against a tendency to affirm the "invisible" church as the true church, then Massey's warning is proper. If he wants only to put a positive spin on the church's many faces, he still must respond more fully to Lohfink's critique of the church's historical division.

[29] See Barry L. Callen, *Radical Christianity* (Nappanee, IN: Evangel Publishing House, 1999).

[30] I am fully aware of many reasons that engender separation besides race, such as denominational loyalties, socio-economic realities, gender and sexual orientation issues, etc.

[31] Callen, *Following the Light*, 18-55.

³²Lohfink, *Does God Need the Church?*, 297-98.

³³William James Jennings, "Wandering in the Wilderness: Christian Identity & Theology Between Context & Race," an essay in *The Gospel in Black & White: Theological Resources for Racial Reconciliation*, edited by Dennis L. Okholm (Downers Grove, Ill.: InterVarsity Press, 1997), 46-47.

³⁴Implementing a strategy focused on outward acts without the corresponding inward transformation by the Spirit is just as pernicious. Life in a reconciled community of the Spirit must resist the idea that the church can be content only with outward acts of piety. Manfred Marquardt says that "Wesley distinguished between the outward performance of good [powered by prevenient grace], which was not without value but nonetheless provisional, and the performance of good that followed the inner renewal by God's grace, prompted and shaped by love. Only this latter activity should...be characterized as good. Only a person who acted out of love was really doing good." [*John Wesley's Social Ethics: Praxis and Principles*. Translated by John E. Steely and W. Stephen Gunter (Nashville, TN.: Abingdon Press, 1992), 103-104]. Hence, we need not therefore insist on a radical separation that too often accompanies much of evangelical and fundamentalist theologies.

³⁵Philip D. Kenneson probes in a provocative way just how dominant aspects of our liberal democratic society serve to undermine the cultivation of the fruit of the Spirit within Christian community. See *Life on the Vine: Cultivating the Fruit of the Spirit in Christian Community* (Downers Grove, Ill.: InterVarsity Press, 1999).

³⁶Rodney Clapp, *Border Crossings: Christian Trespasses on Popular Culture and Public Affairs* (Grand Rapids, Mi.: Brazos Press, 2000), 190. Clapp references a quote of Daniel Payne, elected bishop of the African Methodist Episcopal Church in 1852. "Payne notes a typical response of a runaway slave, of whom Payne inquired if he were a Christian: 'No sir,' replied the runaway, 'white men treat us so bad in Mississippi that we can't be Christians.'" [Clapp, 190-91. Quoted from James H. Cone, *The Spirituals and the Blues* (Maryknoll, N.Y.: Orbis Press, 1972, 1991), 22-23].

³⁷I am reminded of James Cone's polemical theology, *God of the Oppressed*, aimed at the hegemony of Eurocentric theology. While Cone certainly could do theology in that form, he de-legitimated its implicit claim to construct reality. Such theology tended to be so abstract at times that it promoted the status quo, thereby leaving those on the margins of society virtually consigned to subordination to the powers of the world.

³⁸See Barry L. Callen, *Radical Christianity: The Believers Church Tradition in Christianity's History and Future* (Nappanee, In.: Evangel Publishing House, 1999), 175; Cheryl J. Sanders, *Empowerment Ethics for a Liberated People: A Path to African American Social Transformation*, Minneapolis, MN.: Fortress Press, 1995), 1.

³⁹Kenneson, *Life on the Vine*, 205-206.

⁴⁰Richard Hays, *The Moral Vision of the New Testament*, 441.

⁴¹Ibid.
⁴²Callen, *Radical Christianity*, 175-176.
⁴³Clapp, *Border Crossings*, 29.
⁴⁴Stanley Hauerwas, "The Sanctified Body: Why Perfection Does Not Require a Self," a chapter in *Sanctify Them in the Truth: Holiness Exemplified* (Nashville, TN.: Abingdon Press, 1998), 80. [All other page references in the text above.]
⁴⁵James McClendon, *Systematic Theology: Ethics* (Nashville: Abingdon Press, 1986), 177.
⁴⁶Ibid.; quoted from John Howard Yoder, "The Stone Lectures," 28.
⁴⁷James McClendon refers to what he calls "powerful practices" or "corrupt practices." He further equates the New Testament's principalities and powers as the social structures we may also identify as (MacIntyrian) practices (173). *These structures may be religious* (173). McClendon suggests that wherever Christ's victory is proclaimed, the corrupted reign of the powers remain in being. While they are not destroyed nor abolished in between the times, they are "disarmed" or "dethroned" (175).
⁴⁸Joel James Shuman, *The Body of Compassion: Ethics, Medicine, and the Church* (Boulder, CO: Westview Press, 1999), 29. Shuman discusses the relationship of knowledge and power in his effort to show how medicine and bioethics have exercised the power of expert knowledge to define the body and health in ways that eclipse the narrative of the Church community.
⁴⁹Ibid., 32.
⁵⁰Ibid., 44; quotes Foucault, *Truth and Power*, 133.
⁵¹Walter Wink, "Jesus' Third Way", a chapter in *Transforming Violence*, eds. Herr & Herr (Herald Press, 1998), 34.
⁵²Ibid., 35.
⁵³Ibid., 40.
⁵⁴See Barry L. Callen, *Radical Christianity* (Nappanee, IN: Evangel Publishing House, 1999).
⁵⁵ Jennings, "Wanderings in the Wilderness," 48.

Chapter 16

"PLACE" AND HIGHER EDUCATION IN THE HOLINESS TRADITION[1]

by
Merle D. Strege

Many early leaders of the Church of God movement viewed church-related colleges and seminaries as little more than workshops of the devil. The goal of the schools seemed to be to bolster the strength of their sponsoring denominations, training the young to be loyal followers of their individual brands of denominational division. This was viewed as an unacceptable obstacle to Christian unity. Merle D. Strege insists that the social and political locations of institutions of higher education are critical to understanding their characters and emphases. After looking at the distinctives of Anderson University—flagship institution of the Church of God, he concludes that, for all schools whose historic identities lie in the Wesleyan/Holiness tradition, there is a rich "location" worthy of reclaiming. One aspect of this location, highlighted by the Church of God movement, is the placing of experience ahead of rationalistic conceptions of knowledge. This allows the freedom essential for academic inquiry and debate. Originally published in the Wesleyan Theological Journal *(32:1, Spring, 1997). Used here by permission.*

We have before us now a large and growing body of literature that examines the phenomenon of the church-related or Christian colleges. Recent works by leading Evangelical scholars Mark Noll and George Marsden have focused attention respectively on the life of the mind and the secularization of the American university.[2] These two volumes, especially Marsden, have helped us considerably to understand the forces at work on American colleges and universities, including church-related or Christian colleges. In a curious way, both Noll and Marsden themselves bear the marks of such influence. After all, one cannot expect to be taken seriously as an academic unless one's work follows academic conventions and standards.

I wish to pursue a line of thought here which considers an idea related to the following somewhat commonplace observation. Beginning with Stephen Toulmin's observations about the Enlightenment, I want to suggest the importance of "place" in the intellectual life of the colleges and universities sponsored by the Wesleyan-Holiness churches.

In his stimulating and provocative analysis of modernity and its agenda, philosopher-physicist Toulmin fastens on the opening paragraph of the entry on philosopher René Descartes found in *La Grande Encyclopedie*. That entry opens:

> For a biography of Descartes, almost all you need is two dates and two place names: his birth, on March 31, 1596 at La Haye, in Touraine, and his death at Stockholm, on February 11, 1650. His life is above all that of an intellect [esprit]; his true life story is the history of his thoughts; the outward events of his existence have interest only for the light they can throw on the inner events of his genius.[3]

Toulmin continues: "In thinking about Descartes, the authors tell us, we can abstract from their historical context not just the philosophical positions he discusses, and the different arguments he presents, but also his entire intellectual development."[4] Toulmin thinks that the encyclopedia's ahistorical description of Descartes is no accident. As he further explains, the Enlightenment's commitments to universal, timeless, general, and written descriptions predisposed the *Encylopedie's* authors to describe Descartes' work as the product of a disembodied mind. Toulmin challenges this predisposition with his own account of a Cartesian philosophical program profoundly shaped by the tumultuous events of early seventeenth-century France. In his view, one cannot conceive of Descartes' revolutionary philosophy, or the work of any other person, apart from the socio-political location it inhabited.

Below is a tying of Stephen Toulmin's observations on Descartes and the Enlightenment to the theme of place and the university in three ways. (1) I will apply Toulmin's description of Descartes to my own institution, Anderson University, and comparable institutions to say, first, that descriptions of the university abstracted from its social and intellectual location make no more sense than the French encyclopedia's article on

Descartes. Colleges and/or universities are not all alike (at least, we should no think them so); they inhabit different cultural, religious, and socio-political locations. Those institutions which pretend to deny the existence and influence of such locations sever the connections which make them intelligible and distinctive. (2) The second connection will be a prescriptive argument correlative to the first point: universities should practice a politics, a way of being together, that embodies the intellectual traditions of their constituent communities. (3) Thirdly, along the lines of the first two connections, I want to suggest a description of the possible politics of Anderson University, a university sponsored by the Church of God (Anderson, Indiana). It is the holiness movement institution with which I am most familiar. This description will entail the notion that at least some part of our intellectual life will draw upon salient theological notions of the Church of God, resulting in their contribution to the shape of the university's politics. As a part of that description I will offer some illustrations of what these important theological notions might be. Finally, I offer a brief exposition of the biblical story of Daniel and the bright young men of Israel to suggest why these topics merit further consideration.

On the Social and Political Locations of Colleges and Universities

Perhaps it is only in the United States that the standardization of university education is believed to be desirable. Medieval universities differed markedly in subject matter and governance. Bologna, Paris, and Oxford resembled each other hardly at all, each of them giving institutional expression to quite different intellectual and political traditions. In a similar fashion intellectual and political commitments distinguished early twentieth-century European universities from one another. For example, in the 1920s the reigning theology in Göttingen was anathema at Berlin. In the United States, however, and especially among schools that are dominated by undergraduate studies, claims of institutional distinction are based not in intellectual differences, but in assertions of superiority. Does Harvard claim to be different than Yale or Stanford, or is the claim about superiority, one of emphasis on the level of attainment as opposed to difference in tradition or type? Or on another scale, Anderson University claims to be "better" than rather than different from Taylor or Indiana Wesleyan Universities. Unless we are content with this academic version of little boy's comparisons of paternal superiority, we might pause to ask why it is we tend to compare in terms of *degree* rather than *kind*.

I suspect that one answer to this question might be located in the dominance of the academic and professional guilds in American higher education. Accreditation, whether by regional or professional associations, tends to blur institutional distinctiveness as it standardizes the programs offered by its related institutions. To cite but one example, NCATE will have its way, whether at Anderson, Taylor, or Indiana University, which is but another way of saying that as NCATE dictates standards for departments of education, their curricula cannot help but closely resemble each other. The same point obtains concerning virtually all other professional societies and associations. If this is the case, we find ourselves in the rather odd position of saying that, as concerns curriculum—the heart of our universities, need we be reminded—an Anderson education will not differ substantially from what a student might get at Ball State University or Goshen College. Correlatively, the characteristics by which we distinguish ourselves from one another will be secondary matters; at least, they will not pertain to the curriculum. This unfortunate situation forces us to ask whether the primary allegiance is to academic guilds or to the institutions of which we are members.

The present situation of American higher, then, seems a denial of the historical, social, and political particularities of individual colleges and universities. Such a denial is as unfaithful to historical circumstance as it is undesirable. That an ahistorical approach dominates American higher education is, however, not surprising. American culture has deep roots in the Enlightenment, the premium it places on instrumental reason, and its denial of importance to that which "enlightened" thinkers judge to be local, timebound, particular, or oral. For such historical particularities we have substituted a discourse of procedures and means. Such a language may serve industry and business well, although there are growing reservations about its value even there. But thinkers such as Alasdair MacIntyre and Wendell Berry raise very troubling questions about the suitability or even the possibility of a procedural, means-oriented language as the dominant form of university discourse.

In his insightful essay, "The Loss of the University," Berry argues that universities have lost sight of a common goal to which their specific departments might be oriented. Even worse, he contends, is that universities have lost the common language which enabled their members to converse about the ends for which their institutions exist.[5] In his Gifford Lectures of 1988 MacIntyre extends this point, arguing that we can no longer make the assumptions about the encyclopedic nature of knowledge which underwrote such projects as the Gifford Lectures, the ninth edition of the *Encyclopaedia Britannica,* or the Enlightenment version of the institution called a university.[6]

The accuracy of Berry's and MacIntyre's analyses is born out when we ask, What then holds universities together in the absence of a common language? The most common American answer to this question is "the university administration." The common language of the American university then becomes "administrationese": GPA, FTE, FAF, major, minor, GRE, outcomes assessment, and the like. Harold McManus, Roberts Professor of Church History at Mercer University, argues that administrations expand as the inverse function of the university's loss of coherence.[7] The only means of holding together universities which have lost their capacity for conversing about their ends is bureaucratic management. It scarcely need be noticed, however, that such a move gives up the language of ends for the language of instrumental reason.

I submit that it makes no historical sense to deny the very real differences that distinguish American colleges and universities from one another. These differences should be understood as extending beyond the quantifiable, unless we believe that the determinative difference between Anderson and Goshen, for example, is that the library at one of them has more holdings than the other. To deny or even ignore institutional particularities simultaneously denies that we have histories and forces us to the false claim that we are self-generating, all of which flies patently in the face of the facts. Furthermore, that powerful cultural forces such as instrumental reason, the industrial economy, and bureaucratic management combine to press American colleges and universities into bland and homogenized similarity is undesirable. Such homogenization devalues the specific historical and social locations of educational institutions which actually are quite diverse and deserve to be so recognized.

Universities as Embodied Intellectual Traditions

Two years ago my colleague Nancy Fischer offered a lecture to the Anderson University community in which she asked each member of the audience to draw a map of the city of Anderson. She employs this learning exercise in one of her courses, intending to heighten class members' perceptions of and sensitivities to their location. I infer from this exercise that she hopes that students come to a greater appreciation of the role of place in people's lives. If my inference is correct, she shares with Wendell Berry a sense of the importance of local culture.[8] Following Professor Fischer's lead, I have begun recommending to my freshmen students that they eschew the local franchises of MacDonald's and Pizza Hut in favor of such famous Anderson eateries as The Toast, The Lemon Drop, and Art's Pizza No. 1 (even though Art's does not have black olives available as a topping). In this way I want my students to become at least marginally aware of the place where they will live and study for the next several years. I want them to ask questions about the impact of geographic locale upon their education at AU. Even more desirable is that they learn to think about the way place shapes institutions through language and local culture.

Even if one did not know its name, Calvin College's Reformed theological ethos would soon become apparent even to the most insensitive and culturally unaware. Similarly, the Mennonite ethos unmistakably marks Goshen College, even as the intellectual commitments of the Society of Jesus shape Jesuit colleges and universities. It seems to me that such variety in American higher education is highly desirable. To recognize this variety is to acknowledge the historicity of these various institutions and begin to appreciate the real differences by which they are to be distinguished from one another and other institutions as well. If I might be permitted a rhetorical question, who wants to live in an educational culture where all cats are gray? I would like to believe that Calvin, Goshen, and Jesuit colleges and universities are the rule rather than the exception. Unfortunately, it would appear that they are not.

I am not suggesting that we flout the recommendations and standards imposed by our learned societies, professional and regional accrediting associations. But is it not reasonable to ask that the moral, religious, and intellectual traditions of any particular college or university modify or contextualize those external forces, thereby adapting them to particular institutional landscapes. In the case of church-related colleges and universities this means that their work will need to be informed in some way by the theological traditions of the sponsoring church groups. I am not issuing a call for each and every course to have a religious or a spiritual component. Neither is it desirable that religion be the only acceptable discourse on the campus. Mine is no appeal for "Christian Swimming" or "Biblical Business." I appeal, rather, for the necessity of theology and its critique of the intellectual commitments and presuppositions of the university curricula which have such traditions.

In his book *The Fragility of Knowledge,* Edward Farley argues that theological tradition, along with intuitive imagination and praxis, serve crucial roles as correctives in the modern university. Such universities conform to what Farley terms the "Enlightenment tradition" with its ideals of critically acquired knowledge and empirical demonstration. In the name of intuition, Romantics have criticized such universities' perpetuation of abstraction for the sake of rigor, evidence and precision. On the other hand, praxis critics challenge modern universities for forgetting that "…institutions of pure reason…hide from themselves their complicity in societal agendas of power."[9]

Theological criticisms of the Enlightenment university, Farley observes, have taken several lines of attack. The more superficial of these lines exposes and asserts the limited worldview of commitments to critical principles, empirical demonstration and instrumental reason. A more fundamental challenge rests in the theological tradition's argument that "…the corporate experience of past ages and peoples can produce a wisdom that is illuminating and pertinent beyond the past. If this is true, the task of knowledge is confronted not just by the facts about the present to be explained but by sediments of past culture to be interpreted."[10]

Farley's work underlines the importance of a theological critique of the university curriculum. Such traditions may also contribute to the institution's life in another way. Valparaiso University professor Mark Schwehn argues that certain religious virtues bear a marked similarity to certain academic virtues commonly hoped to be developed in our students.[11] One thinks, for example, of the virtue of humility. I work at helping my students to appreciate St. Augustine's intellectual achievement and his arguments so they will not prematurely dismiss his conclusions about free will and predestination with the sophomoric and arrogant prejudice that "Augustine was stupid." The awareness that we do not and cannot know everything strongly resembles the religious virtue of humility. Since that is so, we are warranted in thinking that the presence of theological traditions which prize the virtue of humility should also have positive intellectual application.

Even as the Reformed and Mennonite theological traditions are resources for the intellectual work of scholars at Calvin and Goshen, respectively, so ought the theological traditions of the Church of God (Anderson) inform the general intellectual life of Anderson University. I say "ought" because, in my judgment, this has not frequently been the case or, if so, in ways marginal to the university's intellectual life. As stated earlier, I suspect that many other church-related and/or Christian colleges fit this description. Somewhat ironically, then, those that have strong relationships to sponsoring churches describe themselves as institutions that are tightly connected to their churches politically, but only marginally as far as intellectual matters are concerned. What might some of these intellectual/theological currents be? Could there be a positive role for them to play in the intellectual life of church-related and/or Christian colleges? As a case study familiar to this writer, I will respond to these questions with reference to Anderson University and the Church of God (Anderson).

Theological Traditions of The Church of God (Anderson)

Notions such as the categories of experience, community, holiness, and vocation have been important elements in the theological tradition of the Church of God. They also have affinities with other colleges and universities of the holiness tradition. I suggest that they also might inform intellectual life and institutional politics at Anderson University.

"Holiness" surely is an idea deserving of informing ethics and moral philosophy, but perhaps also courses in public policy or political science. To be sure, the Church of God (Anderson) along with many other holiness groups has, in the main, conceived the idea of holiness in moralistic and individualist terms. But in Walter Brueggemann's recently published volume, *Old Testament Theology*, we find an example of how such traditional and conservative notions of holiness might be enlarged to undergird important political, economic, and ethical themes. Brueggemann demonstrates the relationships between Israel's conception of God, its understanding of its own social location "among the nations," and God's evolving commitment to justice and righteousness as expressions of God's holiness.[12] Brueggemann connects this insight to Israel's perception of the importance of the cry of suffering to the life of God. The cry of pain, i.e., the notice Israel takes of the dysfunctional, is its protest against the normative theology of its surrounding world, a theology which it partially embraced and which taught Israel to trust in the system to provide solutions to the people's dilemmas. To follow Brueggemann's lead will mean that the idea of holiness, whether of God or God's people, will inform discussions in areas such as ethics, economics, theories of management, and public policy. Space will not permit further digression into Brueggemann's stimulating and provocative analysis;

here it sufficiently serves to illustrate how discussions of theological themes such as the holiness of God have broad applicability in a liberal arts curriculum.

Another illustration of the applicability of the idea of holiness to AU's curriculum lies in the idea of "wellness." Wendell Berry explores the connections between health and various aspects of human being in an essay entitled "Health Is Membership."[13] He touches on the etymological connections of such words as "health," "wholeness," and "holiness" in order to explore the manifold influences which contribute to people's health. Indeed, Berry argues that such connectedness is vital to a person's health. These connections extend, obviously, to other people, but they also include land, culture, and spirit. Moreover, health ultimately is situated in communities of love. In Berry's careful assessment, "health" bears a marked resemblance to the biblical ideal of shalom, peace in the most comprehensive of understandings. Institutions such as Anderson, contemplating wellness programs, might develop their programs out of their historical commitments to the idea of holiness, now broadened to be understood as wholeness, especially when such wholeness rests on the presence of the kind of love which St. Paul said is poured into our hearts by the Holy Spirit.

Berry's sense of health's dependence on vital human relationships leads to another of the Church of God movement's deep theological commitments—the idea of the church as a gathered community. Ideas associated with the notion of community provide very fertile ground for research and reflection in the social sciences. Indeed, the communitarian movement is presently demonstrating the value of such notions to national political life. Had Anderson University taken its own theological traditions seriously at an earlier point in its history, it might have found itself poised to enter more fully into the current national debate about a good society.

Anderson University professors such as Willard Reed (philosophy) have interpreted the Church of God movement's theological idea of experience in a manner which bears directly on the university's intellectual life. Reed observes that the Church of God has long maintained an epistemology that places experience ahead of rationalistic conceptions about knowledge. Furthermore, he contends that, insofar as faith is concerned, members of Anderson University need not be threatened by rationalistically framed propositions since they cannot threaten religious experience. Reed has interpreted a salient theological idea of the Church in a manner which clearly underwrites the freedom essential to academic inquiry and debate. To be quite sure, the Church of God is a conservative Protestant church group, but its emphasis on the category of experience has created at AU a degree of freedom unusual in colleges sponsored by such groups.

The surest illustration of my point is that no Anderson faculty appointment is conditional on a signature of confession or creed. That faculty members are not required to sign a belief statement is not due to the Enlightenment-based notion that one's religious commitments are private. Rather, it is precisely because Anderson University is shaped by the ethos of the Church of God that the university says that one's religious experience cannot be reduced to a set of propositions and, therefore, faculty members will not be required to sign a creed. The same could not be said at all member institutions of the Coalition for Christian Colleges and Universities. My point here is not to claim some superiority for my own institution. Rather, it is to illustrate the manner in which specific characteristics rise out of the particularities of institutional historical locations.

One last theme important to the theological life of the Church of God has been the tradition of vocation. It is, of course, the case that the idea of calling has been important throughout Christianity. I am not claiming that the concept is unique to the Church of God. But the idea has nevertheless received considerable stress and broad interpretation among us. The Church of God has thought of people's vocations largely in terms of the ministry; men and women receive a "call to full-time Christian service," as we often have said. But vocation could also be extended beyond the sacred to the secular, and in its earlier years AU played an important role in broadening the meaning of vocation to include gainful employment in service to a particular place. It would not be difficult to make a case for certain professors' understanding of their work at Anderson University as a calling, professors of accounting, economics, art, or physical education. One need not teach in the Seminary or the Department of Religious Studies to be said to have a vocation. In the past the idea of practicing one's work as a vocation extended throughout the institution to include all its members. Two custodians, for example, Charlie Kissel and Leonard Warren, are examples of people who understood themselves to have been called to their work of cleaning the buildings of Anderson College (University).[14] They may have been janitors, but they worshipped and entered into the life of the college as fully as any professor. Why? Because Kissel and Warren understood themselves to have a vocation here, and the institution recognized their self-understanding. We must consider the possibility that the university flourished in part through their faithful service as these two men taught generations of Anderson students the idea of work as a calling rather than a utilitarian means to pursue the transient goods of this earth.

This last reference to the theological tradition of vocation illustrates further the possibility that such traditions contribute to the shape of an institution's polity, i.e., its way of ordering the life together of its members. Language, after all, possesses the power to shape—if not create—the social realities we inhabit. Theological discourse, then, like any other, then will have such power if it is included as a conversation partner. Because language possesses this kind of reality-making power, it is very troubling to observe the increased use of market, corporate, and advertising metaphors as descriptions of colleges and universities in general, and especially those which claim a religious center. Metaphors and forms of discourse certainly have legitimacy in their own social spheres. However, metaphors of one sphere rarely translate well to other spheres of life. Instead, one sphere colonizes another as its language transforms the basic relationships of the latter. Consider, for example, the unfortunate consequences of the application of the market metaphor to marriage partners. Similarly, reference to the university as a corporate machine will eventually transform colleagues into cogs.

These reflections on language call to mind Donald Thorsen's stimulating attempt to recover the word "scholarship." Thorsen means to use this word to bridge the customary distinction between research and religion.[15] "Research" commonly refers to the kind of knowledge we produce under Enlightenment rubrics, that which can be demonstrated scientifically and objectively. Paul Giurlanda effectively demonstrates the extent to which such knowledge, as every other form of knowledge, depends on faith.[16] If that is the case, then Thorsen's suggestion is significant. The scholarship of holiness colleges and universities can and should embrace the theological and moral considerations of teaching as well as the pursuit of knowledge in specialized ("scientific") fields of inquiry. Our knowledge, our faith, and our communities interpenetrate. "Scholarship" names our efforts to introduce others into that life.

To stress the intellectual and political significance of the theological traditions of sponsoring churches should not be taken as underwriting a policy that requires all faculty members to deny time to their research in order to ponder only such matters as those outlined here. Nevertheless, we should expect to find these fibers woven through the intellectual fabric of our colleges and universities. Important institutional courses hinge on our decision to accept or ignore the theological traditions which are woven into that fabric. In the final analysis, such traditions, and others drawing from the ideas of service and liberal education, vitally inform our discourse about the ends for which the university exists and which we encourage our students to pursue throughout the course of their lives. It is the moral and theological shape of this discourse which gives Anderson, and comparable colleges and universities, its unique character. The alternative to such uniqueness is the attempt to be a university without a context, and that is the academic version of *USA Today*—news from nowhere. To follow such a nowhere alternative will also be to give ourselves over to a politics of means, a politics alien to the life and spirit of universities constituted as intellectual communities.

Daniel and the Bright Young Men of Israel

As one final means of making my point and also considering a possible fate if we ignore the traditions which are our historical and political contexts, let me offer a reading of the story of Daniel and his fellow Israelites as told in Daniel 1. After all, this text comes from a book which is determinative for our scholarly life together in Donald Thorsen's sense of that term.

The story is familiar. The children of Israel have been invaded, defeated, their capital laid waste, and many of them deported to Babylon. There they exist only at the sufferance of their masters, on the very fringes of an alien society where they have been made to eat the tasteless bread of exile. But King Nebuchadnezzar has a plan for this people. He wishes to bring the best and the brightest of the Israelite young men into the palace and train them in the ways of the Babylonians. After their training these "best and brightest" will enter the royal bureaucracy.

The focal point of the story, interestingly enough, is food. The king insists that these young men eat the food served at court, but they refuse. The royal table is laden with food seasoned with socio-political expectations. To be sure, it is wonderful, tasty beyond the wildest dreams of impoverished, hopelessly dependent exiles. But this food may be eaten only by Israelites willing to pay a terrible price. That is precisely why this food sticks in the throats of Daniel and his friends. It is rich food prepared for the rich and powerful, and its price is forgetfulness. This rich Babylonian food will blur Israelite memories of exile and their brothers and sisters still dwelling in the camps and shanty-towns on the outskirts of the city. The loss of this kinship of memory inevitably will carry with it the loss of identity of Daniel and his friends, for we can answer the question "Who am I?" only by answering the prior question, "Of what stories am I a part?"

One may read Nebuchadnezzar's invitation as a wonderful opportunity. The king has offered these young men a chance to move to the right side of the tracks where power, privilege, and respectability abound. It is an invitation to "upward social mobility," a chance for some displaced Israelite captives actually to become movers and shakers in Babylonian society. The king has invited Israel's best and brightest to learn the system which keeps society in order and rewards its powerful members. The young Israelites might be tempted to accept such an invitation selfishly and use it as a means of their own advancement. They might prize the invitation as an opportunity to ameliorate Israel's plight as strangers in a strange land.

But the king's invitation is laden with potential for disaster. One cannot expect to employ, even for a good cause, the king's wealth and power without compromising attachments. Sooner or later, the language of means must be circumscribed and controlled by the language of ends. Daniel and his three friends understand that they cannot eat the king's food without becoming the king's possessions. If these best and brightest of Israel would remain members of the people of God, they must eat the simple food of Israelites. They must remember the traditions which enable them to answer fundamental questions of identity and ethics.

Like Daniel and his friends, we appear to face a choice between two modes of being: either we will ground ourselves in the traditions and politics of our larger church communities or we will speak the discourses of systems which claim to provide the solution to our problems. Daniel and his friends had to choose whether to eat the bread of exiles, a food which empowered them to live out of their identity as Israelites, or eat the rich food of a royal bureaucracy which promised "success." In the final analysis, Daniel and his friends were confronted with a situation that required them to own their people and the socio-political location which gave them their identity. Out of that identity they were able to answer the question, "What are we to do?"

Today institutions of higher education should be answering the same vital question. For those colleges and universities whose historic identities lie in the Wesleyan/Holiness tradition, there is richness to be recovered, an important location to be reclaimed, stories out of which institutions can and should be living.

Notes

[1] The bulk of this article was originally developed as a paper read to the Anderson University faculty in March, 1995. Elements of that paper were also developed for papers read to the faculty of Point Loma Nazarene College faculty in August, 1996. I wish to thank both faculties for the invitations to produce papers which required me to think about these matters.

[2] Cf. Mark A. Noll, *The Scandal of the Evangelical Mind* (Grand Rapids: William B. Eerdman's Publishing Company, 1994) and George M. Marsden, *The Soul of the American University* (New York: Oxford University Press, 1994).

[3] Quoted in Stephen Toulmin, *Cosmopolis: The Hidden Agenda of Modernity* (New York: Macmillan, 1990), 45.

[4] Ibid.

[5] Cf. Wendell Berry, "The Loss of the University" in *Home Economics* (San Francisco: North Point Press, 1987), 77-97.

[6] *Three Rival Versions of Moral Enquiry: Encyclopedia, Genealogy, and Tradition* (Notre Dame: University of Notre Dame Press, 1990).

[7] "Community and Governance in the Christian University" (Nashville: The Committee of Southern Churchmen, 1983).

[8] Cf. Wendell Berry, "The Work of Local Culture" in *What Are People For?* (San Francisco: North Point Press, 1990), 153-169.

[9] Edward Farley, *The Fragility of Knowledge: Theological Education in the Church and the University* (Philadelphia: Fortress, 1988), 6-9, passim.

[10] Ibid.

[11] *Exiles from Eden: Religion and the Academic Vocation* (New York: Oxford University Press, 1993).

[12] Walter Brueggemann, *Old Testament Theology: Essays on Structure, Theme, and Text*, edited by Patrick D. Miller (Minneapolis: Fortress Press, 1992), 22-44.

[13] Published in *Another Turn of the Crank* (Washington, D. C.: Counterpoint, 1995), 86-109.

[14] References to the significance of Kissel and Warren, and many others, is found in Barry L. Callen, *Guide of Soul and Mind: The Story of Anderson University* (Anderson, Ind.: Anderson University and Warner Press, 1992).

[15] Donald Thorsen, "Reuniting the Two So Long Disjoined: Knowledge and Vital Piety," *Wesleyan Theological Journal*, vol. 31, no. 2 (Fall, 1996), 192-209.

[16] Paul Giurlanda, *Faith and Knowledge* (Lanham, MD: University Press of America, 1987).

Chapter 17

Relevance of the Nineteenth-Cetnury Holiness Paradigm

by
Douglas M. Strong[1]

The experience of holiness has been central to the assumptions of the Church of God movement (Anderson) concerning the goal of Christian life and the possibility of authentic Christian unity. The movement's understanding of holiness came from the Bible as read in the context of the American holiness movement of the late nineteenth century. Douglas M. Strong now looks for what there is from that paradigm in the past that is relevant for today's church. The current Wesleyan/Holiness Consortium, with the Church of God as an active participant, is convinced of such relevance, as seen in its publication of the "Holiness Manifesto" (reproduced in various places, including as Appendix D in the 2008 autobiography of the Church of God leader Barry L. Callen titled A Pilgrim's Progress*). Strong concludes that we "postmodernists" are learning our deep need for connectedness with God and each other. This opens the door to recalling and recreating the experiences of 19th-century women and men who promoted the transforming immediacy of God's presence. Originally published in the* Wesleyan Theological Journal *(35:1, Spring, 2000).*

How important, really, was the emphasis on sanctification within the wider context of nineteenth-century American history? What difference does the nineteenth-century Holiness heritage mean for the broader understanding of the Wesleyan tradition? Or, for that matter, what does that heritage mean in relation to the pastoral concerns and challenges of the new millennium? What, if anything, is the retrievable or "usable" past that can be gleaned from the nineteenth-century holiness paradigm?

There are different levels of response to these "so what" questions. On the most basic level, church historians need to continue to tell the story of the Holiness Movement so that secular scholars will understand the significance of our tradition within the larger historical narrative. On another level, the response to the relevancy question becomes an historiographical enterprise—an attempt to sort out the Wesleyan legacy. Was the Holiness message faithful to John Wesley or were there two different so-called "Wesleyan" trajectories, one eighteenth century and one nineteenth century? And if there were two trajectories, has the supposed difference between the two centuries been exaggerated? On a still deeper level, our response to these questions becomes central to our theological task, for the ways in which we interpret the Holiness message will shape our understanding and our communication of the gospel in the next century. In the end, then, I am asking the most basic of scholarly questions: Why do I study what I do, in my case the nineteenth century? And why do we, as Wesleyan/Holiness scholars, continue to look to the nineteenth-century Holiness heritage as a source for our theologizing?

Three Critical Analyses of Nineteenth-Century Wesleyans

As we begin to address this issue of relevancy, we must first come to terms with several substantive critiques of nineteenth-century Wesleyan thought. These interpretative judgments must be addressed squarely before there can be any apologetic for the nineteenth-century paradigm or any retrieval of nineteenth century themes for contemporary theology. The three major critical analyses of nineteenth-century Wesleyanism have been: the Calvinist critique, the liberal critique, and the post-liberal critique.

1. The Calvinist Critique. The first critical evaluation—the Calvinist critique—was the theological challenge that American Methodism confronted from its very beginnings on this continent. Since Calvinist forms of Christianity predominated within early American religion, Meth-od-ism was considered to be a theological intruder in relation to the dominant spirituality of the early Republic.

Interestingly, this Calvinist critique has re-emerged among historians in the latter half of the twentieth century, articulated by self-proclaimed guardians of evangelical orthodoxy, nearly all of whom hail from Calvinistic or Calvinistically-inclined Baptist traditions and see the Wesleyan heritage as theologically dangerous. These neo-evangelical historians interpret nineteenth-century American religious history primarily as the story of fanatical emotionalism, anti-intellectualism, and works righteousness.[2] They agree that the nineteenth century was the "Methodist century," as some religious historians have called it.[3] But they believe that this fact was exactly the problem with the nineteenth century.

Although this generic, late twentieth century, Baptistified neo-evangelicalism is not at all theologically congenial to the Wesleyan message, nevertheless many Holiness churches have been assimilated under its all-embracing umbrella. Holiness churches, for example, have happily participated in the burgeoning prosperity of American neo-evangelicalism. Ironically, although Holiness churches were long resistant to cultural accommodation, they have now fully identified with the consumerism that typifies today's American evangelicals. It seems that late twentieth-century Holiness churches have forgotten their nineteenth-century roots. Many of them have largely lost their distinctiveness—thriving numerically, but without their saltiness. This may be what Keith Drury is referring to when he states that the Holiness Movement is dead.[4] It is dead because, on the popular level, it has accepted the Calvinist neo-evangelical paradigm in place of its own.

2. The Liberal Critique. If the first critique of the Wesleyan/Holiness message in America came from the Calvinists in the early part of the nineteenth century, the second critique came later, and it came from the liberal, bourgeois wing of Gilded Age Methodism. Since Holiness advocates often came from socially marginalized contexts and exhibited ecstatic, Spirit-filled faith expressions, the rising middle class of Methodism disdained this enthusiastic reminder of their own unsophisticated frontier past.

By the twentieth century, most Methodist leaders viewed Holiness institutions as a relic of a bygone era, soon (they hoped) to fade away into the woods. Thus, many of the newly-gentrified, mainline Methodists dealt with the Holiness message and Holiness people by simply ignoring them. This was not too difficult to do theologically since most early twentieth-century liberal Methodists had no interest in appropriating what they considered to be Wesley's antiquated ideas. Mainline scholars in the first half of this century did not consider the older Wesleyan theological tradition as something that had any currency for the modern world. When Holiness people claimed that they were the ones who were consistent Wesleyans, their affirmations fell on deaf ears.[5] Mainliners were not interested in who was being faithful to Wesley but, rather, who was most accepting of progressive theological trends. According to Methodist liberals, then, the Holiness movement was deemed irrelevant because it had not engaged sufficiently with the claims of modernity.

3. The Post-liberal Critique. If the liberal contention is that Holiness advocates were not modern enough, then the post-liberal contention is that Holiness advocates were too modern. As the third major group of nineteenth-century critics, the post-liberal critique has arisen relatively recently, in conjunction with more generalized negative appraisals of modernity. Among United Methodists, the post-liberal perspective has developed in combination with the late twentieth-century resurgence of Wesleyan studies, which, following the lead of Albert Outler, rediscovered Wesley as a theological mentor. In the process of reclaiming Wesley, Outler and other scholars judged the nineteenth-century American articulation of the Wesleyan message to be inadequate. For many of these scholars, nineteenth-century Methodism was so hopelessly flawed by modifications made to the original Wesleyan message that they intended to leapfrog right over the nineteenth century and go directly back to the eighteenth.[6]

David Lowes Watson, for example, states quite bluntly that American Methodism failed by the mid-nineteenth century. This failure was due to the relaxation of its original religious discipline, as evidenced by the Church's accommodation to slavery, by its acceptance of worldly wealth and power and, especially, by the gradual decline of the class meeting as a mechanism for mutual accountability. Robert Chiles saw the problem as one of theology more than praxis, but he also identified Methodist modifications to Wesley's message as the major culprit. Similarly, Randy Maddox views the problem as one of shifting views of moral psychology.[7]

Many of these criticisms are directed at the compromises of mainline nineteenth-century Methodism, particularly the liberal emphasis on moral development rather than the traditional Wesleyan stress on the new creation in Christ, and the nurturing platitudes characteristic of the Sunday School replacing the spiritual disciplines that were characteristic of the class meeting. In addition, Nathan Hatch asserts that mainline Methodists appealed "to the petty bourgeoisie, [to] people on the make." Hatch believes that because the Methodist church participated so uncritically in an accommodation to the emerging capitalist society, it became thoroughly "domesticated," and became "the prototype of a religious organization taking on market form." Mainline Methodism, according to Hatch, represented "the bland, uninspired middle of American society."[8] In part, the agenda of the Holiness Movement was a response to these notorious aspects of mainline Methodism's capitulation to modernity. Holiness folks, for instance, condemned Methodism's neglect of the marginalized as well as Methodism's acceptance of liberal theology.

The Holiness Movement Paradigm

Despite the Holiness rebuke of mainline Methodism, the Holiness Movement has also received a negative judgment from the postliberal critique. The critics assert that the Holiness Movement must admit its share of responsibility in the nineteenth-century alteration of Wesleyanism. As both Watson and Maddox point out, Holiness people substituted the Wesleyan stress on the disciplined life of habitual affections with a series of individuated spiritual experiences.[9] For many men and women within the Holiness churches, the pattern of repetitious, guilt-induced times of consecration produced a cycle of spiritual fluctuations that often led to burnout, frustration, a dependence on emotions, and legalistic moralism.

Given this pattern of spirituality, post-liberal historians and theologians want to lift up the eighteenth-century model and reject the nineteenth-century model. One of the speakers at a recent Wesleyan Theological Society meeting, for example, called on us to "rid ourselves of the exclusively Western, nineteenth-century, now lifeless concept of holiness."[10] There are ways in which this is a very persuasive appeal, and I have been won over by the force of many of the arguments regarding the problems of the Victorian mindset. Once we perceive certain concepts such as the intellectualist moral psychology, the Enlightenment individualism, the American triumphalism, the unintended reification of experience, and the unbounded, romantic faith in human potential, it is evident that an uncritical appropriation of the nineteenth century cannot be supported.

But despite the accuracy of interpretations that see additions and accretions to Wesley's message, and despite the problems inherent in the nineteenth-century adoption of modern categories of thought, I am still convinced that there are important lessons to be learned by studying the Holiness Movement—and not only as a negative example of sincere but misguided souls. Put simply, I accept the need to evaluate critically American accommodations to Enlightenment thought, but it is not essential that we throw out the Holiness baby with the bath water of modernity.

Let us grant, for instance, that Wesley's message was modified somewhat by his nineteenth-century heirs. Should that surprise us? Should it even bother us? Who would want a repristinated Wesleyanism that was not relevant to the current situation? Wesley—always the practical theologian—would not have tolerated such irrelevancy. Rather than deny the differences, then, I would like to plumb their depths.

Indeed, as an historian, I am drawn to study and even to appropriate certain characteristics of American Wesleyanism. Perhaps what is most intriguing to me about the nineteenth-century Holiness Movement is the way in which it was simultaneously both very modern and not very modern at all. In fact, the claim—both by postliberals and by Calvinist neo-evangelicals—that nineteenth-century folks were uncritically captured by modernity fails to comprehend the nuanced approach to modernity by Holiness people. Similarly, the typical liberal assertion that Holiness people were unsophisticated, unthinking backwoodsmen who failed to engage with the challenges of modernity misses the Holiness point altogether. The Holiness Movement displayed a more subtle interplay with its culture than is often recognized, accepting certain aspects of modernity while deftly excluding others.

Let us take the early nineteenth-century proclivity toward optimism, for example. It is true that antebellum Wesleyans were postmillennial optimists regarding the possibility of reform. They truly believed that God's kingdom could come on earth—that the nation could be converted to Christ and that Christ's reign of justice could be effected soon: "within three years" was the famous assertion by Charles Finney. Such an idea obviously represented the Enlightenment belief in the goodness and progress of human potential. But before we dismiss this antebellum concept as naively quixotic, let us remember that it was precisely this conviction that motivated sanctified abolitionists to popularize the crusade against slavery—a crusade that had, until then, been perceived by the public as being merely an idiosyncratic notion of the Quakers. This postmillennialism also led many Wesleyans to champion women's rights, temperance, and other social reforms. They may not have ushered in the Kingdom, but they did help to move America toward a more just society.

But even this is not the whole story, for at the same time that antebellum Methodist theology was presenting the possibility of God's soon-arriving Kingdom, it was also "pessimistic about human nature" because of its belief in the persistence of sin.[11] Antebellum Wesleyans knew the difference between the optimism of grace and the optimism of culture. This subtle, but important theological discernment is evident when we survey the religious history of the postbellum period. While mainline

Methodists eventually transformed their religious optimism into a modernist notion of self-help and an unquestioning acceptance of American global expansionism, Holiness advocates began to have doubts about the inevitable progress of human society. Eschatologically, they became premillennialists. That is, Holiness advocates embraced modern concepts of human potential early in the nineteenth century when those concepts coincided with Wesleyan views of the optimism of grace, but then rejected the trends of religious modernity and liberal progressivism later in the nineteenth century and early in the twentieth century when those positions were unable or unwilling to be critical of the surrounding culture.

Twentieth-century liberalism, which downplayed the inherence and pervasiveness of sin,[12] construed the Holiness pessimism about social progress as defensive backwardness. Perhaps we should recognize, however, that the mixed Holiness appraisals of social potential were closer to reality than the uncritical optimism of the liberals.

Another debated emphasis of nineteenth century spirituality was the importance placed on making individual decisions for Christ, particularly as those decisions were related to the key soteriological events of the new birth and entire sanctification. This trend toward particularly-defined experiences was heightened by the Methodists' appropriation of the rather un-Wesleyan, but typically nineteenth century stress on free will.[13] Did this emphasis on volitional actions represent a capitulation to Enlightenment-inspired "common sense" categories of moral psychology? Did the stress on free will eclipse the traditional Wesleyan stress on free grace, and thus move dangerously close to Pelagianism? The answer, in this case, is yes.

But, again, what is a problematic issue on the one hand has positive elements on the other. The decisionistic spiritual formula is less troublesome when one looks at it in terms of Christian praxis and not only as a theological system. This stress on volitional choice is the kind of piety expressed in the hymn "Once to Every Man and Nation Comes the Moment To Decide," a great statement of religious commitment and moral courage. This hymn was written during the Mexican War when Wesleyan Methodists and other sanctification-motivated Christians decried the racism implicit in the war effort. My own dissertation research examined how the decision to accept the grace of entire sanctification became the primary impetus for direct political action against slavery. Just as the new birth was often connected to the acceptance of abolition, so the deeper commitment of entire sanctification was connected to the deeper antislavery commitment of political advocacy.[14]

Yet another factor needs to be considered in regard to the stress on volitional decision. Although nineteenth-century Christians insisted on certain momentary spiritual events, the reality of religious life for Holiness people was a continual religious enthusiasm. When we study the lived religious experience of participants and not just the doctrinal pronouncements of leading theologians, we come to realize that the central factor for nineteenth-century Wesleyans was the immediacy of the power of God through the Holy Spirit—the present experience of God. Roger Finke and Rodney Stark, in their study of growing religious movements, report that thriving churches are always indicated by a "vital otherworldliness," or what I would prefer to refer to as a vital sense of God's pres-ence.[15] Immediate access to God meant that their faith was vibrant, often ecstatic. Holiness spirituality simultaneously affirmed and rejected aspects of modernity; by stressing experiential faith, they affirmed the Enlightenment need for empirical verifiability; but that experience was with a radically transcendent God, a God who breaks into the lives of human beings. In a very un-modern manner, the Holiness Movement was a master at making the extraordinary ordinary, for they were unwilling to domesticate grace and the radical otherness of God.

The primary religious phenomenon for the revivalists was the overwhelming grace of God as experienced in regeneration. As we sing in the words of the nineteenth-century hymn: "What wondrous love is this, O my soul, O my soul." It was a love that one could feel and know and participate in, thus creating a spirituality based on relationality. The nineteenth-century gospel message promoted connectedness with God and with one another. To know God was to be transformed, so that the vital, intimate relationship with Jesus modeled an intimate relationship with others. The faith life of Holiness men and women consisted of God's indwelling leading to concrete ethical action. For example, the abolitionists of the 1840s with whom my own research has centered drew from the deep spiritual well of God's relational love in Christ in order to advocate a social construction that enhanced relationships. The inclusive fellowship of the nineteenth-century Holiness folk was evident, for instance, in the ecstasy of the campmeeting, where, at least initially, gender, racial, and class barriers were dismantled at the altar. Such overturning of traditional distinctions offered participants a glimpse of God's new creation—a model of personal and social transformation. Many have interpreted the campmeeting experience as highly individualistic when, in fact, it was a thoroughly social—and often multicultural—occasion. The religion of nineteenth-century revivalism was intensely personal, but never private.[16]

Holiness Ethos: A Usable Past

The problems with the nineteenth century are easily identifiable. Optimism could lead to a liberal stress on human sufficiency; decisionism could lead to Pelagianism; experiential immediacy could lead to emotional fanaticism; moral earnestness could lead to legalism; and inclusive fellowship could lead to sectarian separatism. But it is important to lift up commendable qualities, as well. In my quest for a usable past, I have tried to discern the characteristic marks or features of nineteenth-century spirituality that have value for us. Rather than simply a particular doctrinal emphasis, Holiness men and women expressed an ethos, a vision, a distinctive spirituality.[17]

But how do we describe this Holiness ethos? Once, while researching an obscure revival preacher named Cary Allen, I found a phrase used by his nineteenth-century biographer. Allen was said to have had a "sanctified eccentricity." This expression conveys the best of nineteenth century emphases. Eccentricity was a common designation among revivalist preachers, for they gloried in their peculiarity and scoffed at pretension and ascribed status.[18]

"Eccentricity" refers to something off center, someone who deviates from the established pattern of accepted conduct. An accusation of being "eccentric" was considered a badge of honor among those who saw themselves as challengers of existing structures. Like many of the Holiness preachers who followed Cary Allen, those dismissed by modern religious society as "holy rollers" may have actually been making an important ideological statement by their behavior. Eccentrics were deliberately contrasting themselves with the polished mores and religious sophistication of genteel culture—values that represented the privileges only available to a few. They challenged the hierarchical power structures of their day, and especially the institutionalism of the mainline churches.[19]

As Methodists, for example, became more affluent and refined, Holiness people became more countercultural and eccentric. One contemporary observer noted that the disheveled appearance of a Holiness preacher was not the result of careless slovenliness, but rather exhibited his desire to be "independent from the changeable fashions of this age of superfluities." [20] Reform-minded Wesleyans resisted the aspects of modernity that contradicted the gospel as they understood it, such as the modern stress on economic efficiency over interpersonal relationships or the racist notion of social Darwinism over the Biblical notion of ethnic equality—in short, any emphasis on progress at the expense of people.

It is typical to dismiss the Holiness ambivalence regarding the benefits of progress by describing it as evidence of their cultural backwardness. While some Holiness disdain for modern values may have been a conservative resistance to change, for others it was a radical refusal to accommodate the claims of the gospel to the debilitating effects of consumerist culture, which undermined faith in God and community with others by encouraging the sins of envy, greed, pride, and indulgence. Holiness men and women repudiated what they considered to be anti-Christian aspects of commercialized enculturation.

Because we have been accepted by God, Holiness people declared, then we are called to accept others. The converts at the campmeetings welcomed the strangers in their midst—those left aside by the larger society. They were able to be so open-hearted because their spiritual union with Christ impelled them to move beyond themselves toward others. Just as Christ does not exist merely for himself but extends himself for the sake of human beings, so Christian believers are truly human when we move outside of our own self-centeredness. Theologically, this self-limiting vulnerability becomes evident initially in the life of Jesus—what Barth intriguingly calls Christ's "eccentric" existence—and is then mirrored in our own human "eccentricity." Through our self-limitation we are set free to love the Other. "The human person," Barth writes, "experiencing the power of the divine....cannot exist for [self alone]...but...awakened rather to genuine humanity,...also exists eccentrically."[21] To be fully human, we step outside of the circle of ourselves in order to bring others into the larger circle of reconciliation. Eccentricity is the very nature of Christ, and thus, it should be so of us.

Seen from this renewed perspective, the "sanctified eccentricity" of the nineteenth-century Holiness paradigm offers us a living tradition from which to draw, one that is particularly well-suited for the postmodern world. Those who were transitioning from a pre-modern to a modern society provide examples for us as we struggle with the transition from a modern to a postmodern society. That is, we share with our friends from one hundred and fifty years ago a suspicion that modern assumptions have their limitations. We suspect that quality of life in the postmodern world will no longer depend solely on the modern capacity to change structures or to produce more.

In important respects, today's postindustrial America more closely resembles the preindustrial America Alexis de Tocqueville wrote about than the industrial America of big business, big labor, big government, and big institutions. Today, we seem to be returning to a country more like the one that Tocqueville so well described. Centralization, hierarchy, and secularism, which historian Robert Wiebe identifies as the dominant characteristics of American life for most of the twentieth century, are yielding to decentralization, equality, communitarianism, and an interest in religious faith. In this new, yet old America, the rules are different from those most of us grew up with.[22]

As postmoderns who acknowledge continuity with our past, we can strip away the modern blinders that have prevented us from seeing clearly our need for genuine connectedness with God and one another. In so doing, we will be able to re-create the experiences of women and men who promoted the immediacy of God's presence for the sake of God's world—a sanctified eccentricity. It is in the recovery of this ethos that our nineteenth-century Holiness forebears can help us the most.

Notes

[1] This article was the presidential address delivered by Dr. Strong to the annual meeting of the Wesleyan Theological Society convened at Southern Nazarene University in March, 1999.

[2] John H. Gerstner, "The Theological Boundaries of Evangelical Faith," in David F. Wells and John D. Woodbridge, *The Evangelicals* (Nashville: Abingdon Press, 1975), 26-28; Mark A. Noll, *The Scandal of the Evangelical Mind* (Grand Rapids: Eerdmans, 1994), 110, 115-31, 142, 249; Douglas W. Frank, *Less Than Conquerors: How Evangelicals Entered the Twentieth Century* (Grand Rapids: Eerdmans, 1986), 103-66. For a similar interpretation from the British perspective, see Boyd Hilton, *The Age of Atonement: The Influence of Evangelicalism on Social and Economic Thought, 1795-1865* (Oxford: Clarendon, 1988).

[3] C. C. Goen, "The 'Methodist Age' in American Church History," *Religion in Life* 34 (1965): 562-72; Winthrop S. Hudson, "The Methodist Age in America," *Methodist History* 12 (April 1974): 3-15.

[4] Keith Drury, "The Holiness Movement is Dead," *Holiness Digest* 8.1 (Winter 1994): 13-15.

[5] In the first half of the twentieth century, the few mainline Methodists who bothered to comment on entire sanctification or other Wesleyan themes articulated by the Holiness Movement were usually people who had defected from Holiness churches and repudiated the Holiness heritage. See, e.g., John L.

Peters, *Christian Perfection and American Methodism* (New York: Abingdon, 1956).

[6]Albert C. Outler, ed., *John Wesley* (New York: Oxford, 1964), 31, 51.

[7]David Lowes Watson, *The Early Methodist Class Meeting* (Nashville: Abingdon, 1987), 145- 47; Robert E. Chiles, *Theological Transition in American Methodism* (New York: Abingdon, 1965); Randy L. Maddox, "Reconnecting the Means to the End" *Wesleyan Theological Journal* 33:2 (Fall 1998), 29-66.

[8]Nathan O. Hatch, "The Puzzle of American Methodism," *Church History* 63:2 (June 1994): 180, 186, 188; A. Gregory Schneider, *The Way of the Cross Leads Home: The Domestication of American Methodism* (Bloomington: Indiana University Press, 1993), xxii-xxiii.

[9]Watson, 145-47; Maddox, "Reconnecting the Means to the End."

[10]Michael J. Christensen, "Theosis and Sanctification," paper delivered at Wesleyan Theological Society, Nampa, Idaho, November 1995, 18.

[11]James H. Moorhead, "Social Reform and the Divided Conscience of Antebellum Protestantism," *Church History* 48 (December 1979): 416-30; Leonard I. Sweet, "The View of Man Inherent in New Measures Revivalism," *Church History* 45 (June 1976): 206-21.

[12]Chiles, 115-43; Thomas A. Langford, *Practical Divinity: Theology in the Wesleyan Tradition* (Nashville: Abingdon, 1983), 170-96.

[13]The transition within American Methodism from Wesley's original stress on "free grace" to the nineteenth-century stress on "free will" is narrated in Chiles.

[14]Douglas M. Strong, *Perfectionist Politics: Abolitionism and the Religious Tensions of American Democracy* (Syracuse: Syracuse University Press, 1999). Though "Once to Every Man and Nation" was written by a Unitarian (James Russell Lowell), it nonetheless reflected many popular concepts held by evangelical abolitionists.

[15]Roger Finke and Rodney Stark, *The Churching of America, 1776-1990: Winners and Losers in Our Religious Economy* (New Brunswick: Rutgers University Press, 1992).

[16]Dickson D. Bruce, Jr., *And They All Sang Hallelujah: Plain-Folk Camp-Meeting Religion, 1800-1845* (Knoxville: University of Tennessee Press, 1974), 86-87.

[17]Henry H. Knight III, *A Future for Truth: Evangelical Theology in a Postmodern World* (Nashville: Abingdon Press, 1997), 19.

[18]William Henry Foote, *Sketches of Virginia, Historical and Biographical, Second Series* (Philadelphia: J. B. Lippincott and Co., 1855), 223-40; Lorenzo Dow, *History of Cosmopolite: or the Writings of Rev. Lorenzo Dow: Containing His Experiences and Travels, in Europe and America, up to near His Fiftieth Year. Also, His Polemic Writings. To Which is Added, The "Journey of Life," by Peggy Dow.* Revised and Corrected with Notes, 6th ed. (Philadelphia: H. M. Rulison, 1855).

[19]Donald W. Dayton, *Theological Roots of Pentecostalism* (Peabody, Mass.: Hendrickson, 1987); Finke and Stark, 153-69.

[20]Marilla Marks, ed., *Memoirs of the Life of David Marks, Minister of the Gospel* (Dover, NH: Free-Will Baptist Printing Establishment, 1846).

[21] Karl Barth, *Church Dogmatics* (Edinburgh: T & T Clark), IV, 2, 547-48.

[22] Alexis de Tocqueville, *Democracy in America*, ed. J. P. Mayer and Max Lerner (New York: Harper and Row, 1966; original edition, 1835); Michael Barone, "The Road Back to Tocqueville," *Washington Post* (7 January 1996): C1-2; Robert H. Wiebe, *The Search for Order, 1877-1920* (New York: Hill and Wang, 1967).

Index of Persons

A
Adams, Robert 97,
Adams, Mary Still 164, 166–71
Allen, Cary 339
Aquinas, Thomas 19
Aristotle 141–42, 148
Arminius, Jacobus 18
Asbury, Francis 189, 202, 214, 219
Augustine 18, 19, 193, 323

B
Barr, James 276, 291
Barth, Karl 19, 340
Bassett, Paul 217–18, 228, 259, 262
Bastian, Donald N. 52, 54
Bentley, William H. 94
Berry, Robert L. 246,
Berry, Wendell 320–22, 325
Blewitt, C. J. 245–46
Booth, William 198, 200
Bowman, Roger 95
Brent, Charles H. 260
Brereton, Virginia 165, 173–74
Bresee, Phineas F. 191, 197–203
Bridges-Johns, Cheryl 262
Brooks, John P. 50
Brown, Charles E. 42, 63, 116, 238, 243–45, 251
Bruce, F. F. 150
Brueggemann, Walter 254, 324
Bultmann, Rudolf 250–51, 252
Bundy, David 219
Burroughs, Nannie H. 106
Byers Andrew L. 43, 196
Byers, J. W. 57
Byrum, Enoch E. 71, 74–79

Byrum, Noah 79–81
Byrum, Russell R. 243, 256
Cagle, Mary Lee 164–169, 170–71, 173
Callen, Barry L. 1–3, 6, 7, 11, 29, 39, 42, 49, 65, 211, 219–22, 237, 246, 297, 301, 305, 307, 331
Calvin, John 14, 23, 252, 322–23
Campbell, Alexander 57
Campbell, Robert 119–23
Campbell, Thomas 45
Caughlan, G. W. 35
Cheatham, W. H. 59, 117
Chiles, Robert 334
Clapp, Rodney 304, 308
Clear, Val 37, 44
Cole, Mary 163–74
Cooke, Sarah 164, 166–67, 169–70, 173
Cox, Leo 228
Cubie, David L. 65, 181, 217, 223, 262
Cunningham, Floyd T. 218

D
Davidson, Phebe 164
Dayton, Donald W. 197, 215, 217–19, 223–25, 259, 262
Demaray, Donald 262
Descartes 318–19
DeYoung, Curtiss Paul 284–85
Dieter, Melvin 33–34, 40
Doty, Thomas 35
Drury, Keith 333

E
Evans, Louis 249

F
Fischer, Nancy 321–22
Fisher, Allie 38
Fisher, Joseph 32
Fitch, George 60
Fletcher, Mary 165–66
Foggs, Edward L 237, 248
Fox, George 239

G
Gaither, Bill 253

Gaither, Gloria 253
Geisler, Normal 25
Giurlanda, Paul 327
Glaser, Mary A. 164, 166–73
Godbey, W. B. 51
Gossard, J. Harvey 45
Graham, Billy 182
Gros, Jeffrey 217, 268
Guyon, Madame 165–66
Gyertson, David 214

H
Haines, G 30–31
Harkness, Georgia 153, 156
Hartshorne, Charles 20
Hatch, Clarence W. 246, 262, 334
Hauerwas, Stanley 254, 308
Haynes, W. A. 60
Hays, Richard 307
Hazzard-Gordon, Katrina 103
Henry, Carl F. H. 37, 50, 62, 86–87, 116, 192
Hill, F. E. 199
Hills, A. M. 202
Hines, Samuel G. 237, 249
Howard, J. N. 53, 88, 98, 117, 218, 249, 282, 284, 291, 309
Howland, C. L. 68
Haney, M. L. 35
Harris, Robert L. 169
Henry, W. J. 116

J
James, Janet Wilson 172, 177
Jennings, Theodore W., Jr. 20,
Jennings, William J. 27, 303–304, 311, 314
Jones, Charles Edwin 44, 46, 123
Jones, Pearl Williams 104, 112

K
Kant, Immanuel 21
Kenneson, Philip D. 306, 314
Kern, Richard 44, 68
Kilpatrick, A. J. 117
Kinnamon, Michael 220
Kissel, Charlie 326

Knapp, Martin Wells 51, 119–200, 202

L
Lee, Luther 190, 200, 207
Leonard, Juanita Evans 326
Lewis, B. Scott 113
Lewis, James W. 293
Lewis, Juanita 262
Linn, Otto F. 246, 250, 251, 254
Lohfink, Gerhard 294–97, 302
Long, Leon 45
Luther, Martin 6

M
Macarius 13
MacIntyre, Alasair 73, 320–21
Maddox, Randy L. 17, 334–35
Mannoia, Kevin 65
Marsden, George 317–18
Marshall, I. Howard 170, 283, 291
Martin, Ralph P. 51, 119, 140, 200, 202, 283, 291
Marty, Martin E. 235
Mason, C. H. 104
Massey, James Earl 42, 64, 85, 116, 211, 275
McClendon, James W. 73–74, 309
McGregor, R. K. 26
McKenna, David L. 53, 65
McManus, Harold 321
Meadows, Philip R. 16
Mellen, Elizabeth H. 4, 211
Meyer, Louis 262
Miley, John 190
Moody, Dwight L. 182, 192
Morris, Leon 283, 291
Morrison, John A. 39, 46
Morrison, Henry Clay 50
Muller, Richard 28
Murphy, Joseph M. 99–101, 105

N
Naylor, Charles W. 271
Neal, Montford L. 119
Nelson, Douglas 114–18, 120
Newberry, Gene W. 261–62
Niebuhr, Richard 291

Noll, Mark A. 317–18
North, James B. 69–70, 220–21, 256, 312
Northcutt, A. C. 201

O
O'Kelly, James 189
Otto, Rudolf 246, 250–51, 254

P
Padgett, Alan 154–159
Palmer, A. B. 57, 69
Palmer, Phoebe 167, 175, 177
Parham, Charles 113, 123
Paris, Arthur E. 99, 111
Paris, Peter J. 90, 94
Pearson, Robert W. 65
Pearson, Sharon Clark 131, 163
Peters, John Leland 46, 342
Phillips, Harold 30, 262
Philo 147
Pinnock, Clark 11–25
Plutarch 144
Purkiser, W. T. 95

R
Reardon, E. A. 243
Reardon, Robert H. 44
Reed, Willard 325
Rees, Seth 200, 202
Richardson, Alan 291
Richardson, Harry V. 94
Riggle, Herbert 61, 63, 75, 121–22, 239, 241–43, 249
Roark, M. N. 120
Roberts, Benjamin T. 57–61, 321
Rogers, Hester Ann 165–66
Rowe, K. A. 25
Royster, James 262

S
Sanders, Cheryl J. 97, 237, 249, 305, 314
Sanders, John 25–27
Schell. W. G. 75, 241, 242
Scholer, David 138
Schwehn, Mark 323

Seymour, William J. 113–23
Shank, Robert 14
Shofner, Lena 238
Shopshire, James M. 99–101, 104–105
Smith, Amanda 175–7
Smith, Frederick G. 69, 241
Smith, John W. V. 41–47, 74, 92, 95, 118, 125, 211, 216, 218, 237, 246, 262, 298–299
Smith, Timothy L. 94
Snyder, Howard 53
Stafford, Gilbert 42, 64–65, 211, 216, 222, 238, 247, 259, 262
Stanley, John 45, 47
Stanley, Susie C., 155, 163, 176, 211, 219, 232, 259, 262
Staples, Russell 218
Starr, William 33
Steele, Daniel 50
Stone, Barton W. 191, 297
Strege, Merle D. 36, 42, 71, 116, 121, 237, 317
Strong, Douglas M. 331
Synan, Vinson 114, 219

T
Tanner, Paul 248
Tasker, George P. 243
Taylor, J. Paul 50, 68
Taylor, Vincent 278, 283, 291
Teasley, D. O. 75
Thompson, Ralph 228
Thorsen, Don 154–55, 259, 327, 330
Thurman, Howard 282, 284–85, 291
Tinney, James S. 98–99, 115, 117

V
VanValin, Clyde 65, 70

W
Wakefield, Samuel 190
Warner, Daniel S. 5–6, 29–34, 40, 42–50, 55–56, 68–69, 72, 75, 77, 116, 122–23, 181, 185, 219, 239–241, 298
Warner, Sarah 31–32
Warren, Barney 41, 47
Warren, Leonard 326
Washington, Booker T. 91, 97, 237, 249
Welch, Douglas 127

Wesley, Charles 240
Wesley, John 6, 12–16, 20, 22, 52, 165, 182–86, 194, 203, 223, 259, 269, 294, 332
White, Alma 164, 167–76
Whitefield, George 12, 182
Wickersham, Henry C. 37, 45, 62, 72, 76–77
Williams, Colin 17, 27
Williams, Jane 125
Winebrenner, John 32, 38, 191
Wirt, Sherwood 87
Wynkoop, Mildren Bangs 16, 85

Y
Yoder, John Howard 218, 309, 310
Yong, Amos 28

Z
Zahniser, Clarence 46
Zinzendorf, Nicholas 74, 75, 182

CONTRIBUTORS

Barry L. Callen
Dean and Vice-President Emeritus, Anderson University and its School of Theology; Editor of Anderson University Press and the *Wesleyan Theological Journal*.

David L. Cubie
Professor Emeritus of Religion, Mount Vernon Nazarene University, and past president of the Wesleyan Theological Society.

B. Scott Lewis
President, Kingswell Theological Seminary, Ohio, and LifeGroup Director of LifePoint Vineyard Church.

James W. Lewis
Professor of Theology and Ethics, Associate Dean, Director of the Doctor of Ministry Studies program, Anderson University School of Theology.

James Earl Massey
Dean Emeritus of Anderson University School of Theology and Dean of the Chapel, Tuskegee University. Author, teacher, and preacher, he is a recipient of the Lifetime Achievement Award of the Wesleyan Theological Society.

Elizabeth H. Mellen
Retired Associate Director of the Graymoor Ecumenical and Interreligious Institute and chairperson of the board of directors of the *Journal of Ecumenical Studies*.

Sharon Clark Pearson
Former Professor of New Testament Studies, Anderson University Department of Religious Studies and School of Theology, and past president of the Wesleyan Theological Society.

Cheryl J. Sanders
Senior Pastor of Third Street Church of God, Washington, D.C., author, and Professor of Ethics, Howard University School of Divinity.

Gilbert W. Stafford
The late Associate Dean and Professor of Christian Theology, Anderson University School of Theology.

Susie C. Stanley
Professor of Historical Theology at Messiah College, longtime executive director of the Wesleyan/Holiness Women Clergy, and past president of the Wesleyan Theological Society.

Merle D. Strege
Professor of Church History, Department of Religious Studies of Anderson University, and Historian of the Church of God (Anderson).

Douglas M. Strong
Dean of the School of Theology, Seattle Pacific University, and past president of the Wesleyan Theological Society.

www.ingramcontent.com/pod-product-compliance
Lightning Source LLC
Chambersburg PA
CBHW021830220426
43663CB00005B/197